LANGUAGE, WRITING, AND THE COMPUTER

Readings from

SCIENTIFIC AMERICAN

LANGUAGE, WRITING, AND THE COMPUTER

With an Introduction by

William S-Y. Wang

University of California, Berkeley

W. H. Freeman and Company

New York

Some of the SCIENTIFIC AMERICAN articles in *Language, Writing, and the Computer* are available as separate offprints. For a complete list of articles now available as offprints, write to W. H. Freeman and Company, 41 Madison Avenue, New York, New York 10010.

Library of Congress Cataloguing in Publication Data

Main entry under title

Language, writing, and the computer.

Bibliography: p.
Includes index.
1. Psycholinguistics—Addresses, essays, lectures.
2. Writing—Addresses, essays, lectures. 3. Linguistics —Data processing—Addresses, essays, lectures.
I. Wang, William S-Y., 1933– .
P37.L37 1985 401′.9 85-20454
ISBN 0-7167-1771-9
ISBN 0-7167-1772-7 (pbk.)

Printed in the United States of Ameraica

1 2 3 4 5 6 7 8 9 0 KP 4 3 2 1 0 8 9 8 7 6

CONTENTS

Note on cross-references to SCIENTIFIC AMERICAN *articles:* Articles in this book are referred to by title and page number; articles not included in this book but available as offprints are referred to by title and offprint number; articles not included in this book and not available as offprints are referred to by title and date of publication.

INTRODUCTION

In any list of our most important inventions, the three that make up the title of this book must rank among the highest. Each has profoundly determined the development of the human species. However, although language, writing, and the computer are closely linked to each other, they emerged at different times.

When exactly language emerged is still in question. The anthropologist Edward Sapir, writing sixty years ago, believed that it "antedated even the lowliest developments of material culture, that these developments, in fact, were not strictly possible until language, the tool of significant expression, had itself taken shape." If we follow this line of thought, then the roots of human language must date back some two million years, since the making of stone tools occurred at least as long ago. Many experts today, however, hesitate to accept so ancient a date.

In any case, the search for a single date is futile, since language probably (i) emerged independently not only at several sites but at different times in the course of human evolution, and (ii) the transition from the crude signals of our primitive ancestors, gradual and incremental, required numerous millenia. Language arose from the earliest pantomimes and gestures, hoots and calls, and traces of these humble origins remain in it to this day. For example, we continue to modulate modern consonants and vowels with distinct sentence melodies, which are intonations, and we still raise our eyebrows and wave our hands when we talk, even into a telephone.

Whenever it originated, the emergence of language meant that cultural evolution could take place side by side with biological evolution. For with language, human beings acquired the power to reason not only within themselves, but also to communicate and collaborate with others of the species. No longer a passive product molded, as the myriad other species on this planet, by ecological forces, we turned the table on nature and began increasingly to modify the world to our needs.

The Machinery for Language

Yet we are still beneficiaries of our biological legacy. In Geschwind's article, which begins this volume, the author sets forth a bold theory of how language may be organized in our nervous system. Perhaps more than anyone else in recent years, Geschwind has developed a precise view on how different language functions are localized to specialized regions of the cortex.

Some of his theory is still intensely debated. For example, it is often difficult to determine questions of relative priority: whether neural structures are exclusively specialized for language *per se*, or whether language evolved because these structures showed proficiency in certain relevant skills. Thus, such abilities as resolving sequences of very rapid acoustic events, storing thousands of distinct semantic patterns in memory, finely coordinating motor activities of dozens of respiratory and masticatory muscles may have evolved to a high degree prior to the emergence of language. Nonetheless, whether language is the result of adaptation or of preadaption, the cogency and influence of Geschwind's views concerning the neurological basis of language are unquestionable.

The next article, by Eimas, is completely compatible with Geschwind's ideas. To not be overwhelmed by the overly rich amount of variation in the speech signal, we need to fit the signal to a small number of categories—the phonemes of the language. The remarkable results of Eimas and his associates show that the ability of categorical perception appears very early in infants in a universal way and then narrows to specific ways as babies become accultured to their particular language.

Bickerton's evidence from Creole languages strengthens the view that we are biologically predisposed for language. Creole languages arise in complex situations of language contact; that is, children learning them do not have a well-defined linguistic model and hence enrich the surrounding pidgin speech by elaborating their own inner resources.

Bickerton shows the existence of striking similarities among widely scattered Creoles, irrespective of the adult languages with which they have come in contact. These similarities lead him to conclude that children are endowed with a linguistic "bioprogram" which surfaces when no dominant linguistic model is present in the environment.

The Invention of Writing

Many millenia had elapsed after language emerged before our ancestors realized the spoken word could be written down: marks on clay could capture the transient sounds of speech, and these marks could then travel across great distances, or be preserved for another time. As Schmandt-Besserat tells us in her article, this realization originated no more than 10,000 years ago, when the earliest precursors of writing were used in western Asia. (Independent invention of writing may also be documented in many other sites throughout the ancient world.)

The use of the word *precursor* in the title of Schmandt-Besserat's article is salient here, since no one has shown that the marks she discusses are systematically related to spoken language in the way all modern orthographies are. Significantly, these first uses of writing in western Asia emerged in a commercial context: people used marks to count objects and to indicate ownership.

The script from the Indus Valley civilization of some four thousand years ago is more advanced. In his article, Fairservis argues persuasively the hypothesis that seal impressions and graffiti on pottery represent an ancient Dravidian language. The Dravidian peoples have long since moved southward down the Indian subcontinent. Furthermore, their modern orthographies are all based on Sanskrit. For these reasons, the script Fairservis discusses has died out, leaving no descendents. Nonetheless, it appears that the writers of it had begun using symbols for conventionalized phonetic values, via the rebus principle.

This single step—from symbols representing meaning to ones representing sound—describes the critical transition to a true writing system. Only by taking this step can written symbols mirror speech, and, by doing so, harness the intricacies and evoke the expressive power of spoken language. The relation between symbol and sound need not be alphabetic, though, of course, the alphabetic relation is typical for the common European languages. In some writing systems, however, such as Chinese characters or

Japanese kana, phonetic symbols correspond to entire syllables, rather than to the consonants and the vowels that make up these syllables.

The discovery of the Chinese oracle bone writing at the beginning of this century is one of the most romantic episodes in the history of archaeology. Specimens of ox bones and turtle shells bearing ancient Chinese characters are shown in the article by Wang. They exemplify a writing system, used extensively over thirty-five hundred years ago, the significance of which was lost for many centuries.

Unlike the marks discovered in western Asia and in the Indus Valley, these oracle bone characters are part of a fully developed system, indicating that Chinese script emerged millenia earlier. Some scholars believe that the lineage of this system can be traced back to the neolithic inscriptions of Banpo, which would double the time depth of Chinese characters to about 7000 B.P. (Like speech, written language undergoes change. The mid-1950s saw the extensive simplification of Chinese characters to facilitate their learning and use.)

My article on Chinese provides a link between language and the computer, and as such, takes us to the third part of the present volume, showing how the computer is used to parse a Chinese sentence and to find English translations for it. Given a restricted and precise subject matter for input, nuclear physics in this example, translation by computer is feasible. It is practicable if we are willing to surrender a little quality in output to achieve high quantity in yield. An entirely different challenge, however, occurs if input is unrestricted. Some of the major problems of this challenge are discussed by Winograd.

The Advent of the Computer

Unlike written and spoken language, computers have had an incredibly short history. The beginning of electrical communication—the first telegram sent by Samuel Morse in 1844—occurred a mere 150 years ago. As a graduate student in the 1950s, I used computers that were clumsy racks of wires and vacuum tubes—hot, slow, and unreliable. In the annals of computer technology, they were antedeluvian.

Since 1960, hardware costs have dropped at a rate of 30 percent per year, amounting to an overall cost reduction of a factor of 1000+ for the same level of performance. In the 1950s, an IBM 650 processed 700 instructions per second, a puny number when compared with a 1970s IBM 370/3135, capable of processing 150,000 instructions per second. In two short decades, then, as prices dropped precipitously and processing power sharply rose, the computer came to dominate the marketplace and to influence our lives in a multitude of ways.

During the same time, words like *input, output, program, interface,* and *network* moved from the specialized lexicon of computer science into mainstream vocabulary. Furthermore, to enhance the transition of information, dramatic computer graphics increasingly complement words, in weather forecasts, lectures on neuroanatomy, or movies about galactic conquests, among other things.

The advancements in computer graphics have also enabled word processing in a variety of scripts, as Becker discusses in his article. Such developments in computer technology fundamentally affect how we perceive, think, and behave in ways we can only dimly understand. Communicating with computer graphics, for instance, extends significantly our conceptual horizons. It provides efficient ways of coding and transmitting certain ideas which words cannot easily do. In this respect, the advantage of computer graphics is like that mathematical symbols provide.

Artificial intelligence is the name given to the attempts to understand human behavior by simulating it with a computer. The remaining articles in this volume suggest the ongoing concerns of researchers in some of these areas. The deeper we delve into various aspects of human behavior, as we try to teach them to the computer, the more we marvel at the awesome complexity and power of "human intelligence." That we can now contrast these two forms of intelligence, thereby gaining renewed respect for our biological heritage, is in itself a gift the computer has brought.

Nowhere is the power of human reason better revealed than in the understanding of sentences, that is, in the extraction of meaning from sequences of words. When examined literally, many types of ambiguity riddle the typical sentence, as Winograd discusses. Such ambiguity is presumably present to a comparable degree in all natural languages, since the mechanisms of sentence formation are largely the same for each.

The difficulty that ambiguity presents for computer analysis is horrendous; yet in everyday communication we barely notice its presence. The mind yokes our knowledge of the real world and effortlessly filters out numerous other possible interpretations of a sentence. How it does this is a question that probes the very core of intelligence. The same question arises, with only minor variations, in our efforts to teach computers to play games, as Waltz discusses.

It arises too when we teach computers to recognize spoken language. Out of a host of alternative possibilities and under extremely noisy conditions, we can still discern phrases that make sense. Just as impressive is our ability to recognize the voice of someone from the distant past, from a simple "hello" on the telephone.

As the discussion by Levinson and Liberman clearly demonstrates, computers have still a way to go in their speech recognition performance. Nonetheless, this technology is already proving itself invaluable in a variety of situations, from assisting test pilots, whom it frees to use their hands (which they need to do constantly), to typing letters for handicapped people unable to control their limbs.

It is fitting that this volume on language should conclude with a discussion of programming languages, as in Tesler's article. The ancients foresaw the tremendous proliferation of languages, as reflected in the biblical story of the Tower of Babel. Current estimates of the world's languages number well above five thousand, and these languages continue to diversify.

Languages for computers also undergo diversification. The older programming languages from the 1960s, BASIC and FORTRAN, have each evolved dialects according to different hardware and software environments. And more and more powerful languages are emerging in rapid succession as our wisdom accumulates concerning the most efficient ways for projecting the human mind onto circuit boards.

Even more striking is the growing tendency to tailor computers to these powerful languages. Initially, they were tailored to satisfy some individual application, such as designing a special chip to do arithmetic. Gradually, the idea generalized to a variety of applications, resulting today, in computers which are increasingly specialized. So it is now possible to find LISP machines, PROLOG machines, and the like, built to harness the conceptual advantages of special languages. The software is shaping the hardware; the language has come to dominate the machine.

The Future Language Machine

The journey began long ago, when some prescient hominids conveyed crude meanings with approximate gestures of the mouth. Eventually, humans wrote down sounds with symbols of various sorts, making it possible for knowledge from distant parts of the world to accumulate through the ages. With writing, civilization began.

The computer came into being a few short decades ago. The machine joined man as the symbol user *par excellence,* and many programming languages were invented for it.

The most recent step forward on our ever-accelerating journey is the reversal of this symbiotic relationship—making machines according to the requirements of language instead of vice versa. The first efforts have been based on the rather restrictive models of programming languages, such as LISP and PROLOG. An inevitable extension will pattern computers after the richness and subtlety of natural languages.

With such dizzying progress, it is nearly impossible to predict the exact course of the journey. Dare we hope that, before the next century, there will be English computers and Chinese computers and so forth, which can communicate with us in *our* languages rather than in *theirs?*

William S-Y. Wang
April 1985

SUGGESTED FURTHER READING

Bickerton, D. 1984. "The Language Bioprogram Hypothesis." *The Behavioral and Brain Sciences* 7, pages 173–221.

Carter, M. L. and K. N. Schoville, eds. 1984. *Sign, Symbol, Script: An Exhibition on the Origins of Writing and the Alphabet.* (Department of Hebrew and Semitic Studies) University of Wisconsin-Madison.

Schank, R. C. and P. G. Childers. 1984. *The Cognitive Computer: On Language, Learning, and Artificial Intelligence.* Reading, Mass.: Addison-Wesley Publishing Company.

Wang, W. S-Y., ed. 1982. *Human Communication: Language and Its Psychobiological Bases.* New York: W. H. Freeman and Company.

Specializations of the Human Brain

1

by Norman Geschwind
September 1979

Certain higher faculties, such as language, depend on specialized regions in the human brain. On a larger scale the two cerebral hemispheres are specialized for different kinds of mental activity

The nervous systems of all animals have a number of basic functions in common, most notably the control of movement and the analysis of sensation. What distinguishes the human brain is the variety of more specialized activities it is capable of learning. The preeminent example is language: no one is born knowing a language, but virtually everyone learns to speak and to understand the spoken word, and people of all cultures can be taught to write and to read. Music is also universal in man: people with no formal training are able to recognize and to reproduce dozens of melodies. Similarly, almost everyone can draw simple figures, and the ability to make accurate renderings is not rare.

At least some of these higher functions of the human brain are governed by dedicated networks of neurons. It has been known for more than 100 years, for example, that at least two delimited regions of the cerebral cortex are essential to linguistic competence; they seem to be organized explicitly for the processing of verbal information. Certain structures on the inner surface of the underside of the temporal lobe, including the hippocampus, are apparently necessary for the long-term retention of memories. In some cases the functional specialization of a neural system seems to be quite narrowly defined: hence one area on both sides of the human cerebral cortex is concerned primarily with the recognition of faces. It is likely that other mental activities are also associated with particular neural networks. Musical and artistic abilities, for example, appear to depend on specialized systems in the brain, although the circuitry has not yet been worked out.

Another distinctive characteristic of the human brain is the allocation of functions to the two cerebral hemispheres. That the human brain is not fully symmetrical in its functioning could be guessed from at least one observation of daily experience: most of the human population favors the right hand, which is controlled by the left side of the brain. Linguistic abilities also reside mainly on the left side. For these reasons the left cerebral hemisphere was once said to be the dominant one and the right side of the brain was thought to be subservient. In recent years this concept has been revised as it has become apparent that each hemisphere has its own specialized talents. Those for which the right cortex is dominant include some features of aptitudes for music and for the recognition of complex visual patterns. The right hemisphere is also the more important one for the expression and recognition of emotion. In the past few years these functional asymmetries have been matched with anatomical ones, and a start has been made on exploring their prevalence in species other than man.

In man as in other mammalian species large areas of the cerebral cortex are given over to comparatively elementary sensory and motor functions. An arch that extends roughly from ear to ear across the roof of the brain is the primary motor cortex, which exercises voluntary control over the muscles. Parallel to this arch and just behind it is the primary somatic sensory area, where signals are received from the skin, the bones, the joints and the muscles. Almost every region of the body is represented by a corresponding region in both the primary motor cortex and the somatic sensory cortex. At the back of the brain, and particularly on the inner surface of the occipital lobes, is the primary visual cortex. The primary auditory areas are in the temporal lobes; olfaction is focused in a region on the underside of the frontal lobes.

The primary motor and sensory areas are specialized in the sense that each one is dedicated to a specified function, but the functions themselves are of general utility, and the areas are called on in a great variety of activities. Moreover, homologous areas are found in all species that have a well-developed cerebral cortex. My main concern in this article is with certain regions of the cortex that govern a narrower range of behavior. Some of these highly specialized areas may be common to many species but others may be uniquely human.

A series of experiments dealing with learning in monkeys illustrates how fine the functional distinction can be between two networks of neurons. A monkey can be taught to choose consistently one object or pattern from a pair. The task is made somewhat more difficult if the objects are presented and then withdrawn and the monkey is allowed to indicate its choice only after a delay during which the objects are hidden behind a screen. It has been found that performance on this test is impaired markedly if a small region of the frontal lobes is destroyed on both sides of the brain. Difficulty can also be introduced into the experiment by making the patterns complex but allowing a choice to be made while the patterns are still in sight. Damage to a quite different area of the cortex reduces ability to carry out this task, but it has no effect on the delay test.

These experiments also illustrate one of the principal means for acquiring information about the functions of the brain. When a particular site is damaged by disease or injury, a well-defined deficiency in behavior sometimes ensues. In many cases one may conclude that some aspects of the behavior affected are normally dependent on the part of the brain that has been destroyed. In man the commonest cause of brain damage is cerebral thrombosis, or stroke: the occlusion of arteries in the brain, which results in the death of the tissues the blocked arteries supply. By 1920 the study of patients who had sustained such damage had led to the identification of several functional regions of the brain, including the language areas.

The study of the effects of damage to the brain is still an important method of investigating brain function, but other techniques have since been developed. One of the most important was brought to a high level of development by the German neurosurgeon Otfrid Foerster and by Wilder Penfield of the Montreal Neurological Institute. They studied the responses in the conscious patient un-

CAPABILITIES OF THE TWO HEMISPHERES of the human cerebral cortex were tested in a subject whose hemispheres had been surgically isolated from each other. The surgical procedure consisted in cutting the two main bundles of nerve fibers that connect the hemispheres: the corpus callosum and the anterior commissure. In the test each of the patterns in the middle column was presented to the subject, who was asked to reproduce it by assembling colored blocks. The assembly was carried out either with the right hand alone (which communicates mainly with the left hemisphere) or with the left hand alone (which is controlled primarily by the right hemisphere). Errors were equally frequent with either hand, but the kinds of error typical of each hand were quite different. The results suggest that each side of the brain may bring a separate set of skills to bear on such a task, a finding consistent with other evidence that the hemispheres are specialized for different functions. What is equally apparent, however, is that neither hemisphere alone is competent in the analysis of such patterns; the two hemispheres must cooperate. The test was conducted by Edith Kaplan of the Boston Veterans Administration Hospital.

dergoing brain surgery that follow electrical stimulation of various sites in the brain. In this way they were able to map the regions responsible for a number of functions. Apart from the importance of this technique for the study of the brain, it is of clinical benefit since it enables the surgeon to avoid areas where damage might be crippling.

Surgical procedures developed for the control of severe epilepsy have also contributed much information. One method of treating persistent epileptic seizures (adopted only when other therapies have failed) is to remove the region of the cortex from which the seizures arise. The functional deficits that sometimes result from this procedure have been studied in detail by Brenda Milner of the Montreal Neurological Institute.

The specializations of the hemispheres can be studied in people who have sustained damage to the commissures that connect the two sides of the brain, the most important of these being the corpus callosum. In the first such cases, studied at the end of the 19th century by Jules Déjerine in France and by Hugo Liepmann in Germany, the damage had been caused by strokes. More recently isolation of the hemispheres by surgical sectioning of the commissures has been employed for the relief of epilepsy. Studies of such "split brain" patients by Roger W. Sperry of the California Institute of Technology and by Michael S. Gazzaniga of the Cornell University Medical College have provided increasingly detailed knowledge of the functions of the separated hemispheres. Doreen Kimura, who is now at the University of Western Ontario, pioneered in the development of a technique, called dichotic listening, that provides information about hemispheric specialization in the intact human brain.

The specialized regions of the brain that have been investigated in the greatest detail are those involved in language. In the 1860's the French investigator Paul Broca pointed out that damage to a particular region of the cortex consistently gives rise to an aphasia, or speech disorder. The region is on the side of the frontal lobes, and it is now called the anterior language area, or simply Broca's area. Broca went on to make a second major discovery. He showed that whereas damage to this area on the left side of the brain leads to aphasia, similar damage to the corresponding area on the right side leaves the faculty of speech intact. This finding has since been amply confirmed: well over 95 percent of the aphasias caused by brain damage result from damage to the left hemisphere.

Broca's area is adjacent to the face area of the motor cortex, which controls the muscles of the face, the tongue, the jaw and the throat. When Broca's area is destroyed by a stroke, there is almost always severe damage to the face area in the left hemisphere as well, and so it might be thought that the disruption of speech is caused by partial paralysis of the muscles required for articulation. That some other explanation is required is easily demonstrated. First, damage to the corresponding area on the right side of the brain does not cause aphasia, although a similar weakness of the facial muscles results. Furthermore, in Broca's aphasia it is known that the muscles that function poorly in speech operate normally in other tasks. The evidence is quite simple: the patient with Broca's aphasia can speak only with great difficulty, but he can sing with ease and often with elegance. The speech of a patient with Broca's aphasia also has features, such as faulty grammar, that cannot be explained by a muscular failure.

Another kind of aphasia was identified in 1874 by the German investiga-

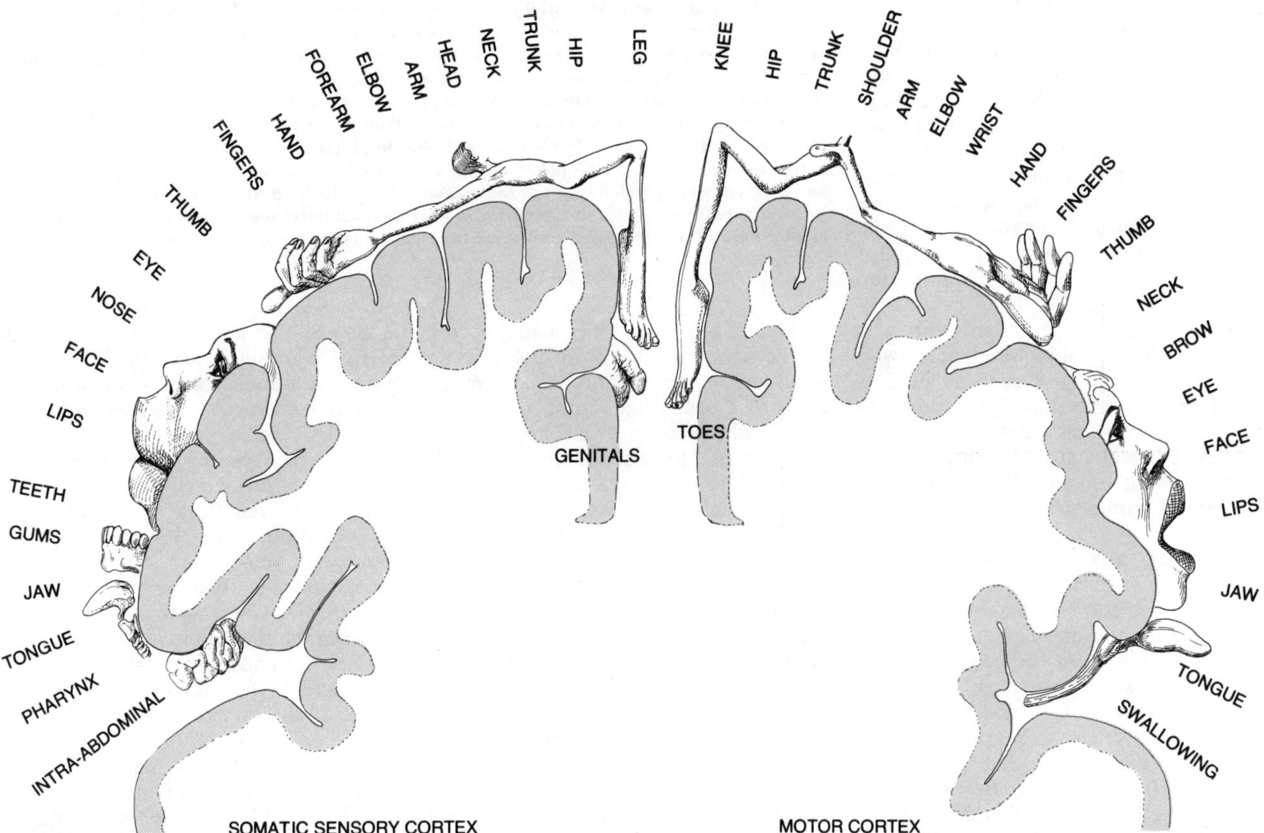

SOMATIC SENSORY AND MOTOR REGIONS of the cerebral cortex are specialized in the sense that every site in these regions can be associated with some part of the body. In other words, most of the body can be mapped onto the cortex, yielding two distorted homunculi. The distortions come about because the area of the cortex dedicated to a part of the body is proportional not to that part's actual size but to the precision with which it must be controlled. In man the motor and somatic sensory regions given over to the face and to the hands are greatly exaggerated. Only half of each cortical region is shown: the left somatic sensory area (which receives sensations primarily from the right side of the body) and the right motor cortex (which exercises control over movement in the left half of the body).

tor Carl Wernicke. It is associated with damage to another site in the cortex, also in the left hemisphere, but in the temporal lobe rather than the frontal lobe. This region, which is now called Wernicke's area, lies between the primary auditory cortex and a structure called the angular gyrus, which probably mediates between visual and auditory centers of the brain. It has since been learned that Wernicke's area and Broca's area are connected by a bundle of nerve fibers, the arcuate fasciculus.

A lesion in either Broca's area or Wernicke's area leads to a disruption of speech, but the nature of the two disorders is quite different. In Broca's aphasia speech is labored and slow and articulation is impaired. The response to a question will often make sense, but it generally cannot be expressed as a fully formed or grammatical sentence. There is particular difficulty with the inflection of verbs, with pronouns and connective words and with complex grammatical constructions. As a result the speech has a telegraphic style. For example, a patient asked about a dental appointment said, hesitantly and indistinctly: "Yes... Monday... Dad and Dick... Wednesday nine o'clock... 10 o'clock... doctors... and... teeth." The same kinds of errors are made in writing.

In Wernicke's aphasia speech is phonetically and even grammatically normal, but it is semantically deviant. Words are often strung together with considerable facility and with the proper inflections, so that the utterance has the recognizable structure of a sentence. The words chosen, however, are often inappropriate, and they sometimes include nonsensical syllables or words. Even when the individual words are correct, the utterance as a whole may express its meaning in a remarkably roundabout way. A patient who was asked to describe a picture that showed two boys stealing cookies behind a woman's back reported: "Mother is away here working her work to get her better, but when she's looking the two boys looking in the other part. She's working another time."

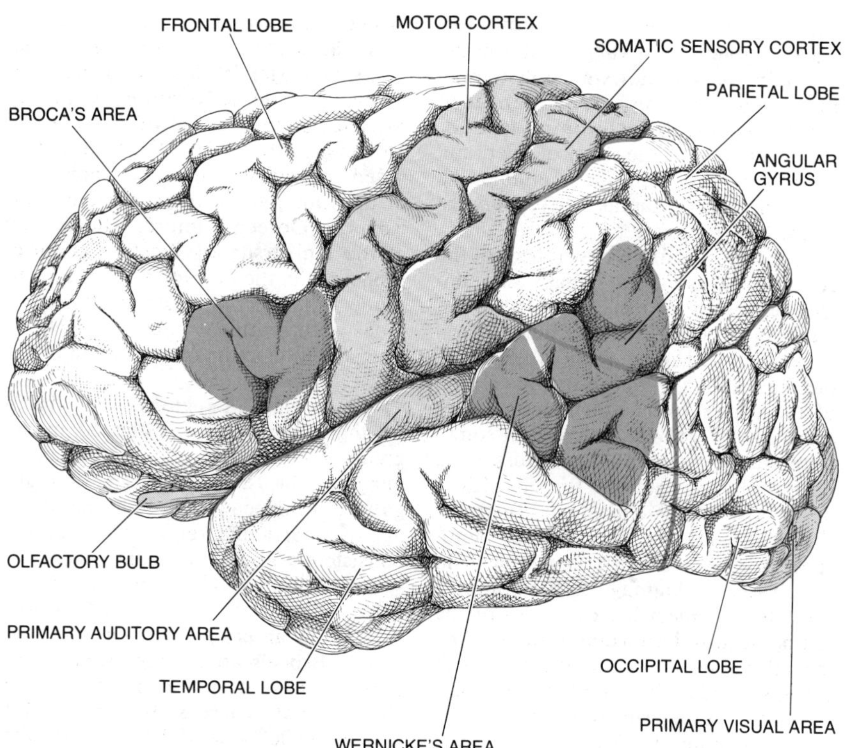

MAP OF THE HUMAN CORTEX shows regions whose functional specializations have been identified. Much of the cortex is given over to comparatively elementary functions: the generation of movement and the primary analysis of sensations. These areas, which include the motor and somatic sensory regions and the primary visual, auditory and olfactory areas, are present in all species that have a well-developed cortex and are called on in the course of many activities. Several other regions (*dark color*) are more narrowly specialized. Broca's area and Wernicke's area are involved in the production and comprehension of language. The angular gyrus is thought to mediate between visual and auditory forms of information. These functional specializations have been detected only on the left side of the brain; the corresponding areas of the right hemisphere do not have the same linguistic competence. The right hemisphere, which is not shown, has its own specialized abilities, including the analysis of some aspects of music and of complex visual patterns. The anatomical regions associated with these faculties, however, are not as well defined as the language areas. Even in the left hemisphere the assignment of functions to sites in the cortex is only approximate; some areas may have functions in addition to those indicated, and some functions may be carried out in more than one place.

From an analysis of these defects Wernicke formulated a model of language production in the brain. Much new information has been added in the past 100 years, but the general principles Wernicke elaborated still seem valid. In this model the underlying structure of an utterance arises in Wernicke's area. It is then transferred through the arcuate fasciculus to Broca's area, where it evokes a detailed and coordinated program for vocalization. The program is passed on to the adjacent face area of the motor cortex, which activates the appropriate muscles of the mouth, the lips, the tongue, the larynx and so on.

Wernicke's area not only has a part in speaking but also has a major role in the comprehension of the spoken word and in reading and writing. When a word is heard, the sound is initially received in the primary auditory cortex, but the signal must pass through the adjacent Wernicke's area if it is to be understood as a verbal message. When a word is read, the visual pattern (from the primary visual cortex) is transmitted to the angular gyrus, which applies a transformation that elicits the auditory form of the word in Wernicke's area. Writing a word in response to an oral instruction requires information to be passed along the same pathways in the opposite direction: from the auditory cortex to Wernicke's area to the angular gyrus.

This model explains many of the symptoms that characterize the aphasias. A lesion in Broca's area disturbs the production of speech but has a much smaller effect on comprehension. Damage to Wernicke's area, on the other hand, disrupts all aspects of the use of language. The effects of certain rarer lesions are also in accord with the model. For example, destruction of the arcuate fasciculus, disconnecting Wernicke's area from Broca's area, leaves speech fluent and well articulated but semantically aberrant; Broca's area is operating but it is not receiving information from Wernicke's area. Because the latter center is also functional, however, comprehension of spoken and written words is almost normal. Writing is disrupted in all aphasias where speech is abnormal, but the neural circuits employed in writing are not known in detail.

Lesions in the angular gyrus have the effect of disconnecting the systems involved in auditory language and written language. Patients with injuries in certain areas of the angular gyrus may speak and understand speech normally, but they have difficulty with written language. The comprehension of a written word seems to require that the auditory form of the word be evoked in Wernicke's area. Damage to the angular gyrus seems to interrupt communication between the visual cortex and Wernicke's area, so that comprehension of written language is impaired.

Although the partitioning of linguistic functions among several sites in the cortex is now supported by much evidence, the rigidity of these assignments should not be overemphasized. The pessimistic view that damage to tissue in these areas inevitably leads to a permanent linguistic impairment is unwarranted. Actually a considerable degree of recovery is often observed. The neural tissue destroyed by an arterial thrombosis cannot be regenerated, but it seems the functions of the damaged areas can often be assumed, at least in part, by other regions. In some cases the recovery probably reflects the existence of an alternative store of learning on the opposite side of the brain, which remains dormant until the dominant side is injured. In other cases the function is taken over by neurons in areas adjacent to or surrounding the damaged site. Patrick D. Wall of University College London has shown that there is a fringe of such dormant but potentially active cells adjacent to the somatic sensory cortex, and it seems likely that similar fringe regions exist throughout the brain. Jay P. Mohr, who is now at the University of Southern Alabama, and his co-workers have shown that the prospects for recovery from Broca's aphasia are quite good provided the region destroyed is not too large. One interpretation of these findings suggests that regions bordering on Broca's area share its specialization in latent form.

Although the detailed mechanism of recovery is not known, it has been established that some groups of patients are more likely than others to regain their linguistic competence. Children, particularly children younger than eight, often make an excellent recovery. Left-handed people also make better progress than right-handers. Even among right-handers those who have left-handed parents, siblings or children are more likely to recover than those with no family history of left-handedness. The relation between handedness and recovery from damage to the language areas suggests that cerebral dominance for handedness and dominance for language are not totally independent.

A disorder of the brain that is startling because its effects are so narrowly circumscribed is prosopagnosia; it is a failure to recognize faces. In the normal individual the ability to identify people from their faces is itself quite remarkable. At a glance one can name a person from facial features alone, even though the features may change substantially over the years or may be presented in a highly distorted form, as in a caricature. In a patient with prosopagnosia this talent for association is abolished.

What is most remarkable about the disorder is its specificity. In general it is accompanied by few other neurological symptoms except for the loss of some part of the visual field, sometimes on both sides and sometimes only in the left half of space. Most mental tasks, including those that require the processing of visual information, are done without particular difficulty; for example, the patient can usually read and correctly name seen objects. What he cannot do is look at a person or at a photograph of a face and name the person. He may even fail to recognize his wife or his children. It is not the identity of familiar people that has been lost to him, however, but only the connection between the face and the identity. When a familiar person speaks, the patient knows the voice and can say the name immediately. The perception of facial features is also unimpaired, since the patient can often describe a face in detail and can usually match a photograph made from the front with a profile of the same person. The deficiency seems to be confined to forming associations between faces and identities.

The lesions that cause prosopagnosia are as stereotyped as the disorder itself. Damage is found on the underside of both occipital lobes, extending forward to the inner surface of the temporal lobes. The implication is that some neural network within this region is specialized for the rapid and reliable recognition of human faces. It may seem that a disproportionate share of the brain's resources is being devoted to a rather limited task. It should be kept in mind, however, that the recognition of people as individuals is a valuable talent in a highly social animal, and there has probably been strong selectional pressure to improve its efficiency.

Similar capacities probably exist in other social species. Gary W. Van Hoesen, formerly in my department at the Harvard Medical School and now at the University of Iowa College of Medicine, has begun to investigate the neurological basis of face recognition in the rhesus monkey. So far he has demonstrated that the monkeys can readily discriminate between other monkeys on the basis of facial photographs. The neural structures called into play by this task have not, however, been identified.

Until recently little was known about the physiological basis of memory, one of the most important functions of the human brain. Through the study of some highly specific disorders, however, it has been possible to identify areas or structures in the brain that are involved in certain memory processes. For example, the examination of different forms of anterograde amnesia—an inability to learn new information—has revealed the role of the temporal lobes in memory. In particular, the striking disability of a patient whom Milner has studied for more than 25 years demonstrates the importance in memory of structures on the inner surface of the temporal lobes, such as the hippocampus.

In 1953 the patient had submitted to a radical surgical procedure in which

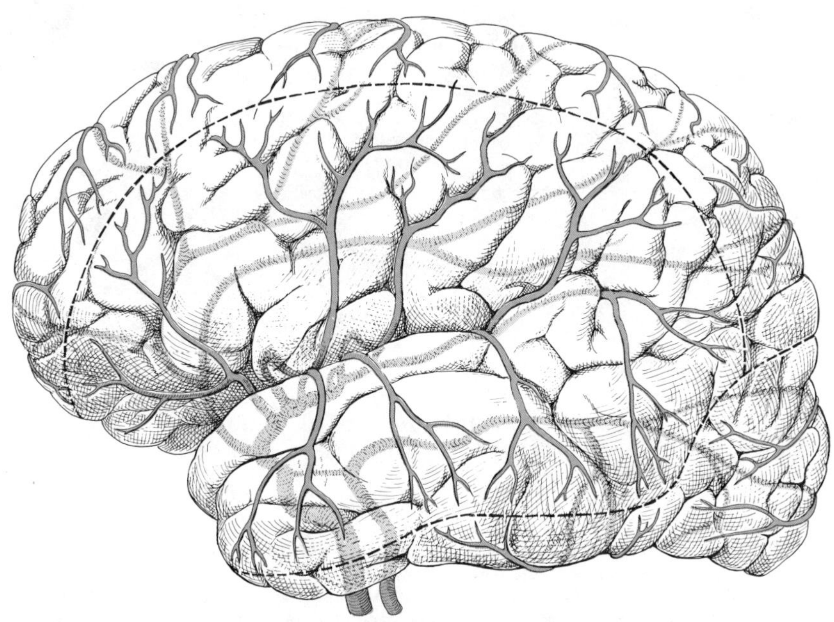

VASCULAR SYSTEM OF THE BRAIN has had an important part in the mapping of functional regions in the cerebral cortex. The normal functions of an area can often be inferred from the disturbance or impairment of behavior that results when the area is damaged. The commonest cause of such damage is the occlusion of an artery supplying the cortex, which leads to the death of the tissue nourished by that artery. Broca's area and Wernicke's area were identified in this way about 100 years ago, when patients with distinctive aphasias, or speech defects, were found by postmortem examination to have damage in those areas of the left hemisphere.

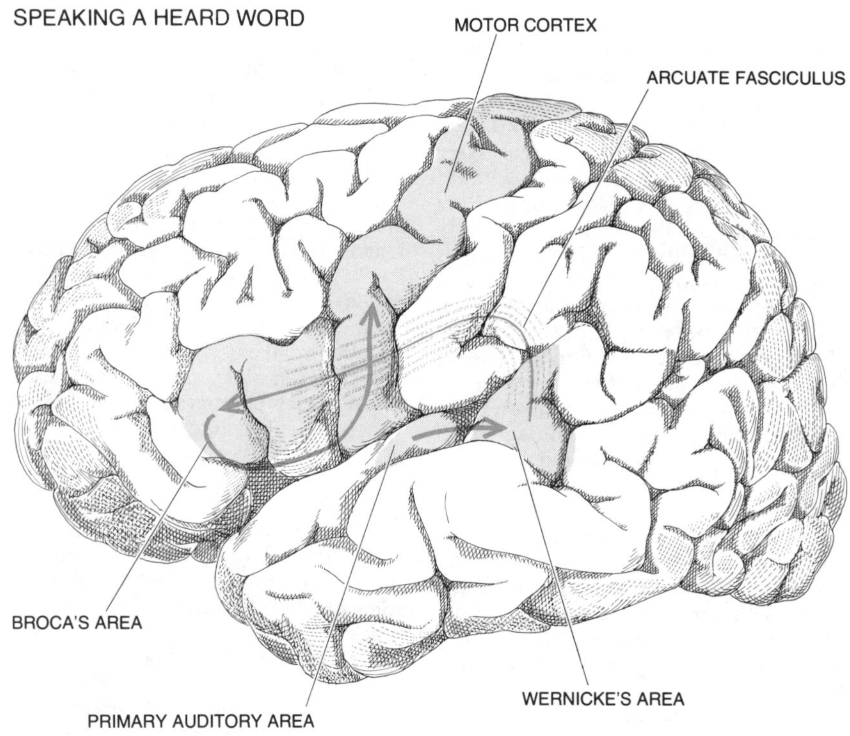

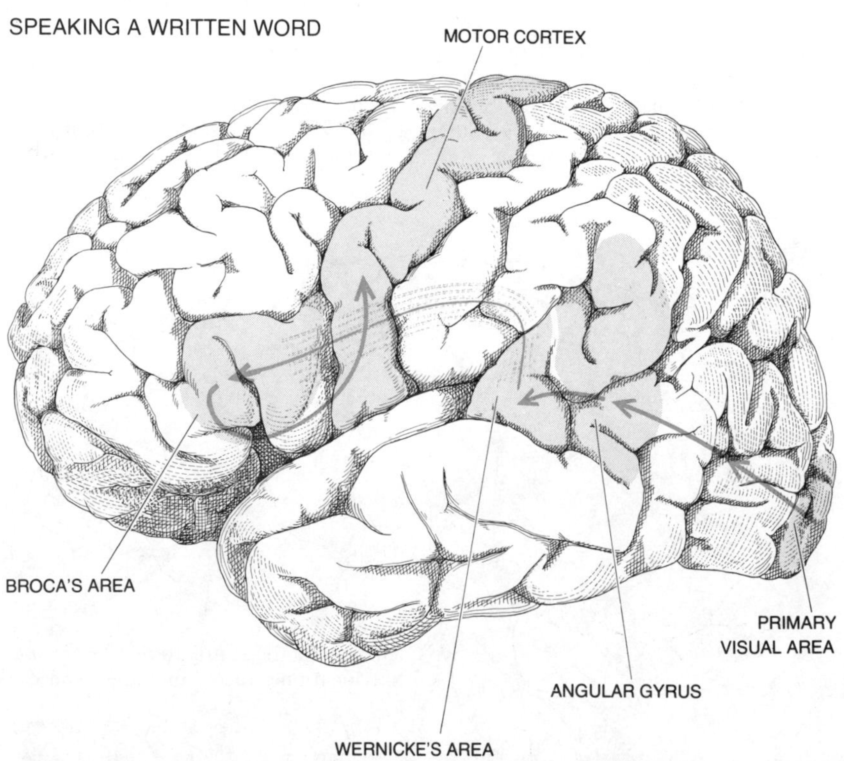

LINGUISTIC COMPETENCE requires the cooperation of several areas of the cortex. When a word is heard (*upper diagram*), the sensation from the ears is received by the primary auditory cortex, but the word cannot be understood until the signal has been processed in Wernicke's area nearby. If the word is to be spoken, some representation of it is thought to be transmitted from Wernicke's area to Broca's area, through a bundle of nerve fibers called the arcuate fasciculus. In Broca's area the word evokes a detailed program for articulation, which is supplied to the face area of the motor cortex. The motor cortex in turn drives the muscles of the lips, the tongue, the larynx and so on. When a written word is read (*lower diagram*), the sensation is first registered by the primary visual cortex. It is then thought to be relayed to the angular gyrus, which associates the visual form of the word with the corresponding auditory pattern in Wernicke's area. Speaking the word then draws on the same systems of neurons as before.

much of the hippocampus and several associated structures in both temporal lobes were destroyed. After the operation the skills and knowledge the patient had acquired up to that time remained largely intact, and he was and still is able to attend normally to ongoing events. In fact, he seems to be able to register limited amounts of new information in the usual manner. Within a short time, however, most of the newly learned information ceases to be available to him.

Milner has interviewed and tested the patient at intervals since the operation, and she has found that his severe anterograde amnesia has changed very little during that time. He has also exhibited an extensive although patchy retrograde amnesia (about the years before the operation), but that has improved appreciably. In the absence of distraction he can retain, say, a three-digit number for many minutes by means of verbal rehearsal or with the aid of an elaborate mnemonic device. Once his attention has been momentarily diverted, however, he cannot remember the number or the mnemonic device to which he devoted so much effort. He cannot even remember the task itself. Living from moment to moment, he has not been able to learn his address or to remember where the objects he uses every day are kept in his home. He fails to recognize people who have visited him regularly for many years.

The bilateral surgery that resulted in this memory impairment is, for obvious reasons, no longer done, but similar lesions on the inner surface of the temporal lobes have occasionally resulted from operations on one side of the brain in a patient with unsuspected damage to the opposite lobe. Comparable memory deficits result, and so the role of the inner surface of the temporal lobes in memory function is now widely accepted. Moreover, the fact that these patients generally retain their faculties of perception supports the distinction made by many workers between a short-term memory process and a long-term process by which more stable storage of information is achieved. It is clearly the second process that is impaired in the patients described above, but the nature of the impairment is a matter of controversy. Some think the problem is a failure of consolidation, that is, transferring information from short-term to long-term storage. Others hold that the information is transferred and stored but cannot be retrieved. The ultimate resolution of these conflicting theories will require a clearer specification of the neural circuitry of memory.

At a glance the brain appears to have perfect bilateral symmetry, like most other organs of the body. It might therefore be expected that the two halves of the brain would also be functionally equivalent, just as the two kid-

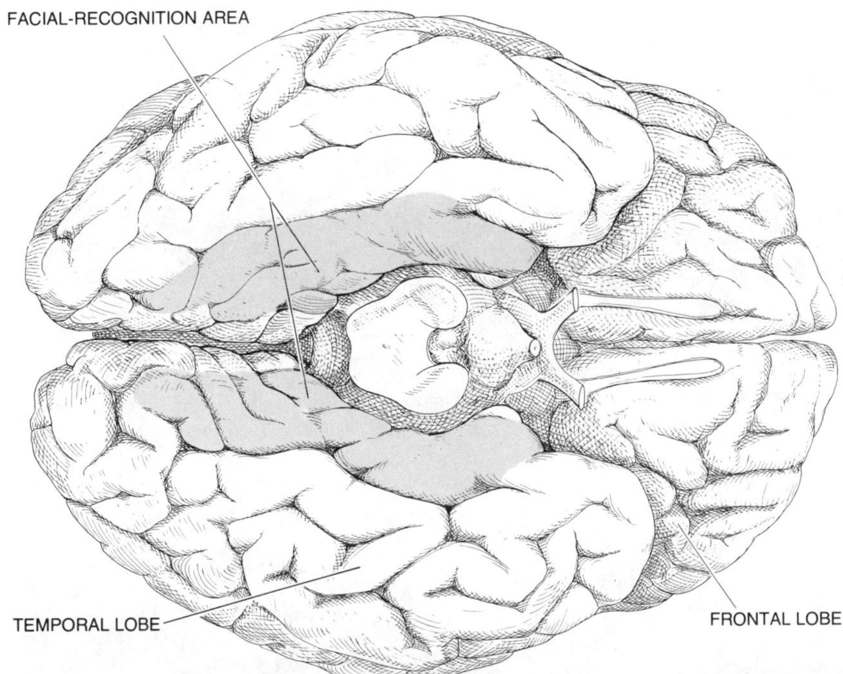

RECOGNITION OF FACES is a faculty that seems to be governed by regions on the underside of the temporal and occipital lobes on both sides of the cortex, which is seen here from below. A lesion that destroys this area impairs the ability to identify a person by facial features but has almost no other effects. There is often some loss of vision, but the patient can read, can name objects on sight and can even match a full-face portrait with a profile of the same person. People can also be recognized by their voices. The only ability that is lost is the ability to recognize people by their faces, and that loss can be so severe that close relatives are not recognized.

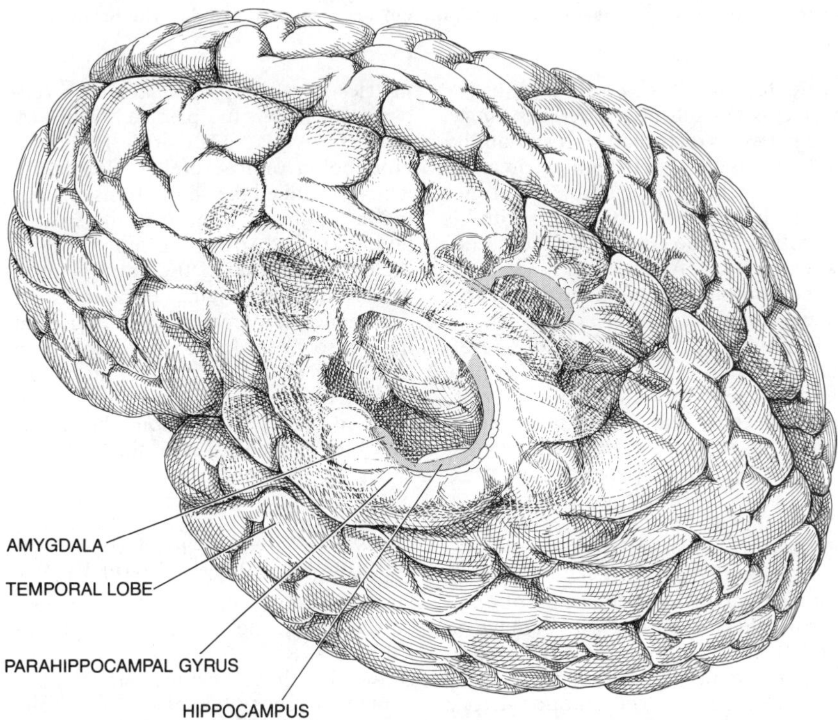

CERTAIN MEMORY PROCESSES appear to be associated with structures on the inner surface of the temporal lobes, such as the hippocampus (*color*). Bilateral lesions of these areas have been shown to cause a severe and lasting memory disorder characterized by the inability to learn new information. Patients with lesions of this type appear to have undiminished powers of perception, but they are largely incapable of incorporating new information into their long-term store. Acute lesions in this region of a single temporal lobe sometimes result in similar but less persistent memory disorders that reflect the contrasting specializations of the hemispheres: the type of information that cannot be learned varies according to the side the lesion is on.

neys or the two lungs are. Actually many of the more specialized functions are found in only one hemisphere or the other. Even the apparent anatomical symmetry turns out to be illusory.

In the primary motor and sensory areas of the cortex the assignment of duties to the two hemispheres follows a simple pattern: each side of the brain is concerned mainly with the opposite side of the body. Most of the nerve fibers in the pathways that radiate from the motor and somatic sensory areas cross to the opposite side of the nervous system at some point in their course. Hence the muscles of the right hand and foot are controlled primarily by the left motor cortex, and sensory impulses from the right side go mainly to the left somatic sensory cortex. Each ear has connections to the auditory cortex on both sides of the brain, but the connections to the contralateral side are stronger. The distribution of signals from the eyes is somewhat more complicated. The optic nerves are arranged so that images from the right half of space in both eyes are projected onto the left visual cortex; the left visual field from both eyes goes to the right hemisphere. As a result of this pattern of contralateral connections the sensory and motor functions of the two hemispheres are kept separate, but they are largely symmetrical. Each half of the brain is concerned with half of the body and half of the visual field.

The distribution of the more specialized functions is quite different, and it is profoundly asymmetrical. I have indicated above that linguistic ability is dependent primarily on the left hemisphere. There is reason to believe the right side of the brain is more important for the perception of melodies, one item of evidence being the ease with which aphasic patients with left-hemisphere damage can sing. The perception and analysis of nonverbal visual patterns, such as perspective drawings, is largely a function of the right hemisphere, although the left hemisphere also makes a distinctive contribution to such tasks. These asymmetries are also reflected in partial memory defects that can result from lesions in a single temporal lobe. A left temporal lobectomy can impair the ability to retain verbal material but can leave intact the ability to remember spatial locations, faces, melodies and abstract visual patterns.

In everyday life this lateralization of function can seldom be detected because information is readily passed between the hemispheres through several commissures, including the corpus callosum. Even when the interconnections are severed, the full effects of cerebral dominance can be observed only in laboratory situations, where it is possible to ensure that sensory information reaches only one hemisphere at a time and that a motor response comes from only one hemisphere. Under these conditions a

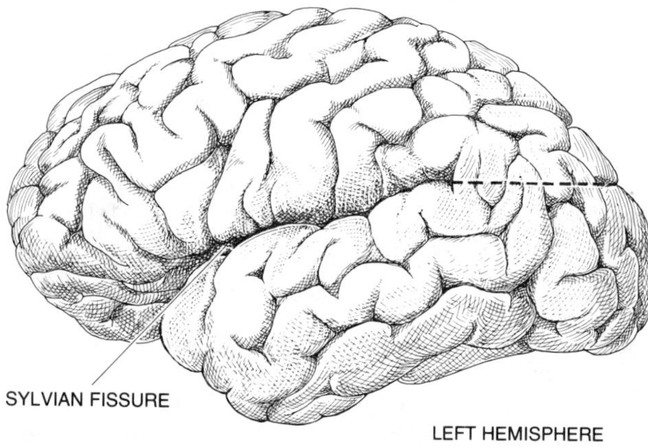

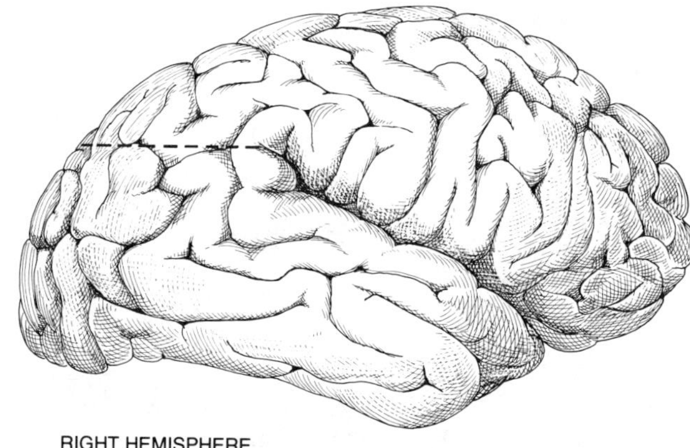

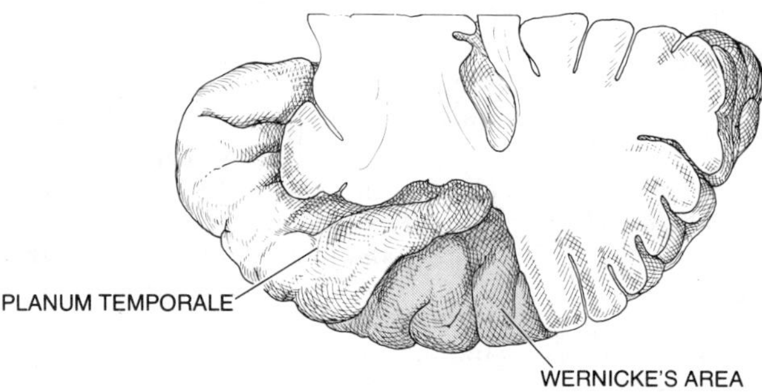

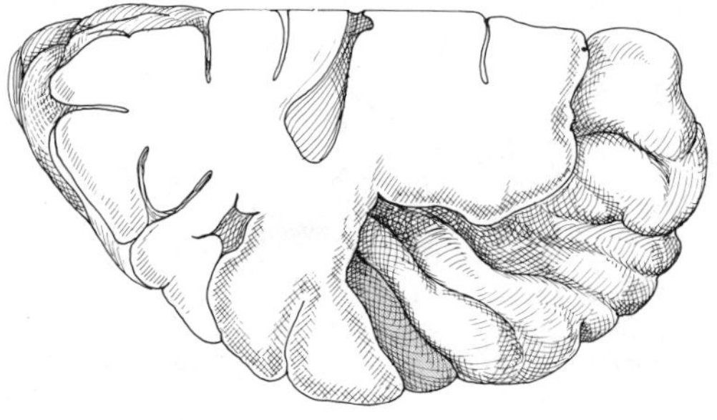

ANATOMICAL ASYMMETRY of the cortex has been detected in the human brain and may be related to the distinctive functional specializations of the two hemispheres. One asymmetry is readily observed in the intact brain: the sylvian fissure, which defines the upper margin of the temporal lobe, rises more steeply on the right side of the brain. A more striking asymmetry is found on the planum temporale, which forms the upper surface of the temporal lobe, and which can be seen only when the sylvian fissure is opened. The posterior part of the planum temporale is usually much larger on the left side. The enlarged region is part of Wernicke's area, suggesting that the asymmetry may be related to the linguistic dominance of the left hemisphere. The distribution of the asymmetries varies with handedness.

remarkable pattern of behavior is observed. If an object is placed in a patient's left hand or if it is presented only to his left visual field, he cannot say its name. The failure is not one of recognition, since the patient is able to match related objects, but the perception received only in the right hemisphere cannot be associated with a name that is known only to the left hemisphere.

The specialization of the isolated hemispheres should not be overstated, however. The right half of the brain does have some rudimentary linguistic ability. Moreover, there are doubtless many tasks where the two hemispheres ordinarily act in concert. In one test administered after surgical isolation of the hemispheres the patient is asked to reproduce a simple pattern by assembling colored blocks. In some cases errors are frequent whether the task is completed with the left hand or the right, but they are characteristically different kinds of errors. It appears that neither hemisphere alone is competent in this task and that the two must cooperate.

One of the most surprising recent findings is that different emotional reactions follow damage to the right and left sides of the brain. Lesions in most areas on the left side are accompanied by the feelings of loss that might be expected as a result of any serious injury. The patient is disturbed by his disability and often is depressed. Damage in much of the right hemisphere sometimes leaves the patient unconcerned with his condition. Guido Gainotti of the Catholic University of Rome has made a detailed compilation of these differences in emotional response.

Emotion and "state of mind" are often associated with the structures of the limbic system, at the core of the brain, but in recent years it has been recognized that the cerebral cortex, particularly the right hemisphere of the cortex, also makes an important contribution. Lesions in the right hemisphere not only give rise to inappropriate emotional responses to the patient's own condition but also impair his recognition of emotion in others. A patient with damage on the left side may not be able to comprehend a statement, but in many cases he can still recognize the emotional tone with which it is spoken. A patient with a disorder of the right hemisphere usually understands the meaning of what is said, but he often fails to recognize that it is spoken in an angry or a humorous way.

Although cerebral dominance has been known in the human brain for more than a century, comparable asymmetries in other species have been recognized only in the past few years. A pioneer in this endeavor is Fernando Nottebohm of Rockefeller University, who has studied the neural basis of singing in songbirds. In most of the species he has studied so far, but not in all of them, the left side of the brain is more important for singing. Examples of dominance in mammals other than man have also been described, although in much less detail. Under certain conditions damage to the right side of the brain in rats alters emotional behavior, as Victor H. Denenberg of the University of Connecticut has shown. Dominance of the left cerebral cortex for some auditory tasks has been discovered in one species of monkey by James H. Dewson III, who is now at Stanford University. Michael Petersen and other investigators at the University of Michigan and at Rockefeller University have shown that the left hemisphere is dominant in the recognition of species-specific cries in Japanese macaques, which employ an unusual variety of such signals. So far, however, no definitive example of functional asymmetry has been described in the brains of the great apes, the closest relations of man.

For many years it was the prevailing view of neurologists that the func-

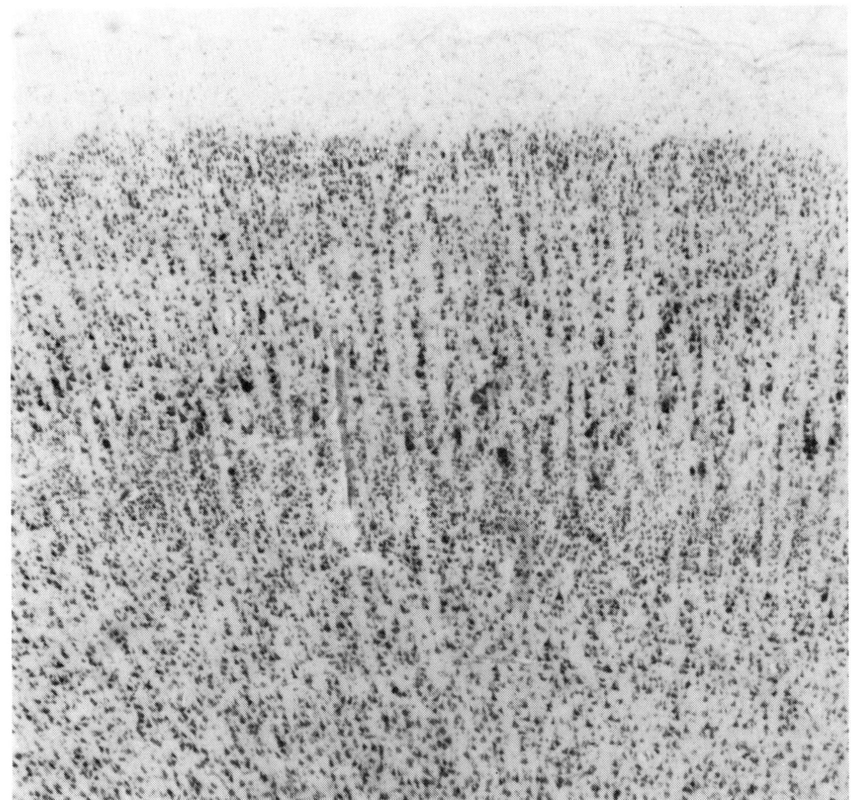

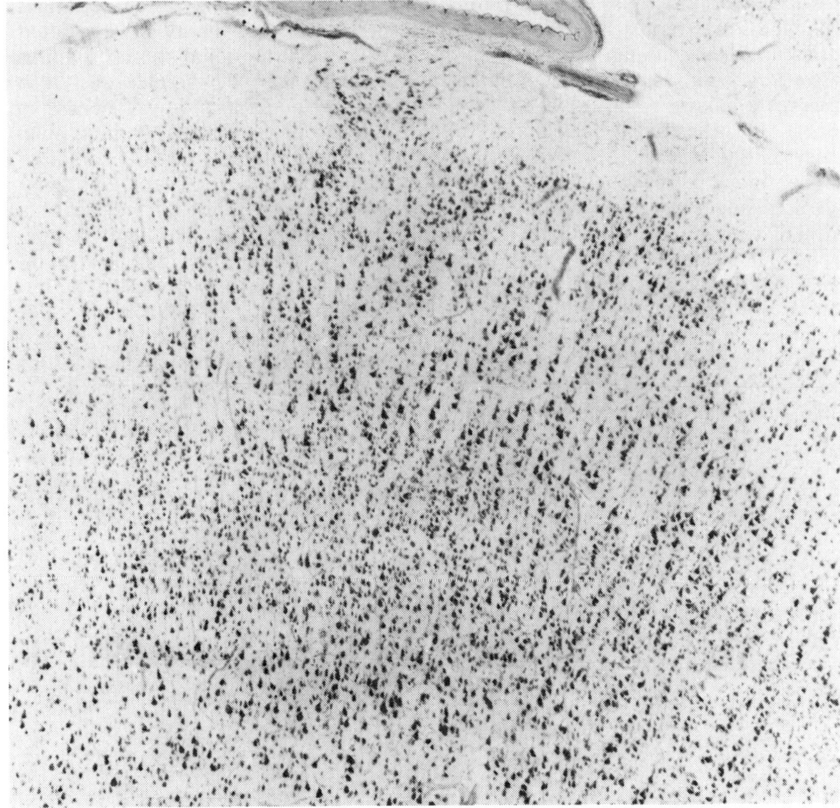

ABNORMAL CELLULAR ARCHITECTURE has been found in a language area of a patient with a developmental reading disorder. The top photomicrograph is a section of the normal cortex from the posterior portion of the planum temporale, the region that makes up part of Wernicke's area. Several layers can be perceived and the cells have a characteristic columnar organization. The bottom photograph is a section from the same region in a patient with dyslexia. One peculiarity is the presence of nerve-cell bodies in the most superficial layer (*near top of photograph*), where they are normally absent. Moreover, throughout the tissue the arrangement of cells is disrupted. The abnormality was found by Albert M. Galaburda of the Harvard Medical School and Thomas Kemper of the Boston University School of Medicine.

tional asymmetries of the brain could not be correlated with anatomical asymmetries. If there were any significant differences between the hemispheres, it was assumed, they would have been noted long ago by surgeons or pathologists. About 10 years ago my colleague Walter Levitsky and I decided to look into this matter again, following some earlier observations by the German neurologist Richard Arwed Pfeifer. We examined 100 human brains, paying particular attention to a region called the planum temporale, which lies on the upper surface of the temporal lobe and is hidden within the sylvian fissure that runs along each side of the brain. Our study was concerned only with gross anatomy, and we employed no instruments more elaborate than a camera and a ruler; nevertheless, we found unequivocal evidence of asymmetry. In general the length and orientation of the sylvian fissures is different on opposite sides of the head. What is more significant, the posterior area of the planum temporale, which forms part of Wernicke's area, is generally larger on the left side. The differences are not subtle and can easily be seen with the unaided eye.

Juhn A. Wada of the University of British Columbia subsequently showed that the asymmetry of the planum temporale can be detected in the human fetus. It therefore appears that the enlargement of the left planum cannot be a response to the development of linguistic competence in childhood. On the contrary, the superior linguistic talent of the left hemisphere may result from the anatomical bias.

More recently my colleague Albert M. Galaburda has discovered that the enlargement of the left planum can be explained in terms of the cellular organization of the tissue. On the planum is a region with a distinctive cellular architecture, designated *Tpt*. Galaburda found that the extent of the *Tpt* region is considerably greater in the left hemisphere; in the first brain he examined it was more than seven times as large on the left side as it was on the right.

Galaburda and Thomas Kemper of the Boston University School of Medicine also examined the brain of an accident victim who had suffered from persistent dyslexia. He found that the *Tpt* areas in the two hemispheres were of approximately equal size. Furthermore, the cellular structure of the *Tpt* area on the left side was abnormal. The neurons in the normal cortex are arranged in a sequence of layers, each of which has a distinctive population of cells. In the brain of the dyslexic the strata were disrupted, one conspicuous anomaly being the presence of cell bodies of neurons in the most superficial layer of the cortex, where they are normally absent. Islands of cortical tissue were also found in the white matter of the brain, where they do not belong. Although no firm conclusion can be drawn from a single case, it does seem striking that a structural abnormality would be found in the language area of a patient who was known to have a linguistic disability.

A new line of research on brain asymmetry has lately been opened by my colleague Marjorie J. LeMay. She has devised several methods for detecting anatomical asymmetry in the living person. One of these methods is cerebral arteriography, in which a substance opaque to X rays is injected into the bloodstream and the distribution of the substance is monitored as it flows through the cranial arteries. Arteriography is often employed in the diagnosis of brain tumors and other brain diseases, and the arteriograms LeMay examined had been made for diagnostic purposes. One of the cranial arteries (the middle cerebral artery) follows the groove of the sylvian fissure, and LeMay showed that the position of the artery in the arteriogram reveals the length and orientation of the fissure. She found that in most people the middle cerebral artery on the right side of the head is inclined more steeply and ultimately ascends higher than the corresponding artery on the left side.

LeMay has also detected brain asymmetries by computed axial tomography, the process whereby an image of the skull in cross section is reconstructed from a set of X-ray projections. In these images a peculiar, skewed departure from bilateral symmetry is observed. In right-handed people the right frontal lobe is usually wider than the left, but the left parietal and occipital lobes are wider than the right. The inner surface of the skull itself bulges at the right front and the left rear to accommodate the protuberances.

LeMay has even reported finding asymmetries in cranial endocasts made from the fossil skulls of Neanderthal man and other hominids. A ridge on the inner surface of the skull corresponds to the sylvian fissure; where the ridge is preserved well enough to make an impression in an endocast LeMay finds the same pattern of asymmetry that is observed in modern man, suggesting that hemispheric dominance had already emerged at least 30,000 years ago. LeMay and I have shown that asymmetries of the sylvian fissures exist in the great apes but not in monkeys. (Grace H. Yeni-Komshian and Dennis A. Benson of the Johns Hopkins University School of Medicine have reported similar findings.) If a functional correlative to this anatomical bias can be discovered, an animal model of cerebral dominance in the anthropoid apes would become available.

One of the most commonplace manifestations of cerebral dominance is also one of the most puzzling: the phenomenon of handedness. Many animals exhibit a form of handedness; for example, if a monkey is made to carry out a task with only one hand, it will consistently use the same one. In any large population of monkeys, however, left- and right-handed individuals are equally common. In the human population no more than 9 percent are left-handed. This considerable bias toward right-handedness may represent a unique specialization of the human brain.

The genetics and heritability of handedness is a controversial topic. In mice Robert V. Collins of the Jackson Laboratory in Bar Harbor, Me., has shown that continued inbreeding of right-handed animals does not increase the prevalence of right-handedness in their offspring. The pattern in man is quite different. Marian Annett of the Lanchester Polytechnic in England has proposed a theory in which one allele of a gene pair favors the development of right-handedness, but there is no complementary allele for left-handedness. In the absence of the right-favoring allele handedness is randomly determined.

Studies undertaken by LeMay and her co-workers have revealed that the distribution of brain asymmetries in left-handed people is different from that in right-handers. In right-handed individuals, and hence in most of the population, the right sylvian fissure is higher than the left in 67 percent of the brains examined. The left fissure is higher in 8 percent and the two fissures rise to approximately equal height in 25 percent. In the left-handed population a substantial majority (71 percent) have approximate symmetry of the sylvian fissures. Among the remainder the right fissure is still more likely to be the higher (21 percent v. 7 percent). The asymmetries observed by tomography also have a different distribution in right-handers and left-handers. Again in the left-handed segment of the population the asymmetries tend to be less pronounced. These findings are in qualitative agreement with the theory proposed by Annett.

If functions as narrowly defined as facial recognition are accorded specific neural networks in the brain, it seems likely that many other functions are represented in a similar way. For example, one of the major goals of child rearing is to teach a set of highly differentiated responses to emotional stimuli, such as anger and fear. The child must also be taught the appropriate responses to stimuli from its internal milieu, such as hunger or fullness of the bladder or bowel. Most children learn these patterns of behavior just as they learn a language, suggesting that here too special-purpose processors may be present. As yet little is known about such neural systems. Indeed, even as the mapping of specialized regions continues, the next major task must be confronted: that of describing their internal operation.

The Perception of Speech in Early Infancy

2

by Peter D. Eimas
January 1985

In perceiving speech human beings detect discrete phonemic categories and ignore much of the acoustic variation in the speech signal. Research with infants suggests the underlying perceptual mechanisms are innate

How is it that a child swiftly and seemingly without much effort learns to speak and understand? The process of language acquisition begins well before the first birthday, and most children use language with considerable skill by their third year. In contrast to the learning of reading or arithmetic, a child masters language without formal teaching; indeed, much of the learning takes place within a fairly limited linguistic environment, which does not specify precisely the rules governing competent language use.

A possible explanation for the swift growth of a child's language skills is that language is not as complex as is generally thought, and consequently that such simple psychological principles as conditioning and generalization account for the speed with which it is learned. But research during the past several decades on the nature of language and the processes by which it is produced and understood has revealed not underlying simplicity but increasing complexity.

Experiments carried out by my colleagues and me at Brown University and by other investigators elsewhere have supported a different explanation, one derived from the view, of which the linguist Noam Chomsky is the most notable exponent, that inborn knowledge and capacities underlie the use of language. In studies of speech perception by infants we have found these young subjects are richly endowed with innate perceptual mechanisms, well adapted to the characteristics of human language, that prepare them for the linguistic world they will encounter.

The search for inborn mechanisms of speech perception developed from studies of the relation of the speech signal to phonemes, the perceptual units that correspond to the consonants and vowels of language. Phonemes are the smallest units of speech that affect meaning: only one phonemic difference sets apart the words *late* and *rate,* yet they are entirely distinct in meaning.

Workers at the Haskins Laboratories in New Haven, the Massachusetts Institute of Technology, Sweden's Royal Institute of Technology and elsewhere have shown that the speech signal is a complex of acoustic units: brief segments bounded by momentary pauses or peaks in intensity. The segments vary in duration and in the frequency, temporal relations and intensity of their constituent bands of concentrated acoustic energy, known as formants, and of noiselike acoustic components known as aspiration and frication. The variation in these acoustic parameters provides the information that is critical to the perception of phonemes.

No direct, one-to-one correspondence holds, however, between individual acoustic segments and the phonemes we perceive. A single acoustic segment may encompass a consonant and a vowel; conversely, two distinct acoustic segments may contribute to a single consonantal sound. Furthermore, there is no direct relation between the segments' frequency and temporal characteristics and the phonemes we hear. A listener may recognize a range of stimuli, varying widely in a number of acoustic traits, as instances of the same phoneme. On the other hand, a small change in a single acoustic cue may in some situations change the phoneme that is perceived.

Consider the acoustic information that is sufficient to signal the distinction between the voiced stop consonant that begins the word *bin* and the voiceless stop consonant in *pin*. In both cases the speaker completely blocks the flow of air through the vocal tract just before the release of the utterance; in *bin,* however, the vocal cords begin to vibrate almost simultaneously with the release of air, whereas in *pin* vocal-cord vibration is delayed. The interval between the release of air and the onset of vocal-cord vibration, or voicing, is known as voice-onset time; it holds the crucial acoustic information that enables a hearer to distinguish *bin* from *pin*. No single value of voice-onset time defines each phoneme, however. Instead hearers typically perceive a range of values, reflecting different speakers, different instances of speech and differences in the surrounding phonemic environment, as examples of the same phoneme.

The acoustic variables that define other phonemes are similarly fluid. For example, many phonemes are differentiated by place of articulation, the site of the constriction of the vocal tract that occurs as the sound is formed; the initial sounds of *bin* and *din* are examples. Among the acoustic cues that correspond to place of articulation and enable a hearer to distinguish such phonemes are the initial frequencies of the second and third formants: the formants that fall second and third from the bottom on a scale of frequency. Again no single value of these acoustic parameters characterizes each phoneme; a range of onset frequencies can signal the same place of articulation. Yet in spite of the variation in the sounds corresponding to each phoneme we have little trouble deciding whether a speaker said *din* or *bin*. We are able in effect to listen through the variation in the signal and make categorical judgments of phonemic quality.

Experimental results confirm that in

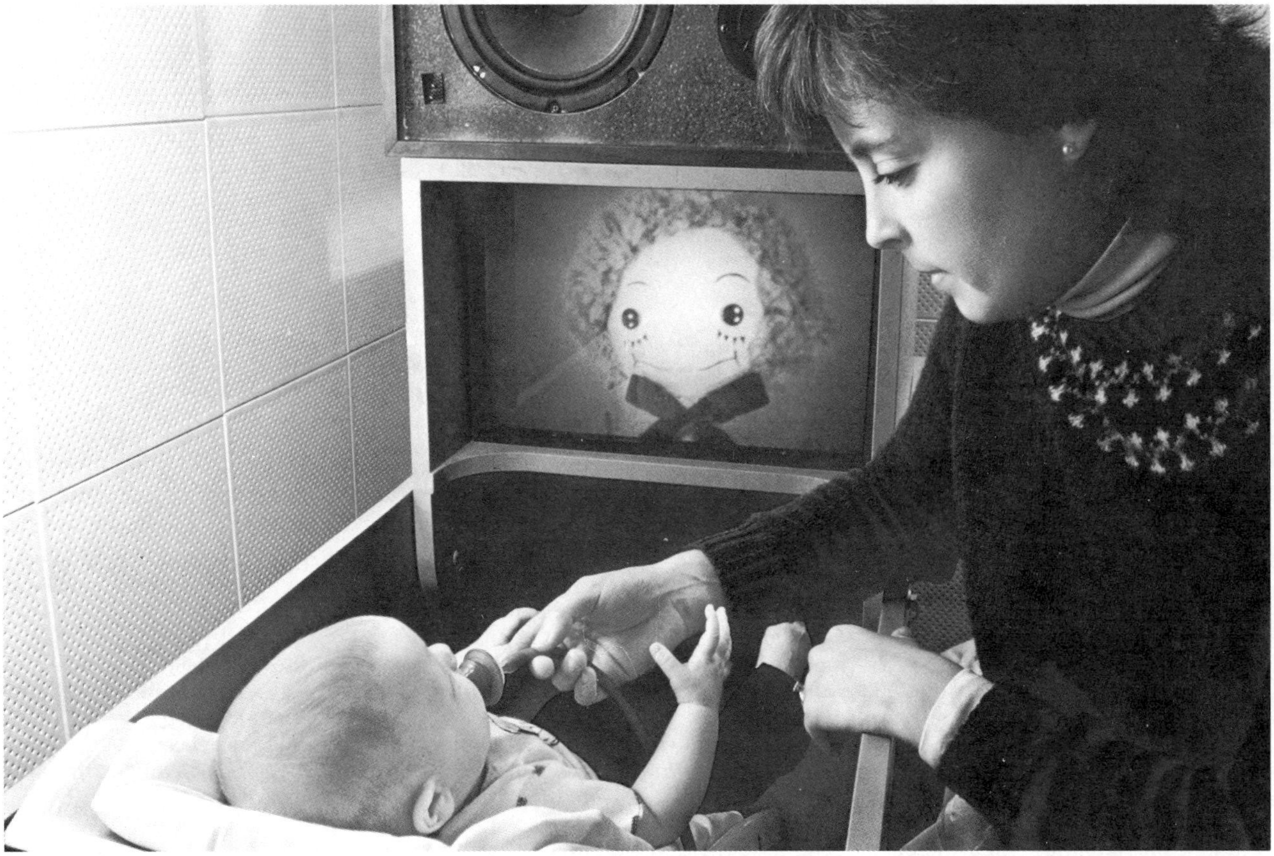

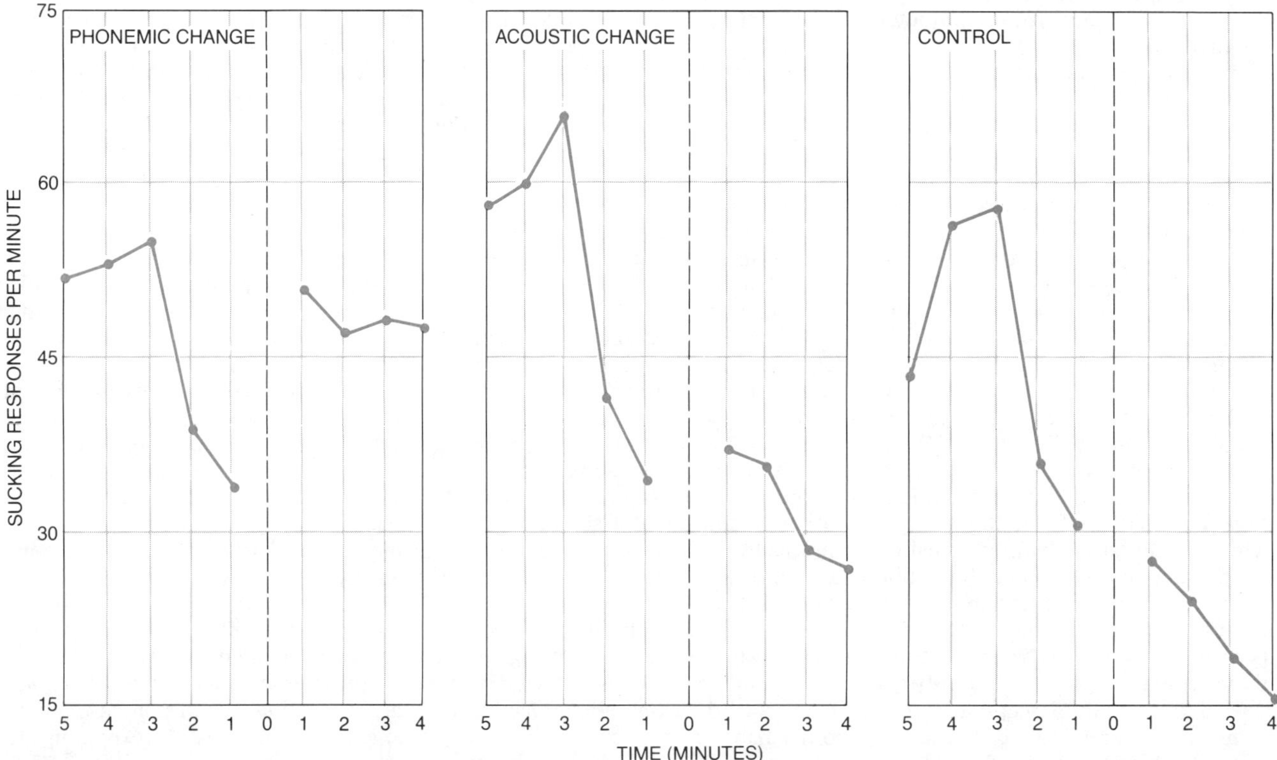

INFANTS' SUCKING RATE indicates their response to a series of speech sounds. In the author's experimental setup (*top*) syllables of synthetic speech were played through the loudspeaker above the screen display of Raggedy Ann while a four-month-old infant sucked on a pacifier connected to recording instruments. Graphs of mean sucking rate (*bottom*), recorded under various experimental conditions with a number of infants, show that when a syllable beginning with a particular consonant was repeated, sucking rate first increased and then decreased as the stimulus became familiar. In some cases the sound changed at a time indicated by the broken line. In one group (*bottom left*) the new sound represented a different consonant; sucking rate increased sharply, showing that the infants perceived a contrast. In a second group (*bottom middle*) the stimulus differed acoustically from the preceding sound but corresponded to the same consonant, and there was little change in sucking rate. A control group of infants (*bottom right*) experienced no change in stimulus.

the perception of speech we are ordinarily aware of discrete phonemic categories rather than of the continuous variation in each acoustic parameter: we perceive speech categorically. In experiments conducted by Leigh Lisker and Arthur S. Abramson of the Haskins Laboratories adults heard computer-generated speech sounds that embodied a range of different values of voice-onset time. In spite of the many variants of voice-onset time the subjects heard nearly all the stimuli either as a voiced phoneme such as the initial consonant of BAH or as a voiceless phoneme such as the consonant that begins PAH. The boundary—the voice-onset time at which listeners began to hear PAH instead of BAH—was situated at about 30 milliseconds following the initial release of air.

To confirm the categorical nature of speech perception the experimenters asked subjects to distinguish pairs of stimuli differing in voice-onset time. If both sounds represented voicing delays of less than 30 milliseconds, the listeners generally heard them as two identical instances of BAH; if the voice-onset times of both were longer than 30 milliseconds, the listeners tended to hear two PAH's, indistinguishable although acoustically different. Only when the stimuli straddled the 30-millisecond boundary could subjects distinguish them consistently. Catherine G. Wolf, then at Brown University, obtained similar evidence of categorical perception in school-age children.

How much of this mechanism of categorical perception, which enables us to perceive speech reliably in spite of the lack of precision of the speech signal, is innate? The fact that speakers of different languages are attuned to somewhat different phonemic distinctions suggests that the influence of the linguistic environment on speech perception is powerful. Japanese speakers fail to perceive the contrast between the phonemes /r/ and /l/, a standard distinction in English; English speakers do not notice a fundamental contrast in voicing that distinguishes certain phonemes in Thai. Yet certain phonemic distinctions are present in languages throughout the world. It seemed possible to my colleagues and me that strong biological determinants, modified by later linguistic experience, might underlie the categorical perception of speech. To find out whether this is the case we did experiments with infants not yet able to speak, in whom one would expect the influence of their parents' language to be minimal.

In 1971 Einar R. Siqueland, Peter W. Jusczyk, James Vigorito and I examined the perception of voice-onset time in one- and four-month-old infants. We exposed the infants to three different pairs of sounds. The voice-onset times of one pair were 20 and 40 milliseconds; thus the stimuli fell on opposite sides of the category boundary recognized by adult speakers of English and other languages. To adult ears the stimuli sounded like the syllables BAH and PAH. In each of the other pairs, with voice-onset times of zero and 20 milliseconds and 60 and 80 milliseconds, both stimuli fell on the same side of the voiced/voiceless boundary; both were instances of BAH or PAH.

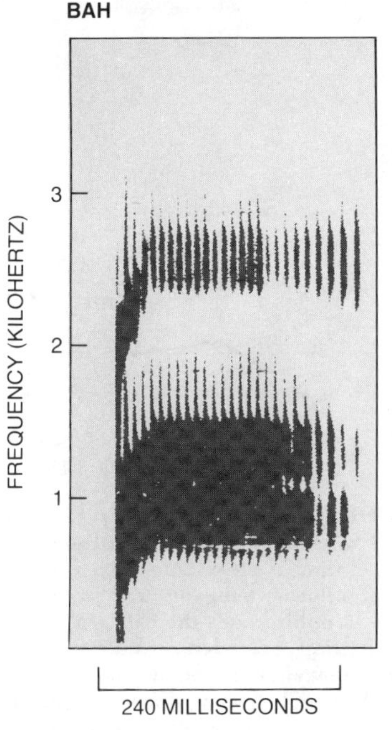

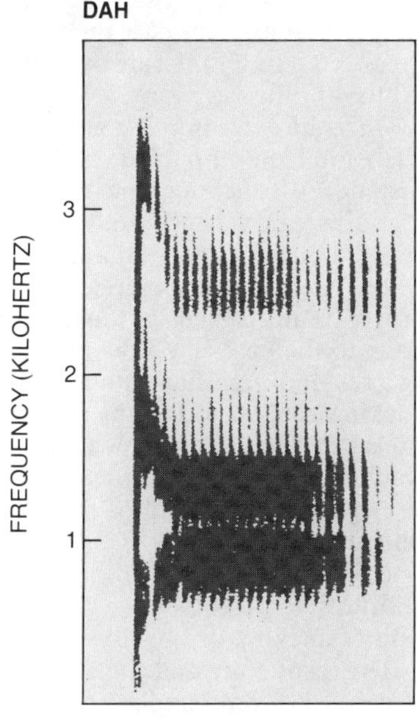

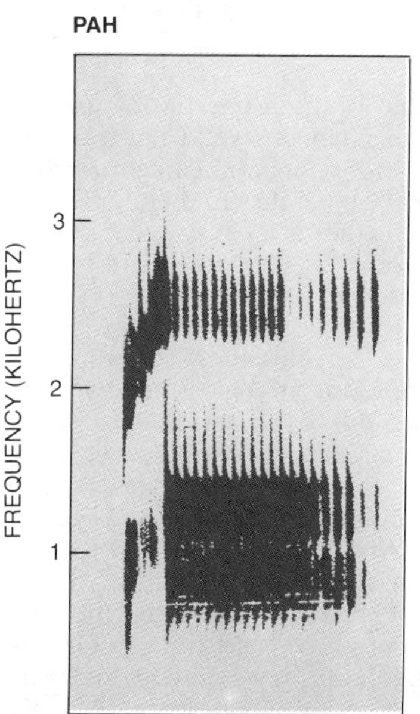

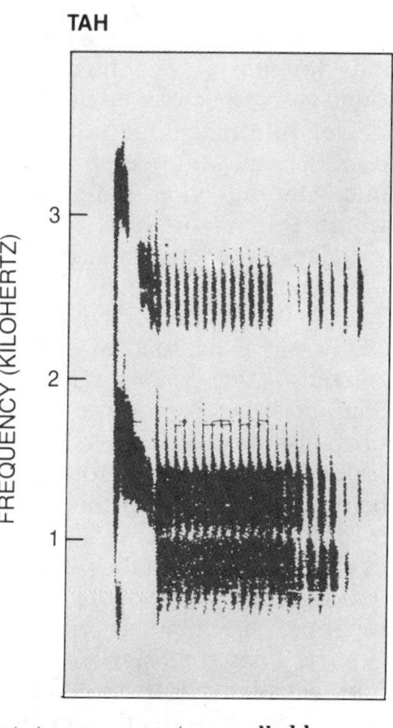

SPECTROGRAMS of syllables beginning with different stop consonants, so called because they require an interruption in the flow of air through the vocal tract, show the underlying differences in acoustic characteristics. The four acoustic signatures differ in the frequency and timing of their component bands of acoustic energy, known as formants. The consonants paired horizontally are distinguished by the frequency at which the formants begin, a reflection of the point within the vocal tract at which constriction occurs. The frequency of the highest formant of the sound BAH, for example, begins at about two kilohertz and then rises, while that of the third formant of DAH begins at about three kilohertz and falls. Consonants paired vertically differ in voice-onset time, a measure of the delay between the release of air and the vibration of the vocal cords. In spectrograms for BAH and DAH a voice-onset time of zero is evident in the presence of periodicity, a series of spiky vertical striations that indicate vocal-cord vibration, at the beginning of all three formants. In spectrograms for PAH and TAH there is a gap before the lowest formant appears and periodicity begins in the two higher formants, reflecting a longer delay in onset of voicing.

Infants a few months old cannot report their perceptions directly. In order to gauge the infants' responses to the stimuli we resorted to a methodology called the high-amplitude sucking procedure. Each infant sucked on a pacifier wired to a pressure transducer, which in turn was connected to recording instruments. We adjusted the setup's sensitivity separately for each infant so that in every case the apparatus recorded a base-line rate of sucking of 20 to 40 times a minute.

Once the experiment was under way, each time the apparatus recorded an instance of sucking one sound of a stimulus pair was played. When an infant encounters a new stimulus, its rate of sucking typically increases for several minutes, then gradually settles back to the base-line rate, presumably as a result of familiarization. When the sucking rates of our subjects fell to a preset level as they grew accustomed to the first sound, we shifted the stimulus to the other sound of the stimulus pair. If an infant grows familiar with one stimulus and then encounters a stimulus it perceives as different, its rate of sucking ordinarily increases.

The results showed that infants, like people who command a language, perceive differences in voice-onset time categorically. When both the sounds to which an infant subject was exposed lay on the same side of the 30-millisecond boundary, the shift from one sound to another evoked no increase in sucking rate. The infants appeared not to notice the change in voice-onset time. On the other hand, when the stimuli fell on opposite sides of the boundary, a sharp increase in sucking rate occurred at the shift, indicating that the infants perceived a change.

Other investigators and I have discovered further perceptual boundaries in infants' responses to the acoustic information in speech. Like adults, they respond categorically to changes in the onset frequency of the second and third formants, an acoustic cue that indicates differences in the place of articulation of a consonant. The same pattern holds in their responses to the acoustic cues that signal the distinctions between nasal and stop consonants, exemplified by the initial sounds of MAH and BAH, and between stop consonants and semivowels such as the initial sound of WAH.

It is difficult to see how learning could account for the mode of perception we have demonstrated in infants. What events during the first few weeks of life would train an infant to respond categorically to gradations of acoustic properties? A simpler view is that categorization occurs because a child is born with perceptual mechanisms that are tuned to the properties of speech. These mechanisms yield the forerunners of the phonemic categories that later will enable the child unthinkingly to convert the variable signal of speech into a series of phonemes and thence into words and meanings.

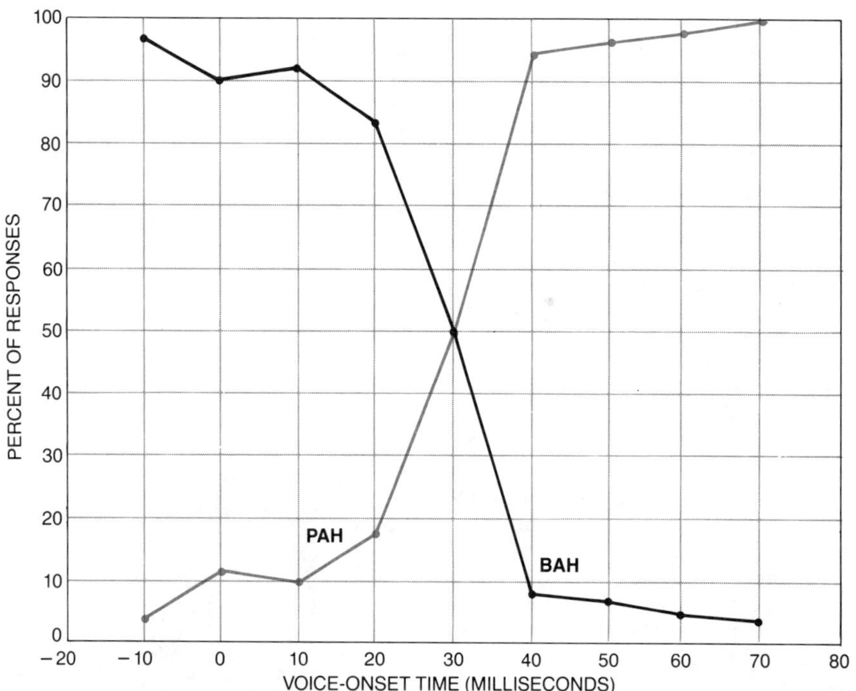

CATEGORICAL PERCEPTION is reflected in curves showing the relative proportions of responses when children were asked to identify a synthetic speech sound with a particular voice-onset time as an instance of a voiced (BAH) or a voiceless (PAH) consonantal sound. Instead of a linear change in the percentages the curves show that at voice-onset times of less than 30 milliseconds the children almost always identified the stimulus as BAH; when voice-onset time exceeded 30 milliseconds, they tended to hear the sound as PAH. The perceptual tendency shifted abruptly at 30 milliseconds. The study, done by Catherine G. Wolf at Brown University, suggests that perceptual categories, rather than continuous gradations in the acoustic properties of the speech signal, shape the perception of speech.

If these perceptual mechanisms do represent a biological endowment, they should be universal. The same perceptual patterns should occur in infants of every linguistic background. In research reported in 1975 Robert E. Lasky, Ann Syrdal-Lasky and Robert E. Klein, then at the Institute of Nutrition in Panama, investigated the perception of voice-onset time by Guatemalan infants, born into a Spanish-speaking environment. The group's experimental methods differed from those used in our 1971 study: in place of changes in sucking rate they used changes in heart rate as the gauge of infants' response to the speech patterns. The study also tested sensitivity to a voicing category we had omitted, one found among stop consonants at the beginning of syllables in Thai and in a number of other languages although not in English. In this so-called prevoiced category the vocal cords begin to vibrate up to 100 milliseconds before the release of air, in a kind of prefatory hum.

Lasky and his co-workers exposed the infants to three pairs of stimuli. In the first pair the voice-onset times fell at 20 and 60 milliseconds after consonantal release; thus the two sounds lay on opposite sides of the voiced/voiceless boundary recognized by speakers of English and other languages, although as it happens not by Spanish speakers. The stimuli in the second pair had voice-onset times of 60 and 20 milliseconds prior to consonantal release and fell on opposite sides of the prevoiced/voiced boundary of Thai. In the sounds of the final pair voicing began 20 milliseconds before and 20 milliseconds after consonantal release. Spanish speakers, in contrast to speakers of many other languages, perceive the voiced/voiceless boundary as falling between those two values.

The tracings of heart rate recorded any increases that occurred when the infants, having grown accustomed to the first sound of a stimulus pair, heard the second sound. The data showed the young subjects responded to the prevoiced/voiced distinction, with a boundary between 60 and 20 milliseconds before consonantal release, and also to the voiced/voiceless distinction with a boundary between 20 and 60 milliseconds following release. The voicing distinction peculiar to Spanish evoked no change in heart rate.

In 1976 Lynn A. Streeter, then at the Bell Laboratories, published evidence that infants born into a Kikuyu-speaking culture in Kenya display much the same perceptual pattern as the Guatemalan babies. Richard N. Aslin, David B. Pisoni, Beth L. Hennessy and Alan J. Perey of Indiana University recently completed the study of voice-onset-time sensitivity among infants in English-speaking communities by showing that they respond to the prevoiced/voiced contrast just as they do to the voiced/voiceless distinction. It appears that infants the world over are equipped with an inborn sensitivity to these three categories of voicing, whether or not the distinctions are important in their parent language.

The perception of speech is a complex and subtle process, which the studies of categorical perception described so far probe only in the simplest terms. The acoustic information that enables a listener to perceive distinctions in voicing illustrates the point. So far we have treated the essential information as a single continuum of time measuring the interval between consonantal release and the beginning of voicing. In ordinary speech, however, an interplay of temporal and spectral factors governs the perception of voicing distinctions. These acoustic properties interact in what might be called perceptual trading relations: a change in the value of one property alters the value of another at which the perceptual boundary falls.

For example, because of functional characteristics of the mechanisms of articulation, the frequency of the first, or lowest, formant rises as voice-onset time increases. Our perceptual system seems to be attuned to the relation: a frequency change can substitute for a

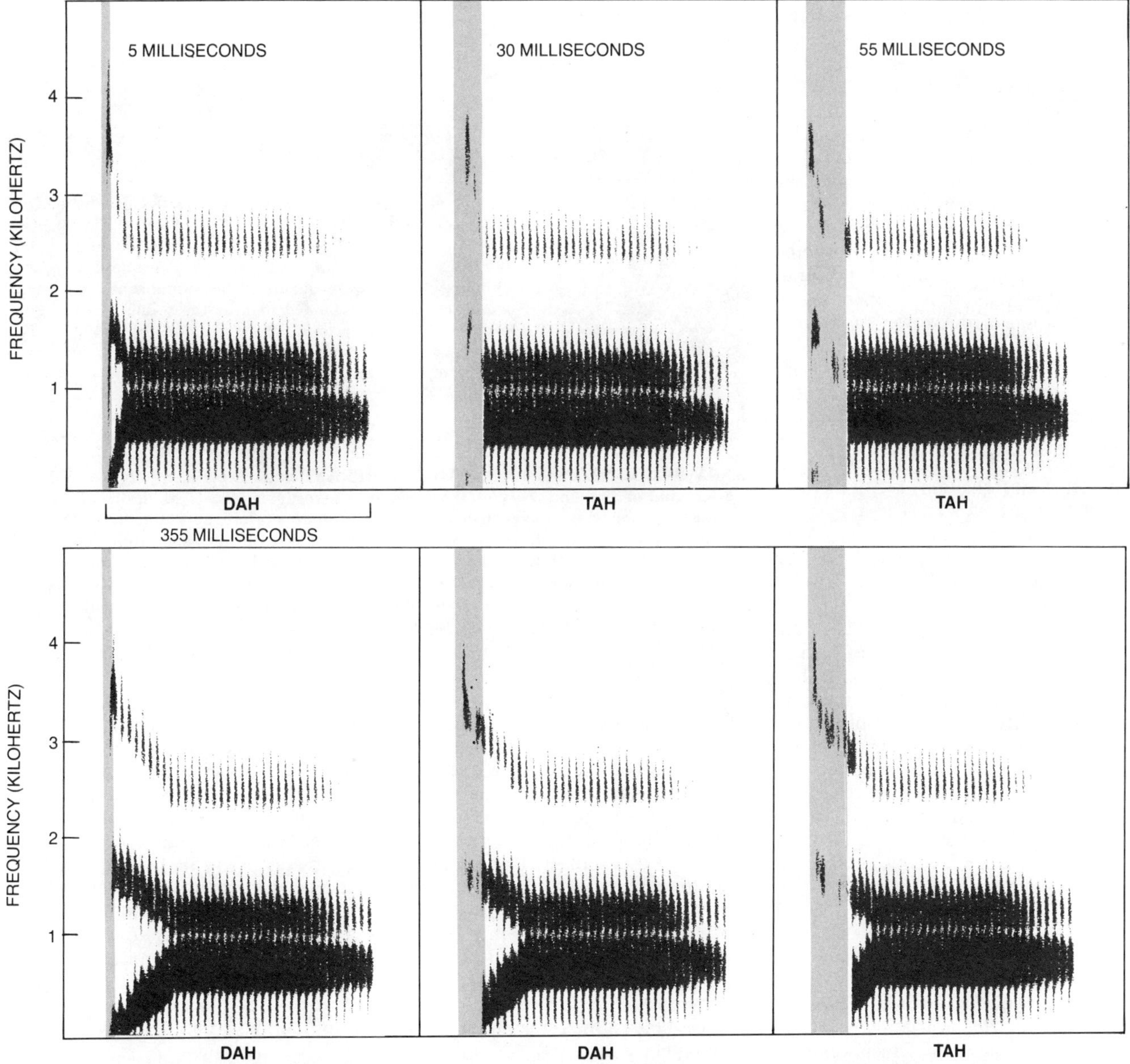

SHIFT IN A PERCEPTUAL BOUNDARY can occur when two acoustic cues are altered independently. The consonants beginning the six syllables shown in spectrographic form vary in voice-onset time and in the onset frequency of the lowest formant; to adult ears the sounds are the syllables DAH and TAH. At a high onset frequency (*top row, visible in second and third spectrograms*) infants detected the DAH/TAH contrast between sounds having voice-onset times of five and 30 milliseconds. When the onset frequency was low (*second and third spectrograms in bottom row*), voice-onset time had to increase to between 30 and 55 milliseconds before the infants reacted to the phonemic contrast. Such interactions between two acoustic variables are known as perceptual trading relations.

change in the temporal cue. When the first formant begins at a higher frequency, the effect is the same as if the voice-onset time had lengthened. As a result, at higher onset frequencies adults perceive the voiced/voiceless boundary earlier in the continuum of voice-onset times.

The same subtleties are apparent in the perceptual systems of infants. In 1983 Joanne L. Miller of Northeastern University and I showed that one perceptual trading relation found in adults also holds in infants' responses. We found that the voice-onset time at which three- and four-month-old infants recognize a shift from the voiced initial sound of the syllable DAH to the voiceless sound of TAH varies with the onset frequency of the first formant.

A second complication in the perceptual process arises from the fact that the category boundaries perceived by adults shift not only as a result of the interplay of multiple cues but also with variations in acoustic context. In this respect as well infants display the forerunners of more mature patterns of perception. Miller and I have shown that infants, like adults, distinguish the stop consonant of BAH and the semivowel of WAH differently depending on the duration of the vowel sound that follows. The acoustic basis of the distinction is the length of the formant transitions: the periods needed for the central frequencies of the formants to reach the values appropriate for the vowel that follows. In the case of BAH the formant transitions are swift; with WAH they are slower. The longer the vowel duration is, however, the slower the formant transitions must be before infants recognize a change in stimulus from BAH to WAH.

Other quite complex effects of context on the categorization of speech by infants have been demonstrated. Jusczyk and his associates at the University of Oregon found a shift in the formant-onset frequencies at which infants detect a distinction between phonemes differing in place of articulation. The boundary value varied depending on whether an additional band of noiselike acoustic energy was present, signaling a fricative rather than a stop consonant.

/A/ . . . /A/ . . . /A/ . . . /A/ . . . /A/ . . . /A/ . . . /A/ . . . /A/ . . . /A/ . . . /A/ . . . /A/ . . . /A/ . . . /A/ . . . /A/

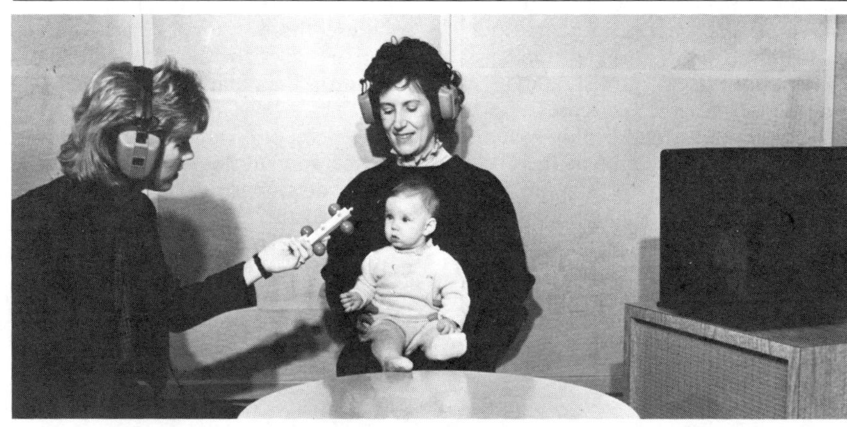

/I/ . . . /I/ . . . /I/ . . . /I/ . . . /I/ . . . /I/ . . . /I/ . . . /I/ . . . /I/ . . . /I/ . . . /I/ . . . /I/ . . . /I/ . . . /I/

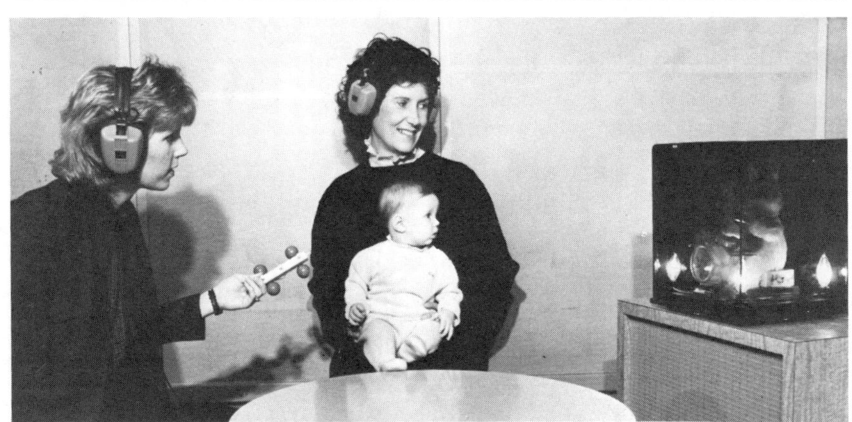

BABY RECOGNIZES A PHONEMIC CONTRAST in an experiment devised by Patricia K. Kuhl of the University of Washington to investigate infants' ability to distinguish contrasting phonemes from acoustically varied instances of the same phoneme. In this case the baby, its attention held by a toy, ignored variations in speaker and intonation among repetitions of the vowel sound / a /, as in POP (*top*). When instances of the vowel / i /, as in PEEP, interrupted the sequence, the infant turned away from the toy and toward the loudspeaker (*bottom*), indicating recognition of the linguistically important contrast. The sight of a mechanical stuffed rabbit, illuminated in its case on top of the loudspeaker when the contrasting phoneme was played, served to reward the infant's accurate response.

The complex mechanism of categorical perception enables an individual to recognize phonemes consistently in spite of great variation in crucial acoustic parameters. Other kinds of variability blur the definition of the speech signal even further. The length of syllables, along with other temporal characteristics of speech, changes with rate of speech and patterns of emphasis; wide variations in the fundamental frequency of voicing and in the spacing of resonant frequencies occur as a result of the speaker's sex, age and emotional state. Some mechanism must enable us to listen through the variation to hear the same phoneme each time it is spoken. This phenomenon of perceptual constancy cannot be investigated directly in infants. But studies of infants' ability to form equivalence classes—groups of stimuli that evoke the same response in spite of obvious differences—suggest infants possess at least the forerunners of perceptual constancy.

Patricia K. Kuhl and her colleagues at the University of Washington have investigated the formation of equivalence classes for the sounds of speech in six-month-old infants. In the first stage of each experiment the Kuhl group trained infants to turn their head 90 degrees toward a loudspeaker whenever a series of contrasting stimuli interrupted a background sound; the sight of a colorful, moving toy that appeared above the loudspeaker as the contrasting sequence was played rewarded successful responses. In one experiment identical instances of the vowel sound / a /, as in POP, served as the background stimulus; identical versions of / i /, as in PEEP, provided the contrast. Once the training was complete the stimuli were varied: the vowels, / a / and / i /, remained the same but the infants now heard both vowels in a variety of voices and intonations. Sequences without contrasting stimuli, in which every sound was a variant of / a /, served as controls.

The infants' success in singling out

contrasting stimuli and ignoring within-category acoustic variations during the control trials was impressive. When both inappropriate head-turnings and missed contrasts were counted, they averaged about 80 percent correct; in seven out of eight cases the infants scored better than if their responses had reflected chance. When Kuhl and her colleagues repeated the experiment with the acoustically less distinctive vowels / a / and / ɔ / (as in PAW), the infants still could detect equivalent sounds, although less reliably; the proportion of correct responses fell to 67 percent and only four out of eight infants bettered the expected score for random responses.

When both the background and the contrasting sequences included arbitrarily chosen variants of both / a / and / i /, however, the infants could not learn to differentiate members of the two sequences, in spite of the reward elicited by a correct response. They could not be trained to recognize an arbitrary grouping of sounds that had no linguistic property in common. They could respond correctly, indicating they had organized diverse stimuli into equivalence classes, only when the background and contrasting sequences represented different categories of speech. The finding is further evidence that long before infants can speak and understand they are particularly sensitive to the acoustic distinctions crucial to the comprehension of speech. It adds weight to the case for a set of inborn mechanisms that are specialized for speech perception.

The diversity among the sound systems of human languages makes it clear that environmental factors affect the perceptual dispositions with which an infant is born. What happens as the linguistic environment created by a child's parents and companions interacts with inborn perceptual mechanisms? It appears that perceptual horizons narrow as a child learns his or her native language. The child retains and probably sharpens those perceptual capacities that correspond to phonemic distinctions in the parental language but loses the ability to detect distinctions that do not occur in the native language.

Studies of voice-onset-time perception testify to the decline in some discriminative powers as the infant develops. While infants from diverse linguistic backgrounds respond to contrasts in prevoiced, voiced and voiceless initial consonants, adult speakers of some languages, including English, recognize only the distinction between the voiced and the voiceless categories. Although native adult Japanese speakers are virtually unable to perceive the distinction between the sounds of / r / and / l / without special training, I have found that the distinction is among those to which American infants—and presumably Japanese infants—have an innate sensitivity. Similarly, research by Janet F. Werker of Dalhousie University in Nova Scotia and Richard C. Tees of the University of British Columbia showed that six- to eight-month-old infants from an English-speaking background readily distinguish phonemic contrasts in Hindi and Salish, a North American Indian language. When they were tested again at the age of 12 months, the same infants, like English-speaking adults, did not detect the contrasts to which they had earlier been sensitive.

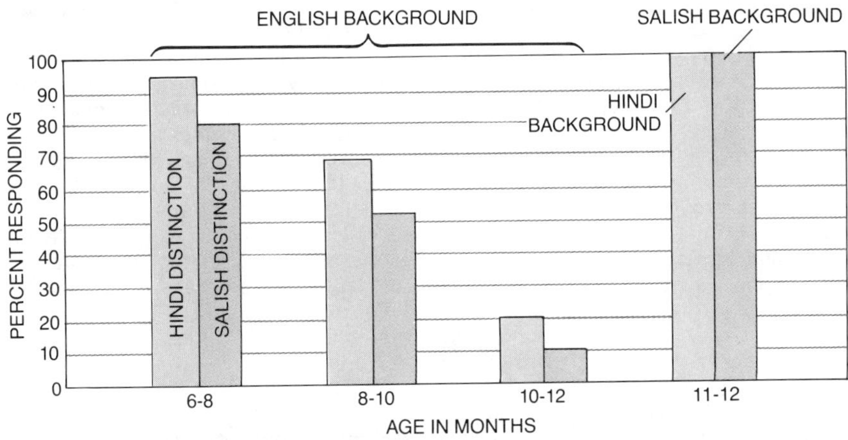

WANING OF UNUSED PERCEPTUAL POWERS is evident in the responses of infants from an English-speaking background to linguistic contrasts that are foreign to English. When Janet F. Werker of Dalhousie University in Nova Scotia and Richard C. Tees of the University of British Columbia simultaneously tested infants in different age groups, the proportion responding to consonantal contrasts from Hindi and Salish, a North American Indian language, fell rapidly with age. One-year-old Hindi and Salish infants, in contrast, retain the capacity to perceive the linguistic contrasts native to their respective languages.

The decline in perceptual abilities through exposure to a restricted environment is familiar. When kittens are raised wearing goggles that limit the visual input of one eye to a series of horizontal stripes and that of the other eye to vertical stripes, corresponding areas of the visual cortex lose their sensitivity to stripes running in other directions. Such losses seem to be irreversible, no matter how varied the animal's later surroundings. In contrast, we can recover at least some of our initial capacities to detect the acoustic information underlying phonemic contrasts. For instance, when the acoustic information critical to phonemic distinctions in Hindi and Salish is embodied in sounds that usually are not heard as speech, English speakers can detect differences to which they are ordinarily insensitive.

Apparently the restricted linguistic environment of one's native language does not inactivate unused perceptual mechanisms completely. We learn to listen primarily for the acoustic distinctions that correspond to phonemic contrasts in our own language. Given the right task or instructions, however, we can detect unfamiliar acoustic distinctions even though we do not perceive them as marking phonemic contrasts. Furthermore, with enough experience the perception of non-native distinctions begins to operate at the phonemic level: after considerable experience with spoken English, native speakers of Japanese can distinguish the phonemes / r / and / l / categorically and almost as accurately as native English speakers. The fact that perceptual mechanisms available to us as infants can still operate in adulthood, after long disuse, confounds hypotheses that early experience with language immutably alters some of the mechanisms of speech perception.

The most dramatic demonstration of the innate mechanisms of perception other workers and I have studied, however, takes place in infancy, as a child begins to learn its parents' language. It is now clear that an infant is born with many of the underpinnings of later speech perception and comprehension. It may be that like the specialized anatomy of the vocal tract and the speech centers in the brain these innate perceptual capacities evolved specifically for the perception and comprehension of speech. They are an evolutionary answer to the need for each infant to acquire its parents' language and culture as early in life as possible. The effectiveness of these mechanisms is reflected in the swiftness with which a child joins the community of language.

3 Creole Languages

by Derek Bickerton
July 1983

These widely scattered languages show striking similarities. The development of Creole in Hawaii suggests children learn a language by first constructing an abstract form of a creole

The ancient Greek historian Herodotus records the story of Psamtik I, pharaoh of Egypt in the seventh century B.C., who set out to discover the original language of humanity. On royal decree two infants were taken away from their parents and put in the care of a mute shepherd, who was instructed to raise the children in isolation from other people. The shepherd was to take note of the first word uttered by the children; "uncorrupted" by the language of their forefathers, Psamtik reasoned, they would begin to speak in the pure tongue from which all other languages were derived. The first intelligible sound the children made was "bekos," which meant bread in the ancient language Phrygian. Therefore, Psamtik maintained, the original language of humanity is Phrygian.

The story has amused generations of linguistics students. Most linguists, who have taken it for granted that no such experiment should ever be carried out, have dismissed the Psamtik experiment as being defective in design and unlikely to yield any useful result. Indeed, the assumption that an "original" vocabulary can be recovered is overoptimistic, and linguistic isolation of the individual, which has been documented in a few cases of severe child abuse, usually results in the absence of language. Nevertheless, a modified form of the experiment has been repeated many times over the past 500 years among the children of slaves and laborers who were pressed into service by the European colonial powers.

These laborers, who were shipped from many parts of the world to tend and harvest crops in Africa, the Indian Ocean region, the Orient, the Caribbean and Hawaii, were obliged to communicate within their polyglot community by means of the rudimentary speech system called pidgin. Pidgin speech is extremely impoverished in syntax and vocabulary, but for the children born into the colonial community it was the only common language available. From these modest beginnings new native languages evolved among the children, which are generically called creole languages. It can be shown that they exhibit the complexity, nuance and expressive power universally found in the more established languages of the world.

Taken at face value, the development of many different creole languages suggests that the search for a single, original language is misguided. For many years, however, scholars have noted a remarkable similarity of structure among all the creole languages. It can now be demonstrated, by considering the origin of creole language in Hawaii, that similarities among creoles cannot be accounted for by contact with other languages, either indigenous or imported. The finding suggests that what is common to creole languages may indeed form the basis of the acquisition of language by children everywhere. There is now an impressive body of evidence to support this hypothesis: between the ages of two and four the child born into a community of linguistically competent adults speaks a variety of language whose structure bears a deep resemblance to the structure of creole languages. Hence, by an ironic stroke of justice, the surviving linguistic remnants of colonialism may offer indispensable keys to the study of our own linguistic heritage.

The historical conditions that favored the development of creole languages are well known. Between 1500 and 1900 England, France, the Netherlands, Portugal and Spain established numerous labor-intensive, agricultural economies on isolated littorals and underpopulated tropical islands throughout the world. The colonies were engaged primarily in monoculture, usually sugar, and their economic viability depended on an abundance of cheap labor imported from distant regions under conditions of chattel slavery. Workers were drawn first from West Africa and later from East Africa, India and the Orient, and they spoke a variety of mutually incomprehensible languages.

Under more salutary conditions of immigration the workers or their children would eventually have learned the language of the local colonial power, but two factors combined to keep them from doing so. First, the number of speakers of the colonial languages rarely exceeded 20 percent of the total population, and it was often less than 10 percent. In other words, there were relatively few people from whom the dominant language could have been learned. Second, the colonial societies were small, autocratic and rigidly stratified. There were few chances for prolonged linguistic contact between field laborers and speakers of the dominant language.

Except in Hawaii, there is little reliable documentary evidence concerning the early linguistic history of the colonial societies. It has generally been assumed that pidgin developed as a contact language solely to allow communication between masters and workers and among workers from various immigrant groups. Creole languages then arose among the children of the workers through the "expansion" of pidgin; there was little occasion for the children to use the ancestral languages of their parents, and they still lacked access to the language of the dominant culture. What is meant by the term "expansion" has remained obscure until my colleagues and I began our studies in Hawaii.

The unique advantage for the study of creole language in Hawaii is that the details of its formation can be reconstructed at least in part from the speech of people still living. Although Hawaiian contact with Europeans goes back to 1778, it was not until 1876 that a revision in the U.S. tariff laws, allowing the free importation of Hawaiian sugar, enabled Hawaiian sugar plantations to increase their output by several hundred percent. A polyglot force of indentured laborers, made up of Chinese, Filipinos, Japanese, Koreans, Portuguese, Puerto Ricans and others, began to be assembled, and by 1900 it outnumbered the other groups in Hawaii, both native and European, by a ratio of two to one.

A pidgin based on the Polynesian language Hawaiian initially served as a means of communication between immigrants and the locally born, but the annexation of Hawaii by the U.S. in 1898 eventually led to the replacement of Hawaiian by English. After 1900 the Hawaiian language declined, and pidgin Hawaiian was replaced as a lingua franca by a pidgin based on English. By the time we began our intensive study of language variation in Hawaii in the early 1970's there were still many survivors, both immigrant and locally born, from the years 1900 until 1920.

Our recordings of locally born people make it clear that the process of creolization was under way by 1900 and was certainly complete by 1920. Most of the linguistic features that characterize Hawaiian Creole English are present in the speech of working-class people born in Hawaii since 1905; before that date the proportion of Creole speakers to the rest of the population falls off rapidly. On the other hand, the speech of immigrants is always some form of pidgin, although just what form it takes depends on the date of the immigrant's arrival in Hawaii as well as the immigrant's language background. The pidgin spoken by the earliest immigrants among our subjects is much more rudimentary than that spoken by the later ones, probably because the latter were exposed to Creole as well as pidgin. Nevertheless, the distinction between pidgin and Creole remains fundamental: anyone familiar with Hawaii can quickly identify the ethnic origins of any immigrant on the basis of speech patterns alone. Without a conversational topic or a person's physical appearance as a guide, however, no one can reliably identify the ethnic origins of any locally born speaker solely on the basis of the speaker's pronunciation or the grammatical structure of the utterances.

One of the main characteristics of pidgin, therefore, is its variability from speaker to speaker. Each immigrant seems to have gone about the task of inventing a makeshift language in some individual way. For example, pidgin speakers of Japanese ancestry generally place the verb at the end of a sentence, as in "The poor people all potato eat" ("All that the poor people ate were potatoes"). Filipino pidgin, however, places the verb before the subject: "Work hard these people" ("These people work hard"). More often word order follows no fixed principle except the pragmatic one that old, shared information is stated near the beginning of a sentence and new information near the end.

It is probably the case that anything expressible in Creole, or in English for that matter, can also be expressed in pidgin. Nevertheless, the pidgin speaker is at a great disadvantage, because pidgin lacks many of the building blocks possessed by all native languages. Such everyday necessities of language as articles, prepositions and auxiliary verbs are either absent or appear sporadically in a quite unpredictable fashion. Pidgin sentences have no subordinate clauses, and single-clause utterances frequently lack verbs.

The first of the following examples

INDENTURED SUGARCANE WORKERS, who spoke a rudimentary language called pidgin, are shown in a photograph made in Hawaii by the late Ray Jerome Baker in 1924. Thousands of such workers from many countries were brought to Hawaii in the late 19th and early 20th centuries to meet the labor demands of large sugarcane and pineapple plantations. Pidgin language developed out of the need for communication among the various language groups within this polyglot labor force; the workers in the photograph, for example, although primarily from the Philippines, originally spoke a variety of mutually incomprehensible languages such as Visayan, Ilocano and Tagalog. The children of pidgin-speaking parents remained largely isolated from speakers of Hawaiian or English, and they inherited no consistent linguistic model from the previous generation that could meet their needs. There arose among these children a language much more sophisticated than pidgin called Hawaiian Creole English, whose vocabulary is primarily English but whose structure, or grammar, is quite distinct from that of English or any other noncreole language. Socioeconomic circumstances similar to those in Hawaii frequently gave rise to pidgin languages throughout the world; these languages were later developed into creole languages by the children of immigrant laborers. The original photograph is in the collection of Ray Jerome Baker and Robert E. Van Dyke in Honolulu.

was recorded from a pidgin-speaking Korean; omitted words are bracketed in the translation: "And a too much children, small children, house money pay" ("And [I had] too many children, small children, [I had] to pay the rent"). The second example was recorded from a Japanese speaker: "Before mill no more Filipino no nothing" ("Before the mill [was built, there were] no Filipinos here at all"). The third example, recorded from the speech of a retired bus driver, illustrates the heroic measures needed to say anything out of the ordinary in pidgin: "Sometime good road get, sometime, all same bend get, enguru [angle] get, no? Any kind same. All same human life, all same" ("Sometimes there's a good road, sometimes there's, like, bends, corners, right? Everything's like that. Human life's just like that").

The language-learning task confronted by the child born into a community of such speakers is far different from the task imposed on the child who is surrounded by linguistically competent adults. The children of English or Chinese parents, for example, are presented with accurate models to follow. Although their mistakes are seldom overtly corrected, they can almost constantly check their own utterances against those of older speakers and adapt them

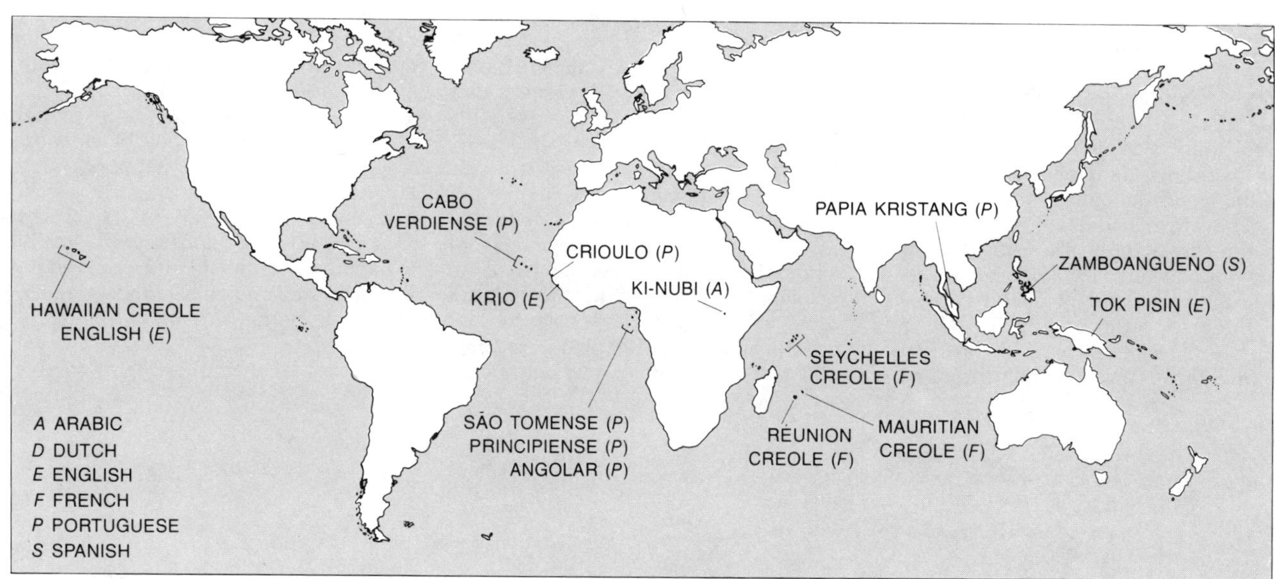

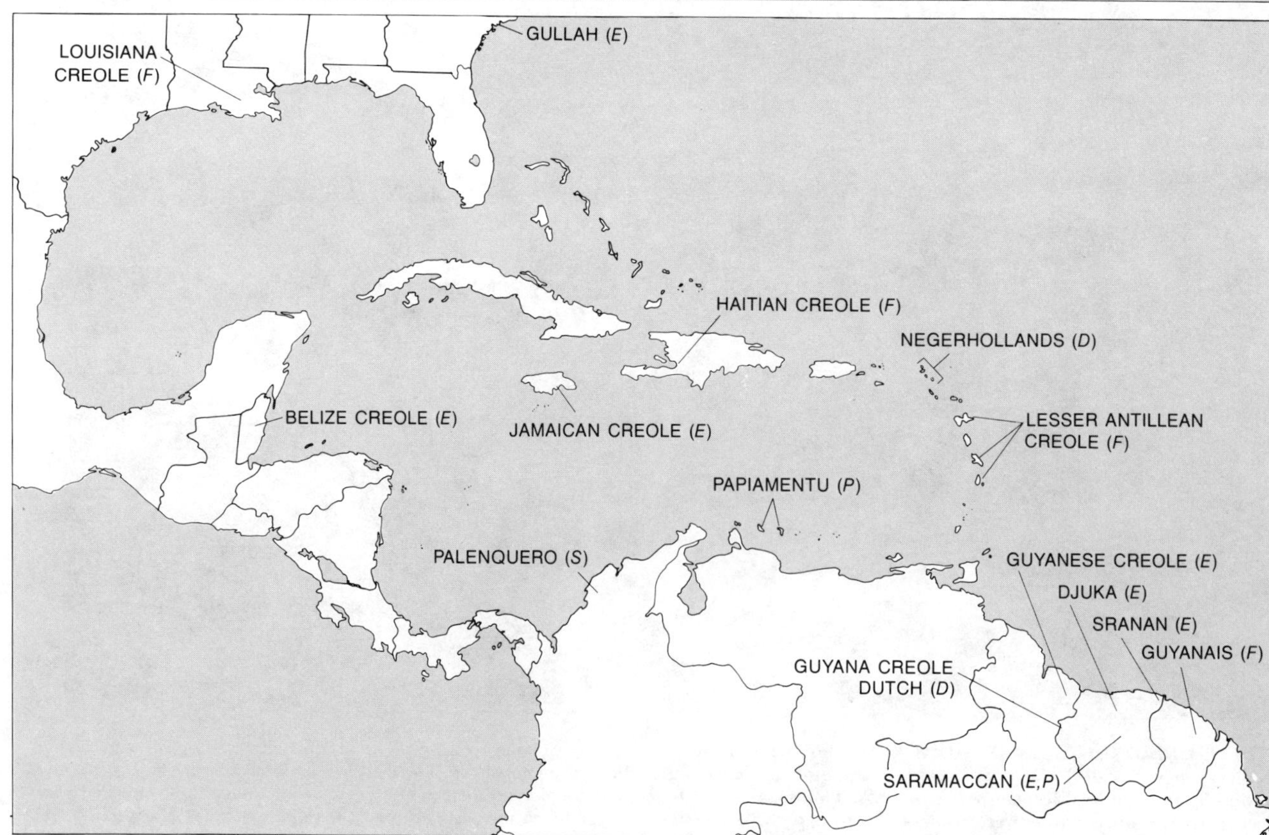

WORLDWIDE DISTRIBUTION of creole languages reflects the historical circumstances of their development. Almost all creoles arose on isolated tropical littorals or islands, where colonial powers had established agricultural economies based on cheap immigrant labor. The geographic dispersion of the colonies suggests that creole languages developed independently of one another. The letters in parentheses after the name of each language indicate the colonial language from which most of the vocabulary of the creole is borrowed.

where necessary. When they have mastered the simpler structures of their language, more complex structures are readily available.

For the Hawaiian-born child of immigrant parents, however, there was no consistent linguistic model for the basic word order of simple sentences and often no model at all for the more complicated structures of language. Many such children were born of interethnic or interracial marriages, and so even at home there was little occasion to speak the native language of either parent. Moreover, even among the children not born of linguistically mixed parents there was considerable incentive to abandon the parents' native language and adopt some version of pidgin in the company of peers and neighboring adults. Like first-generation immigrant children elsewhere, the children of Hawaiian immigrants often became bilingual or even trilingual, and they adopted the common language of their peers as a native language in spite of considerable efforts by their parents to maintain the ancestral tongue.

The historical evidence is consistent with the view that the structure of Creole arose without significant borrowing from other languages. Bilingual or trilingual children of school age need not (and usually do not) mix up the structural features of the languages they speak, and there is no reason to suppose such crossovers were common in Hawaii. The most compelling argument for the autonomous emergence of Creole, however, is its observed uniformity. How, within a single generation, did such a consistent and uniform language develop out of the linguistic free-for-all that was pidgin in Hawaii? Even if all the children of various immigrant groups had begun by learning the languages of their parents, and even if the differences among the various pidgins had been smoothed by interaction and contact among the children, the homogeneity of the language that developed remains in need of explanation. Fifty years of contact among pidgin-speaking adults were not enough to erase the differences among the national language groups; the homogeneity must have resulted from the differences between children and adults.

One might still suppose the structural uniformity of Creole is derived from certain structures of one of the ancestral languages or perhaps from certain structures of English, the language of the plantation owners. There are numerous differences, however, between the structure of Creole and the structure of any of the languages with which Creole speakers might have been in contact. In English, for example, it is possible to refer to an object or a group of objects in a nonspecific way, but English grammar forces the speaker to state in advance whether the number of unspecified objects is one or many, singular or plural. One must say either "I am going to the store to buy a shirt" or "I am going to the store to buy shirts," even though one may not want to commit oneself in advance to buying any particular number of shirts.

In Creole a grammatically neutral marker for number can be employed on the noun "shirt" in order to avoid specifying number: "I stay go da store for buy shirt" ("I am going to the store to buy shirt"). Moreover, in Creole the addition of a definite or an indefinite article to "shirt" changes the meaning of the sentence. In saying "I stay go da store for buy one shirt" the Creole speaker asserts the shirt is a specific one; in the sentence "I stay go da store for buy da shirt" the speaker further presupposes

PIDGIN	HAWAIIAN CREOLE ENGLISH
Building—high place—wall part—time—now-time—and then—now temperature every time give you.	Get one [There is an] electric sign high up on da wall of da building show you what time an' temperature get [it is] right now.
Now days, ah, house, ah, inside, washi clothes machine get, no? Before time, ah, no more, see? And then pipe no more, water pipe no more.	Those days bin get [there were] no more washing machine, no more pipe water like get [there is] inside house nowadays, ah?
No, the men, ah—pau [finished] work—they go, make garden. Plant this, ah, cabbage, like that. Plant potato, like that. And then—all that one—all right, sit down. Make lilly bit story.	When work pau [is finished] da guys they stay go make [are going to make] garden for plant potato an' cabbage an' after little while they go sit down talk story ["shoot the breeze"].
Good, this one. Kaukau [food] any kind this one. Pilipin island no good. No more money.	Hawaii more better than Philippines, over here get [there is] plenty kaukau [food], over there no can, bra [brother], you no more money for buy kaukau [food], 'a'swhy [that's why].

PIDGIN AND CREOLE versions of identical sentences illustrate the structural differences between pidgin and Creole in Hawaii. Pidgin, which is spoken only by immigrants, varies widely from speaker to speaker. Although one can probably say anything in pidgin that can be said in English or Creole, the structure of pidgin is extremely rudimentary. Pidgin sentences are little more than strings of nouns, verbs and adjectives, often arranged to place old, shared information first and new information later in the sentence. Creole arose in Hawaii only among the children of immigrants, and it is much richer in grammatical structure than pidgin. Moreover, the rules of Creole grammar are uniform from speaker to speaker, and they resemble the structural rules of other creoles. English versions of words and phrases are given in brackets.

ENGLISH	HAWAIIAN CREOLE ENGLISH
The two of us had a hard time raising dogs.	Us two bin get hard time raising dog.
John and his friends are stealing the food.	John-them stay cockroach the kaukau.
He doesn't want to play because he's lazy.	He lazy, 'a'swhy he no like play.
How do you expect to finish your house?	How you expect for make pau you house?
It would have been better if I'd gone to Honolulu to buy it.	More better I bin go Honolulu for buy om.
The one who falls first is the loser.	Who go down first is loser.
The man who was going to lay the vinyl had quoted me a price.	The guy gon' lay the vinyl bin quote me price.
There was a woman who had three daughters.	Bin get one wahine she get three daughter.
She can't go because she hasn't any money.	She no can go, she no more money, 'a'swhy.

STRUCTURAL DIFFERENCES between sentences in Hawaiian Creole and their English equivalents show that the grammar of Creole did not originate as a grammar borrowed from English. For example, the past perfect tense of a verb in Creole is expressed by the particles "bin" or "wen," which precede the main verb, instead of by the suffix "-ed." Nonpunctual, or progressive, aspect is expressed by the word "stay" instead of by the suffix "-ing." In the English sentence "The two of us had a hard time raising dogs" the rules of grammar oblige the speaker to indicate that the noun "dog" is either singular or plural. In the Creole version of the sentence, however, neither singular nor plural is implied. There are also relatively insignificant lexical differences between the two languages: "cockroach" is picturesquely employed as a verb, and "kaukau," which may be derived from the Chinese pidgin term "chowchow," is a common word for "food." Equally striking structural differences are found between Hawaiian Creole and other languages, such as Chinese, Hawaiian, Japanese, Korean, Portuguese, Spanish or the Philippine languages, with which speakers of Hawaiian Creole might have been in contact.

that the listener is already familiar with the shirt the speaker is going to buy.

There are many other features of Creole that distinguish it from English. Whereas in English there is a past tense, which is usually marked with the suffix "-ed," in Creole there is a tense called the anterior tense, which is marked with "bin" for older speakers and with "wen" for younger speakers. The anterior tense is somewhat like the English past perfect: "had walked" in English is "bin walk" in Creole, and "walked" in English is simply "walk" in Creole. In order to distinguish irreal, or possible, actions or processes from actual ones, English employs the conditional or the future tense. In Creole all such irreal circumstances are expressed by the particle "go," which is placed before the main verb and marks what linguists call modality. For example, the sentence "If I had a car, I would drive home" is rendered in Creole as "If I bin get car, I go drive home."

There is also a Creole auxiliary verb that marks what linguists call aspect; it too is placed before the main verb and indicates that the action expressed by the verb is nonpunctual, or in other words repeated, habitual, continuing or incomplete. In order to say "I run in Kapiolani Park every evening" in Creole one must say "I stay run in Kapiolani Park every evening." If the particle "stay" is omitted by the Creole speaker, the action is understood to be completed or nonrepetitive.

In English there is no straightforward way to distinguish purposes that have been accomplished from those that have not. The sentence "John went to Honolulu to see Mary" does not specify whether or not John actually saw Mary. In Creole grammar the ambiguity must be resolved. If John saw Mary and the Creole speaker knows that John saw Mary, the speaker must say, "John bin go Honolulu go see Mary." If John did not see Mary or if the speaker does not know whether or not John saw Mary, the speaker must say, "John bin go Honolulu for see Mary."

Similar distinctions could be drawn between the grammatical structure of Creole and the structure of other contact languages, such as Hawaiian, Ilocano (the language spoken in the north of the Philippine island of Luzon) and Japanese. There are also resemblances, but most of them are confined to idiomatic expressions. For example, the Creole expression "O the pretty," which means "How pretty he [she/it] is," is a literal translation of the Hawaiian-language idiom "O ka nani." In the main, however, our investigations strongly suggest that the basic structures of Creole differ from those of other languages. Although it might seem that some children of immigrants could transfer the structures of their parents' native languages onto the evolving Creole language, they did not do so. The structural linguistic input that was available to the children was apparently not used in the development of Creole.

Even if it could be demonstrated that all the grammatical structures of Creole were borrowed, cafeteria-style, from one contact language or another, the uniformity of Creole would present a difficult question: How did the speakers who invented Creole come to agree on which structure to borrow from which language? Without such agreement Creole could not be as uniform as it is. Yet it seems highly implausible that the agreement could have been reached so quickly. If there had been massive borrowing from ancestral languages, differences in the version of Creole spoken by various groups would have persisted at least one generation beyond the first generation of speakers.

There is another dimension to the problem of the uniformity of Hawaiian Creole. It turns out that creole languages throughout the world exhibit the same uniformity and even the same grammatical structures that are observed in Hawaii. The finding is all the more remarkable when it is compared with the rather poor correspondence in structure I have noted between Hawaiian Creole and other contact languages in Hawaii. For example, the distinction made in Hawaiian Creole between singular, plural and neutral number is also made in all other creole languages. Similarly, in all other creole languages there are three invariant particles that act as auxiliary verbs and play the roles that "bin," "go" and "stay" play in Hawaiian Creole.

In Haitian Creole, for example, the word "té" marks the anterior tense of the verb, the word "av(a)" marks irreal modality and the word "ap" marks the aspect of the verb as nonpunctual. Thus in Haitian Creole the phrase "I have been walking" is rendered "m [I] t'ap [té + ap] maché." Similarly, in Sranan, an English-based creole found in Surinam (formerly Netherlands Guiana), the anterior tense marker is "ben," the irreal modality marker is "sa" and the nonpunctual aspect marker is "e." The phrase "He would have been walking" is rendered "A [he] ben sa e waka." Most important, there is a strict order that must be followed in all creole languages when more than one of these markers is present in a sentence. The particle for tense precedes the particle for modality, and the particle for modality precedes the particle for aspect.

Finally, consider the grammatical distinction I have noted between purposes accomplished and unaccomplished. The same distinction, absent in English, is found in all creoles. In Mauritian Creole, a creole based on the French vocabulary that is used on the island of Mauritius, a sentence such as "He decided to eat meat" can be expressed in two ways. If the subject of the sentence carried out his decision, the sentence is rendered "Li ti desid al mâz lavian," which literally means "He decided go eat meat." If the decision was not carried out, the sentence is rendered as "Li ti desid pu mâz lavian," or literally "He decided for eat meat." In Jamaican Creole the sentence "He went to wash" must be rendered either as "Im gaan fi bied" ("He went with the intention of washing") or as "Im gaan go bied" ("He went to wash and completed the task").

These examples only suggest the extent of the structural similarities among creole languages. The similarities seem unaffected by the wide geographic dispersion of the creoles and the variation among the languages such as Dutch, English and French from which they draw the greatest part of their vocabulary. Scholars such as Hugo Schuchardt began to point out the resemblance in the 19th century, and in the 1960's many examples were explored in detail by Douglas Taylor, by Robert Wallace Thompson of the University of the West Indies and by Keith Whinnom of the University of Exeter. Thus even before the development of Hawaiian Creole was reasonably well understood the grammatical similarities among the creole languages of the world were recognized as an important finding that required explanation.

The linguist's first reaction to such a finding is to look for a common ancestor of the similar languages. For ex-

VERB FORM
BASE FORM ("HE WALKED"; "HE LOVES")
ANTERIOR ("HE HAD WALKED"; "HE LOVED")
IRREAL ("HE WILL/WOULD WALK"; "HE WILL/WOULD LOVE
NONPUNCTUAL ("HE IS/WAS WALKING")
ANTERIOR + IRREAL ("HE WOULD HAVE WALKED" "HE WOULD HAVE LOVED")
ANTERIOR + NONPUNCTUAL ("HE WAS/HAD BEEN WALKING")
IRREAL + NONPUNCTUAL ("HE WILL/WOULD BE WALKING")
ANTERIOR + IRREAL + NONPUNCTUAL ("HE WOULD HAVE BEEN WALKING")

CONJUGATION OF THE VERB is similar in all creole languages, in spite of superficial lexical differences. Moreover, the creole system is quite distinct from the one encountered in English and in most other languages. The table gives conjugations in Hawaiian Creole, Haitian Creole and Sranan (an English-based creole spoken in Surinam, the former Nether-

ample, it has been conjectured that the linguistic ancestor was a contact language that grew out of Portuguese and certain West African languages in the course of the first Portuguese explorations of Africa in the 15th and 16th centuries. According to the hypothesis, this contact language was subsequently spread around the world by Portuguese sailors, changing its vocabulary but not its syntax or semantics as it entered the sphere of influence of another colonial power. Superficially such an explanation might seem to be consistent with the development of Creole in Hawaii, because Portuguese laborers were brought to the islands in large numbers during the late 19th and early 20th centuries.

There are several serious flaws in the account. First, Hawaiian Creole bears scant resemblance to any of the contact languages, including Portuguese. Second, the claims of linguistic similarity between creoles and Portuguese or between creoles and West African languages are grossly exaggerated. Most important, our study of hundreds of Hawaiian speakers has made it clear that Hawaiian Creole almost certainly originated in Hawaii. We found no surviving immigrant who speaks anything approximating a creole language; instead every immigrant we surveyed speaks some variety of pidgin. If Hawaiian Creole was primarily an imported language, it would have been carried by immigrants, and presumably it would have been learned by others among the immigrant population. One must therefore conclude that Hawaiian Creole arose among the children of immigrants, where it is now found. Moreover, if a creole language could develop in Hawaii without ancestry, it can arise anywhere else in a similar way.

The implications of these findings are far-reaching. Because the grammatical structures of creole languages are more similar to one another than they are to the structures of any other language, it is reasonable to suppose most if not all creoles were invented by the children of pidgin-speaking immigrants. Moreover, since creoles must have been invented in isolation, it is likely that some general ability, common to all people, is responsible for the linguistic similarities.

The suggestion that people are biologically predisposed to use language is not a new one: for more than two decades Noam Chomsky of the Massachusetts Institute of Technology has argued that there is an innate universal grammar underlying all human languages. The universal grammar is postulated largely on the grounds that only by its means could children acquire a system as enormously complex as a human language in the short time they do. Studies by the late Eric H. Lenneberg tend to confirm Chomsky's hypothesis. The acquisition of language resembles the acquisition of other complex and flexible aspects of the child's behavior, such as walking, which are undoubtedly controlled to some degree by neurophysiological development. The universal grammar conjectured by Chomsky is a computing device, somehow realized neurologically, that makes a wide range of grammatical models available to the child. According to Chomsky, the child must then "select" which of the available grammatical models matches the grammar of the language into which the child is born.

The evidence from creole languages suggests that first-language acquisition is mediated by an innate device of a rather different kind. Instead of making a range of grammatical models available, the device provides the child with a single and fairly specific grammatical model. It was only in pidgin-speaking communities, where there was no grammatical model that could compete with the child's innate grammar, that the innate grammatical model was not eventually suppressed. The innate grammar was then clothed in whatever vocabulary was locally available and gave rise to the creole languages heard today.

The implications of this hypothesis call into question an idea that most linguists, including Chomsky, have tacitly accepted for many years, namely that no one of the world's languages is easier or harder for the child to acquire than any other. If there is a creole grammar somehow imprinted in the mind, creole languages should be easier to acquire than other languages. How is it, then, that not all children grow up speaking a creole language? The answer is they do their best to do just that. People around them, however, persist in speaking English or French or some other language, and so the child must modify the grammar of the native creole until it conforms to that of the local language.

Two kinds of linguistic evidence are relevant for testing the hypothesis. First, if some grammatical structure of creole is at variance with the corresponding grammatical structure of the local language, one should find that children

NONSTATIVE VERBS			STATIVE VERBS		
HAWAIIAN CREOLE	HAITIAN CREOLE	SRANAN	HAWAIIAN CREOLE	HAITIAN CREOLE	SRANAN
HE WALK	LI MACHÉ	A WAKA	HE LOVE	LI RÊMÊ	A LOBI
HE BIN WALK	LI TÉ MACHÉ	A BEN WAKA	HE BIN LOVE	LI TÉ RÊMÊ	A BEN LOBI
HE GO WALK	L'AV(A) MACHÉ	A SA WAKA	HE GO LOVE	L'AV(A) RÊMÊ	A SA LOBI
HE STAY WALK	L'AP MACHÉ	A E WAKA	—	—	—
HE BIN GO WALK	LI T'AV(A) MACHÉ	A BEN SA WAKA	HE BIN GO LOVE	LI T'AV(A) RÊMÊ	A BEN SA LOBI
HE BIN STAY WALK	LI T'AP MACHÉ	A BEN E WAKA	—	—	—
HE GO STAY WALK	L'AV AP MACHÉ	A SA E WAKA	—	—	—
HE BIN GO STAY WALK	LI T'AV AP MACHÉ	A BEN SA E WAKA	—	—	—

lands Guiana) for stative and nonstative verbs. Stative verbs are verbs such as "like," "want" and "love," which cannot form the nonpunctual aspect; in English, for example, one cannot add "-ing" to a finite stative verb. The base form of the verb refers to the present for stative verbs and to the past for nonstative verbs. The anterior tense is roughly equivalent to the English past tense for stative verbs and to the English past perfect tense for nonstative verbs. The irreal mode includes the English future, conditional and subjunctive. In all the creole languages the anterior particle precedes the irreal particle, and the irreal particle precedes the nonpunctual particle. In Hawaiian Creole, however, "He bin go walk" has come to mean "He walked" instead of "He would have walked," and the forms "He bin stay walk," "He go stay walk" and "He bin go stay walk," although they were widespread before World War II, are now almost extinct because of the growing influence of English in Hawaii. The bracketed English translations are provided only as a rough guide to the meaning.

CHILD LANGUAGE	ENGLISH CREOLES
Where I can put it?	Where I can put om? (Hawaii)
Daddy throw the nother rock.	Daddy t'row one neda rock'tone. (Jamaica)
I go full Angela bucket.	I go full Angela bucket. (Guyana)
Lookit a boy play ball.	Luku one boy a play ball. (Jamaica)
Nobody don't like me.	Nobody no like me. (Guyana)
I no like do that.	I no like do that. (Hawaii)
Johnny big more than me.	Johnny big more than me. (Jamaica)
Let Daddy get pen write it.	Make Daddy get pen write am. (Guyana)
I more better than Johnny.	I more better than Johnny. (Hawaii)

SENTENCES SPOKEN BY CHILDREN between two and four years old, all born of English-speaking parents, are strikingly similar to sentences in English-based creole languages. The similarities among creole languages and the likelihood that the languages arose independently of one another suggest that creoles develop among children whenever there is no adequate native language to serve as a model. The author conjectures that if children were removed from their native English-language community at the age of about two, they would grow up speaking a language whose vocabulary would be primarily English but whose grammar would be a creole.

make systematic errors with respect to the structure of the local language. On the other hand, if the two grammatical structures tend to agree, one should find extremely early, rapid and errorless acquisition of the local-language structure.

Consider the systematic error observed by David McNeill of the University of Michigan in the speech of a four-year-old boy. In one of McNeill's observing sessions the boy complained, "Nobody don't like me," and the boy's mother responded by correcting the sentence: "Nobody likes me." The boy then repeated his sentence and the mother repeated her correction no fewer than eight times. Finally, the child altered his sentence and shouted in exasperation, "Nobody don't likes me."

The error is found in many English-speaking children between three and a half and four years old, including children who are not exposed to dialects of English that employ double negatives. There are many languages, such as French and Spanish, that also employ double negatives, but the only languages that allow negative subjects with negative verbs are creoles. For example, in Papia Kristang, the Portuguese-based creole language of the Malay Peninsula, one can say, "Angkosa nte mersimentu," or literally, "Nothing not-have value." In Guyanese Creole, which is based on English and found in Guyana (formerly British Guiana), one can say, "Non dag na bait non kyat," or literally, "No dog did not bite no cat."

A second instance of systematic error is found in the formation of children's questions. Children learning English often indicate questions only by their intonation; the subject and the auxiliary verb are almost never reversed. For example, children repeatedly say things such as "You can fix this?" even though they have heard countless questions such as "Can you fix this?" Similarly, no creole language distinguishes questions and statements on the basis of word order; the difference is marked by intonation alone.

Consider the sentence "A gon' full Angela bucket." Although such a sentence is unacceptable in English, it is perfectly acceptable in Hawaiian Creole, Guyanese Creole or any of several other creoles related to English. It is synonymous with the sentence "I'm going to fill Angela's bucket," but it differs from the structure of the English sentence in the following ways. First, the first-person pronoun "I" is reduced to "A"; second, the auxiliary verb "am" is omitted; third, the forms "go" or "gon" are used to mark the future tense; fourth, the word "to" in the infinitive is omitted; fifth, the adjective "full" is employed as if it were a transitive verb, and sixth, the possessive marker "-'s" is omitted. All these features are characteristics of creoles, but this sentence was not uttered by a creole speaker. It was spoken by the three-year-old daughter of an English-speaking linguist.

When a feature of the local language matches the structure of creole, children avoid making errors that would otherwise seem quite natural. For example, children learning English acquire the suffix "-ing," which expresses duration, at a very early age. Even before the age of two many children say things such as "I sitting high chair," where the verb expresses a continuing action. One would expect that as soon as the suffix was acquired it would be applied to every possible verb, just as the suffix "-s" that marks the English plural is frequently overgeneralized to nouns such as "foot" and "sheep."

One would therefore expect children to utter ungrammatical sentences such as "I liking Mommy" and "I wanting candy." Remarkably, such errors are almost never heard. Children seem to know implicitly that English verbs such as "like" and "want," which are called stative verbs, cannot be marked by the suffix "-ing" to indicate duration. The distinction between stative and nonstative verbs is fundamental to creole languages, however, and no marker of continuing action can be employed with a stative verb in creoles either.

The distinction between specific and nonspecific reference, which I have already discussed, is an important feature of creole languages. In English the distinction can be subtle, but young children nonetheless acquire it with ease. Michael P. Maratsos of the University of Minnesota constructed a series of sentences for children to complete, for which the completions depended on the distinction between specific and nonspecific reference. For example, the sentence "John has never read a book," which makes nonspecific reference to the noun "book," can be completed by the phrase "and he never will read a book"; it cannot be completed by the phrase "and he never will read the book." Similarly, the sentence "John read a book yesterday," in which a specific book is presupposed, can be completed by the phrase "and he enjoyed the book"; it cannot be completed by the phrase "and he enjoyed a book." Children as young as three years were able to make such distinctions correctly about 90 percent of the time.

Many more studies of language acquisition will have to be carried out before the structure of creole languages can be firmly accepted as the basis of first-language acquisition. Daniel Isaac Slobin of the University of California at Berkeley has suggested that there is a set of processes children apply to any language they hear, which he calls basic child grammar. Slobin's most recent work, which is not yet published, cites evidence from several languages for the hypothesis, and it now appears that basic child grammar and creole languages may have much in common.

If creole languages represent the manifestation of a neurologically determined program of child development, then Psamtik was by no means the fool he has been taken for. It may be possible to discover, at least in general outline, the structure of human language in the early stages of its development. Moreover, in attempting to reconstruct such a language linguists may be able to answer questions the pharaoh did not even ask: How did human language originate? What are the minimum prerequisites for such a thing as language to arise in a species? If such questions can be answered or even formulated in a precise and coherent way, we shall be much closer to understanding what makes the human species different from others.

The Earliest Precursor of Writing

4

by Denise Schmandt-Besserat
June 1978

Long before the Sumerians invented writing, accounts in western Asia were kept with clay tokens of various distinctive shapes. It appears that the tokens gave rise to the Sumerian ideographs

What led to writing? The art itself is a good example of what students of the past call independent invention, since systems of writing have evolved in isolation at different times in different parts of the world. For example, one system—the Chinese ideogram—can be traced to its origin in archaic signs engraved on the scapular bones of sheep or the shells of turtles in the second millennium B.C. as a means of asking questions of heaven. Roughly 1,000 years later an entirely independent system of writing arose halfway around the world in Mesoamerica. It combined a simple system of numerical notation with complex hieroglyphs and was principally used to indicate the dates of various events according to an elaborate calendrical system.

Both Chinese and Maya writing were relatively late inventions. Some one system of writing must have been the earliest, and it is from such an initial point that we may begin the search for the antecedents of the art. The credit for being the first to write texts is usually given to the Sumerians of Mesopotamia. By the last century of the fourth millennium B.C. the officials of such Sumerian city-states as Uruk had developed a system of recording numerals, pictographs and ideographs on specially prepared clay surfaces. (A pictograph is a more or less realistic portrayal of the object it is supposed to represent; an ideograph is an abstract sign.)

At Uruk a team of German archaeologists directed by Julius Jordan turned up many examples of these archaic records in 1929 and 1930. The texts, about 1,000 of them, were first analyzed by Adam Falkenstein and his students. Today additional discoveries have increased the total number of Uruk and Uruk-style texts to about 4,000, and Falkenstein's pioneer efforts are being continued mainly by Hans J. Nissen of the Free University of Berlin and his associate Margaret W. Green.

Although the clay blanks used by the Uruk scribes are universally referred to as tablets, a word with the connotation of flatness, they are actually convex. Individual characters were inscribed in the clay by means of a stylus made of wood, bone or ivory, with one end blunt and the other pointed. The characters were basically of two kinds. Numerical signs were impressed into the clay; all other signs, pictographs and ideographs alike, were incised with the pointed end of the stylus. The repertory of characters used by the Uruk scribes was large; it is estimated at no fewer than 1,500 separate signs.

Hypotheses about the origin of writing generally postulate an evolution from the concrete to the abstract: an initial pictographic stage that in the course of time and perhaps because of the carelessness of scribes becomes increasingly schematic. The Uruk tablets contradict this line of thought. Most of the 1,500 signs (Falkenstein compiled 950 of them) are totally abstract ideographs; the few pictographs represent such wild animals as the wolf and the fox or items of advanced technology such as the chariot and the sledge. Indeed, the Uruk texts remain largely undeciphered and an enigma to epigraphers. The few ideographic signs that have been identified are those that can be traced back stage by stage from a known cuneiform character of later times to an archaic Sumerian prototype. From the fragmentary textual contents that such identities allow it appears that the scribes of Uruk mainly recorded such matters as business transactions and land sales. Some of the terms that appear most frequently are those for bread, beer, sheep, cattle and clothing.

After Jordan's discovery at Uruk other archaeologists found similar texts elsewhere in Mesopotamia. More were found in Iran: at Susa, at Chogha Mish and as far off as Godin Tepe, some 350 kilometers north of Uruk. In recent years tablets in the Uruk style have been unearthed in Syria at Habuba Kabira and Jebel Aruda, nearly 800 kilometers to the northwest. At Uruk the tablets had been found in a temple complex; most of the others came to light in the ruins of private houses, where the presence of seals and the seal-marked clay stoppers for jars indicate some kind of mercantile activity.

The fact that the Uruk texts contradict the hypothesis that the earliest form of writing would be pictographic has inclined many epigraphers to the view that the tablets, even though they bear the earliest-known writing, must represent a stage in the evolution of the art that is already advanced. The pictographic hypothesis has been revived anew. The fact that no writing of this kind has yet appeared at sites of the fourth millennium B.C. and even earlier is explained away by postulating that the writing of earlier millenniums was recorded exclusively on perishable mediums that vanished long ago, such as parchment, papyrus or wood.

I have an alternative proposal. Research into the first uses of clay in the Near East over the past several years suggests that several characteristics of the Uruk material provide important clues to what kinds of visible symbols actually preceded the archaic Sumerian texts. These clues include the choice of clay as a material for documents, the convex profile of the Uruk tablets and the appearance of the characters recorded on them.

Nuzi, a city site of the second millennium B.C. in Iraq, was excavated by the American School of Oriental Research in Baghdad between 1927 and 1931. Nearly 30 years later, reviewing an analysis of the Nuzi palace archives, A. Leo Oppenheim of the Oriental Institute of the University of Chicago reported the existence of a recording system that made use of "counters," or tokens. According to the Nuzi texts, such tokens were used for accounting purposes; they were spoken of as being "deposited," "transferred" and "removed."

Oppenheim visualized a kind of dual bookkeeping system in the Nuzi texts; in addition to the scribes' elaborate cuneiform records the palace administration had parallel tangible accounts. For

example, one token of a particular kind might represent each of the animals in the palace herds. When new animals were born in the spring, the appropriate number of new tokens would be added; when animals were slaughtered, the appropriate number of tokens would be withdrawn. The tokens were probably also moved from one shelf to another when animals were moved from one herder or pasture to another, when sheep were shorn and so forth.

The discovery of a hollow egg-shaped tablet in the palace ruins supported Oppenheim's hypothesis. The inscription on the face of the tablet turned out to be a list of 48 animals. The hollow tablet rattled, and when one end of it was carefully opened, 48 tokens were found inside. Presumably the combination of a written list and countable tokens represented a transfer of animals from one palace service to another. Unfortunately we have no accurate description of the tokens; they were subsequently lost.

The Nuzi archives are dated to about 1500 B.C. The great Elamite site, Susa, has levels that are more than 1,500 years older. The digging at Susa, undertaken by French investigators, began in the 1880's and continues to this day. Six years after Oppenheim's 1958 report Pierre Amiet of the Musée du Louvre was able to confirm the existence of a similar accounting system at Susa. The token containers at Susa, unlike the container from Nuzi, were hollow clay spheres. Amiet called them "bullae"; so far about 70 of them have been found. The tokens they contain are clay modeled in a variety of geometric forms, including spheres, disks, cylinders, cones and tetrahedrons.

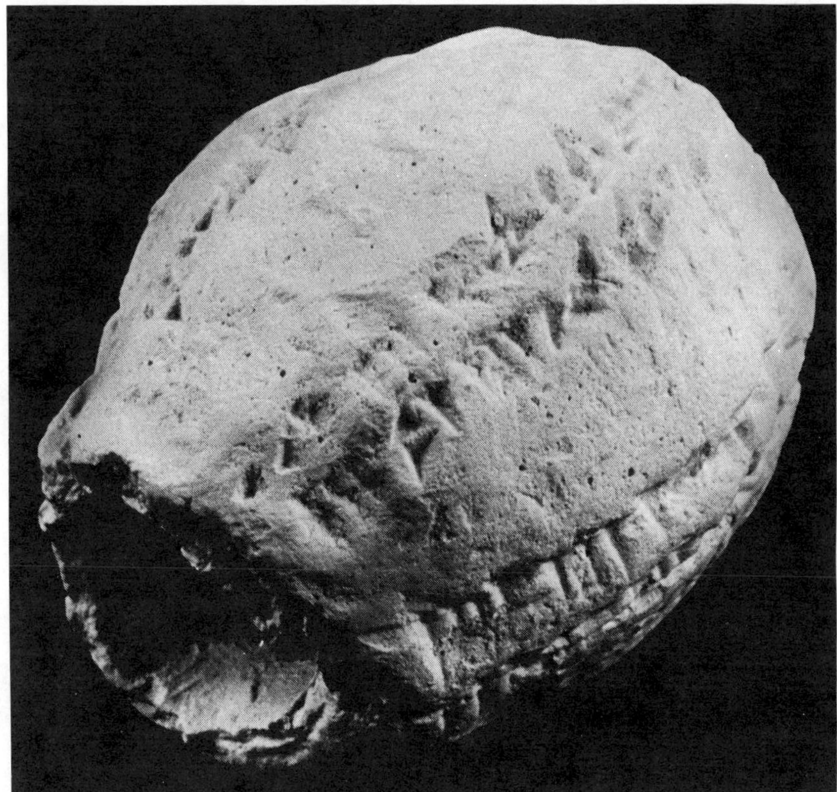

EGG-SHAPED HOLLOW TABLET was found in the palace ruins at Nuzi, a Mesopotamian city site of the second millennium B.C. The cuneiform inscription on its surface lists 48 animals. On being opened the tablet was found to contain 48 counters. The counters were lost before an accurate description had been prepared, but Nuzi texts suggest their use for reckoning.

Amiet's finding was one of great significance; not only did it demonstrate that bullae and tokens were in existence at least a millennium and a half before they appeared at Nuzi but also it showed that they were as old or older than the earliest written records at Uruk. Indeed, it later became clear that the tokens, at least, were very much older.

In 1969 I began a research project with the objective of discovering when and in what ways clay first came to be used in the Near East. The making of pottery is of course the most familiar use of clay, but before the appearance of pottery man was making clay beads, modeling clay figurines, molding bricks out of clay and using clay for mortar. As a start on my project I visited museums in the U.S., in Europe and in various Near Eastern cities that had collections of clay artifacts dating back to the seventh, eighth and ninth millenniums B.C. This interval of time, beginning around 11,000 years ago and ending a little more than 8,000 years ago, saw the firm establishment of the first farming settlements in western Asia.

In the museum collections, along with the beads, bricks and figurines I had expected to find, I encountered what was to me an unforeseen category of objects: small clay artifacts of various forms. As I later came to realize, the forms were like those Amiet had found inside his Susa bullae: spheres, disks, cones, tetrahedrons, ovoids, triangles (or crescents), biconoids (double cones joined at the base), rectangles and other odd shapes difficult to describe. Could these artifacts, some of them 5,000 years older than the tokens from Susa, also have served as tokens?

I began to compile my own master catalogue of these oddities, listing each token that was known to have come from a specific site. In summary, I found that whereas all of them were small, measuring on the average from one centimeter to two centimeters in their greatest dimension, many were of two distinct sizes. For example, there were small cones about a centimeter high and large cones three to four centimeters high. There were also thin disks, only three millimeters thick, and thick ones, as much as two centimeters thick. Other variations were evident. For example, in addition to whole spheres I found quarter-, half- and three-quarter spheres. Some of the tokens had additional features. Many were incised with deep lines; some had small clay pellets or coils on them and others bore shallow circular punch marks.

The tokens had all been modeled by hand. Either a small lump of clay had been rolled between the palms of the hands or the lump had been pinched between the fingertips. The clay was of a fine texture but showed no sign of special preparation (such as the addition of tempering substances, a practice in pottery making that enhances hardness after firing). All the tokens had, however, been fired to ensure their durability. Most of them varied in color from buff to red, but some had become gray and even blackish.

I found that the tokens were present

CLAY TOKENS FROM SUSA, a city site in Iran, are seen in the composite photograph on the opposite page. The tokens, in the collection of the Musée du Louvre, are about 5,000 years old. The five tokens in the top row represent some of the commonest shapes: a sphere, a half-sphere, a disk, a cone and a tetrahedron. The more elaborate tokens in the next row have been marked with incisions or impressions. Unperforated and perforated versions of similar tokens appear in the third and fourth rows. Tokens in the bottom two rows vary in shape and marking; some can be equated with early Sumerian ideographs ***(see illustration on pages 38 and 39).***

SPHERICAL BULLA, an envelope of clay with tokens enclosed, was excavated from levels of the third millennium B.C. at Tepe Yahya, a site in south-central Iran halfway between the Indus Valley and lower Mesopotamia. Three tokens (*right*) were enclosed: a cone and two spheres.

in virtually all museum collections of artifacts from the Neolithic period in western Asia. An extreme example of abundance is provided by the early village site of Jarmo in Iraq, first occupied some 8,500 years ago. Jarmo has yielded a total of 1,153 spheres, 206 disks and 106 cones. Reports generally indicate that the excavators found the tokens scattered over the floors of houses located in various parts of a site. If the tokens had once been kept in containers, such as baskets or pouches, these had disintegrated long ago. Nevertheless, there is evidence suggesting that the tokens were segregated from other artifacts and even implying what their function was. The reports indicate that many were found in clusters numbering 15 or more and that the clusters were located in storage areas within the houses.

As I reviewed the museum collections and the related site reports I became increasingly puzzled by the apparent omnipresence of the tokens. They had been found in sites from as far west as Beldibi in what is now southwestern Turkey to as far east as Chanhu Daro in what is now Pakistan. Tokens had even been unearthed at an eighth-millennium-B.C. site on the Nile near Khartoum.

At the same time I found that some site reports failed to take note of the tokens that had been collected, or men-

BULLA FROM SUSA shows two rows of surface impressions that match in number and shape the tokens it contained (*foreground*): one large cone, three small cones (*bottom row*) and three disks (*top row*). Tablets with incised representations of tokens probably evolved next.

tioned them only casually. When the tokens were noted, the heading might read "objects of uncertain purpose," "children's playthings," "game pieces" or "amulets." As an example, the tokens from Tello in Iraq were interpreted by their discoverer, Henri de Genouillac, as amulets that expressed the residents' desire for "personal identification." Another example appears in Carleton S. Coon's report on Belt Cave in Iran: "From levels 11 and 12 come five mysterious . . . clay objects, looking like nothing in the world but suppositories. What they were used for is anyone's guess."

The realization that the tokens were all artifacts of the same kind was also hampered because, when they were listed at all in the site reports, they usually appeared under not one heading but several headings depending on their shape. For example, cones have been described as schematic female figurines, as phallic symbols, as gaming pieces and as nails, and spheres were mostly interpreted as marbles or as sling missiles.

Having studied at the École du Louvre, I was familiar with the work of Amiet. Nevertheless, I had compiled a catalogue of hundreds of tokens before I at last realized how much like Amiet's tokens from Susa these far earlier clay artifacts were. At first it seemed impossible that the two groups could be related; a minimum of 5,000 years separated the tokens of Neolithic times from those of Bronze Age Susa. As I extended my investigations to include later clay artifacts, dating from the seventh millennium B.C. to the fourth millennium and later, I found to my surprise that similar clay tokens had been found in substantial numbers at sites representative of the entire time span. Evidently a system of accounting that made use of tokens was widely used not only at Nuzi and Susa but throughout western Asia from as long ago as the ninth millennium B.C. to as recently as the second millennium.

The system appears to have been much the same as many other early, and even not so early, methods of account keeping. Classical scholars are familiar with the Roman system of making "calculations" with pebbles (*calculi* in Latin). Up to the end of the 18th century the British treasury still worked with counters to calculate taxes. For that matter, the shepherds of Iraq to this day use pebbles to account for the animals in their flocks, and the abacus is still the standard calculator in the markets of Asia. The archaic token system of western Asia was if anything only somewhat more complex than its later counterparts.

Considered overall, the system had some 15 major classes of tokens, further divided into some 200 subclasses on the basis of size, marking or fractional vari-

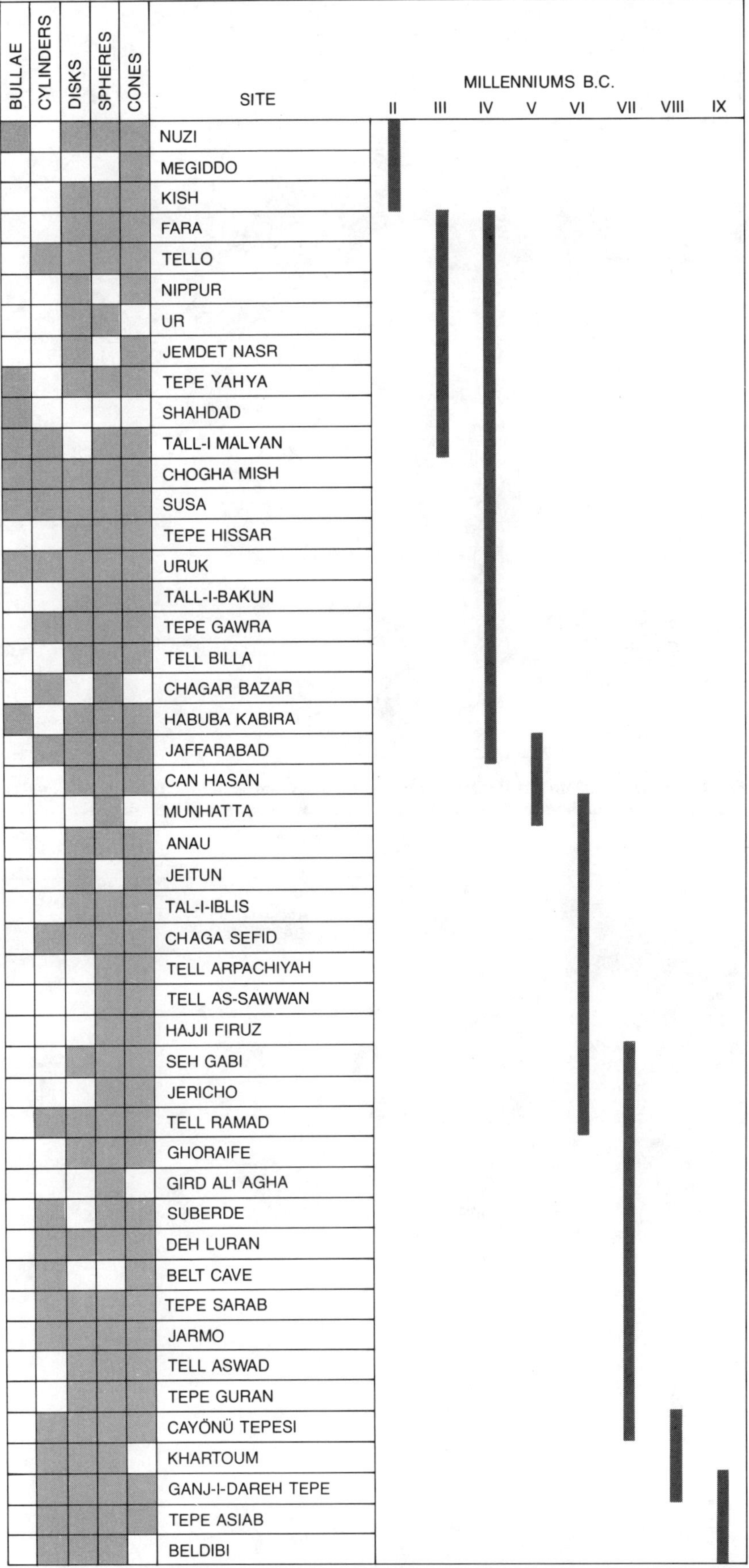

SITES WHERE TOKENS APPEAR represent a span of time from the ninth millennium B.C. to the second. As many as 20 variations on four basic token shapes are present at the earliest sites. Clay envelopes as containers for tokens do not appear before the fourth millennium B.C.

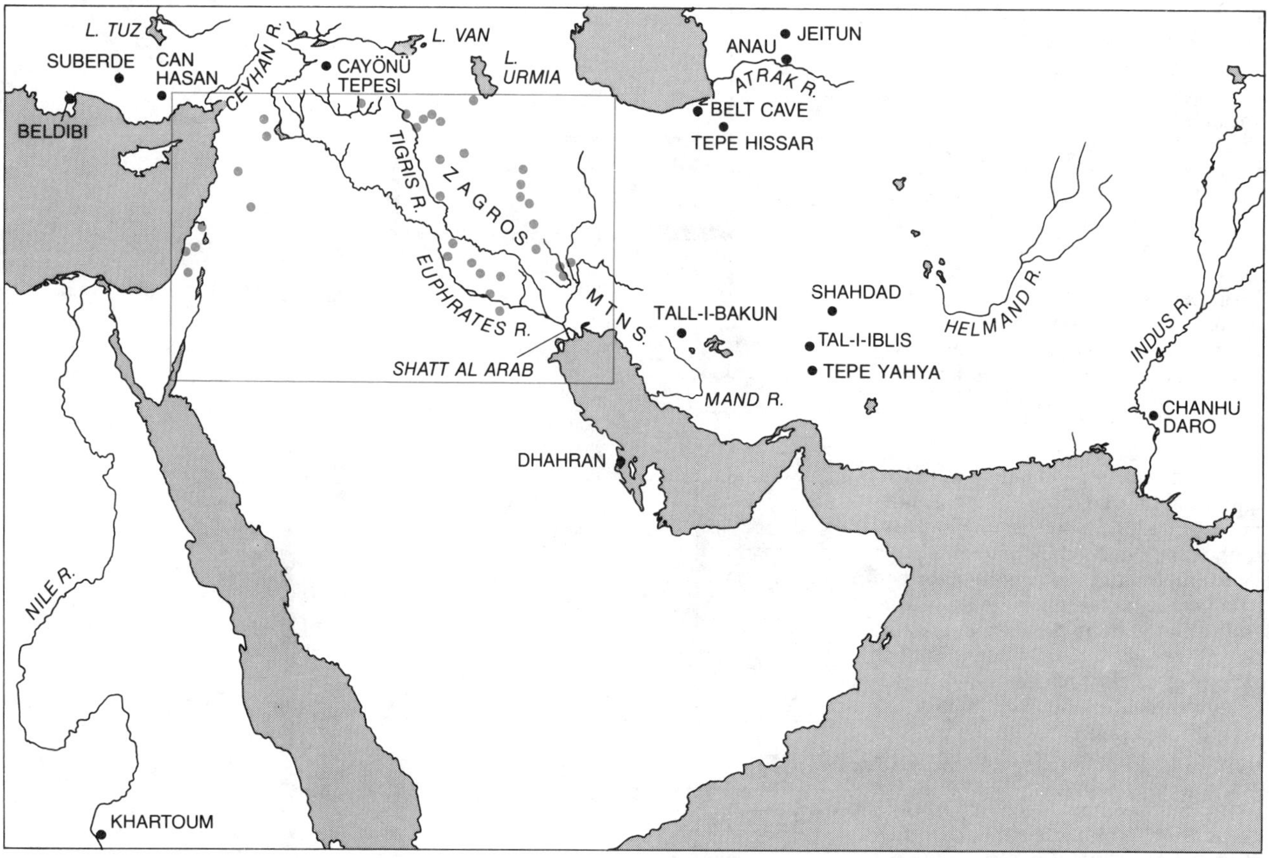

GEOGRAPHICAL DISTRIBUTION of tokens extends from as far north as the Caspian border of Iran to as far south as Khartoum and from Asia Minor eastward to the Indus Valley. Sites identified only by dots (*color*) within a rectangle here are named in the map below.

CLUSTERING OF SITES in the drainage of the upper and lower Tigris and the lower Euphrates and in the Zagros region of Iran is more a reflection of the availability of study collections than a measure of the actual extent and frequency of token use in the area.

ation, as in the case of the quarter-, half- and three-quarter spheres. Evidently each particular shape had a meaning of its own; a few appear to represent numerical values and others specific objects, commodities in particular.

It is not necessary to theorize about some of these meanings; a number of ideographs on the Uruk tablets almost exactly reproduce in two dimensions many of the tokens. For example, Uruk arbitrary signs for numerals, such as a small cone-shaped impression for the number one, a circular impression for the number 10 and a larger cone-shaped impression for the number 60 are matched by tokens: small cones, spheres and large cones. Further examples of ideographs that match tokens include, under the general heading of commodities, the Uruk symbol for sheep (a circle enclosing a cross), matched by disk-shaped tokens incised with a cross, and the Uruk symbol for a garment (a circle enclosing four parallel lines), matched by disk-shaped tokens incised with four parallel lines. Still other examples are ideographs for metal and oil and more clearly pictographic symbols for cattle, dogs and what are evidently vessels; each tablet sign can be matched with a similarly shaped and marked token. In addition, the forms of many still unread Sumerian ideographs appear to match other tokens.

Why did such a repertory of three-dimensional symbols come into existence? It cannot simply be a coincidence that the first tokens appear early in the Neolithic period, a time of profound change in human society. It was then that an earlier subsistence pattern, based on hunting and gathering, was transformed by the impact of plant and animal domestication and the development of a farming way of life. The new agricultural economy, although it undoubtedly increased the production of food, would have been accompanied by new problems.

Perhaps the most crucial would have been food storage. Some portion of each annual yield had to be allocated for the farm family's own subsistence and some portion had to be set aside as seed for the next year's crop. Still another portion could have been reserved for barter with those who were ready to provide exotic products and raw materials in exchange for foodstuffs. It seems possible that the need to keep track of such allocations and transactions was enough to stimulate development of a recording system.

The earliest tokens now known are those from two sites in the Zagros region of Iran: Tepe Asiab and Ganj-i-Dareh Tepe. The people of both communities seem to have tended flocks and were possibly experimenting with crops around 8500 B.C., although at the same time they continued to hunt game and gather wild plants. The clay tokens they made were quite sophisticated in form. There were four basic types of token: spheres, disks, cones and cylinders. In addition there were tetrahedrons, ovoids, triangles, rectangles, bent coils and schematic animal forms. Subtypes included half-spheres and cones, spheres and disks with incisions and with punch marks. The set totaled 20 individual symbols.

The Neolithic period and the succeeding Chalcolithic period, or Copper Age, in western Asia lasted about 5,000 years. Over this substantial span one finds surprisingly few changes in the tokens, a fact that may indicate how well suited to the needs of an early agricultural economy this recording system was. In about 6500 B.C., 2,000 years after the rise of the first Zagros farming communities, another Iranian village, Tepe Sarab, began to flourish. The token inventory from excavations at Tepe Sarab shows no increase in the number of main types and an increase in subtypes from 20 only to 28, among them a four-sided pyramid and a stylized ox skull that is probably representative of cattle.

Perhaps it was during the Chalcolithic period that the agricultural surpluses of individual community members came to be pooled by means of taxes in kind, with the supervision of the surplus put into the hands of public officials such as temple attendants. If that is the case, the need to keep track of individual contributions evidently failed to bring any significant modification in the recording system. The tokens unearthed at four sites that flourished between 5500 and 4500 B.C.—Tell Arpachiyah and Tell as-Sawwan in Iraq and Chaga Sefid and Jaffarabad in Iran—reflect no more than minor developments. A new type of token, the biconoid, appears, and among some of the subtypes painted black lines and dots have taken the place of incisions and punch marks.

Early in the Bronze Age, between 3500 and 3100 B.C., there were significant changes in the recording system. This period saw an economic advance quite as remarkable in its own way as the rise of the farming economy that laid the foundation for it. The new development was the emergence of cities. Surveys of ancient sites in western Asia indicate a drastic increase in the population of Iraq and Iran; urban centers with many inhabitants begin to appear close to the earlier village settlements.

Craft specialization and the beginnings of mass production appear at this time. The bronze smithies and their products gave the age its name, but craftsmen other than smiths also arose, concentrated in various areas. The invention of the potter's wheel allowed the development of a pottery industry, and the output of various mass-production kilns came to be distributed over great distances. A similar trend is apparent in the manufacture of stone vessels, and the development of an expanded trade network is indicated by the appearance in Iraq of such exotic materials as lapis lazuli.

The development of an urban economy, rooted in trade, must have multiplied the demands on the traditional recording system. Not only production but also inventories, shipments and wage payments had to be noted, and merchants needed to preserve records of their transactions. By the last century of the fourth millennium B.C. the pressure of complex business accountancy on the token system becomes apparent both in the symbols and in how the tokens were used.

To consider the symbols first, six sites of the late fourth millennium B.C. in Iraq (Uruk, Tello and Fara), in Iran (Susa and Chogha Mish) and in Syria (Habuba Kabira) have yielded tokens representative of the full range of early shapes. In addition, some new shapes appear, among them parabolas, rhomboids and replicas of vessels. Even more significant than the appearance of new shapes, however, is the great proliferation of subtypes indicated by a variety of incised markings on the tokens. It is also now that a few of the tokens begin to have appliqué markings: added pellets or coils of clay.

The six sites have yielded a total of 660 tokens dating to about 3100 B.C. Of this number 363, or 55 percent, are marked with incisions. Most of the incisions are deep grooves made with the pointed end of a stylus; the grooves are placed conspicuously and with a clear concern for symmetry. On rounded tokens such as spheres, cones, ovoids and cylinders the incisions usually run around the equator and are thus visible from any aspect. On flat tokens such as disks, triangles and rectangles the incisions appear only on one face.

Most of the incisions present a pattern of parallel lines, although incised crosses and crisscross patterns are also found. The number of parallel lines would not seem to be random: there can be as many as 10 incisions, and the frequency of one-stroke, two-stroke, three-stroke and five-stroke patterns is conspicuous. It is noteworthy that with the exception of two-stroke patterns odd-numbered patterns are the most frequent.

Although incised patterns are by far the most abundant, 26 of the tokens (some 4 percent of the total) show circular impressions apparently made by punching the clay with the blunt end of a stylus. Some of the punched tokens bear a single impression. Others show a cluster of six punches, arranged either in a single row or in two rows with three impressions each.

As for changes in how the tokens were used, it is significant that 198 of them, or 30 percent of the total, are perforated. The perforated tokens run the gamut of types and include subtypes of the unmarked, incised and punched variety. In effect this means that tokens of any type or subtype were available in both unperforated and perforated forms. The perforations are so small that only a thin string could have passed through them. Of the explanations that come to mind one is that all 15 types of tokens and their 250 subtypes are nothing more than individual amulets that the early Bronze Age urban folk of western Asia wore on strings around their neck or wrist. I reject this explanation on two grounds. First, none of the perforated tokens that I have examined shows any evidence of being used as an amulet, such as wear polish or erosion around the string hole. Second, it seems preposterous that such a complex repertory of forms, so widespread in geographical distribution and manufactured with such remarkable uniformity, should have served as personal adornment in 30 percent of the cases and for some other purpose in the remaining 70 percent.

I prefer the hypothesis that some tokens representative of a specific transaction were strung together as a record. It seems at least plausible that the complexity of record keeping in an urban economy might have given rise to duplicate tokens suitable for stringing.

The stringing of tokens, if that is what the perforated tokens imply, would be only one change in how these symbolic bits of clay were used at the end of the fourth millennium B.C. A much more significant change is the first appearance at this time of clay bullae, or envelopes, such as those Amiet found as containers of tokens at Susa. The existence of a bulla is clear-cut direct evidence of the user's desire to segregate the tokens rep-

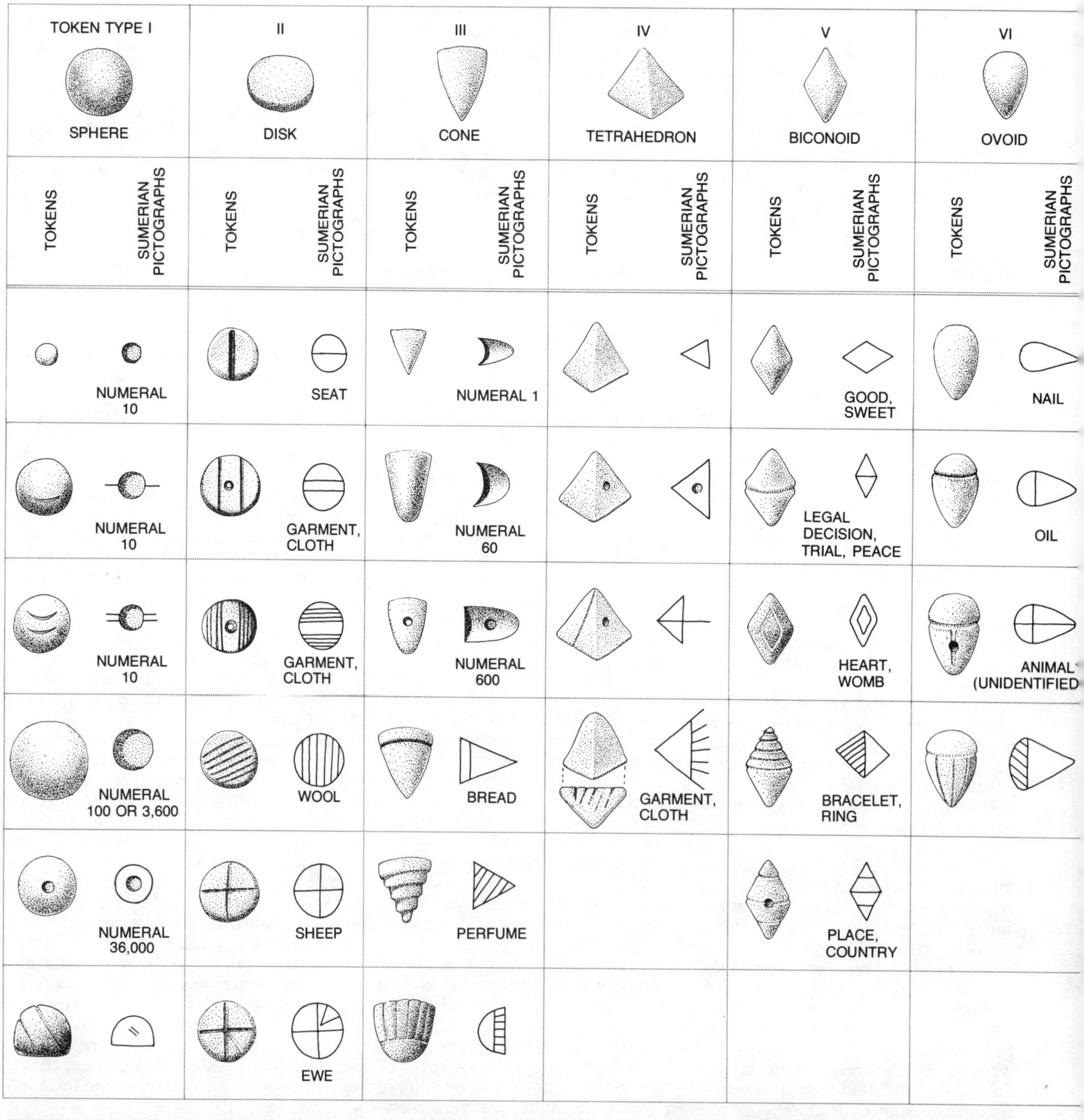

TOKEN TYPE I SPHERE		II DISK		III CONE		IV TETRAHEDRON		V BICONOID		VI OVOID	
TOKENS	SUMERIAN PICTOGRAPHS	TOKENS	SUMERIAN PICTOGRAPHS	TOKENS	SUMERIAN PICTOGRAPHS	TOKENS	SUMERIAN PICTOGRAPHS	TOKENS	SUMERIAN PICTOGRAPHS	TOKENS	SUMERIAN PICTOGRAPHS
	NUMERAL 10		SEAT		NUMERAL 1				GOOD, SWEET		NAIL
	NUMERAL 10		GARMENT, CLOTH		NUMERAL 60				LEGAL DECISION, TRIAL, PEACE		OIL
	NUMERAL 10		GARMENT, CLOTH		NUMERAL 600				HEART, WOMB		ANIMAL (UNIDENTIFIED)
	NUMERAL 100 OR 3,600		WOOL		BREAD		GARMENT, CLOTH		BRACELET, RING		
	NUMERAL 36,000		SHEEP		PERFUME				PLACE, COUNTRY		
			EWE								

FIFTY-TWO TOKENS, representative of 12 major categories of token types, have been matched here with incised characters that appear in the earliest Sumerian inscriptions. Most of the inscriptions cannot be read. Here, if the meaning of the symbol is known, the

resenting one or another transaction. The envelope could easily be made by pressing the fingers into a lump of clay about the size of a tennis ball, creating a cavity large enough to hold several tokens; the envelope could then be sealed with a patch of clay.

There is no doubt in my mind that such bullae were invented to provide the parties to a transaction with the kind of smooth clay surface that according to Sumerian custom could be marked by the personal seals of the individuals concerned as a validation of the event. The fact that most of the 350 bullae so far discovered bear the impressions of two different seals lends support to my conviction. Amiet has suggested that the Susa bullae may have served as bills of lading. In this view a rural producer of, say, textiles would consign a shipment of goods to an urban middleman, sending along with the shipment a bulla that contained a number of tokens descriptive of the kind and quantity of merchandise shipped. By breaking the bulla the recipient of the shipment could verify the makeup of the shipment; moreover, the need to deliver an intact bulla would inhibit the carrier from tampering with the merchandise in transit. This sealed transfer of tokens between trade partners represents an entirely new way of using the ancient recording system.

The innovation had one serious drawback. The seals impressed on the smooth exterior of the bulla served to validate each transmission, but if the seal impressions were to be preserved, the bulla had to remain intact. How, then, could one determine what tokens were enclosed and how many? A solution to the problem was soon found. The surface of the bulla was marked so that in addition to the validating seal impressions, it bore images of all the enclosed tokens.

The most striking example of this

equivalent word in English appears. The Sumerian numerical symbols equated with the various spherical and conical tokens are actual impressions in the surface of the tablet. In two instances (*sphere*) incised lines are added; in a third (*cone*) a circular punch mark is added.

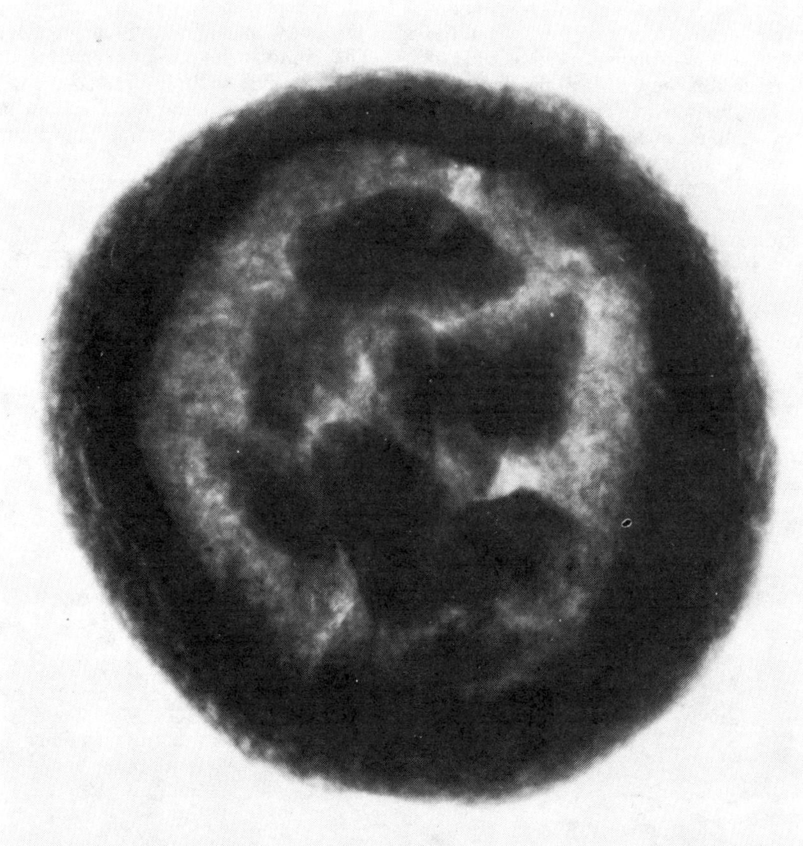

X RAY OF UNOPENED BULLA reveals tokens, some apparently cones and others ovoids. Age of the bulla is unknown; it was an isolated surface find near Dhahran in Saudi Arabia.

stratagem is a bulla that proved to contain six grooved ovoid tokens. Each of the six tokens had been pressed into the surface of the bulla before being stored inside it; they fit the surface imprints exactly. This means of recording the contents of a bulla on its exterior was not, however, universally practiced. On most bullae the impression was made with a thumb or a stylus; a circular impression stood for a sphere or a disk, a semicircular or triangular impression stood for a cone, and so forth.

The bulla markings were clearly not invented to take the place of the token system of record keeping. Nevertheless, that is what happened. One can visualize the process. At first the innovation flourished because of its convenience; anyone could "read" what tokens a bulla contained and how many without destroying the envelope and its seal impressions. What then happened was virtually inevitable, and the substitution of two-dimensional portrayals of the tokens for the tokens themselves would seem to have been the crucial link between the archaic recording system and writing. The hollow bullae with their enclosed tokens would have been replaced by inscribed solid clay objects: tablets. The strings, baskets and shelf loads of tokens in the archives would have given way to representative signs inscribed on tablets, that is, to written records.

The convex profile of the early Uruk tablets may well be a morphological feature inherited from the spherical bullae. Much the same may be true of the selection as a writing surface of a material as unsuitable as clay, a soft and easily smeared medium that must be dried or baked if it is to be preserved. There can be little doubt about the relation between the shapes and markings of the tokens and the supposed arbitrary forms of many Uruk ideographs. No fewer than 33 clear-cut identities exist between the ideographs and two-dimensional representations of tokens and more than twice that many are possible.

TABLETS FROM URUK show the convex shape that may reflect their evolution from hollow bullae. Impressions represent numerals. Tablets are in the Pergamon Museum in Berlin.

To summarize, the earliest examples of writing in Mesopotamia may not, as many have assumed, be the result of pure invention. Instead they appear to be a novel application late in the fourth millennium B.C. of a recording system that was indigenous to western Asia from early Neolithic times onward. In this view the appearance of writing in Mesopotamia represents a logical step in the evolution of a system of record keeping that originated some 11,000 years ago.

On this hypothesis the fact that the system was used without significant modification until late in the fourth millennium B.C. seems attributable to the comparatively simple record-keeping requirements of the preceding 5,000 years. With the rise of cities and the development of large-scale trade the system was pushed onto a new track. Images of the tokens soon supplanted the tokens themselves, and the evolution of symbolic objects into ideographs led to the rapid adoption of writing all across western Asia.

The Script of the Indus Valley Civilization

5

by Walter A. Fairservis, Jr.
March 1983

One of the four earliest civilizations has a script that has long resisted decipherment. A start on deciphering it is now made on the basis of facts and inferences from the archaeological record

The oldest civilizations are those of Sumer, Egypt, China and the Indus Valley in the northwestern part of the subcontinent now occupied by India, Pakistan and Bangladesh. The writings of the first three civilizations can be read; the inscriptions of the fourth one remain largely enigmatic. As a result what is known of the Indus Valley civilization comes solely from the material objects brought to light by archaeology. It is ironic that in a part of the world noted for the antiquity of its literature even the most ancient accounts contain no valid reference to the first great culture that thrived there.

The culture of the Indus Valley civilization is called Harappan, after one of its two great cities: Mohenjo-Daro and Harappa. The difficulties that face those who would decipher Harappan writing seem at first virtually insurmountable. They derive in large part from the Harappans' limited use of their script. Their "texts" consist almost exclusively of brief inscriptions on seals and equally limited graffiti on pottery. No known inscription consists of more than 21 signs and the average text numbers only five or six. This, coupled with the fact that many of the signs are pictographic, has let the imagination of more than a few scholars run riot. Earnest attempts have been made to relate Harappan to Minoan, Canaanite, Hittite and even to the peculiar "writing" of Easter Island. Studies in recent years building on what the archaeological record reveals about Harappan life have now yielded a more rewarding approach to the decipherment problem. It is my intent to outline some of these achievements here.

In the decades since the two great Harappan cities were discovered in the 1920's, and particularly since the end of World War II, archaeologists in India and Pakistan have located nearly 1,000 other Harappan sites. They are spread in a wide arc from western India in the vicinity of the Narmada River northward across Gujarat and Kutch, through the Pakistani regions of Sind and the western Punjab and on into Indian Rajasthan and the eastern Punjab up to the vicinity of Delhi. Other settlements have been found along the coast of the Arabian Sea almost as far as the Iranian border and in Baluchistan; one settlement was even discovered close to the Oxus River, deep in central Asia, by a recent French archaeological mission.

Most Harappan sites are small, covering between two and five acres, and are near rivers or streams. There appear to have been three phases of settlement. Sites of the early phase are in or near the borderlands between the subcontinent and Iran. Those of the mature phase are more widespread. Most are in the valley of the Indus River itself, but such far-flung sites as those in Baluchistan and the one near the Oxus also belong to the mature phase. Those of the later phase tend to be far to the south and east of the Indus. Findings at these later sites also contain evidence that the older Harappan culture was in the process of merging with local pastoral and agricultural peoples. Such findings suggest Harappan civilization did not come to a sudden end but played a role in the development of the style of village life that is so characteristic of the subcontinent today.

What does the archaeological record tell us about Harappan life? First, it indicates that its mainstay was farming. Both grains and garden vegetables were grown, and cattle husbandry was central to the farm economy. Second, it indicates that the material culture of the Harappans was simple but not lacking in rich goods. They used copper and bronze for some tools and weapons and occasionally worked gold and silver into the beads that were their principal form of jewelry. At the same time the bulk of their artifacts consist of wood and bone, shell, flint and clay, all materials that were locally abundant. Among the beads, however, were some skillfully fashioned out of rarer semiprecious stones such as agate, carnelian and lapis. (The site near the Oxus was also close to early lapis mines.)

A further striking aspect of Harappan life was the extent of standardization. In architecture, building bricks were standard in size and were laid in standard ways. Drainage and sewer systems were standard in pattern. Dwellings were standard in dimensions and special structures (possibly public) were positioned with respect to private ones according to standard plans. Other aspects of the same phenomenon included standard weights and measures, pottery that was standard in shape and ornamentation and standardized artifacts such as ladles, loom weights and even toy carts. At the same time certain aspects of Harappan life suggest the later culture of India, for example the use of distinctive headdresses and of multiple bangles and necklaces and even the style of Harappan figurines.

So much for a broad summary of what is known. What is not known may be of equal significance. There is no evidence of rivalry between different Harappan states, of warfare, of major international trade or of the kings and courts and great temple complexes so characteristic of the other ancient civilizations of the Old World. The archaeological evidence reveals next to nothing about Harappan religion or political and social organization. Yet Harappan civilization was important to the civilizations that succeeded it. The Harappans cultivated cotton and perhaps rice, domesticated the chicken and may have invented the game of chess and one of the two great early sources of nonmuscle power: the windmill. (The other was the water wheel.)

When did this enigmatic civilization flourish? Although there is some controversy on the point, the mature Harappan phase seems to have extended from about 2200 to 1700 B.C. Most Harappan sites appear to have been occupied for no more than 200 years; they give the impression of a short-lived development characterized by substantial group organization and regular interaction between contemporaneous settlements.

The task of "reading" the Harappan inscriptions is sufficiently difficult to make many scholars believe it is impossible. The first difficulty arises from the fact that the inscriptions represent the unknown writing of an unknown language for which there are no bilingual texts, such as the Rosetta stone of Egypt or the Behistun monument of Iran. A second difficulty is the absence of long texts. The entire corpus of Harappan writing consists of some 4,000 seals, seal impressions (that is, impressions of seals) and graffiti on pottery; moreover, many of the seals are damaged and many of the pottery graffiti are interrupted by breakage. Still a third difficulty arises from the fact that Harappan civilization was not only geographically remote from the other civilizations of its time but also historically remote from later cultural developments on the subcontinent.

Fortunately the Harappan seals are inscribed with both writing and pictures, and the pictorial motifs can yield clues to what the writing means. Most Harappan seals are square or rectangular pieces of soapstone, a material that is easy to carve. On the back of most of the seals is a raised boss pierced with a hole for a carrying string; on the front is a combination of a negative picture and an inscription. The carvings presumably

SEAL OF THE HARAPPAN CULTURE in the archaeological collection of the National Museum of Pakistan in Karachi displays a zebu bull. The four signs across the top of the seal are among those that appear on the grid on pages 64 and 65. They are, from left to right, the triple stroke of the numeral 3, which also has the meaning "foremost"; a pipal-leaf figure and an arrow, with the meaning "mother" or "mistress"; a stick figure with "horns," indicative of a high-ranking personage, and a pot with handles, an honorific suffix with the meaning "high" or "superior." The seal evidently belonged to a high-ranking member of Harappan society, possibly a woman.

identified the owner of the seal, so that when the seal was pressed into soft clay, the imprinted object was recognized as somehow associated with the owner.

A majority of Harappan seals display one or the other of two distinct pictorial motifs. The first involves an animal. It is usually a long-horned bull, but humped zebus are also portrayed, as are water buffaloes, goats, short-horned bulls, rhinoceroses, tigers, gavials (the river crocodiles of India) and elephants. Whatever the animal, an object was shown in place before it. The object shown with wild or dangerous animals is platterlike. The object shown with the domestic animals is either a basket or (particularly in front of the long-horned bull) a "stem" emblem such as one also shown being carried in processions.

A few of the animal seals show their subjects in groups. One well-known example is centered on an anthropomorphic figure, sometimes called the "Lord of the Beasts," seated cross-legged and wearing a water-buffalo headdress. To the right of the figure are an elephant and a tiger; to the left are a rhinoceros and a water buffalo. The seal is damaged but below and to the left of the central figure's feet can be seen a goat looking over its shoulder and to the right are what may be the horns of a matching goat figure, otherwise obliterated. A less elaborate seal centers on a pipal, or sacred fig tree (*Ficus religiosa*); the heads of two long-horned bulls are shown growing up from its trunk.

Another "animal group" depiction appears on one prismatic seal. (A few Harappan seals were made in the shape of a prism and a few others were cylindrical.) In a row on one of its three faces are an elephant, a rhinoceros and a tiger; a fourth figure in the row is too worn to identify. Presumably this is the "wild animal" face of the seal. On the second face is another four-animal procession, none of them apparently "wild." On both faces, however, a fifth animal is depicted above the animal procession. It is a gavial, self-evidently a member of the "wild" group. On the "wild animal" face the gavial is shown with a recognizable fish in front of its snout and what may be a fish behind it. On the second face no recognizable fish appears.

A fourth seal, even more elaborate than the "Lord of the Beasts," introduces a "worshiper" element. It repeats the depiction of a pipal tree, this time at its upper right corner. Between the branches of the tree stands a horned anthropomorphic figure. Facing the horned figure is a kneeling one, skirted and thus presumably female; to the left of the kneeling figure is a large goat. Seven skirted figures occupy the bottom half of the seal, their hair dressed in some kind of long "ponytail." A rather gruesome depiction on a fifth seal shows several similarly coiffed figures, one of

"LORD OF THE BEASTS," a famous seal in the archaeological collection of the National Museum of India in New Delhi, shows a human figure seated cross-legged and wearing a water-buffalo headdress. The "beasts" associated with the figure are a rhinoceros and a water buffalo (*left*), an elephant and a tiger (*right*) and a goat with its head turned (*bottom*). The goat may originally have been one of two, the second being lost when the seal was broken. The inscription can be rendered as "The Black One, the Black Buffalo *an-i(l)*, the High One, the Lord of Chiefs."

GRAFFITI ON POTTERY, such as those on these sherds found in Baluchistan, are a second source of Harappan signs. They are not as numerous as the inscriptions on seals and seal impressions, but they indicate that the inscriptions were meant to be read from right to left.

them wearing a skirt, being attacked by a water buffalo.

These motifs suggest something about Harappan social organization: that individual seal-bearers belonged to groups that transcended normal familial lines. For example, all individuals with a rhinoceros on their seal may have had some social tie in common. What was held in common could have been membership in some superfamilial group such as a clan or a club. The existence of procession scenes on a few seals, where animal effigies seem to be carried as standards, adds strength to this concept of superfamilial groups. The groups in turn may have been part of a larger two-part grouping, as is suggested by the motif of the "Lord of the Beasts" on the one hand and the motif of the "Pipal-deity worshipers" on the other. Such a possible structure is familiar to anthropologists as what is termed a moiety: a society characterized by the classification of clans or similar subsidiary organizations into two groups, "halves" that usually intermarry.

If one accepts the working hypothesis that the pictorial material on each seal identifies its bearer as to clan and moiety, it logically follows that the part of the seal devoted to Harappan script could be concerned with identifying the bearer as an individual. The script might, for example, give the individual's name, occupation, place of residence, rank or title and similar information. In support of such an interpretation the study of seal texts reveals considerable variation in the sequence of individual signs and yet a frequent repetition of certain of them. The hypothesis gives the would-be decipherer some basis on which to proceed. Just as Michael Ventris knew that at least some of the Linear B texts found on Crete were inventories of material objects, so the decipherer of Harappan script can assume that what to search for are proper names and their embellishments or other statements identifying the individual.

As long ago as the 1930's the British scholar G. R. Hunter had identified a total of 396 separate Harappan signs. More recent work has added another 23, so that the script is now known to incorporate a total of 419 signs. Statistical analysis shows that they occur 13,376 times in 2,290 known texts. Of the 419, 113 signs occur only once, 47 occur twice and 59 occur fewer than five times. In effect this means that the remaining 200 signs were in more or less general service, and analysis shows that fully half of them are combinations of the remaining half.

These findings demonstrate that Harappan writing was neither alphabetic, as Sanskrit is, nor logographic (that is, having one character for each word), as Chinese is. This places Harappan writing in the category known as logo-syllabic, meaning that some signs represent words and others serve purely for their syllabic values, or sounds. Other examples of this kind of writing are Egyptian hieroglyphs, early Sumerian ideographs and modern Japanese. The fact that half of the Harappan signs in common use were combinations of other commonly used ones suggests that the writers exploited such combinations to express ideas (as the Chinese do when they pair the characters for sun and moon to represent the word "brightness") and to combine syllabic sounds to "spell out" a word.

A crucial part of any writing system is the series of devices used to indicate gender, to distinguish between singular and plural, to establish the case of a verb and so on. The identification of these devices goes a long way toward establishing the relations between the graphemes, or individual components, of words and the language the graphemes represent. Now, the Harappan texts exhibit certain regularly paired signs, much as in the English reiteration of titles such as "His Majesty" and "Her Grace." It is also notable that certain signs appear in the middle of a text but rarely at the beginning or the end, whereas with other signs the reverse is true.

The usual ordering of signs and the identity of characteristic pairings may be established with a grid. Since the Harappan inscriptions are commonly brief, such a grid can consist of a relatively limited number of vertical columns. In fact, 14 columns were found to be sufficient. Of the first 17 inscriptions selected for horizontal grid display, most consisted of only five or six signs; thus they were entered near the center of the column array, allowing any longer lines to extend to the right or the left.

On entering the texts on the grid it became evident that certain signs appeared regularly in most of them. Con-

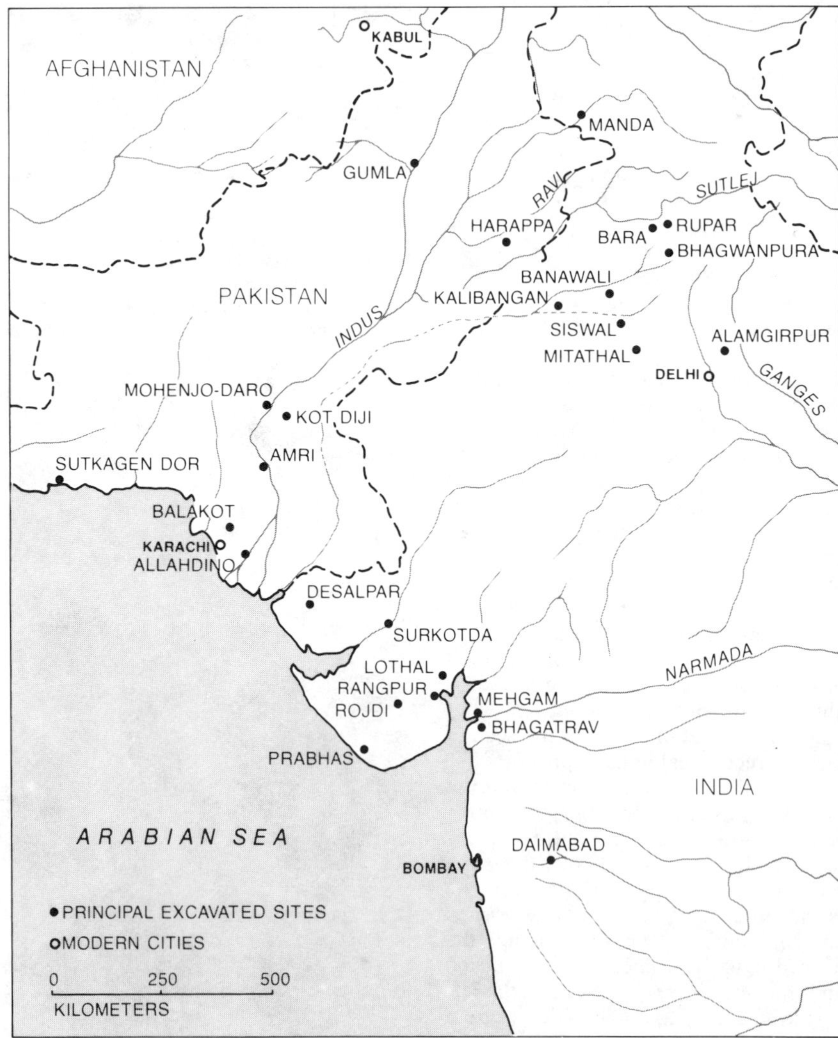

HARAPPAN SITES have been found from almost as far south as Bombay to as far north as central Asia and from as far west as Baluchistan to as far east as Delhi. Twenty-five of the principal excavated sites are shown on this map, including the great cities of the civilization: Mohenjo-Daro and Harappa. Most Harappan sites are small, covering between two and five acres.

sider the "pot" signs in column 5, the "loom twist" signs in column 8 and the "two-stroke" signs in column 10. When two of these three signs appear in the same text (as in lines *b, e, h* and *p*), they are always in the same right-to-left order with respect to each other no matter what other signs are included in the inscription. Regularity of position evidently governed their relations. Accordingly in setting up the Harappan grid such signs were placed in the columns noted above even when only one of them appeared in a particular text.

What then became clear was that these signs were the most numerous among those in the 17 selected texts. The pot sign in column 5 appears there 10 times, and three variants appear in two other columns. The loom-twist sign in column 8, variants included, appears six times, and the two short vertical strokes of column 10, variants included, appear eight times. Certain other signs utilizing vertical strokes are not as fixed in their relative positions. Whereas the group of one or two short single strokes can be accommodated in column 10, those groups consisting of one, two, three or more long strokes fall outside the central columns of the grid.

By now, acquainted with the appearance of some 50 Harappan signs as they are displayed on the analytical grid, the reader may be wondering in which horizontal direction they are to be "read." On the basis of seal inscriptions alone this might have been a hard question to answer. Fortunately the graffiti inscribed on pottery supplied an answer. Studies by B. B. Lal and I. Mahadevan of the Archaeological Survey of India have shown that some graffiti have overlapping strokes. The overlaps demonstrate that the direction of writing was from right to left. That is why column 14 of the grid appears at its left margin and column 1 at its right margin. The reversal puts the reading order in the more familiar left-to-right pattern.

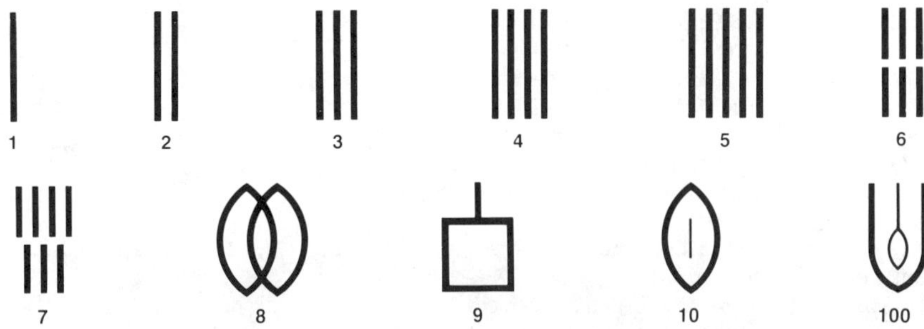

HARAPPAN NUMERALS, perhaps originally part of a system with a base of eight, are a plausible set of vertical strokes for 1 through 5 and a sextuplet of short strokes for 6. The sign for 7 is a similar set of short strokes. The signs for 8 and 9 are respectively pictographs of a double sun and a "foundation post." The sign for 10 is a single sun with a short stroke inside it. One other identified numeral, the sign for 100, is a pictograph of a mortar and pestle.

We now come to the most complex part of the decipherment problem: What was the Harappan language? When Ventris identified the language of Linear B as Greek, he had overcome his greatest difficulty. The archaeological record of the region offers something of the same kind of help to those trying to pick a candidate for the unknown tongue. For example, the record shows that Harappan civilization was no sudden development. It had a long ancestry in the Indo-Iranian borderland, spread widely and eventually made its own contribution to the emergence of village India. This sequence suggests that the language spoken by the Harappans cannot have completely disappeared from the subcontinent.

Accepting such an assumption, which of the three principal families of languages spoken in the region might be related to Harappan? One candidate is Munda, a family of languages (spoken largely in eastern India) that seems affiliated with certain languages of Southeast Asia. Studies of the earliest forms of Munda, however, find little in its vocabulary that comports with what archaeology tells us about the culture of the Harappans. Another candidate is Indo-Aryan, a family of languages that traditionally came to India in the middle of the second millennium B.C. Its earliest literary expression, the Rig-Veda, however, describes a basically central-Asian culture quite different from the Harappan. The third candidate is Dravidian, a language now spoken mostly in southern and southeastern India but also still found in pockets in northern India and in Baluchistan.

A fourth possibility, of course, is that Harappan is related to none of the above. It is nonetheless worthwhile to consider the candidacy of Dravidian more closely than that of either Munda or Indo-Aryan. In addition to the northern forms (Kuruḵẖ, Malto and Brahui) about 25 Dravidian languages are still spoken. Indeed, the major families (Tamil, Malayalam, Kannaḍa and Telegu) are spoken by more than 100 million people. Thanks again to the archaeological record it is not necessary to accept the candidacy of Dravidian blindly.

In 1974 excavations at the Harappan site of Allahdino, near Karachi, unearthed an ivory fragment with a half-circular cross section. There were holes on one side, apparently drilled to hold pegs; on the other side were two lengthwise parallel grooves. The object was

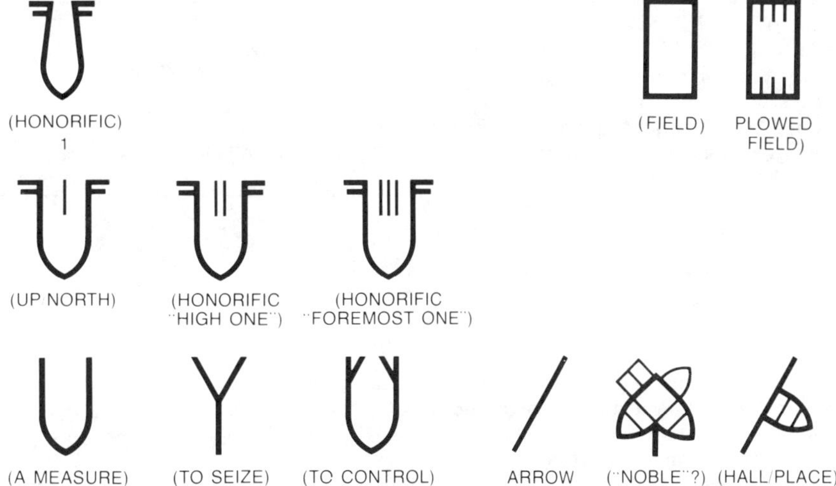

COMBINED SIGNS make up half of the total of the 200 signs most frequently encountered in the Harappan script. Four examples are given here. At the top left is one of the commonest script signs, a pictograph of a pot with handles (labeled with the Arabic numeral 1). Below it are three combined signs: the sign labeled *1* plus signs like those for the Harappan numerals 1, 2 and 3 but consisting of short strokes. Under each of these three signs appears its sense in English. Below the combined signs are seen, from left to right, the pictographs for a container and for a forked stick, and a third sign combining them. At the top right is the pictograph for a field, a simple rectangle. Beside it is a sign that combines the field sign with the strokes of the Harappan numeral 6 to form a new pictograph with the apparent sense of "plowed field." At the bottom right, from left to right, are pictographs for "arrow" and for "pipal-tree leaf." The third sign, combining "arrow" with a partial "pipal leaf," seems to indicate "hall" or "place."

similar to a large number of ivory rods or sticks excavated in the 1930's by one of the later workers at the great Harappan city of Mohenjo-Daro, E. J. H. Mackay. The Mohenjo-Daro ivories were not, as has been asserted, merely gaming pieces. For example, one of them, square in cross section, had a series of alternating circles and crescents cut into one side.

On some of the Mohenjo-Daro ivories is a sign seen in the grid (column 6, line *c*) and another sign resembling some form of plant. In various seal texts these two signs are associated with vertical strokes that range from one to seven in number and with five other signs. (Two appear on the grid at column 7, line *c*, and column 11, line *q*.) Like the second sign on the Mohenjo-Daro ivories, the sign at column 6, line *c*, appears to represent a plant, probably a stalk of grain. Considering the association of both signs in the seal inscriptions with what appear to be numbers and the marking of one of the ivories with circles and crescents that approximate in number a lunar (crescent) month of 30 solar (circle) days, the two plant signs might logically be taken to represent a word meaning both grain and month (or moon). Furthermore, the vertical strokes associated with both signs end after reaching a total of seven, suggesting that some other sign served for the number eight and possibly that the Harappan number system was to the base eight.

What language has a word for grain that also means month or moon and is associated with a base-eight numerical system? On the first point *nel* means rice in five Dravidian languages and *nilā* or *nela* means moon in three of the same five and in five others as well. It is also the word for month in some of the same languages. On the second point, a student of Dravidian language, Kamir V. Zvelebil, has pointed out that the original Dravidian number system was indeed probably to the base eight: the count to 10, used for conformity with the base-10 number system today, goes literally (in translation) "one," "two," "three," "four," "five," "six," "seven," "number," "many minus one" and "many."

Over the years scholars have noted in Dravidian a number of homophones: words with the same sounds but with different meanings. For example, the word for the shoulder pole from which pots are suspended is *kā*. It is also the word meaning guardian, or protector. The common word for fish is *mīn*, which is also the word for star. The word for 100 is *nūṟu*, which is also the word meaning to grind or to powder.

The homophonic, or rebus, principle is found in a number of ancient languages, including the hieroglyphs of Egypt. The key aspect of the homo-

		14	13	12	11
a	FEMD 606				
b	HAR 16				
c	HAR 99				
d	HAR 72				
e	FEMD 590				
f	MD-31 121				
g	MD-31 46				
h	MD-31 26				
i	HAR 110				
j	HAR 102				
k	FEMD 111				
l	MD-31 69				
m	HAR 69				
n	MD 650				
o	MD 405				
p	FEMD 48				
q	ME-31 110				

ANALYTICAL GRID 14 columns wide contains 17 seal texts that range in length from two signs to nine. When "pot" signs were all assigned to column 5, "loom twist" signs and their variants to column 8 and the signs made up of two short vertical dashes to column 10, it became apparent that when two or more of these three signs appeared in an inscription, they always appeared in the same right-to-left order with respect to one another regardless of what other signs might appear in the text. Lines *b, e, h* and *p* provide four examples. The single short verti-

10	9	8	7	6	5	4	3	2	1

cal dashes in column 10 (lines *b, d* and *j*) reveal an inflectional quality. The same sign also appears in combining form in column 12, line *d*, as an addition to a "sun" sign; in column 11, line *k*, as an addition to a "man" sign, and in column 9, lines *n* and *o*, as additions to "pot" signs. The sense of the single sign and its combination (lines *i, n* and *o*) appears to be that of a possessive; the sense of the double-dash sign appears to be that of a locative. Two of the texts, lines *l* and *m*, do not fall within the "normal" central grid distribution. Thus it can be assumed that they are not texts of the usual formulation. When two signs are found in one grid cell, the placement indicates that the signs are regularly found paired in seal texts. Readings of four of these 17 texts (lines *d, e, g* and *k*) are shown at the bottom of the next page.

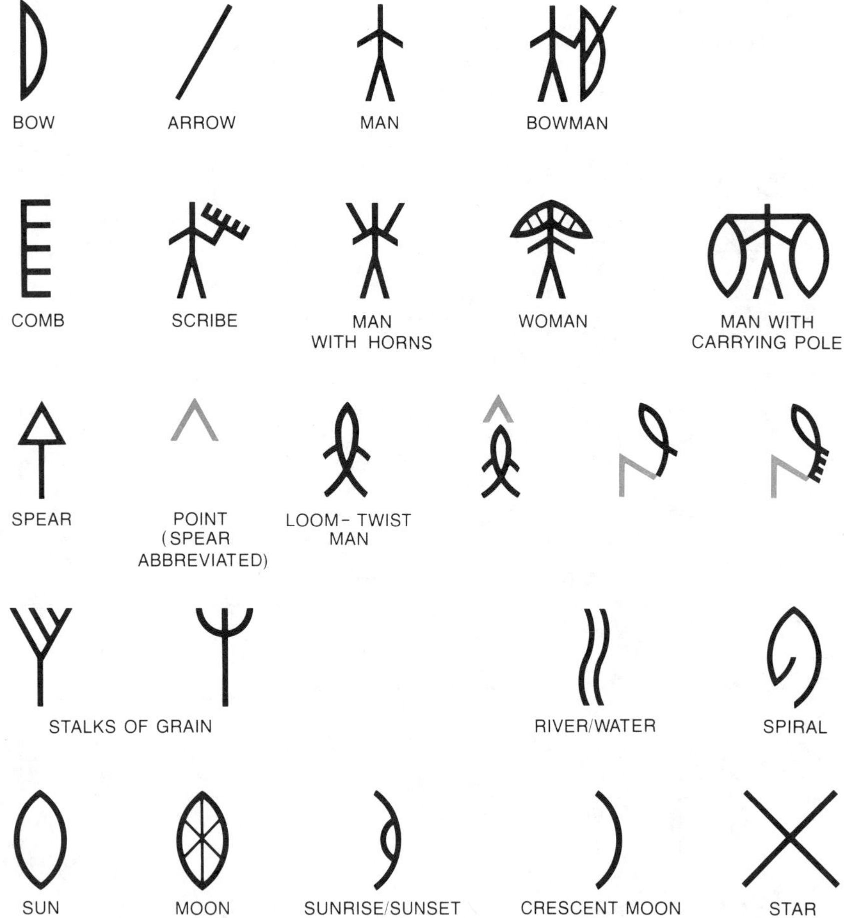

ADDITIONAL PICTOGRAPHS to be found on the grid on the next two pages include those illustrated here together with some combined forms. In the top row, from left to right, are "bow," "arrow," "man" and the combination "bowman." In the second row are "comb," a third human stick figure holding a comb (a combination that appears to indicate "scribe"), a fourth stick figure with "horns," a fifth stick figure with an elaborate coiffure ("woman") and a stick figure with a loaded shoulder pole (a combination appearing to indicate "guardian"). In the third row, from left to right, are "spear" and the shorthand for "spear," "point" (*color*), an honorific; a "loom twist" plus human arms, a second honorific pertaining to rulership, and the two signs combined. In the fourth row are two stalks of grain (both signs have the interchangeable sense of "grain" or "month"), a sign with the sense of "river" or "water" and a spiral with the sense of "surround" or "surrounding." In the bottom row are five astronomical pictographs. From left to right are seen the sun, the moon, sunrise or sunset, the crescent moon and a star.

phonic principle is that it seeks a syllabic equivalent (say a picture of an eye to mean "I") rather than merely being a picture of something. For example, an early Egyptian ruler, Nr-mr, was represented in hieroglyphs by the sign for a catfish (*nr*) and the sign for a chisel (*mr*). The representation was not meant to suggest that he be called "the catfish-chisel one" but rather that his name sounded like "catfish-chisel."

Does this suggest a basis for deriving a Harappan syllabary? I shall put the point to trial in what follows, first warning that the acid test of any decipherment is its consistency. If a decision is made to declare a certain symbol equivalent to a selected sound or sense, it cannot later be shifted to represent some other sound or sense. Inner logic is basic to all writing systems; when decipherers arbitrarily alter the values of symbols in order to fit the model they prefer, their work is spoiled.

For a start consider the sign shown in column 7, line *h*. Pictographically it could be taken to represent a mortar and pestle. Linguistic reconstructions suggest that this utensil was given the syllabic value *nūṟu* in Dravidian. This, as we have seen, is also the sound of the verb to grind or powder and the numerical noun "100." Next consider the sign that figures so prominently in column 5 of the grid. Some years ago Mahadevan conjectured that this sign, which most frequently appears at the end of seal texts, was a pictographic representation of a pot with handles. He went on to point out that various Dravidian words for this kind of pot were homophones of words meaning male, including the common honorific suffix *aṉ* used with male personal names at least as long ago as early in the Christian Era. The fact that such a sign terminates seal texts hypothesized to contain personal names strengthens Mahadevan's conjecture.

Now, another terminal sign on the grid (column 5, line *f*) is a pictograph of a human figure carrying a shoulder pole with a pot at each end. As we have seen, the syllable for a pole with pots alone, *kā*, is a homophone of the Dravidian words meaning "to guard" or "to protect." Furthermore, a common Dravidian word for man is *āḷ*. The combination of these would allow the reconstruction of the sign at column 5, line *f*, as a two-syllable word, *kā-āḷ*. In the Dravidian languages, for the sake of euphony, such adjacent vowels are separated by a consonant, either a *v* or a *y*. Thus the restored word, *kāvāḷ*, could be translated as "one who guards or protects," a statement of personal identity suitable for entry on a private seal.

To give two further examples before turning to trial readings of some of the seal texts on the grid, two of the "number" signs—the sign in column 12, line *k*, presumably meaning three, and a second sign consisting of four vertical strokes, presumably meaning four—also have plausible homophones. The first homophone, *mu*(*n*), equates with the Dravidian word meaning "foremost" (*muṉ*); the second homophone, *nāl*, equates with the word meaning "good" (*nal*), both logical titular adjectives.

Let us now consider two short and two longer seal texts from the grid. The text designated Mohenjo-Daro 31 46 (line *g*) consists of three signs, putatively a musical instrument, a spear and a comb. The assigned Dravidian syllabic values are, in the same order, *pan, ār* and *ki*(*r*), in translation the word "sing," a third-person honorific and the word "mark," read as *Panār-ki*(*r*). The proposed translation is "Panar's seal," or literally "The singer's mark." Next, the text designated FEMD 590 (line *e*) consists of four signs. The first sign, a diamond shape, has the three-syllable value *āra-man*, the second, two short vertical lines, has the value *i*(*l*), the third, a "loom twist," has the three-syllable value *piri*(*key*) and the fourth is the same honorific *ār* as in the preceding text. This is read as *Āra-man-i*(*l*) *pirikeyār*, with the proposed translation "Belonging to the noble house (of the) Pirikeyar" ("pirs" and "pirikeys" are chiefs).

The third text, Harappa 72 (line *d*), consists of seven signs: an initial spiral (*cur*), an oval enclosing a short vertical dash (*paṭă*), a pipal leaf and an arrow combined (*ambara*), a short vertical dash alone (*ă*), a twist with a point above it (*āra-pirikey*), pincers combined with the sign for the sun (*paṭu-kāru*) and, as the terminal sign, the pot with handles (*aṉ*). This is a mouthful: *Cur paṭămbara-ă āra-pirikey paṭu-kāran*. The pro-

HARAPPAN CONTACT WITH MESOPOTAMIA is evidenced by the discovery of Harappan seals in the region. The one shown here, with the seal at the left and the sealing impression at the right, was uncovered in 1975 in the ruins of a house of the Kassite period at Nippur, an ancient city in Iraq, by McGuire Gibson of the Oriental Institute of the University of Chicago.

posed translation is "Patukaran, powerful (noble) chief of the surrounding settlements." The fourth text, FEMD 111 (line *k*), is one of the longest of the translated seal inscriptions, consisting of nine signs. In the interest of brevity, only the syllables and their proposed translation will be given: *Munālă-i(l) nūr̠u cār̠uvara amban ārōru malya,* or "Belonging to Munala, mistress of 100 plowed fields, noble first lady."

So far syllabic values have been assigned to nearly 100 seal and pottery signs and appropriate Dravidian homophones have been found for each. Translations such as those given here have been proposed for more than 100 seal texts. They range from such simple statements as "water-holder" (probably a proper name) to such sonorities as "Arasamban, High Chief (of) Chiefs of the Southwest, lineage of the Moon."

What such readings demonstrate about the Harappans is that a number of individuals (Arasamban among them) traced their lineage to such major figures of the cosmos as the Sun, the Moon and the Stars and perhaps also the Monsoon Rain. These may represent distinctions within each clan. Chiefs were associated with *aramani,* or chiefs' houses, which may have had both residential and administrative functions. In addition there was a high place (the "citadels" identified by archaeologists?) that served a special but so far undetermined function. An assembly area—an open court or a pillared hall (both known archaeologically)—suggests that an assembly of chiefs was a basic part of Harappan political organization.

Among other kinds of leaders known from the seals were heads of associations (guilds?) such as that of the coppersmiths, storehouse overseers, irrigation supervisors and landowners, a category that as we have seen included women. Religious references, however, are scarce. There is a possible "horned deity," referred to as "the copper one" or "the red one," and a possible "mother deity," but at the moment these distinctions are not confirmed. Lesser figures included drummers and singers, the drummers perhaps to summon assemblies and the singers perhaps to entertain or perform at ceremonies.

The seals attest further to a class of scribes, to people in charge of weights and measures and to supervisors of the distribution of stores, the grinding of flour and probably hunting operations. There were also captains of boats and custodians of fire. Many seals bear the sign *kā,* referring to guardianship, not in a military sense but more in terms of a responsibility for the care of crops and the preservation of herds and flocks. One of the gratifying near-proofs that the decipherments are on the right track comes from the prismatic seal where a gavial is twice seen above an array of "clan" animals. In Dravidian the word for crocodile is *mutalai.* The Dravidian word for first chief, *mutali,* is a close homophone.

Thus it appears that the language of Mohenjo-Daro and Harappa some 4,000 years ago was an early Dravidian tongue and that the Harappan scribes struggled to put that language into graphic form as a method of identifying the elite of the Indus Valley civilization. The Harappan civilization, however, was geographically so widespread that a number of non-Dravidian words must have entered the language, just as Dravidian words were later borrowed by the speakers of Indo-Aryan.

A great deal of additional decipherment remains to be done and no doubt what has been put forth here will be found to have flaws. What remains to be done is even more exciting. It leads toward a goal that until recently seemed impossible to attain: cohesive information on Harappan polity, social organization and ideology, and perhaps even stronger evidence that, as the parent of the village India of today, the Harappan culture never did disappear.

a
pan -ār ki(r)

b
āra-man i̠(l) pirikey -ār

c
cur paṭă ambara ằ āra-pirikey patu-kāru -an̠

d
mun āl-ằ i(l) nūr̠u cār̠uvara amban -ār ōru malya

FOUR SEAL INSCRIPTIONS appear together with the syllabic value of each sign in Dravidian, a surviving family of early languages of the region. The shortest inscription (*a*), in the author's reading, is "The singer's mark." The next inscription (*b*), which repeats the third-person honorific "spear" sign, *ār,* is read as "Belonging to the noble house (of the) Pirikeyar." The next inscription (*c*) is seven signs long and includes a variant of the "loom twist" sign of inscription *b.* It is read as "Patukaran, powerful (noble) chief of the surrounding settlements." The last inscription (*d*) is nine signs long and includes the two-stroke sign *i(l)* of inscription *b* and an abbreviation of the "spear" signs in both *a* and *b* (*color*). It is read as "Belonging to Munala, mistress of 100 plowed fields, noble first lady." More than 100 seal texts have now been read. The majority of the readings accord with the hypothesis that the seal signs identify individuals.

6 The Chinese Language

by William S-Y. Wang
February 1973

This melodious tongue is spoken by more people than any other. Although the Chinese system of writing is complex, the basic structure of the language is remarkably simple

To people who are familiar only with the common European languages the Chinese language is strikingly different. Yet today Chinese is spoken by more people than any other language, and Chinese literature is the world's oldest, spanning a period of 35 centuries. When we examine the structure of the Chinese language, we find that it is not conspicuously complex; indeed, in many ways it is simpler than the Western languages. But since Chinese does differ from the European languages in fundamental respects, some knowledge of its structure and historical development is indispensable to a general understanding of the nature of human language.

To the Western eye the writing system of the Chinese is altogether novel: instead of neat rows of simple alphabetic letters there are thousands of unique characters, many of which seem incredibly intricate. To the ear the language sounds rather melodious, perhaps a little like singing. When one peers below the surface, there are more surprises. The language has virtually no conjugation for its verbs and no declension for its nouns. The inevitable paradigms that Western schoolchildren have come to dread in their grammar books are totally absent in a grammar of Chinese. For the various forms of the verb "to buy," such as "buy," "buys," "bought" and "buying," Chinese has the single form *mǎi*. (The mark over the *a* signifies that the syllable is spoken in a tone that falls and then rises. There are three other vowel marks for tones, as in *á* indicating a rising tone, *à* indicating a falling tone and *ā* indicating a level high tone.) For "book," "books," "to the books" and "of the books" the Chinese is *shū*. Most of the time it is quite clear from the context what tense or mood is intended for a verb and what number or case is intended for a noun. Hence the Chinese language does not bother much with this particular type of redundancy in its grammar. Perhaps it is this structural simplicity of the language that moved the anthropologist and linguist Edward Sapir to characterize it as "soberly logical."

The Antiquity of Chinese

Chinese is often termed a very old language. In a sense such a statement is misleading. All human languages go back to the dim uncertainty of prehistory, and at present we have no way of knowing whether or not they can all be traced back to the same root. Four thousand years ago the ancestors of the Chinese peoples spoke an early form of the Chinese language in much the same way that the ancestors of the English-speaking peoples were using an early form of the English language. Since almost nothing is known about the emergence of language in the human species, we are not in a position to say which of the world's languages evolved earlier and which later. It is rather that in the course of history some languages have been renamed more often than others (as a result of events such as migration or conquest) and the newness of the names gives the illusion that the thing being named is new.

There is one sense, however, in which Chinese is a very old language. Sumerian is the only language we know of that has extant written materials that antedate Chinese ones. Sumerian cuneiform writing dates back some 5,000 years; the earliest Chinese writing in existence today dates back 3,500 years. But Sumerian and its derivative orthographies died out long before the beginning of the Christian Era. Chinese orthography has continued to this day, although there have been major stylistic changes.

The earliest Chinese writings are incisions on bone and tortoise shell. Most of the inscriptions are oracular, dealing with political or religious events or with the weather or warfare. Discovered toward the end of the 19th century in Chinese drugstores, where they were being sold as "dragon bones" for their medicinal value, the story of these inscriptions is a colorful chapter in the history of Chinese archaeology and philology. More than 100,000 inscribed pieces have now been found. Even though the total number of written characters on the pieces is more than a million, the number of different characters is small. The texts of the oracular inscriptions dealt with a very limited range of topics, and the same characters are repeated over and over again. Of the 2,000 to 3,000 characters on the shells and bones, about half can be read today.

Through the centuries Chinese characters have been preserved in many different mediums: metal vessels, stone drums, jade jewelry, coins, metal mirrors, bricks and tiles. The central line of development, however, has been the use of the brush on silk, bamboo, wood and ultimately on paper. A brush can produce variations in thickness whereas a stylus cannot. Such variations give the

SYMBIOTIC RELATION between painting and writing in Chinese art is elegantly exemplified by a detail from "Flowering Plants and Trees" on the opposite page. The characters were written in the traditional format: in columns and from right to left. The portion of the poem that is framed by the pine branches is translated: "Jade strands hang limp in the wind. Crimson berries sparkle bright against the snow." The painting was made by Ch'en Shun in the 16th century during the Ming dynasty. It is part of the Avery Brundage Collection at the Center of Asian Art and Culture in San Francisco.

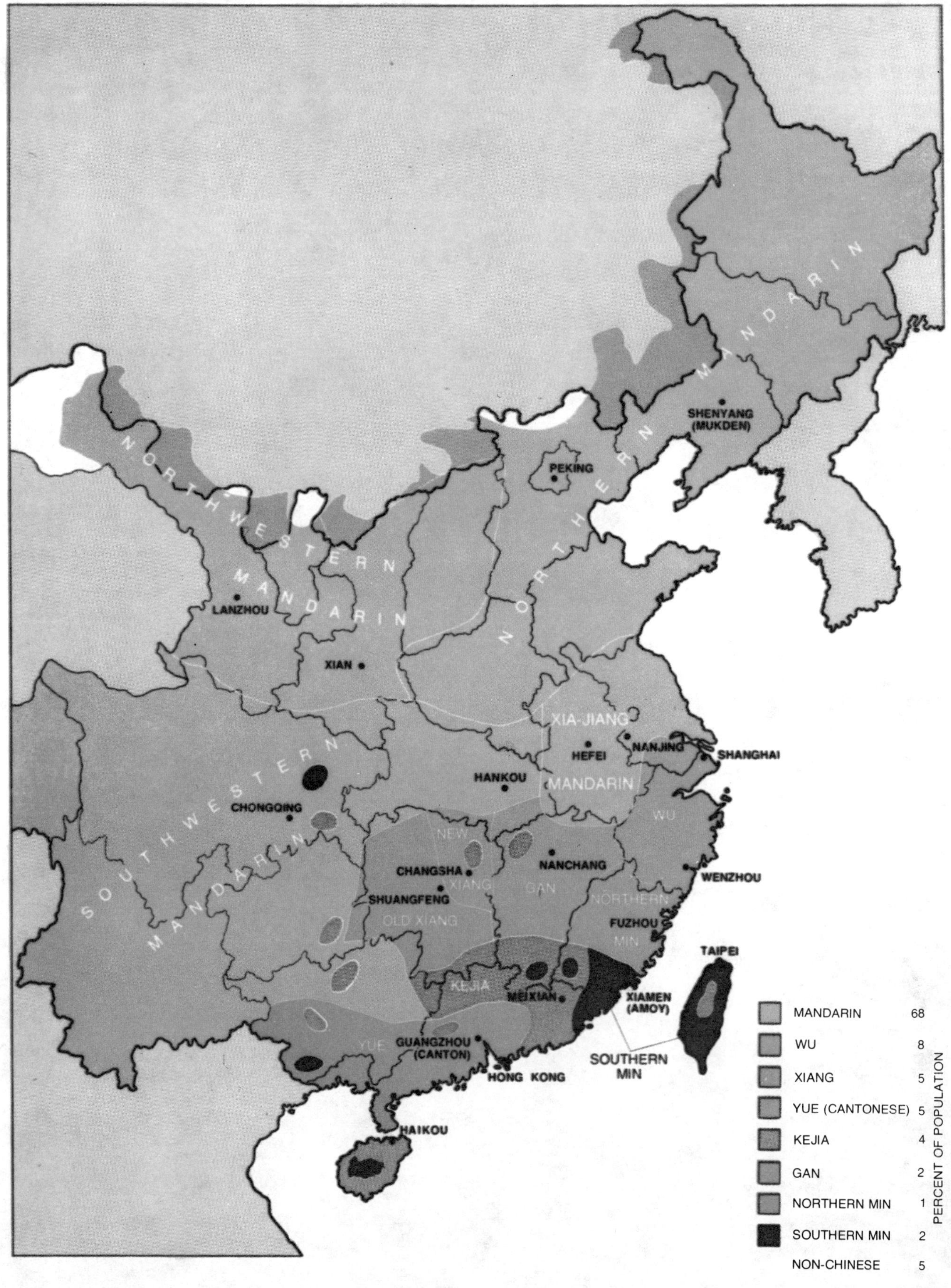

MAP OF CHINA shows the distribution of the major dialects of the Chinese language. More than two-thirds of the Chinese population speak one of the Mandarin dialects, of which the speech of Peking is the standard. It is the dialects along the southern coast, however, that have been carried to many parts of the world by Chinese emigrants. There are also several non-Chinese linguistic stocks within China. The regions to the north and west are dominated by non-Chinese languages such as Mongolian and Tibetan.

writer a much greater artistic freedom in rendering his characters.

Some of the earliest written Chinese characters were pictographic. The character for "rain" was several columns of broken lines, and the one for "horse" looked like a horse, complete with mane and four legs [*see illustration on page* 59]. Pictographs, however, are only a minority in the total vocabulary of Chinese. Most of the words in the language cannot be suggested by a simple picture.

Calligraphy, the elegant rendering of characters, is a highly cultivated art form that has long been prized in Chinese culture, much as painting is valued in the Western world. For the Chinese there is a close relation between painting and calligraphy. Typically a silk scroll is covered with a picture and a few lines of characters, the two carefully balanced against each other. Because of their artistic values and their long history, Chinese characters have a much greater range of variability in their size and shape than the characters of any other writing system.

The Writing System

The Chinese writing system underwent major changes in 1956, when the government of the People's Republic of China decided to simplify the characters and also to adopt a system of spelling Chinese words in Latin letters. Both measures are intended to make the reading and writing of Chinese easier to learn, a crucial step in promoting linguistic unity and raising the standard of literacy in China.

In order to understand the nature of Chinese characters and their simplification, we must first examine their internal structure. Each character is made up of two types of smaller unit called the stroke and the radical. Roughly speaking, a stroke is a line, either straight or curved, that is completed every time the pen leaves the paper. For example, the character for "sun," which is pronounced *rì*, looks like:

日

It is built up of four strokes [*see top illustration on page 55*]. Both the order and the geometric position of the strokes are important. There are approximately 20 distinct strokes in the language, so that strokes are the closest counterparts to the 26 letters of the Latin alphabet. There is no counterpart of the radicals in the orthography of other languages. The traditional set consists of 214 radicals, and these radicals are found in almost all

ORACLE-BONE INSCRIPTIONS, dating from 1300 B.C., are among the earliest-known examples of Chinese writing. They were made on ox bones and tortoise shells and were used for divination. The photograph, provided through the courtesy of Bernhard Karlgren and Jan Wirgin, shows specimens in the Museum of Far Eastern Antiquities in Stockholm.

Chinese dictionaries. A dictionary published in 1971, however, has merged some radicals, reducing the number to 189. Most radicals are also characters; for example, the "sun" radical and the character for "sun" are identical. There are thousands of characters in regular use, and the majority of them are not radicals. Each character contains only one radical, with or without a remainder.

The character for "star," pronounced *xīng*, is written:

星

There is a literary character referring to the morning sun, pronounced *lóng*, that is written:

昽

Now it can be seen that both characters contain the "sun" radical:

日

"Star" has the radical on top and a remainder, which is pronounced *shēng*, that looks like this:

生

"Morning sun" has the "sun" radical to the left; its remainder is pronounced *lóng* and is written:

龙

Almost all the recent Chinese dictionaries and reference books arrange their characters by radicals. Take for example the character for "star." To look it up one first goes to the section marked by the "sun" radical:

日

In this section all the characters that contain the "sun" radical are ordered by the number of strokes in the remainder, which is:

生

This remainder is only moderately complex, with five strokes. We would expect to find it in about the middle of the section.

A key process in the construction of characters can be illustrated with "star" and "morning sun":

星 昽

Their meanings are clearly related to the meaning of the "sun" radical. In these characters the radical is called the signific and the remainders are the phonetics. The phonetics indicate how the characters are to be pronounced. In "morning sun" the phonetic is *lóng:*

龙

It gives its pronunciation to the character. On the other hand, there are characters that are not pronounced like their phonetic, often for reasons of historical sound change. The phonetic in the character "star" is:

生

The phonetic is pronounced *shēng*, but the pronunciation for "star" is *xīng*.

As another example of a phonetic we can take the character for "horse." It is pronounced *mǎ* and is written:

马

When the phonetic for "horse" is combined with the signific for "woman," we have *mā*, which means "mother":

妈

When the "horse" phonetic is combined with the signific for "jade," we have *mǎ*, which means "agate":

玛

Combined with the signific for "insect," the meaning becomes "ant," and again it is pronounced *mǎ:*

蚂

When there are two "mouth" significs hovering over the "horse" phonetic, the meaning becomes "to scold," and it is pronounced *mà:*

骂

There are a large number of characters in Chinese that are constructed on the phonetic-signific plan. Thus underlying many Chinese characters there is a phonetic principle. The average Chinese can often pronounce correctly a character he has never seen before simply by making a shrewd guess at its phonetic. For example, examine the following:

钅龙

The signific portion means "gold." The phonetic portion is pronounced *lóng* and is written:

龙

There would be no problem in agreeing that the character should be the name of a metal or metallic compound and should be pronounced like *lóng*, even though such a character does not exist in the language.

Another fictitious character was sent to me recently by a friend as a riddle. The character has three components:

女 上 下

The first component means "woman." The second and third components also are independent characters; they are pronounced *shàng* and *xià* and respectively mean "up" and "down." We assigned the signific to the "woman" component, and the character looked like this:

女上下

For the character as a whole we settled on the meaning "elevator girl." However, there is no intuitive way of pronouncing the character, since the last two components do not constitute a phonetic. The solution of pronouncing it with two syllables, *shàng-xià*, breaks a general rule of Chinese orthography, namely that for one character there is one syllable. Although reformers of the Chinese language have occasionally proposed polysyllabic characters, no such reform has ever been successful.

Chinese dictionaries and rhyme books may list tens of thousands of characters, but a knowledge of 4,000 to 7,000 characters is sufficient for, say, reading a newspaper. The form of the characters has been built up unsystematically through the centuries, and some are very intricate, requiring 30 or more strokes to write. The Chinese government's plan of simplification has gone a long way toward standardizing the form of the characters and reducing the average number of strokes per character. The net gain has been dramatic. A text written in simplified characters can contain fewer than half as many strokes as the same text written before 1956. This simplification makes the task of learning the written language considerably easier. An average of five or six strokes per character is not significantly different from the average of five or six letters per English word.

Since it is not the primary purpose of

the characters to represent sounds, the Chinese written language has been largely independent of the evolutionary changes that have taken place in the spoken language. This independence has made it possible for the written language to provide a literary continuity across thousands of years and to serve as a cohesive force binding the diverse cultures of China together.

The Evolution of the Language

The evolution of spoken Chinese, like the evolution of all other living languages, has been constant. Therefore many of the beautiful poems of the Táng dynasty of the seventh to 10th centuries no longer rhyme. If Confucius, who lived in the fifth century B.C., were to give a lecture anywhere in China today, he would not be understood. Within the large area of China dialects have evolved so far apart in their sounds that a man from Peking cannot be sure of being able to order a dinner in a Cantonese restaurant. Compared with the change in sounds, the written characters have changed little. Most of the characters Confucius used are still in books today, and many of these characters have their original meanings. The writing of Confucius is more intelligible to a modern Chinese than, say, a page of *Beowulf* is to an American. By the same token, although the Táng poems no longer rhyme, they are still enjoyed throughout China because their visual message remains the same. When the poems are read aloud by people in Peking, Shanghai or Canton, the poems sound altogether different because of the various dialects. It is rather like hearing "6 + 7 = 13" being read aloud in English, German and Norwegian. Even in Japan a Chinese with no knowledge of Japanese can manage to communicate reasonably well by writing. Chinese characters were also a significant medium of communication in Korea and in Vietnam. The independence of the characters from the spoken language has enabled them to serve as a core of culture in much of East Asia for many centuries.

A written Chinese character has a more direct connection with its meaning than a written word in English does. The sequence of letters spelling "horse" has meaning only through the mediation of the sounds they represent. The shape of the letters has no relation to the concept "horse." Little would be changed if English-speaking peoples were to take up the Cyrillic alphabet and the sounds for "horse" were represented *xopc*. To a Chi-

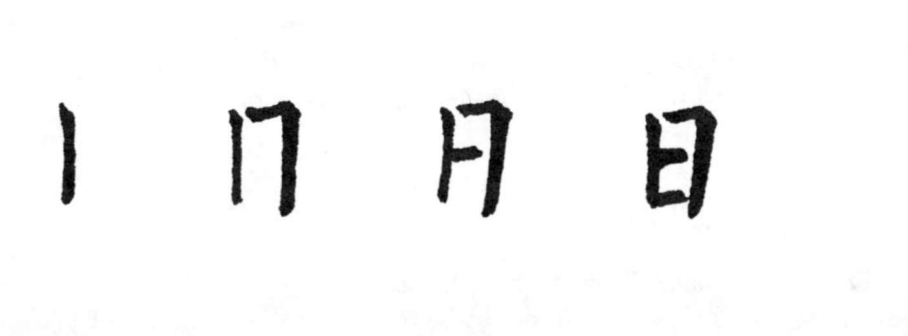

CHARACTER FOR "SUN" is built up with four brushstrokes: first a vertical, then a turning stroke, then the inside and finally the closure. Order and the geometric position of the strokes are important. All the components of a character should fit roughly into a square.

	OLD	SIMPLIFIED
SUN (rì)	日	日
STAR (xīng)	星	星
MORNING SUN (lóng)	曨	昽
HORSE (mǎ)	馬	马
MOTHER (mā)	媽	妈
AGATE (mǎ)	瑪	玛
ANT (mǎ)	螞	蚂
TO SCOLD (mà)	罵	骂

SIMPLIFIED CHARACTERS were introduced in 1956 by the government of the People's Republic of China. Simple characters, such as the first two, were not affected. The remaining characters, somewhat more complex, were each reduced by six strokes.

nese the character for "horse" means horse with no mediation through the sound *mă*. The image is so vivid that one can almost sense an abstract figure galloping across the page:

马

The other major linguistic decision made by the Chinese government was to adopt a spelling system based on the Latin alphabet. This system is called Pinyin, which literally means "spell sound." All the Chinese words spelled out in Latin letters in this article are written in Pinyin. The government has been careful to point out that Pinyin is not intended to replace the characters but rather to serve as an aid in learning pronunciation. To discontinue the use of the Chinese characters would deprive coming generations of Chinese of a rich and meaningful cultural heritage.

Standard Chinese

To discuss the Pinyin system of spelling we need to examine the sound system of what is called standard Chinese, which is based on the Peking dialect and is now being taught in all parts of China. It is a straightforward system, simpler in many ways than the easy syllables of Spanish. There is really only one aspect unfamiliar to those who speak European languages: the tones. The musical quality of the spoken Chinese language is due to the fact that almost every syllable must carry one of four basic tones. These tones are indicated by diacritical marks over the vowels. The phenomenon of tones seems to be confined to Chinese and to some of the languages of Southeast Asia that have been heavily influenced by Chinese.

One of the earliest references in the literature to tones dates back to the sixth century. When the emperor of Liáng asked one of his scholars, Zhōu Shě, what was meant by the four tones, Zhōu responded with an elegant illustration:

天 子 圣 哲

It means "The son of heaven is divine and wise." (Chinese emperors have traditionally been regarded as sons of heaven and divine, whether or not they were wise.) The beauty of Zhōu's response lies in the fact that the first word of his phrase illustrates the first tone in the speech of that time, the second word the second tone, and so on.

Essentially every Chinese syllable has a characteristic pitch pattern (tone). Changing the tone alters the meaning just as much as changing a consonant or a vowel in English changes the meaning. In English we use a rising pitch pattern for "Jóhn?" and a falling pitch pattern for "Jòhn!" The different tones convey different attitudes, but the meaning of the word remains the same. In Chinese, however, *má* with a rising pitch pattern means "hemp" and *mà* with a falling pitch pattern means "to scold." The two meanings are no more related to each other than they would be if we were to change the vowel to get *mì*, which means "honey," or if we were to change the consonant to get *pà*, which means "to fear."

Standard Chinese has a total of four tones: rising, falling, level and dipping [*see illustration at left*]. In addition to the tone every syllable must also have a nucleus to carry the tone, usually a vowel. The tone and the nucleus are the two obligatory components of the Chinese syllable. There are also three optional components of a syllable: the initial component, which is usually a consonant; the medial component, which is a glide, and the ending, which may be either a glide or a consonant from a restricted class. There are eight possible forms a syllable can take.

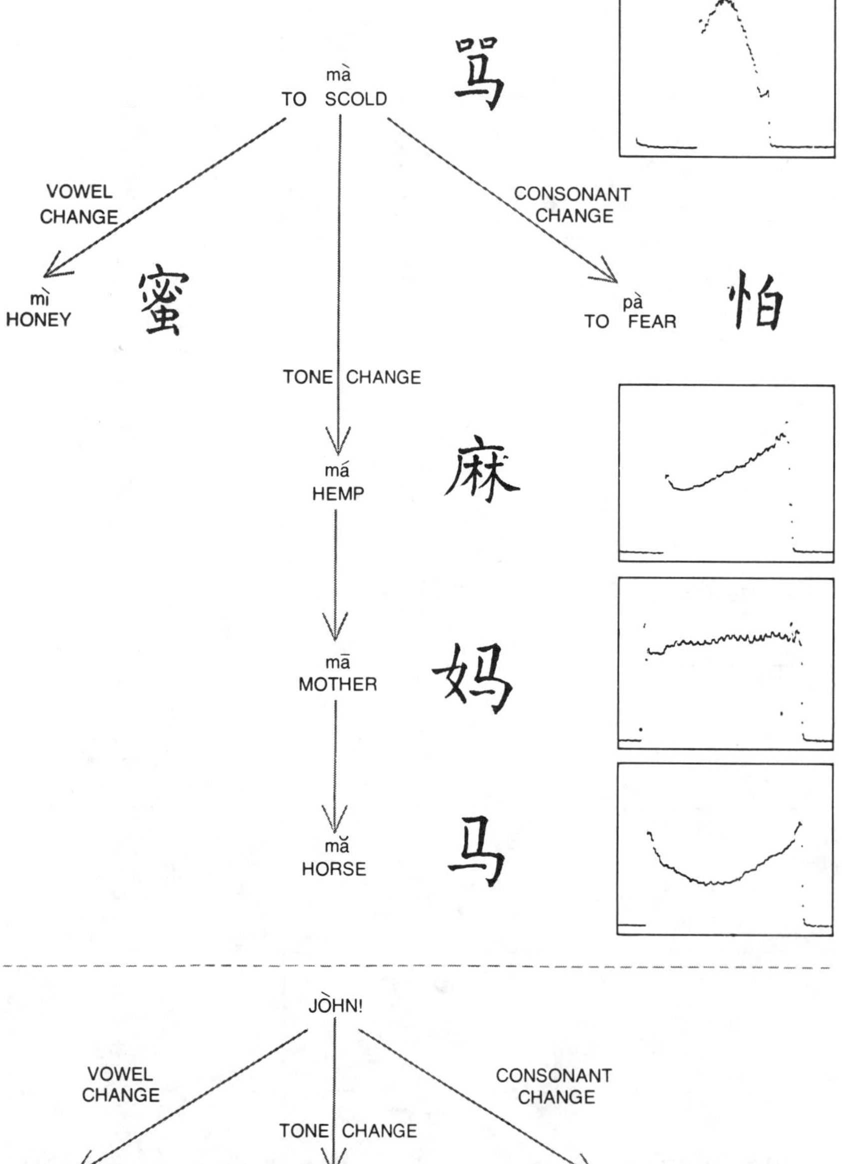

TONES are used to alter the meaning of Chinese words. Standard Chinese has only four tones: falling (as in *mà*), rising (*má*), level (*mā*) and dipping, or falling and then rising (*mǎ*). The oscillograph traces at right show the fundamental frequency of the author's voice as he spoke the words. In English, on the other hand, variation in tone is used to convey different moods; the meaning of the word being spoken does not change. In Chinese changing tone has same kind of effect on meaning of word as changing a vowel or a consonant.

	PINYIN	PHONETIC	INITIAL CONSONANT	FINAL		
				MEDIAL, GLIDE	NUCLEUS, VOWEL	ENDING, VOWEL OR CONSONANT
FACE	liǎn	ljɛ̆n	●	●	●	●
IRON	tiě	t^{h}jɛ̆	●	●	●	
TO GROW	zhǎng	tʂăŋ	●		●	●
HORSE	mǎ	mă	●		●	
EYE	yǎn	jɛ̆n		●	●	●
MOON	yuè	yɛ̀		●	●	
HIDDEN	yǐn	ɪ̆n			●	●
CHAIR	yǐ	ɪ̆			●	

COMPONENTS OF A CHINESE SYLLABLE that are obligatory are the tone and the nucleus (usually a vowel) to carry the tone. There are three optional components in a syllable: the initial, which is usually a consonant; the medial, which is a glide, and the ending, which may be either a glide or a consonant. All together there are eight possible forms that a Chinese syllable can take.

One striking feature of Chinese words in comparison with most European words is the lack of clusters of consonants before and after the nuclear vowel. When Western words with consonant clusters are represented in Chinese, they are typically broken up so that each consonant has its own syllable. "Marx" is conventionally rendered:

马克思

It is pronounced *mă-kè-sī*. The first character is the one for "horse," which also happens to be a prevalent Chinese surname.

Although the Pinyin system and standard Chinese are taught in all parts of China, the languages of ethnic minorities are given full consideration. According to *The Nationalities in China,* a book published in Peking in 1961, there are about 30 million people belonging to minority groups. The minorities occupy about a third of the land of China, mostly in the west and northwest. Some of the groups are large: the Zhuàngs are close to eight million in number and the Uighurs about four million. The languages of some of these groups are related genetically to Chinese but belong to other linguistic families such as Altaic and Austroasiatic.

A 1956 report by the Chinese Academy of Sciences estimated that the total number of people in China who spoke one or another of the Chinese dialects was more than 500 million. Of the dialects, Mandarin has by far the most speakers: more than two-thirds of the total [*see illustration on page 52*]. The Western name "Mandarin" derives from the fact that the dialect was the speech of government officials, or mandarins. It corresponds to the Chinese term *Guān-huà,* which means "official speech." Standard Chinese is a conventionalized variety of this dialect and is known as *Guóyŭ,* or "national language." It also is referred to as *Bĕifānghuà,* which means "northern speech," or as *Pŭtōnghuà,* "common speech."

Outside China standard Chinese plays a much less important role. The dominant dialects among the 15 million Chinese in Southeast Asia are Yue and Southern Min, because it was people from the southern coastal provinces who migrated into the area. In the U.S. the Chinese are relative newcomers; they date back to 1850, when they were first drawn across the Pacific Ocean by the discovery of gold in California. Later these immigrants made up the core of the labor force that built the railroads in the American West. The ancestry of the great majority of the several hundred thousand Chinese now in the U.S. can be traced back to a small cluster of villages around Canton, all within a radius of 100 miles or so. The speech patterns of these villages are definitely of the Yue dialect group, but they differ markedly from one another. We can be sure that significant differences have arisen in the past 100 years between the speech of the American Chinese and the speech of the source villages around Canton.

Word Formation

Every language has a stock of several thousand morphemes: the bearers of the basic semantic and grammatical content. An expression such as "can openers" comprises four morphemes: "can," "open," "-er" and "-s." Some morphemes in English have more than one syllable (as in "open" and "adamant"), whereas others, such as the "-s" in "cats" and the "-t" in "slept," are single consonants. In Chinese most morphemes are exactly one syllable long. The usual division of morphemes into three major categories—noun, verb and adjective—applies to Chinese quite well. Thus in Chinese *shū* ("book") is a noun, *măi* ("buy") is a verb and *guì* ("expensive") is an adjective. These morphemes are known as contentives, in that they carry independent semantic meanings.

There is also a class of morphemes called functives. They are usually attached to contentives to modify their meaning in systematic ways and to show the relations the contentives have to one another. For example, functives attached to the contentive "prove" change its meaning: "proves," "proved," "proving," "disprove," "unproved" and "proof." Although conjugational and declensional paradigms are important in English, they are negligible in Chinese. There is, however, a sizable amount of derivational morphology in Chinese, where nouns are derived from verbs by changing the tone. Thus *shŭ* is a verb meaning "to count," and *shù* is a noun meaning "number." The verb *lián* means "to connect," and the noun *liàn* means "a chain." *Mó* is "to grind," and *mò* is "a grindstone." To derive a noun in these cases one simply changes the syllable to a falling tone. A similar example from English is deriving a noun from a verb by devoicing the final consonant: "prove"–"proof," "bathe"–"bath," "house"–"house."

The device of derivation by tone change is no longer productive in standard Chinese, but it is suspected that tonal derivation was an important process in the earlier stages of development

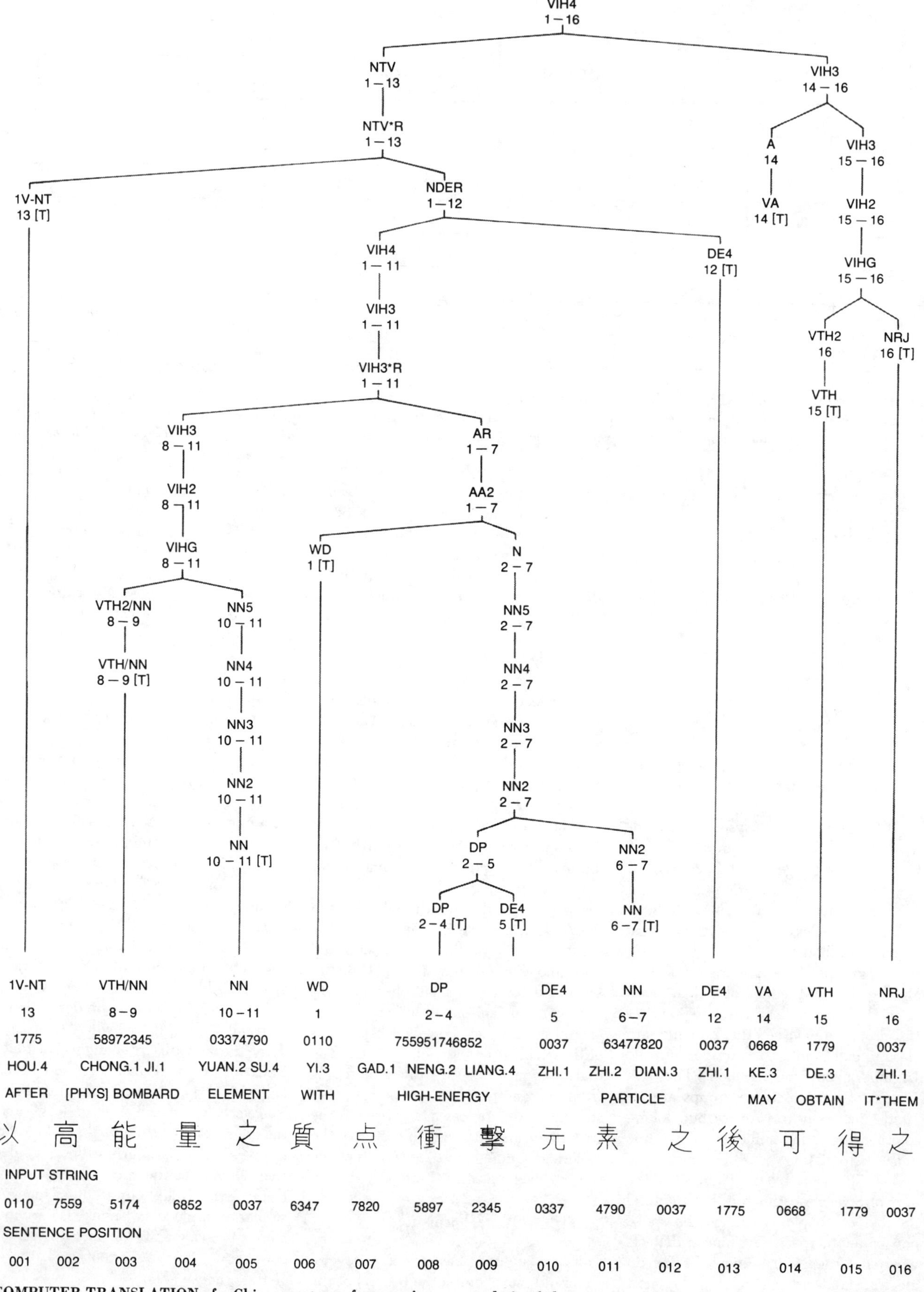

COMPUTER TRANSLATION of a Chinese sentence from a scientific text produces a reasonably accurate and understandable result. The string of Chinese characters is entered into the computer using a numeric code for each character. The position of each character in the sentence is also entered. The computer searches its memory for the meaning of each character and then performs syntactic analysis of the sentence. In converting the sentence into English the computer makes permutations of the word order. The sentence means: "It may be obtained after bombarding the element with high-energy particles." Research into computer analysis of Chinese is being conducted by the author and his colleagues at the phonology laboratory of the University of California at Berkeley.

of the Chinese language. In the Cantonese dialect, however, the process is still very productive. The Cantonese use tone change for forming diminutives: "candy" from "sugar," "daughter" from "female" and so on.

A common derivational device in Chinese is reduplication. Applied to nouns, it carries the meaning "every." Hence although *rén* means "person," *rénren* means "every person," *tiān* means "day" and *tiāntian* means "every day." Applied to verbs, it adds a transitory meaning to the action: *kàn* means "to look," whereas *kànkan* means "to take a look," *zǒu* means "to walk" and *zóuzou* means "to take a walk." Adverbs can be derived from adjectives by reduplication and the addition of a *de* suffix. Thus *kuài* is "quick" and *kuàikuàide* is "quickly," *lǎn* is "lazy" and *lánlǎnde* is "lazily."

The manner in which two-syllable adjectives reduplicate is different. Whereas a two-syllable verb, *tǎolùn* ("to discuss"), reduplicates as *tǎolùntǎolùn* ("to discuss a little"), an adjective, say *gāoxìng* ("happy"), becomes *gāogāoxìngxìngde* ("happily"). A verb reduplicates by the entire word, but the adjective reduplicates in terms of its constituent syllables.

Another device for word formation in Chinese is the conjoining of antonyms. "Buy" and "sell" combine to form "business," *mǎimài.* "Long" and "short" combine to form "length," *chángduǎn.* The derived meaning is not always straightforward. For example, *fǎn* means "turned over" and *zhèng* means "right side up." Put together, *fǎnzhèng* means "in any case."

Classifiers are a linguistic feature peculiar to Chinese and its neighboring languages. Articles, numerals and other such modifiers cannot directly precede their associated noun; there has to be an intervening classifier, which usually has negligible semantic content. In Chinese one cannot say *sān shū* ("three books") or *nèi māo* ("that cat"). One has to say *sān běn shū* ("three piece book") or *nèi zhī māo* ("that piece cat"). The terms *běn* and *zhī* here are translated as "piece" for the lack of a better counterpart in English. Such classifiers are absolutely necessary in Chinese expressions. This feature has been carried over into many pidgin and Creole languages based on Chinese, in which "three bananas" or "this man" are rendered as "three piece banana" or "this fellow man."

Sentence Formation

The basic sentence in Chinese has the order subject-verb-object, as in English. Thus the sentence *wǒmen chī jī* is word for word "We eat chicken." There is a tendency in Chinese to delete either the subject or the object. Hence *wǒmen chī* ("We eat") or *chī jī* ("Eat chicken") are both common sentences. To focus attention on the object, the Chinese speaker will move it to the beginning of the sentence. *Jī wǒmen chī,* for instance, means "We eat chicken," but it is normally used to contrast with something else we do not eat. Suppose subject deletion and moving the object to the initial position both operated on the sentence *wǒmen chī jī.* First we front the object and get *jī wǒmen chī,* and then we delete the subject and get *jī chī.* The resulting sentence would mean something like "Chicken *A* eats," and the identity of *A* normally would be clear from the context. But *jī chī* of course also means something like "The chicken eats," where *jī* is the subject of the verb. In other words, *jī chī* is an ambiguous sentence, its ambiguity arising from object fronting and subject deletion.

There is no evidence that Chinese allows either more ambiguity than English or less. In an English sentence such as "It is too hot to eat," the "it" can refer to the weather, to the food or to the animal that is doing the eating. Moreover, "hot" could mean "high in heat content" (which in Chinese is *tàng*) or it could mean "spicy" (which in Chinese is *là*).

The Chinese language as an object of study goes back as far as the beginning

	REGULAR FORMS: TIGER	REGULAR FORMS: DRAGON	SCRIPT FORMS: TIGER	SCRIPT FORMS: DRAGON	
ANCIENT GRAPHS ABOUT 2000 B.C.					
SHELL-AND-BONE CHARACTERS jiǎgǔwén ABOUT 1400-1200 B.C.					
GREAT SEAL dàzhuàn ABOUT 1100-300 B.C.					
SMALL SEAL xiǎozhuàn 221-207 B.C.					
SCRIBE CHARACTER lìshū ABOUT 200 B.C.-A.D. 200					DOCUMENTARY SCRIPT zhāngcǎo ABOUT 200 B.C.-A.D.1700
STANDARD CHARACTERS kǎishū ABOUT A.D. 100 -PRESENT					RUNNING STYLE xíngshū ABOUT A.D. 200 -PRESENT
SIMPLIFIED CHARACTERS jianzì ABOUT A.D. 100 -PRESENT					SIMPLIFIED SCRIPT CHARACTERS liánbǐ jiǎnzì ABOUT A.D. 100 -PRESENT
					"MODERN" SCRIPT jīncǎo ABOUT A.D. 300 -PRESENT
					ERRATIC SCRIPT kuángcaǒ ABOUT A.D. 600-1700

HISTORICAL DEVELOPMENT of pictographic characters for the two most powerful animals in Chinese mythology, the tiger and the dragon, are shown in their various stages. The earliest-known pictographic forms of the animals are at the top in red. The illustration is from *Introduction to Chinese Cursive Script,* by F. Y. Wang of Seton Hall University.

of the Christian Era. At that time the Chinese had already produced sophisticated works in dialectology and in semantic classification. The foundations for the historical study of Chinese sounds were laid during the 17th and 18th centuries by the great scholars of the Qīng dynasty, and it is on their shoulders that modern Chinese linguists stand.

The key to how a language sounded centuries ago lies in how it sounds today. The basic method is to compare the pronunciation of morphemes in contemporary dialects and to infer what their ancestral pronunciations might have been. The inference is not just a guess but is made on the basis of documentary evidence and knowledge of the general linguistic principles underlying sound change.

Given the nonphonetic nature of the Chinese writing system, it may seem an impossible task to reconstruct how the language was spoken many centuries ago. One might think that the sounds of alphabetic languages, such as Old Church Slavic or Sanskrit, would be much easier to reconstruct. Actually it is not much easier, because there is no direct way to determine how a letter was pronounced. With alphabetic languages the phonetic values must also be arrived at by inference.

Chinese has the great advantage of an abundance of ancient writings that reach back continuously in time further than the literature of any other language in the world. The fact that the form of Chinese characters is often not much influenced by changes in pronunciation is quite a convenience in helping linguists to determine which morphemes are etymologically related.

The study of Chinese dialects has been hampered in the past by an overabundance of data, which tended to make research procedures cumbersome and time-consuming. The advent of large computers has facilitated the manipulation of the data. Chin-Chuan Cheng and I, with the help of several colleagues, have developed a dialect dictionary on computer, which we call DOC. The program is in operation at the computer centers of the University of California at Berkeley and of the University of Illinois. It incorporates the pronunciation of more than 2,000 morphemes in each of 20 Chinese dialects.

Evidence is accumulating from our work with DOC that changes in language proceed in ways that are essentially parallel to biological evolution, as Charles Darwin noted in *The Descent of Man.* In both cases the mechanism of change resides in variation. When two or more variants appear, the rival forms compete for survival. For instance, in American speech the vowel in "room" varies between that of "pool" and that of "put," and the *s* in "disobey" varies between an *s* and a *z*. The major selective force, which is constant across time as well as across languages, is the ease with which the forms can be pronounced and properly perceived. This selective force determines what forms of speech will survive.

With the aid of computer programs such as DOC we have been able to run through large pools of data to locate ongoing sound changes of special interest. Some changes are just beginning, some are in midstream and some are ending. In the Cháozhōu dialect, for example, there is a change from one tone to another that has so far affected about half of the vocabulary. By having access to a large number of well-defined types of sound change, we are now in a position to study much more effectively the selective force that determines the direction of language evolution.

Another aspect of the Chinese language that has been subjected to intensive computer study is its morphology and syntax. With the collaboration of Stephen W. Chan, Benjamin K. Tsou and others, we have developed a machine dictionary with more than 70,000 entries, together with the necessary programs for translation from Chinese into English. A good measure of how well we understand the structure of a language is how well we can break it apart in a way that is suitable for translation by machine. Although we are an indefinite distance away from being able to translate a Táng poem into English without losing its exquisite sensitivity, we can do a reasonably accurate job with scientific texts [*see illustration on page 58*].

Now that relations between the People's Republic of China and Western nations are becoming more normal, interest in the Chinese language is increasing at an accelerating tempo. Considering that the Chinese language has the largest number of speakers in the world and the greatest time depth in its literature, this interest is long overdue. With the increase in interest we may look forward to deeper probings into the history and the structure of the language, and into the influence the language has had on the cultural and intellectual development of the Chinese people. These studies will surely lead to a better general understanding of the nature of human language.

7

Computer Software for Working with Language

by Terry Winograd
September 1984

Programs can manipulate linguistic symbols with great facility, as in word-processing software, but attempts to have computers deal with meaning are vexed by ambiguity in human languages

In the popular mythology the computer is a mathematics machine: it is designed to do numerical calculations. Yet it is really a language machine: its fundamental power lies in its ability to manipulate linguistic tokens—symbols to which meaning has been assigned. Indeed, "natural language" (the language people speak and write, as distinguished from the "artificial" languages in which computer programs are written) is central to computer science. Much of the earliest work in the field was aimed at breaking military codes, and in the 1950's efforts to have computers translate text from one natural language into another led to crucial advances, even though the goal itself was not achieved. Work continues on the still more ambitious project of making natural language a medium in which to communicate with computers.

Today investigators are developing unified theories of computation that embrace both natural and artificial languages. Here I shall concentrate on the former, that is, on the language of everyday human communication. Within that realm there is a vast range of software to be considered. Some of it is mundane and successful. A multitude of microcomputers have invaded homes, offices and schools, and most of them are used at least in part for "word processing." Other applications are speculative and far from realization. Science fiction is populated by robots that converse as if they were human, with barely a mechanical tinge to their voice. Real attempts to get computers to converse have run up against great difficulties, and the best of the laboratory prototypes are still a pale reflection of the linguistic competence of the average child.

The range of computer software for processing language precludes a comprehensive survey; instead I shall look at four types of program. The programs deal with machine translation, with word processing, with question answering and with the adjuncts to electronic mail known as coordination systems. In each case the key to what is possible lies in analyzing the nature of linguistic competence and how that competence is related to the formal rule structures that are the theoretical basis of all computer software.

The prospect that text might be translated by a computer arose well before commercial computers were first manufactured. In 1949, when the few working computers were all in military laboratories, the mathematician Warren Weaver, one of the pioneers of communication theory, pointed out that the techniques developed for code breaking might be applicable to machine translation.

At first the task appears to be straightforward. Given a sentence in a source language, two basic operations yield the corresponding sentence in a target language. First the individual words are replaced by their translations; then the translated words are reordered and adjusted in detail. Take the translation of "Did you see a white cow?" into the Spanish "*¿Viste una vaca blanca?*" First one needs to know the word correspondences: "*vaca*" for "cow" and so on. Then one needs to know the structural details of Spanish. The words "did" and "you" are not translated directly but are expressed through the form of the verb "*viste*." The adjective "*blanca*" follows the noun instead of preceding it as it does in English. Finally, "*una*" and "*blanca*" are in the feminine form corresponding to "*vaca*." Much of the early study of machine translation dwelt on the technical problem of putting a large dictionary into computer storage and empowering the computer to search efficiently in it. Meanwhile the software for dealing with grammar was based on the then current theories of the structure of language, augmented by rough-and-ready rules.

The programs yielded translations so bad that they were incomprehensible. The problem is that natural language does not embody meaning in the same way that a cryptographic code embodies a message. The meaning of a sentence in a natural language is dependent not only on the form of the sentence but also on the context. One can see this most clearly through examples of ambiguity.

In the simplest form of ambiguity, known as lexical ambiguity, a single word has more than one possible meaning. Thus "Stay away from the bank" might be advice to an investor or to a child too close to a river. In translating it into Spanish one would need to choose between "*orilla*" and "*banco,*" and nothing in the sentence itself reveals which is intended. Attempts to deal with lexical ambiguity in translation software have included the insertion of all the possibilities into the translated text and the statistical analysis of the source text in an effort to decide which translation is appropriate. For example, "*orilla*" is likely to be the correct choice if words related to rivers and water are nearby in the source text. The first strategy leads to complex, unreadable text; the second yields the correct choice in many cases but the wrong one in many others.

In structural ambiguity the problem goes beyond a single word. Consider the sentence "He saw that gasoline can explode." It has two interpretations based on quite different uses of "that" and "can." Hence the sentence has two possible grammatical structures, and the translator must choose between them [*see bottom illustration on page 64*].

An ambiguity of "deep structure" is subtler still: two readings of a sentence can have the same apparent grammatical structure but nonetheless differ in meaning. "The chickens are ready to eat" implies that something is about to eat something, but which are the chickens? One of the advances in linguistic

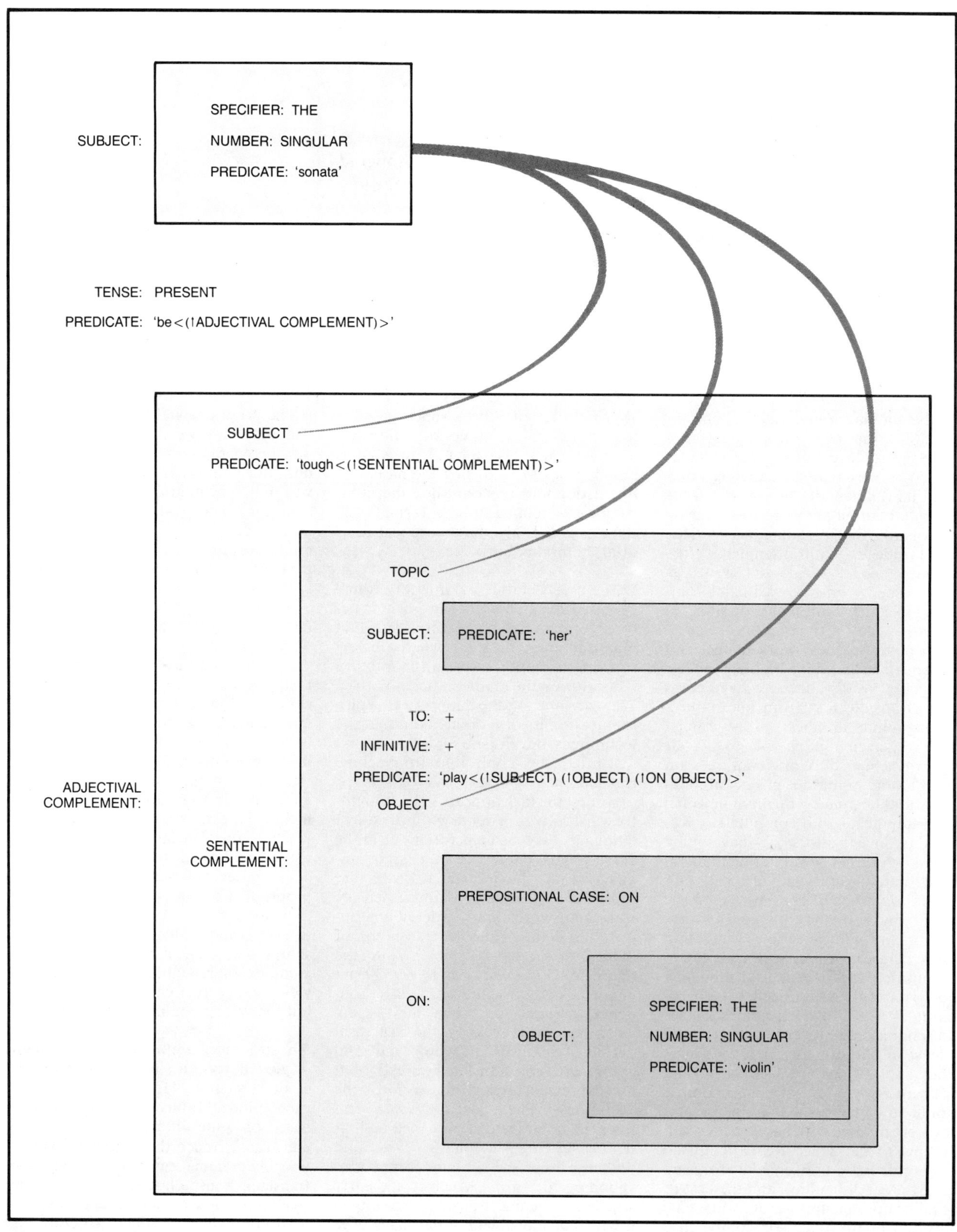

REPRESENTATION OF A SENTENCE in a way that makes explicit the linguistic relations among its parts has been a goal of the science of linguistics; it is also a necessary aspect of the effort to design computer software that "understands" language, or at any rate can draw inferences from linguistic input. In this illustration a sentence is given in "functional structure" form, which has the property that when part of a sentence plays a role in another part, the former is "nested" in the latter. The nesting is shown by placing one box in another, or (in three places) by a "string." The sentence was analyzed by Ronald M. Kaplan and Joan Bresnan of Stanford University and the Xerox Corporation's Palo Alto Research Center. Another functional-structure diagram appears in the illustration on pages 52–53.

theory since the 1950's has been the development of a formalism in which the deep structure of language can be represented, but the formalism is of little help in deducing the intended deep structure of a particular sentence.

A fourth kind of ambiguity—semantic ambiguity—results when a phrase can play different roles in the overall meaning of a sentence. The sentence "David wants to marry a Norwegian" is an example. In one meaning of the sentence the phrase "a Norwegian" is referential. David intends to marry a particular person, and the speaker of the sentence has chosen an attribute of the person—her being from Norway—in order to describe her. In another meaning of the sentence the phrase is attributive. Neither David nor the speaker has a particular person in mind; the sentence simply means that David hopes to marry someone of Norwegian nationality.

A fifth kind of ambiguity might be called pragmatic ambiguity. It arises from the use of pronouns and special nouns such as "one" and "another." Take the sentence "When a bright moon ends a dark day, a brighter one will follow." A brighter day or a brighter moon? At times it is possible for translation software to simply translate the ambiguous pronoun or noun, thereby preserving the ambiguity in the translation. In many cases, however, this strategy is not available. In a Spanish translation of "She dropped the plate on the table and broke it," one must choose either the masculine "*lo*" or the feminine "*la*" to render "it." The choice forces the translator to decide whether the masculine "*plato*" (plate) or the feminine "*mesa*" (table) was broken.

In many ambiguous sentences the meaning is obvious to a human reader, but only because the reader brings to the task an understanding of context. Thus "The porridge is ready to eat" is unambiguous because one knows porridge is inanimate. "There's a man in the room with a green hat on" is unambiguous because one knows rooms do not wear hats. Without such knowledge virtually any sentence is ambiguous.

Although fully automatic, high-quality machine translation is not feasible, software is available to facilitate translation. One example is the computerization of translation aids such as dictionaries and phrase books. These vary from elaborate systems meant for technical translators, in which the function of "looking a word up" is made a part of a multilingual word-processing program, to hand-held computerized libraries of phrases for use by tourists. Another strategy is to process text by hand to make it suitable for machine translation. A person working as a "pre-editor" takes a text in the source language and creates a second text, still in the source language, that is simplified in ways facilitating machine translation. Words with multiple meanings can be eliminated, along with grammatical constructions that complicate syntactic analysis. Conjunctions that cause ambiguity can be suppressed, or the ambiguity can be resolved by inserting special punctuation, as in "the [old men] and [women]." After the machine translation a "post-editor" can check for blunders and smooth the translated text.

The effort is sometimes cost-effective. In the first place, the pre-editor and post-editor need not be bilingual, as a translator would have to be. Then too, if a single text (say an instruction manual) is to be translated into several languages, a large investment in pre-editing may be justified because it will serve for all the translations. If the author of the text can be taught the less ambiguous form of the source language, no pre-editor is needed. Finally, software can help in checking the pre-edited text to make certain it meets the specifications for input to the translation system (although this is no guarantee that the translation will be acceptable).

A machine-translation system employing pre- and post-editing has been in use since 1980 at the Pan-American Health Organization, where it has translated more than a million words of text from Spanish into English. A new system is being developed for the European Economic Community, with the goal of translating documents among the official languages of the community: Danish, Dutch, English, French, German, Greek and Italian. Meanwhile the theoretical work on syntax and meaning has continued, but there have been no breakthroughs in machine translation. The ambiguity pervading natural language continues to limit the possibilities, for reasons I shall examine more fully below.

I turn next to word processing, that is, to software that aids in the preparation, formatting and printing of text. Word processors deal only with the manipulation and display of strings of characters and hence only with superficial aspects of the structure of language. Even so, they pose technical problems quite central to the design of computer software. In some cases the end product of a word-processing program is no more than a sequence of lines of text. In others it is a complex layout of typographic elements, sometimes with drawings intercalated. In still others it is a structured document, with chapter headings, section numbers and so on, and with a table of contents and an index compiled by the program.

The key problems in designing word-processing software center on issues of representation and interaction. Representation is the task of devising data structures that can be manipulated conveniently by the software but still make provision for the things that concern the user of the system, say the layout of the printed page. Interaction takes up the issue of how the user expresses instructions and how the system responds.

Consider the fundamental problem of employing the data-storage devices of a computer to hold an encoded sequence of natural-language characters. The first devices that encoded text were card-punch and teletype machines, and so the earliest text-encoding schemes were tailored to those devices. The teletype machine is essentially a typewriter that converts key presses into numerical codes that can be transmitted electronically;

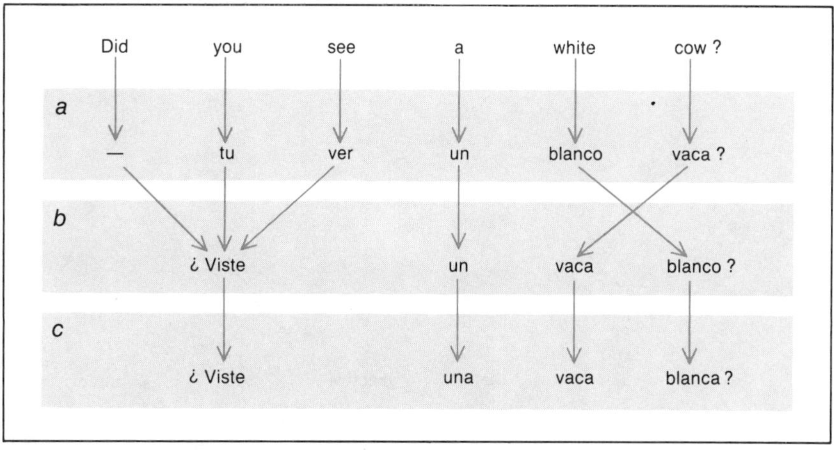

MACHINE TRANSLATION of text from one language into another was thought to be quite feasible in the 1950's, when the effort was undertaken. In the first step of the process (*a*) the computer would search a bilingual dictionary to find translations of the individual words in a source sentence (in this case Spanish equivalents of the words in the sentence "Did you see a white cow?"). Next the translated words would be rearranged according to the grammar of the target language (*b*). The changes at this stage could include excision or addition of words. Finally, the morphology of the translation (for example the endings of words) would be adjusted (*c*).

Stay away from the bank.

bank *n* 1. the rising terrain that borders a river or lake.

bank *n* 2. an establishment for the deposit, loan, issuance and transmission of money.

AMBIGUOUS MEANINGS permeate natural languages (that is, languages that people speak and write) and thus subvert the attempt to have computers translate text from one language into another. Here lexical ambiguity, the simplest type of ambiguity, is diagrammed. In lexical ambiguity a word in a sentence has more than one possible meaning. In this case the word is "bank" (*color*), which might equally well refer to either a river or a financial institution. A translator must choose. The following four illustrations show more complex types of ambiguity.

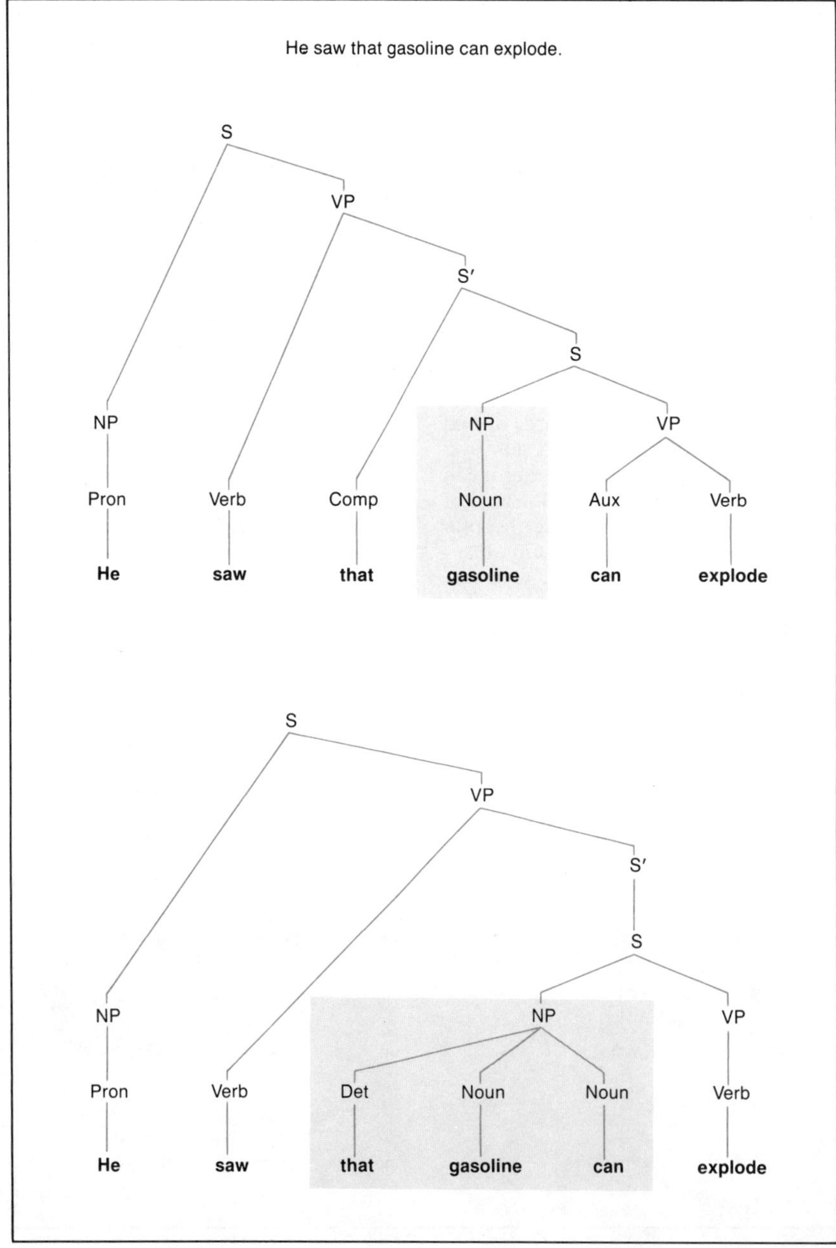

STRUCTURAL AMBIGUITY arises when a sentence can be described by more than one grammatical structure. Here the conflicting possibilities for the sentence "He saw that gasoline can explode" are displayed in the form of grammatical "trees." In one of the trees the sentence has a subordinate clause whose subject is "gasoline" (*color*); the sentence refers to the recognition of a property of that substance. In the other tree "gasoline can" is part of a noun phrase (*NP*) meaning a container of gasoline; the sentence refers to the sight of a specific explosion.

thus there are teletype codes for most of the keys on a typewriter. The codes include the alphabetic characters *A* through *Z*, the digits 0 through 9 and common punctuation marks such as the period and the comma. Standards are harder to establish, however, for symbols such as #, @, ¢ and }. And what about keys that print nothing, such as the tab key, the carriage-return key and the backspace key?

The difficulties that arise in choosing standards can be illustrated by one peculiarity of text encoding. The teletype code distinguishes between a carriage return (which returns the type carriage to the beginning of the line without advancing the paper) and a line feed (which advances the paper without repositioning the carriage). Hence the end of a line is marked by a sequence of two characters: a carriage return and a line feed. One code would suffice, and so some programs eliminate either the carriage return or the line feed, or they replace both characters with another code entirely. The problem is that various programs employ different conventions, so that lines encoded by one program may not be readable by another.

The problems become worse when a full range of characters—punctuation marks, mathematical symbols, diacritical marks such as the umlaut—is considered. Moreover, word processing is now being extended to languages such as Chinese and Japanese, which require thousands of ideographic characters, and to languages such as Arabic and Hebrew, which are written from right to left. Coding schemes adequate for English are useless for alphabets with thousands of characters. It should be said that the schemes continue to vary because political and economic forces play a role in the design of computer systems. A given manufacturer wants to promulgate a standard that suits its own equipment; thus some present-day standards exist because they were offered by a vendor that dominates a market. On the other hand, technical matters such as the efficiency of certain software running on certain hardware perpetuate differences in detail. It will be quite a while before universal standards emerge and users gain the ability to transport text from one word-processing system to any other.

Encoding schemes aside, there is the form of the letters themselves. On a typewriter keyboard an A is simply an A. Typographically, however, an A is an A or an *A* or an **A**. In the new field of digital typography the computer is a tool for the design and presentation of forms of type. Some of the efforts in the field are applied to the forms themselves: in particular the representation of characters as composites of dots and spaces. Additional efforts go into the devising of code for the computer stor-

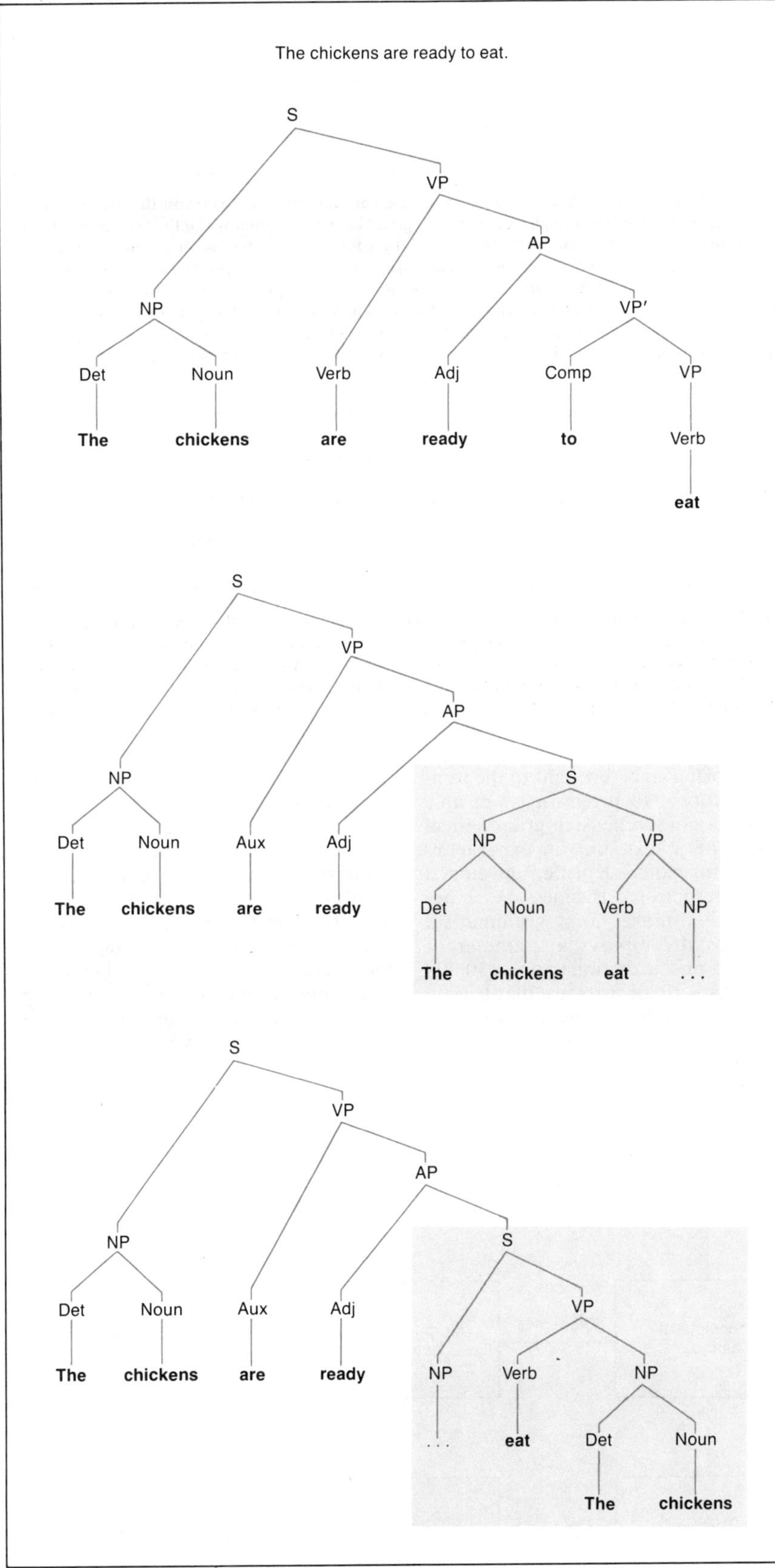

DEEP-STRUCTURAL AMBIGUITY arises when a sentence has a single apparent structure but nonetheless has more than one possible meaning. In this example the sentence is "The chickens are ready to eat." Its grammatical structure (*top*) leaves the role of the chickens ambiguous: in one interpretation they will eat; in the other they will be eaten. Deep-structure trees make the chickens' role explicit: they are the subject of the sentence (*middle*), in which case their food is undetermined, or they are the object (*bottom*), and their eaters are undetermined.

age of text that combines different fonts (such as Times Roman and Helvetica) and different faces (such as *italic* and **boldface**).

So far I have dealt only with stored sequences of characters. Yet one of the major tasks of a word-processing program is to deal with margins and spacing—with the "geography" of the printed page. In the typesetting language called TEX commands that specify nonstandard characters, change the style of type, set the margins and so on are embedded in the text [*see top illustration on page 67*]. A command to TEX is distinguished from ordinary text by the backslash character (\). The stored text is "compiled" by the TEX program, which interprets the embedded commands in order to create a printed document in the specified format.

The compiling is quite complex, and a good deal of computation is often needed to get from code created by means of a word-processing program to code that readily drives a printer or a typesetting machine. An algorithm that justifies text (fills the full width of each line of type) must determine how many words will fit in a line, how much space should be inserted between the words and whether a line would be improved by dividing and hyphenating a word. The algorithm may also take actions to avoid visual defects such as a line with wide interword spacing followed by a line that is very compact. Positioning each line on the page is further complicated by the placement of headings, footnotes, illustrations, tables and so on. Mathematical formulas have their own typographic rules.

TEX and similar programs are primitive with respect to another aspect of word processing: the user interface. The high-resolution display screens becoming available are now making it possible for the computer to display to the user a fair approximation of the pages it will print, including the placement of each item and the typeface to be employed. This suggests that the user should not have to type special command sequences but might instead manipulate page geography directly on the screen by means of the computer keyboard and a pointing device such as a "mouse." The resulting interface between the computer and the user would then fall into the class of interfaces known as WYSIWYG, which stands for "What you see is what you get."

It is worth noting that programs for manipulating text are called different things by different professions. Programmers call them text editors, but in business and publishing they are referred to as word processors; in the latter fields an editor is a person who works to improve the quality of text. Computer software is emerging to aid in this more substantive aspect of editing. It deals with neither the visual format of language nor the conceptual content but with spelling, grammar and style. It includes two kinds of programs: mechanized reference works and mechanized correctness aids.

An example of a mechanized reference work is a thesaurus program designed so that when the writer designates a word, a list of synonyms appears on the display screen. In advanced systems the thesaurus is fully integrated into the word-processing program. The writer positions a marker to indicate the word to be replaced. The thesaurus is then invoked; it displays the alternatives in a "window" on the screen. The writer positions the marker on one of the alternatives, which automatically replaces the rejected word.

The design of such a program involves both linguistic and computational issues. A linguistic issue is that the mechanism for looking up a word should be flexible enough to accept variant forms. For example, the store of information pertaining to "endow" should be accessible to queries about "endowed," "endowing," "endows" and even "unendowed" or "endowment." Recognizing the common root in such words calls for a morphological analysis, which can be done by techniques developed in the course of work on machine translation. Computational issues include devising methods for storing and searching through a thesaurus or a dictionary, which must be fairly large to be useful.

A correctness aid deals with spelling, grammar and even elements of style. The simplest such programs attempt to match each word in a text with an entry in a stored dictionary. Words that have no match are flagged as possible misspellings. Other programs look for common grammatical errors or stylistic infelicities. For example, the Writer's Workbench software developed at AT&T Bell Laboratories includes programs that search for repeated words, such as "the the" (a common typing mistake), for incorrect punctuation such as "?." and for wordy phrases such as "at this point in time." A different correctness aid calls attention to "pompous phrases" such as "exhibit a tendency" and "arrive at a decision" and suggests simpler replacements such as "tend" and "decide." Still another correctness aid searches for gender-specific terms such as "mailman" and "chairman" and suggests replacements such as "mail carrier" and "chairperson."

In addition to searching a text for particular strings of characters, some correctness-aid programs do statistical analyses. By calculating the average length of sentences, the length of words and similar quantities, they compute a "readability index." Passages that score poorly can be brought to the writer's attention. No program is yet able to make a comprehensive grammatical analysis of a text, but an experimental system called Epistle, developed at the International Business Machines Corporation, makes some grammatical judgments. It employs a grammar of 400 rules and a dictionary of 130,000 words. As with all software that tries to parse text without dealing with what the text means, there are many sentences that cannot be analyzed correctly.

Is there software that really deals with meaning—software that exhibits the kind of reasoning a person would use in carrying out linguistic tasks such as translating, summarizing or answering a question? Such software has been the goal of research projects in artificial intelligence since the mid-1960's, when the necessary computer hardware and programming techniques began to appear even as the impracticability of machine translation was becoming apparent. There are many applications

David wants to marry a Norwegian.

$\exists x\ \mathrm{Norwegian}(x) \land \mathrm{Want}(\mathrm{David},[\mathrm{Marry}(\mathrm{David},x)])$

$\mathrm{Want}(\mathrm{David},[\exists x\ \mathrm{Norwegian}(x) \land \mathrm{Marry}(\mathrm{David},x)])$

SEMANTIC AMBIGUITY arises when a phrase can play different roles in the meaning of a sentence. Here the roles of the phrase "a Norwegian" become explicit when the sentence "David wants to marry a Norwegian" is "translated" into a logical form based on the notation called predicate calculus. According to one interpretation, the speaker of the sentence has a particular person in mind and has chosen nationality as a way to specify who. Hence the sentence means: There exists (∃) an *x* such that *x* is Norwegian and (∧) *x* is the person David wants to marry. According to another interpretation, neither David nor the speaker has any particular person in mind. David might be going to Norway hoping to meet someone marriageable.

She dropped the plate on the table and broke it.

She dropped the plate on the table and broke [the plate].

She dropped the plate on the table and broke [the table].

PRAGMATIC AMBIGUITY arises when a sentence is given more than one possible meaning by a word such as the pronoun "it." Suppose a computer is given the sentence shown in the illustration. If the computer has access to stored knowledge of the grammar of English sentences but lacks access to commonsense knowledge of the properties of tables and plates, the computer could infer with equal validity that the table was broken or that the plate was broken.

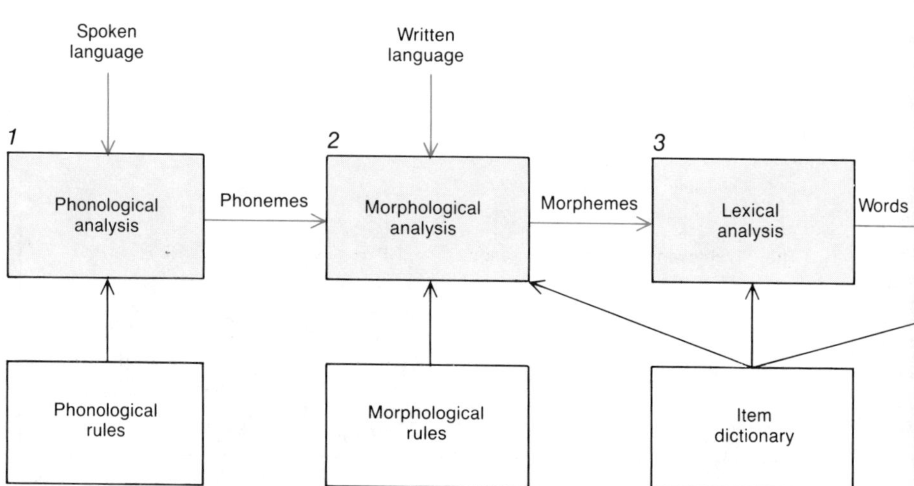

COMPUTERIZED UNDERSTANDING OF LANGUAGE requires the computer to draw on several types of stored data (*white boxes*) and perform several levels of analysis (*colored boxes*). If the language is spoken, the first analysis is phonological (*1*): the computer analyzes sound waves. If the language is written, the first analysis is morphological (*2*): the computer decomposes each word into its root, or basic form, and inflections (for example *-ing*). Next is lexi-

a

\inset
This is a sample of a {\italic justified} piece of text, which contains {\eightpoint small letters {\bold and }} {bigFont big ones}.
It includes foreign words such as \lquote pe\~na\rquote—which is Spanish—and foreign letters like \alpha\ and \aleph,
which can be baffling, and includes one \hskip 1.3in wide space.

b . . .

01110100	01100101	01110010	01110011	00000000	00100111	00101101	11010011	00001000	01100001	01101110	01100100	00000000
t	e	r	s	NEW ENTITY	FONT CODE	X-POSI-TION	Y-POSI-TION	X-INCRE-MENT	a	n	d	NEW ENTITY

00110100	00110001	10110110	00101101	01100010	01101001	01100111	00100000	01101111	01101110	01100101	01101011	00101110
FONT CODE	X-POSI-TION	Y-POSI-TION	X-INCRE-MENT	b	i	g	SPACE	o	n	e	s	•

00000000	00000001	10101111	10110110	00101100	01001001	01110100	00100000	01101001
NEW ENTITY	FONT CODE	X-POSI-TION	Y-POSI-TION	X-INCRE-MENT	I	t	SPACE	i

. . .

c

This is a sample of a *justified* piece of text, which contains small letters **and** big ones. It includes foreign words such as "peña"—which is Spanish—and foreign letters like α and $\aleph$, which can be baffling, and includes one   wide space.

WORD PROCESSING, that is, the computer-aided preparation and editing of text, requires several representations of the text, because the format best for interactions between the software and its user is not efficient for sending instructions to a printing machine, nor can it efficiently give a preview of the result of the printing. In the typesetting language TEX the user's typed input (*a*) includes commands that specify nonstandard characters, change the style of type, set margins and so on. Such commands are distinguished by a backslash (\). The TEX software "compiles" the input, producing computer code that will drive a printing machine (*b*). To that end the code is divided into "entities," each of which specifies the typeface and the starting position for a sequence of words. Coded "*X* increments" space out the words to fill the distance between margins on the printed page; thus they "justify" lines of type. The printed page (*c*) shows the result.

in which the software would be useful. They include programs that accept natural-language commands, programs for information retrieval, programs that summarize text and programs that acquire language-based knowledge for expert systems.

No existing software deals with meaning over a significant subset of English; each experimental program is based on finding a simplified version of language and meaning and testing what can be done within its confines. Some investigators see no fundamental barrier to writing programs with a full understanding of natural language. Others argue that computerized understanding of language is impossible. In order to follow the arguments it is important to examine the basics of how a language-understanding program has to work.

A language-understanding program needs several components, corresponding to the various levels at which language is analyzed [*see illustrations on pages 66–70*]. Most programs deal with written language; hence the analysis of sound waves is bypassed and the first level of analysis is morphological. The program applies rules that decompose a word into its root, or basic form, and inflections such as the endings *-s* and *-ing*. The rules correspond in large part to the spelling rules children are taught in elementary school. Children learn, for example, that the root of "baking" is "bake," whereas the root of "barking" is "bark." An exception list handles words to which the rules do not

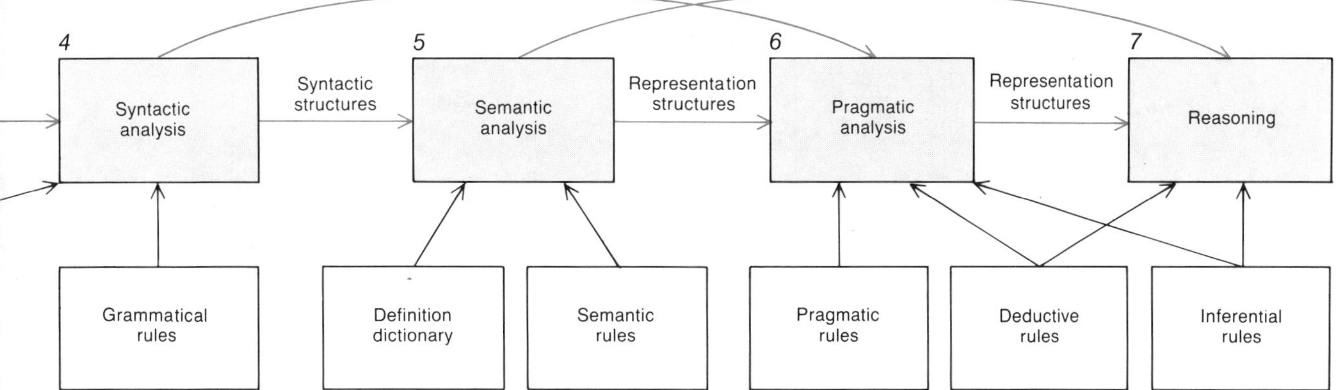

cal analysis (*3*), in which the computer assigns words to their lexical category (noun, for instance) and identifies "features" such as plurals. Then comes syntactic analysis, or parsing (*4*): the application of rules of grammar to yield the structure of the sentence. After that comes semantic analysis (*5*). Here the sentence is converted into a form that makes it amenable to inference-drawing. The final stage is pragmatic (*6*): it makes explicit the context of the sentence, such as the relation between the time at which it is spoken and the time to which it refers. The computer is now in a position to draw inferences (*7*), perhaps in preparation for responding to the sentence.

apply, such as forms of the verb "be." Other rules associate inflections with "features" of words. For example, "am going" is a progressive verb: it signals an act in progress.

For each root that emerges from the morphological analysis a dictionary yields the set of lexical categories to which the root belongs. This is the second level of analysis carried out by the computer. Some roots (such as "the") have only one lexical category; others have several. "Dark" can be a noun or an adjective; "bloom" can be a noun or a verb. In some instances the morphological analysis limits the possibilities. (In its common usages "bloom" can be a noun or a verb, but "blooming" is only a verb.) The output of the morphological and lexical analysis is thus a sequence of the words in a sentence, with each word carrying a quantity of dictionary and feature information. This output serves in turn as the input to the third component of the program, the parser, or syntactic-analysis component, which applies rules of grammar to determine the structure of the sentence.

Two distinct problems arise in designing an adequate parser. The first problem is the specification of a precise set of rules—a grammar—that determines the set of possible sentence structures in a language. Over the past 30 years much work in theoretical linguistics has been directed toward devising formal linguistic systems: constructions in which the syntactic rules of a language are stated so precisely that a computer could employ them to analyze the language. The generative transformational grammars invented by Noam Chomsky of the Massachusetts Institute of Technology were the first comprehensive attempt; they specify the syntax of a language by means of a set of rules whose mechanical application generates all allowable structures.

The second problem is that of the parsing itself. It is not always possible to tell, when a part of a sentence is encountered, just what role it plays in the sentence or whether the words in it go together. Take the sentence "Roses will be blooming in the dark gardens we abandoned long ago." The words "in the dark" might be interpreted as a complete phrase; after all, they are grammatically well formed and they make sense. But the phrase cannot form a coherent unit in a complete analysis of the sentence because it forces "Roses will be blooming in the dark" to be interpreted as a sentence and therefore leaves "gardens we abandoned long ago" without a role to play.

Parsers adopt various strategies for exploring the multiple ways phrases can be put together. Some work from the top down, trying from the outset to find possible sentences; others work from the bottom up, trying local word combinations. Some backtrack to explore alternatives in depth if a given possibility fails; others use parallel processing to keep track of a number of alternatives simultaneously. Some make use of formalisms (such as transformational grammar) that were developed by linguists. Others make use of newer formalisms designed with computers in mind. The latter formalisms are better suited to the implementation of parsing procedures. For example, "augmented-transition networks" express the structure of sentences and phrases as an explicit sequence of "transitions" to be followed by a machine. "Lexical-function grammars" create a "functional structure" in which grammatical functions such as head, subject and object are explicitly tied to the words and phrases that serve those functions.

Although no formal grammar successfully deals with all the grammatical problems of any natural language, existing grammars and parsers can handle well over 90 percent of all sentences. This is not entirely to the good. A given sentence may have hundreds or even thousands of possible syntactic analyses. Most of them have no plausible meaning. People are not aware of considering and rejecting such possibilities, but parsing programs are swamped by meaningless alternatives.

The output of a parsing program becomes the input to the fourth component of a language-understanding program: a semantic analyzer, which translates the syntactic form of a sentence into a "logical" form. The point is to put the linguistic expressions into a form that makes it possible for the computer to apply reasoning procedures and draw inferences. Here again there are competing theories about what representation is most appropriate. As with parsing, the key issues are effectiveness and efficiency.

Effectiveness depends on finding the appropriate formal structures to encode the meaning of linguistic expressions. One possibility is predicate calcu-

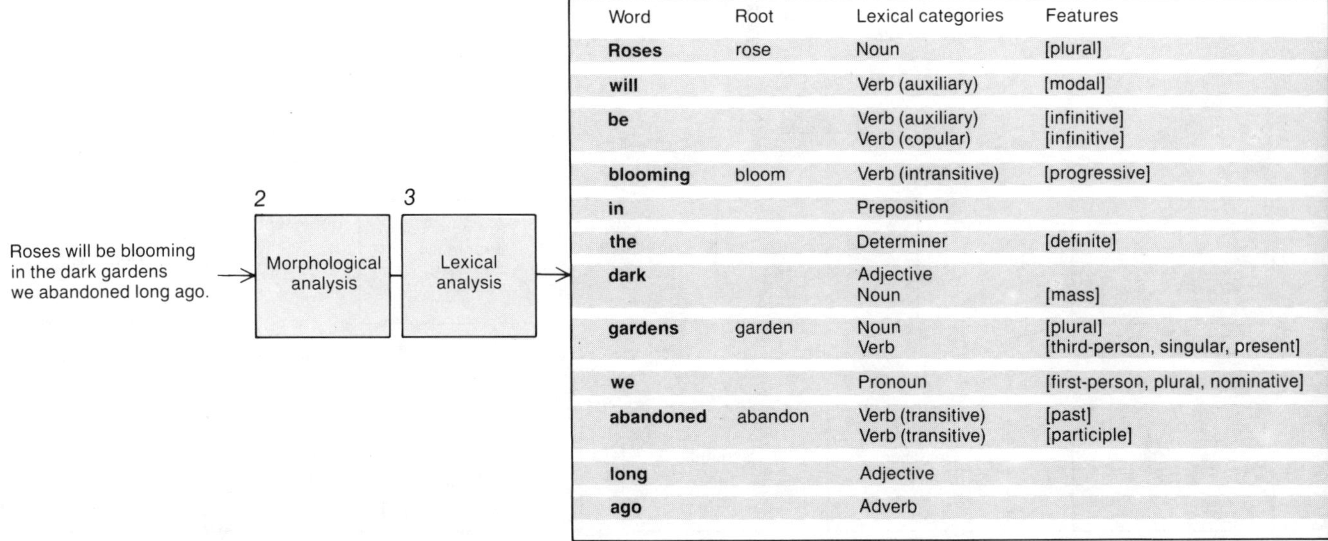

Word	Root	Lexical categories	Features
Roses	rose	Noun	[plural]
will		Verb (auxiliary)	[modal]
be		Verb (auxiliary) Verb (copular)	[infinitive] [infinitive]
blooming	bloom	Verb (intransitive)	[progressive]
in		Preposition	
the		Determiner	[definite]
dark		Adjective Noun	 [mass]
gardens	garden	Noun Verb	[plural] [third-person, singular, present]
we		Pronoun	[first-person, plural, nominative]
abandoned	abandon	Verb (transitive) Verb (transitive)	[past] [participle]
long		Adjective	
ago		Adverb	

SUCCESSION OF ANALYSES done by a hypothetical computer program suggests how software that understands language works. In this illustration the program has been given the sentence "Roses will be blooming in the dark gardens we abandoned long ago." The first analyses (morphological and lexical) yield a list of the words in the sentence, with their roots, their lexical categories and their features. "Blooming," for instance, is a progressive verb: it signifies an act in progress. The data serve as input for the syntactic level of analysis: the parsing of the sentence. Here the surface, or grammatical, structure of "Roses will be blooming..." is put in the form of a tree. Pre-

lus, which employs the quantifiers ∀ to mean "all" and ∃ to mean "there exists." In predicate calculus "Roses will be blooming . . . " is equivalent to the assertion "There exists something that is a rose and that is blooming. . . ." This entails a difficulty. Is one rose adequate to represent the meaning of "roses will be blooming," or would it be better to specify two or more? How can the computer decide? The dilemma is worsened if a sentence includes a mass noun such as "water" in "Water will be flowing. . . ." One cannot itemize water at all. In designing a formal structure for the meaning of linguistic expressions many similar problems arise from the inherent vagueness of language.

Efficiency must also be considered, because the computer will employ the logical form of a sentence to draw inferences that in turn serve both the analysis of the meaning of the sentence and the formulation of a response to it. Some formalisms, such as predicate calculus, are not directly amenable to efficient computation, but other, more "procedural" representations have also been devised. Consider the effort to answer the question "Are there flowers in the gardens we abandoned long ago?" The computer needs to know that roses are flowers. This knowledge could be represented by a formula in predicate calculus amounting to the assertion "Everything that is a rose is a flower." The computer could then apply techniques developed for mechanical theorem-proving to make the needed deduction. A different approach would be to give certain inferences a privileged computational status. For example, basic classificational deductions could be represented directly in data structures [*see bottom illustration on page 70*]. Such deductions are required constantly for reasoning about the ordinary properties of objects. Other types of fact (for example that flowers need water in order to grow) could then be represented in a form closer to predicate calculus. The computer could draw on both to make inferences (for example that if roses do not get water, they will not grow).

A good deal of research has gone into the design of "representation lan-

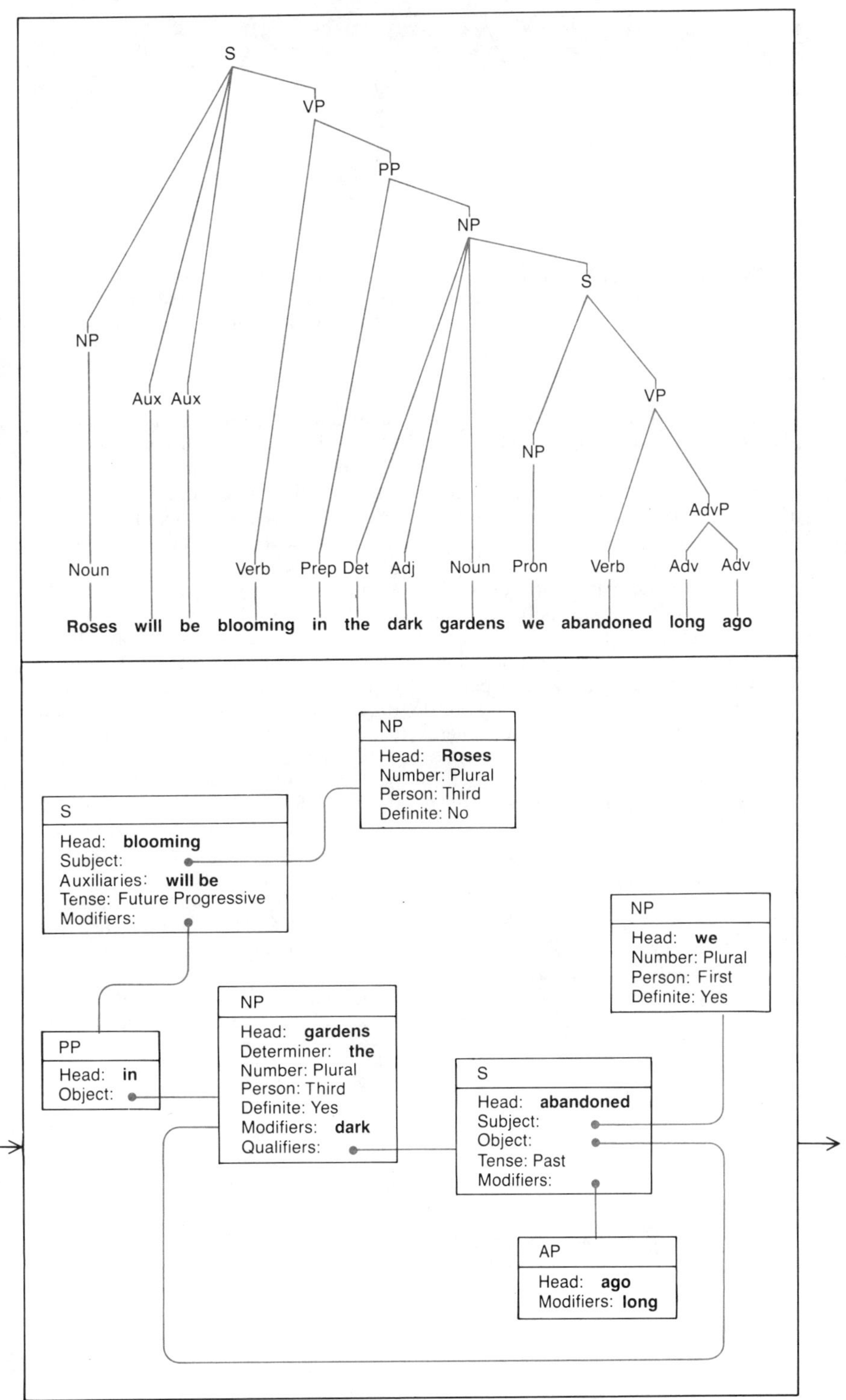

sumably the computer discards numerous incorrect trees. For example, it discards a tree in which "Roses will be blooming in the dark" is construed as a sentence. The deep structure of "Roses will be blooming . . . " is put in the form of a functional-structure diagram. There the relations between the parts of a sentence become explicit; they are shown by strings between boxes. Some relations were explicit in the surface structure (for example that "roses" is the subject of "blooming"). Others were not (for example that "gardens" is the object of "abandoned"). The syntactic analysis is supplied to the final stages of the program, which appear in the bottom illustration on the next page.

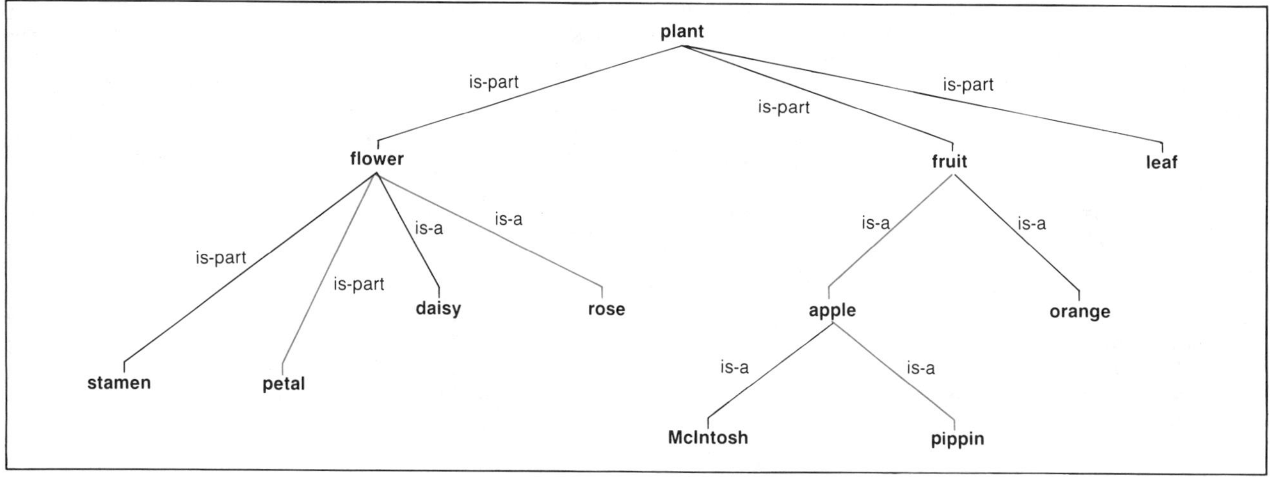

SEMANTIC NETWORK is a specialized form of stored data that represents logical relations so that certain types of inference can be drawn efficiently by a computer. Here a simple tracing of links in the network (*color*) has yielded the inference that a pippin is a fruit and that a rose has petals. Facts not readily represented by a network can be represented in other ways, for example by predicate calculus.

guages" that provide for the effective and efficient encoding of meaning. The greatest difficulty lies in the nature of human commonsense reasoning. Most of what a person knows cannot be formulated in all-or-nothing logical rules; it lies instead in "normal expectations." If one asks, "Is there dirt in the garden?" the answer is almost certainly yes. The yes, however, cannot be a logical inference; some gardens are hydroponic, and the plants there grow in water. A person tends to rely on normal expectations without thinking of exceptions unless they are relevant. But little progress has been made toward formalizing the concept of "relevance" and the way it shapes the background of expectations brought to bear in the understanding of linguistic expressions.

The final stage of analysis in a language-understanding program is pragmatic analysis: the analysis of context. Every sentence is embedded in a setting: it comes from a particular speaker at a particular time and it refers, at least implicitly, to a particular body of understanding. Some of the embedding is straightforward: the pronoun "I" refers to the speaker; the adverb "now" refers to the moment at which the sentence is uttered. Yet even these can be problematic: consider the use of "now" in a letter I write today expecting you to read it three or four days hence. Still, fairly uncomplicated programs can draw the right conclusion most of the time. Other embedding is more complex. The pronoun "we" is an example. "We" might refer to the speaker and the hearer or to the speaker and some third party. Which of these it is (and who the third party might be) is not explicit and in fact is a common source of misunderstanding when people converse.

Still other types of embedding are not signaled by a troublesome word such as "we." The sentence "Roses will be blooming..." presupposes the identification of some future moment when the roses will indeed be in bloom. Thus the sentence might have followed the sentence "What will it be like when we get home?" or "Summer is fast upon us." Similarly, the noun phrase "the dark gardens we abandoned long ago" has a context-dependent meaning. There may be only one instance of gardens in which we have been together; there may be more than one. The sentence presupposes a body of knowledge from which the gardens are identifiable. The point is that a phrase beginning with "the" rarely specifies fully the object to which it refers.

One approach to such phrases has been to encode knowledge of the world in a form the program can use to make inferences. For example, in the sentence "I went to a restaurant and the waiter was rude" one can infer that "the waiter" refers to the person who served the speaker's meal if one's knowledge includes a script, so to speak, of the typical events attending a meal in a restaurant. (A particular waiter or waitress serves any given customer.) In more complex

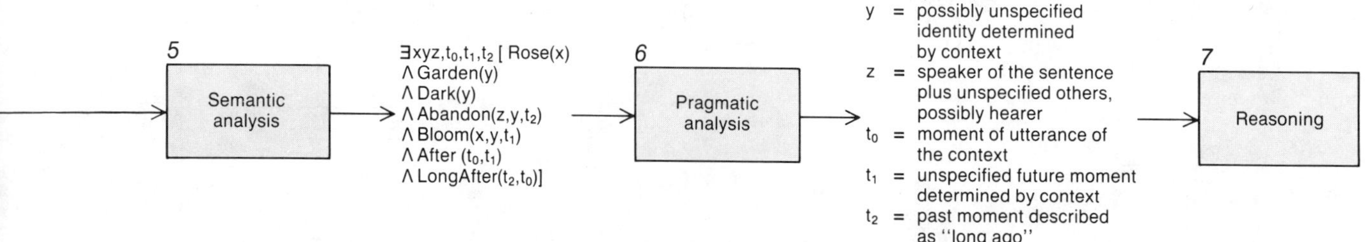

ANALYSES CONCLUDE with the conversion of the syntactic structure of "Roses will be blooming..." into a form from which the computer can draw inferences. In this example the conversion is based on predicate calculus; thus the semantic-analysis module of the hypothetical software represents the logical content of "Roses will be blooming..." by symbols that can be translated as "*x* is a rose and *y* is a garden and *y* is dark...." Finally, the pragmatic-analysis module specifies what is known about the variables *x*, *y*, *z*, t_0, t_1 and t_2. The variable *x*, for example, is "quantified": it declares the existence of something instead of identifying a particular object. In other words, the computer takes "roses" as referring to roses in general, not to particular roses. Hence roses is not a "definite" noun. (That decision was made in the course of semantic analysis.) On the other hand, *z* remains ambiguous because it stands for the ambiguous pronoun "we."

cases an analysis of the speaker's goals and strategies can help. If one hears "My math exam is tomorrow, where's the book?" one can assume that the speaker intends to study and that "the book" means the mathematics text employed in a course the speaker is taking. The approach is hampered by the same difficulty that besets the representation of meaning: the difficulty of formalizing the commonsense background that determines which scripts, goals and strategies are relevant and how they interact. The programs written so far work only in highly artificial and limited realms, and it is not clear how far such programs can be extended.

Even more problematic are the effects of context on the meaning of words. Suppose that in coming to grips with "the dark gardens we abandoned long ago" one tries to apply a particular meaning to "dark." Which should it be? The "dark" of "those dark days of tribulation" or that of "How dark it is with the lights off!" or that of "dark colors"? Although a kernel of similarity unites the uses of a word, its full meaning is determined by how it is used and by the prior understanding the speaker expects of the hearer. "The dark gardens" may have a quite specific meaning for the person addressed; for the rest of us it is slightly mysterious.

At first it might seem possible to distinguish "literal" uses of language from those that are more metaphorical or poetical. Computer programs faced with exclusively literal language could then be freed from contextual dilemmas. The problem is that metaphor and "poetic meaning" are not limited to the pages of literature. Everyday language is pervaded by unconscious metaphor, as when one says, "I lost two hours trying to get my idea across." Virtually every word has an open-ended field of meanings that shade gradually from those that seem utterly literal to those that are clearly metaphorical.

The limitations on the formalization of contextual meaning make it impossible at present—and conceivably forever—to design computer programs that come close to full mimicry of human language understanding. The only programs in practical use today that attempt even limited understanding are natural-language "front ends" that enable the user of a program to request information by asking questions in English. The program responds with English sentences or with a display of data.

A program called SHRDLU is an early example. Developed in the late 1960's, it enables a person to communicate with a computer in English about a simulated world of blocks on a tabletop. The program analyzes requests, commands and statements made by the user and responds with appropriate words or with actions performed in the simulated scene. SHRDLU succeeded in part because its world of conversation is limited to a simple and specialized domain: the blocks and a few actions that can be taken with them.

Some more recent front-end interfaces have been designed with practical applications in mind. A person wanting access to information stored in the computer types natural-language sentences that the computer interprets as queries. The range of the questioning is circumscribed by the range of the data from which answers are formulated; in this way words can be given precise meaning. In a data base on automobiles, for example, "dark" can be defined as the colors "black" and "navy" and nothing more than that. The contextual meaning is there, but it is predetermined by the builder of the system, and the user is expected to learn it.

The main advantage of a natural-language front end is that it presents a low initial barrier to potential users. Someone invited to pose a question in English is usually willing to try, and if the computer proves unable to handle the specific form of the question, the user is probably willing to modify the wording until it works. Over time the user will learn the constraints imposed by the system. In contrast, a person who must learn a specialized language in order to formulate a question may well feel that an inordinate amount of work is being demanded.

I want finally to look at a rather new type of system called a coordinator. In brief it replaces standard electronic mail with a process that aids the generation of messages and monitors the progress of the resulting conversations. Coordinators are based on speech-act theory, which asserts that every utterance falls into one of a small number of categories. Some speech acts are statements: "It's raining." Some are expressive: "I'm sorry I stepped on your toe." Some are requests: "Please take her the package" or "What is your name?" Some are commitments: "I'll do it tomorrow." Some are declarative: "You're fired." (Declaratives differ from statements in that they take effect by virtue of having been said.)

The classification of speech acts is useful because acts in the various categories do not occur at random. Each speech act has "felicity conditions" under which it is an appropriate thing to say and "conditions of satisfaction" under which it is fulfilled. For example, a request or a commitment carries with it, either implicitly or explicitly, a time by which it should be satisfied. Moreover, each speech act is part of a conversation that follows a regular pattern. The regularity is crucial for successful communication.

As with every aspect of language, the full understanding of any given speech act is always enmeshed in the unarticulated background expectations of the speaker and the hearer. The speech act "I'll be here tomorrow" might be a prediction or a promise, and "Do you play tennis?" might be a question or an invitation. In spoken conversation intonation and stress play a prominent part in establishing such meaning.

Coordinator systems deal with the speech acts embodied in messages by specifying what needs to be done and when. The system does not itself attempt to analyze the linguistic content of messages. Instead the word-processing software at the sender's end asks the sender to make explicit the speech-act content of each message. A person may write "I'll be happy to get you that report" in the message itself but must add (with a few special keystrokes) that the message is an ACCEPT of a particular REQUEST. The computer system can then keep track of messages and their interconnections. In particular the system can monitor the completion of conversations, calling the users' attention to cases in which something immediate is pending or in which an agreed-on time for satisfaction has not been met.

From a broad perspective, coordinators are just one member of a large family of software that gives users a structured medium in which language is augmented by explicit indications of how things fit together. Another type of software in this family provides tools for outlining and cross-indexing documents. Still another type is a computerized bulletin board that enables users to store and receive messages not addressed to a specific receiver. The messages are "posted" with additional structure that indicates their content and helps interested readers to find them.

The most obvious prediction about the future of computer software dealing with language is that the decreasing cost of hardware will make applications that are possible but impractical today available quite widely in the future. Yet software that mimics the full human understanding of language is simply not in prospect. Some specific trends can be noted.

The first is that spoken language will get more emphasis. To be sure, the computerized understanding of spoken language presents all the difficulties of written language and more. Merely separating an utterance into its component words can vex a computer; thus hopes for a "voice typewriter" that types text from dictation are just as dim as hopes for high-quality machine translation and language-understanding. On the other hand, many useful devices do not require the analysis of connected speech. Existing systems that can identify a spoken word or phrase from a fixed vocabulary of a few hundred items will improve the interface between users and machines; the recent emergence of inexpensive integrated-circuit chips that process acoustic signals will facilitate the trend. Speech synthesizers that generate understandable utterances (although not in a natural-sounding voice) will also play an increasing role. Improved speech "compression" and encoding techniques will make acoustic messages and acoustic annotation of computer files commonplace.

A second trend in software dealing with language is that constraints on linguistic domain will be handled with increasing care and theoretical analysis. At several points in this article I have noted instances in which computers deal with meaning in an acceptable way because they operate in a limited domain of possible meanings. People using such software quickly recognize that the computer does not understand the full range of language, but the subset available is nonetheless a good basis for communication. Much of the commercial success of future software that deals with language will depend on the discovery of domains in which constraints on what sentences can mean still leave the user a broad range of language.

A third trend lies in the development of systems that combine the natural and the formal. Often it is taken for granted that natural language is the best way for people to communicate with computers. Plans for a "fifth generation" of intelligent computers are based on this proposition. It is not at all evident, however, that the proposition is valid. In some cases even the fullest understanding of natural language is not as expressive as a picture. And in many cases a partial understanding of natural language proves to be less usable than a well-designed formal interface. Consider the work with natural-language front ends. Here natural language promotes the initial acceptance of the system, but after that the users often move toward stylized forms of language they find they can employ with confidence, that is, without worrying about whether or not the machine will interpret their statements correctly.

The most successful current systems facilitate this transition. Some systems (including coordinators) mix the natural and the formal: the user is taught to recognize formal properties of utterances and include them explicitly in messages. Thus the computer handles formal structures, while people handle tasks in which context is important and precise rules cannot be applied. Other systems incorporate a highly structured query system, so that as the user gains experience the artificial forms are seen to save time and trouble. In each case the computer is not assigned the difficult and open-ended tasks of linguistic analysis; it serves instead as a structured linguistic medium. That is perhaps the most useful way the computer will deal with natural language.

Artificial Intelligence

8

by David L. Waltz
October 1982

Computer programs not only play games but also process visual information, learn from experience and understand some natural language. The most challenging task is simulating common sense

The idea that the digital computer will someday match or exceed the intellectual abilities of human beings has been put forward repeatedly ever since the computer was invented. In the early days of computing the assertion was without an empirical basis: the programs of the computer could no more be expected to reason, plan, learn, sense, formulate concepts, use language or think creatively than could their mechanical predecessors in the art of simulation: the puppet, the windup toy soldier and the music box. Moreover, the idea that intelligence itself might require a theoretical framework for its explanation was scarcely acknowledged. Intelligence was considered a transparent concept, and if it were to be recognized in a machine, the intellectual powers of the machine would have to be almost indistinguishable from those of a human being. Thus early computers were called electronic brains, and John von Neumann, one of the architects of the kind of computer in commonest use today, formulated explicit analogies between the computer and the brain. Many people still associate data with human knowledge, the operation of a program with decision making, the trace or ongoing record of the program's operation with the stream of consciousness and the acquisition of data with learning.

In the past 20 or 25 years the new discipline of artificial intelligence has put to rest some of the more naive analogies between the computer and the brain and has begun the task of placing the concept of intelligence on a theoretical footing. For the practitioners of the discipline the computer is a laboratory in which to develop new ways of thinking about thinking. Computer programs written by investigators in artificial intelligence have demonstrated conclusively that in certain activities (including activities most people would say require intelligence, such as playing games) the computer can outperform a human being. Recent programs have demonstrated that the computer can even develop elaborate theories about a limited domain such as arithmetic from a few simple axioms. At the same time the understanding of various features of human intelligence has been considerably enriched by the attempt to describe analogues of those features in the detail necessary for writing a program. As a result the analogy relating the performance of the computer to that of human intelligence has broadened and matured.

Consider learning: In people learning seems to be intimately related to growth and changes in the physical structure of the brain, but the hardware of a computer does not undergo any analogous changes. The programs of a computer, however, can change in a variety of ways: they can accumulate data, organize it and even modify themselves. Hence workers in artificial intelligence have suggested that complex programs, and particularly those that can alter their own operations, may be good models of human learning. Such models, like other models in science, do not duplicate the phenomenon they are meant to represent in all its detail. For example, the operations of a computer that embodies a "learning" program bear no explanatory relation to human learning as it is realized in the firing patterns of brain cells and nerve cells. Nevertheless, the computer model of intelligence is flexible enough to be formulated at whatever level of detail is considered appropriate for highlighting the essential functions of human thinking.

Here I shall attempt to convey an idea of the kinds of results that can be achieved by programs in artificial intelligence. Most of the programs I shall discuss are well-known approaches to major problem areas in the field, and my descriptions are intended primarily to make clear the main contributions of each program. I have therefore favored programs whose operation can be explained succinctly. What follows should be read more as an introduction to the field than as a summary of it.

One of the constant themes in artificial intelligence has been how best to explore a range of possible actions in the pursuit of well-defined goals. In general for every action taken new possible actions become available, and so the planning of a sequence of actions must consider a branching structure of possible states called a search tree. The tree is generally shown inverted, with the root at the top. The root is the current situation, the branches are the possible actions and the ends of the branches are the possible outcomes. One or more of the outcomes may correspond to the goal of the search.

Heuristic Search

Exploring the full range of possible actions in all possible sequences would be equivalent to tracing every branch of the tree and would guarantee that the optimum sequence would be identified. In many cases, however, the search tree is so large that a complete search is not feasible. Therefore in most artificial-intelligence programs heuristic principles, or informal rules of thumb, are incorporated so that the most promising actions are selected for further examination early in the search and the less promising ones are eliminated from full-scale consideration. Heuristic principles are effective and practical in most circumstances and they shorten the search, but their application cannot guarantee that the optimum result will be found. Heuristic-search methods are commonly employed in programs that enable a robot to plan the manipulation of objects or to plan its own movement in space.

Programs that play games such as chess, checkers and backgammon are informative examples of the application of the heuristically guided search. Many of the programs now play at the level of the expert or master human player; a program called Mighty Bee, written by Hans Berliner of Carnegie-Mellon University, defeated the world backgammon champion in 1979. Probably the most intense interest has been focused on programs that play chess, and virtually all chess programs devised since the 1950's are based on a heuristic-search model developed by Claude E. Shannon at Bell Laboratories.

When a chess program is choosing a move, the program must somehow evaluate the position that results from each candidate move. The evaluation can be done by means of a scoring system such as one based on the value of each piece and on the gravity of the threat to any piece that can be captured on the next move [*see illustration on page 76*]. Many programs also incorporate such factors as the strength of the pawns' positions, the degree of control over the center of the board and the number of pieces mobilized. The program plays to maximize the score.

The heuristic principles incorporated into a chess program control the breadth and the depth of the search tree the program explores in looking for the best move. Generally the program calculates the score for every legal move from a given position. It can then consider the opponent's responses to each of these moves and its own range of countermoves for each response. Early in the process, however, some selection of moves must be made or the number of positions to be evaluated will become impractical. It is in making the selection that the heuristic principles are brought to bear. The program might select only the move with the highest score for further study, or it could explore the consequences of, say, the five most promising moves. For the moves still under consideration the program examines the search tree to some specified depth, at which point the heuristic principles determine whether or not to continue the exploration: a line of search is abandoned only if the position reached is reasonably stable. Black then makes the move likely to lead to the highest score, assuming that White makes the best move available at each turn.

In chess the average number of moves that can be made from a given position is 35; an exhaustive search only three moves deep for each player would require the examination of more than 1.8 billion moves. Rigorous methods for pruning the search tree have been devised, but in spite of such methods the essential operation of most computer-chess programs is an extensive exploration of the search tree. The current world champion among programs is Belle, developed by Ken Thompson and Joe Condon of Bell Laboratories. The program runs on a specialized computer with hardware designed specifically to make chess calculations; it examines an average of 160,000 positions per second. Belle plays in tournaments as if it had a chess rating of 2,160 (a rating of 2,000 to 2,199 qualifies a player as an expert), making its level of play higher than that of all but a small fraction of human chess players.

Artificial Intelligence and Psychology

The operation of Belle and similar chess-playing programs illustrates one of the most important questions about the goals of work in artificial intelligence. If one of the primary goals is the simulation of intelligent human behavior, on what level is the simulation to be carried out? In a sense a program that plays chess at the level of an expert chess player, by whatever means, simulates the behavior of the expert human player. On the other hand, if the goal is to emulate the strategic decisions made by a human player, a program such as Belle must be counted a failure.

There is considerable evidence that good human chess players employ processing methods radically different from the ones incorporated into Belle. A human player relies on strategy: he picks a goal, such as capturing a particular piece, then looks for ways to attain the goal. Reaching the goal may in turn call for identifying subgoals and verifying that each of them can be attained. Tests have shown that a good human player examines no more than about 100 board positions before choosing a move; only

"BLOCKS WORLD" is a highly simplified domain that enables workers in artificial intelligence to explore the ways perception, thought and action can be modeled and linked by a computer. The blocks world of the computer is represented by the colored cubes, boxes and pyramids in the illustration. Also part of the blocks world are the standard principles of everyday physical interactions; for example, a pyramid in the blocks world is not allowed to rest balanced on its vertex. The blocks world was devised at the Massachusetts Institute of Technology by Terry A. Winograd, who is now at Stanford University, as a domain of action for a computer program called SHRDLU. SHRDLU simulates the actions and responses of a person with respect to the objects in the world: the program can plan and carry out certain manipulations of the objects according to instructions issued to the computer in ordinary natural language, and it can answer questions about present and past configurations of the world, about actions it has taken or plans to take and about the reasons for its actions. Other investigators have shown how to model the learning of new actions in the blocks world. Scenes from the blocks world have been adapted from Winograd's article "Understanding Natural Language," which first appeared in the journal *Cognitive Psychology*.

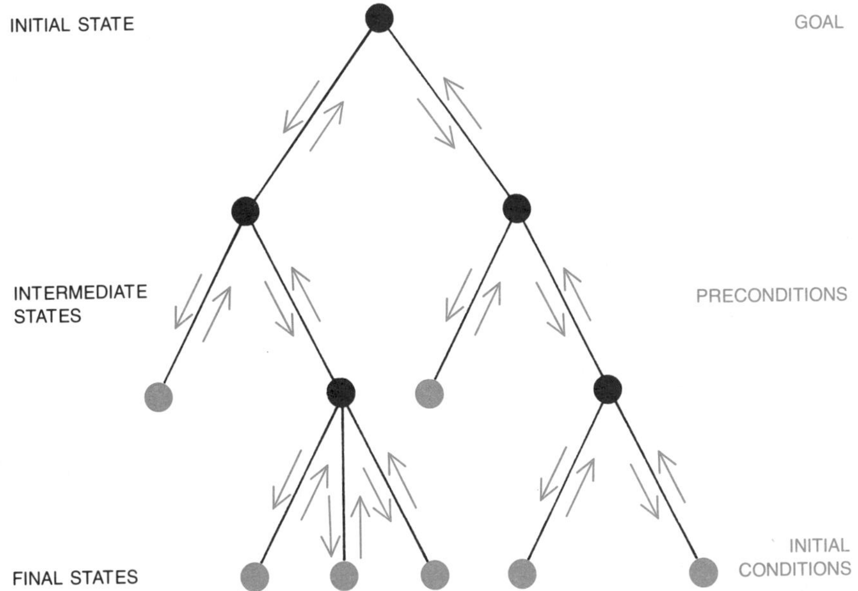

SYSTEMATIC SEARCH of an inverted tree structure proceeds from the top node, or root, along the leftmost branch to a terminal node. The search then returns to the first intermediate node from which it can trace another downward branch and goes on to explore all the terminal nodes from left to right (*colored arrows*). An inverted tree can represent the structure of a variety of problems. The root can represent a given situation, such as a position in a chess game, and each node directly below the root can represent the outcome of some action that is possible in the situation, such as the movement of one of the chess pieces. Still lower nodes can represent the results of possible subsequent actions, such as the countermoves available to a chess opponent after a given move. The root of a tree can also represent a goal, and the immediate branching nodes can represent the preconditions of taking some action that will achieve the goal. A precondition can have preconditions of its own, which are represented by the nodes at the next level. Exploring a tree structure is a serial process, that is, the nodes are examined one at a time.

the most promising lines of attack are considered, but they are explored in relatively great depth. Belle, on the other hand, examines some 29 million positions in the average of three minutes it can allot to each move in a tournament game.

Given Belle's success at the chess board it seems clear that intelligent behavior can result from underlying processes quite different from those of human cognition. Some investigators, however, argue that artificial intelligence is, broadly speaking, a branch of human psychology. They submit that whenever a program simulates some aspect of human intellectual performance, the program constitutes an "existence proof" for the computer model of human intelligence. The operation of the program may diverge so far from human mental processes as to preclude any direct contribution to human psychology. Nevertheless, the program may simulate certain other aspects of human intelligence that seem quite important, such as its unpredictability in performance. Chess programs often play better than the people who write them, and so it is highly misleading to assert, as many people have, that computer intelligence is limited because a computer can do only what it is programmed to do. In many cases the programmer does not know what his program can do until it is run on a computer.

A striking example of the phenomenon was reported recently by Donald Michie and Tim Niblett of the University of Edinburgh and Ivan Bratko of the Edward Kardelj University of Ljubljana. A program developed by the three investigators analyzes certain end games in chess, a part of the game in which most computer programs fare considerably less well than they do in the middle of the game. Master chess players generally memorize a set of rules for the end game, but the program has demonstrated that certain end-game positions once thought to end in a draw actually result in a forced win for one side. In order to force the win, however, one must apply a set of rules too complex to be easily remembered by a human player; the rules are well within the capacity of current computers.

Planning

Although goal-directed planning is not a dominant feature of chess-playing programs, it is easy in principle to write a program that identifies goals and finds ways to attain them. Again the operation of the program can be understood as the exploration of an inverted treelike structure.

The root of the tree represents the goal and the nodes that branch away from the root represent preconditions that may have to be met before the goal can be achieved. (Preconditions that, taken together, are sufficient for achieving the goal are linked, but all the sufficient sets of preconditions are represented in the tree.) Each precondition can in turn become a subgoal with preconditions of its own represented by further branching nodes. The terminal nodes of the tree represent conditions already satisfied by the initial state of affairs. An action that can accomplish a goal or a subgoal is also associated with each nonterminal node. The program explores all the branches of the tree until every precondition is satisfied. It then constructs a plan of action by tracing a path through the tree from the lowest node to the highest one.

A program developed in the late 1960's and early 1970's by Terry A. Winograd, then at the Massachusetts Institute of Technology, illustrates the operation of a planning program in a carefully limited domain. Winograd's program is called SHRDLU, after the seventh through the 12th most frequent letters in English; the domain in which it operates is made up of simple three-dimensional objects such as cubes and pyramids that rest on a table. (The program actually has no facilities for manipulating real objects or even for representing them on a video screen, but it keeps track of their properties and positions internally.) SHRDLU replies to questions typed by an operator, executes commands on the objects in its simple environment, called the blocks world, and reports on the results.

To understand how a plan of action is formulated by SHRDLU, suppose the program could carry out only two actions, called STACK and CLEARTOP. The program executes STACK by grasping an object, moving it to a point above a second object and putting it down on top of the second object. CLEARTOP effects the removal of one object from the top of another; it calls for grasping the upper object, moving it over an unoccupied region of the table and putting it down.

Actually both STACK and CLEARTOP represent a hierarchy of actions. At the next level of detail are subactions such as GRASP, MOVE and PUT. Each of the subactions in turn is made up of a sequence of more detailed steps, until ultimately the steps could be expressed as control signals for such activities as closing mechanical "fingers," sensing contact with an object and rotating a joint. Thus the hierarchy of program statements reflects the hierarchical structure of human actions, from high-level, conscious goals to the detailed sequences of motor control. Hereafter I shall omit all such details of control and discuss the plans formulated by the program only at the highest level.

Before the action STACK can be executed two preconditions must be satisfied: the tops of both the objects that will form the stack must be clear. Similarly, there are two preconditions for the action CLEARTOP. The object whose top is to be cleared must have another object resting on it, and the top of the upper object must itself be clear. In order to select an action that can accomplish a certain goal or subgoal, the program compares the goal or subgoal with a set of "postconditions" associated with each action. The postconditions specify the configuration of the blocks world that the action will bring about. If the configuration satisfies the conditions of the goal or subgoal, the action is proposed as part of the plan.

Suppose a dark green cube is resting on a dark grey one. How can the program exploit the actions STACK and CLEARTOP to achieve the goal of placing the dark grey cube on the dark green one? Beginning with the goal state, the program searches for an action that has postconditions matching the goal and sets up the preconditions of the action as new subgoals. The action STACK could place the dark grey cube on the dark green one (the goal) if the tops of both the dark green and the dark grey cubes were clear. In the given initial state the top of the dark green cube is clear but the top of the dark grey one is not. Hence clearing the top of the dark grey cube becomes a new subgoal.

Backward Chaining

The program continues by searching for actions that will achieve each subgoal and sets up preconditions of each action in turn. To clear the top of the dark grey cube the action CLEARTOP could be applied. Its preconditions are satisfied by the initial state of the blocks world and so the search is complete. The entire process of constructing a sequence of actions from the goal state back to the state in which all the preconditions of the actions necessary to initiate the chain are satisfied is called backward chaining.

The program can now devise a plan of action to achieve the goal by reversing the sequence of actions found during the search. The plan is first to apply CLEARTOP in order to remove the dark green cube from the top of the dark grey one and second to apply STACK in order to place the dark grey cube on the dark green one. One effect of the plan is that the top of the dark grey cube is cleared, a change brought about by the plan that was not one of its explicit

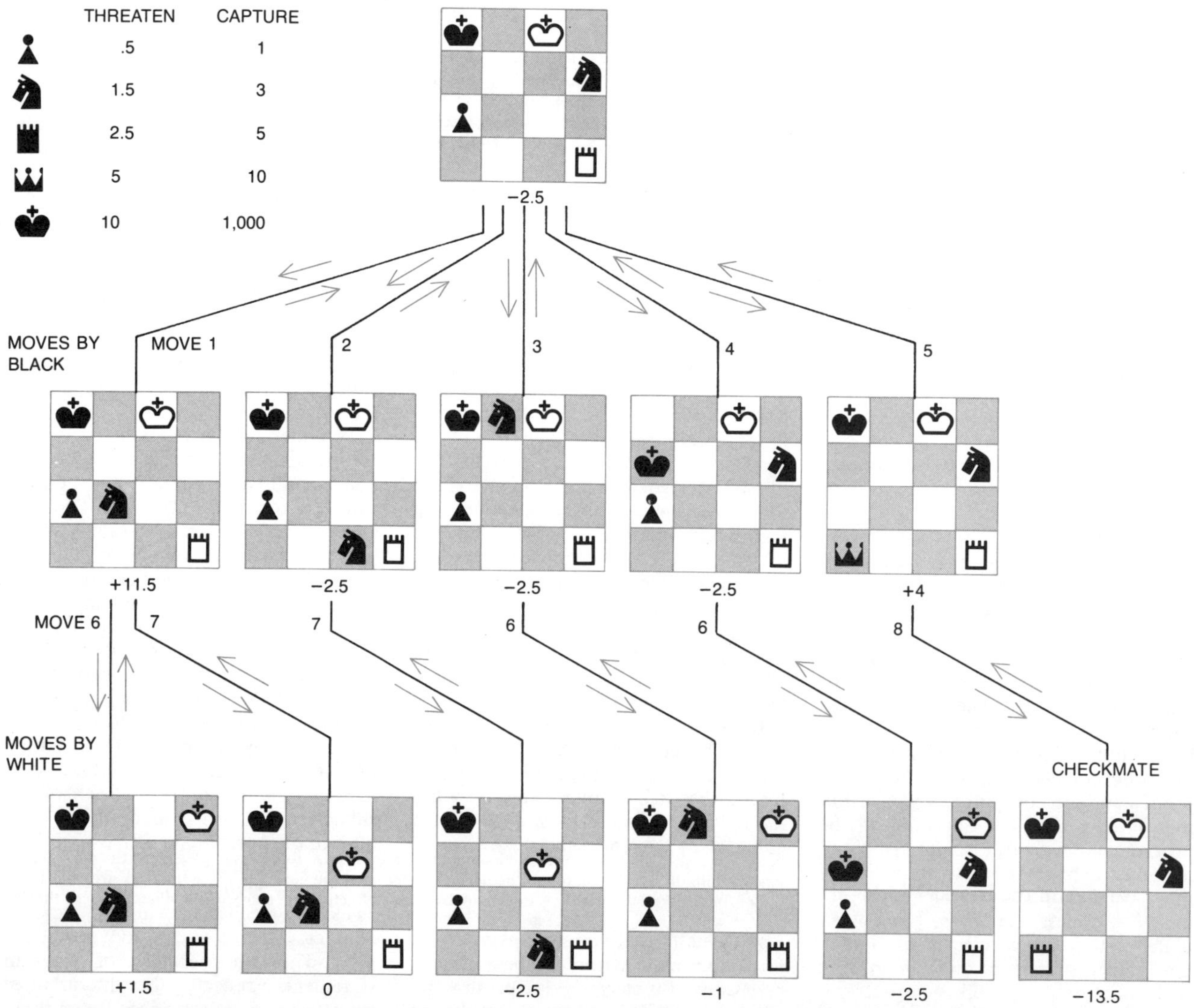

TREE STRUCTURE of a simplified chess game shows how the computer program, here playing Black, determines its next move. The program examines the available moves and the opponent's countermoves one by one, tracing the game tree (*colored arrows*) to a depth determined by heuristic rules. Each position is assigned a score according to an evaluation procedure, such as the one in the table at the upper left. The initial position, shown at the top of the tree, is scored −2.5: a total of 1,004 for the black pieces on the board, −1,005 for the white pieces and −1.5 for the threat to the black knight. The move selected is the one that leads to the highest score for Black at the greatest depth examined, assuming that White will make the best countermove available. In this case Black plays move 1 and assumes White will respond with move 7. The heuristic rules instruct the program to abandon the search whenever one of White's countermoves leads to a better score for White than the best countermove previously considered. Thus the program abandons its examination of moves 2, 3, 4 and 5 as soon as it finds countermoves that lead to positions worth less than 0, the value of the best position available to White after move 1.

goals. Such a change is called a side effect of the plan.

One of the most intriguing recent applications of backward-chaining search methods has been the development of computer programs that draw on expert knowledge and interact with the user. The programs have proved capable of expert performance and are called expert systems. They have been applied to tasks such as medical diagnosis, prospecting for mineral deposits and advising on tax matters. For example, if the goal is the diagnosis of disease, the program works backward from general information about the patient's condition to increasingly specific facts until the chain of facts can justify a fairly plausible inference about what disease is present. Thus the emphasis of an expert system is to develop a plan for making a plausible inference, based on knowledge supplied by the user, rather than to develop a plan of action. The possible inferences are stored as rules in the program, where they have a role analogous to that of the actions in SHRDLU.

A good example of a rule is found in the medical-diagnosis system called MYCIN, written by Edward H. Shortliffe of Stanford University: "If the infection is primary bacteremia, and the site of the culture is one of the sterile sites, and the suspected portal of entry of the organism is the gastrointestinal tract, then there is suggestive evidence (.7) that the identity of the organism is bacteroides."

Such a rule is quite similar in form to the rules people cite to explain their decisions; rules employed by expert systems have therefore been relatively easy for experts to learn to write. It is important that a numerical confidence rating, such as the number .7 in the MYCIN rule for diagnosing bacteroides infection, be assigned to each rule. The confidence rating is the basis of heuristic controls that guide the program's search for a plausible inference, and it is supplied to the user for assessing the validity of various conclusions the program generates. The program must also explain why it reached the conclusion it did; no one would trust a program that simply printed its conclusion without saying why it rejected some other conclusion that seems reasonable.

Learning in the Blocks World

Unless a computer can expand its own capabilities on the basis of "experience," the performance of a program is limited by the knowledge, foresight and available time of the programmer. Learning, therefore, is a particularly important concern in artificial intelligence. A number of investigators have adopted Winograd's blocks world as a kind of laboratory in which to explore various learning strategies.

One kind of learning is based on the "memorization" of a plan formulated after a search by backward chaining; the idea was first developed by Richard E. Fikes and Nils J. Nilsson, both then at the Stanford Research Institute, for the system STRIPS (for the Stanford Research Institute Problem Solver). Suppose a program is to achieve the goal state in which a brown block is resting on a light green one, and it encounters a state in which a light green block is resting on a brown one. Having earlier interchanged the dark grey block and the dark green one, the program stores a representation of the plan it developed for the exchange, namely to employ first the action CLEARTOP and then the action STACK. The representation of the plan must be a generalized one, however, since otherwise it could be applied only

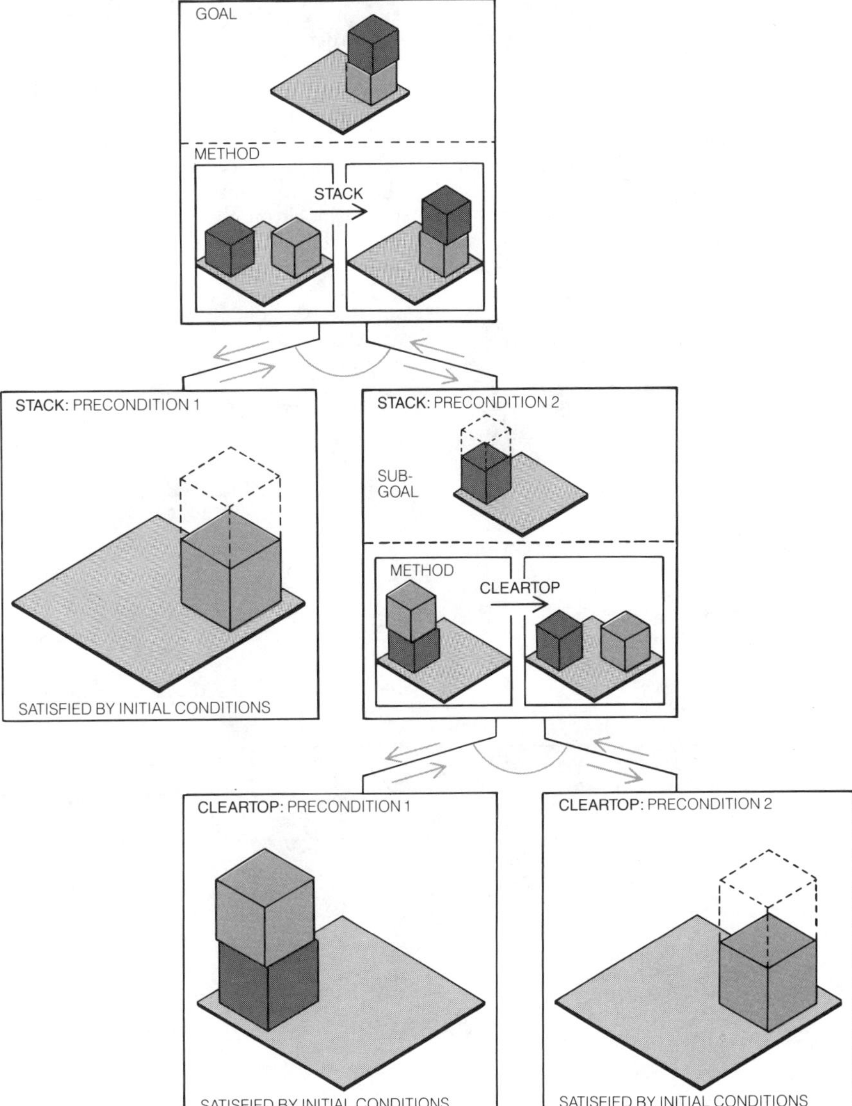

FORMULATING A PLAN in the blocks world calls for identifying a goal and choosing a sequence of actions that will achieve the goal from a given initial state. In the example shown the dark green block is initially resting on top of the dark grey one, and the goal is to place the dark grey block on top of the dark green one. In order to devise a plan of action the program conducts a search that is equivalent to exploring a tree structure. Each node of the tree represents a state of the blocks world; the root is the goal, that is, the state in which a dark grey block rests on top of a dark green one. An action is selected from the repertory of actions available to the program, such as the action STACK. The action selected is the one whose results, or postconditions, match the essential features of the state; the action is also associated with the node. The nodes branching down from a given node represent preconditions, or states in the blocks world that must be attained before the action represented by the given node can be carried out. When multiple preconditions must all be satisfied, they are connected by an arc. Before the action STACK can be undertaken the top of both the dark green block and the dark grey block must be clear. The program determines that the first precondition is met by the initial state but the second precondition is not. To clear the top of the dark grey block, therefore, another action from the repertory must be applied, and its preconditions must in turn be compared with the initial conditions. When all the preconditions of every node that is explored by the program are satisfied by the initial conditions, the sequence of actions encountered during the search is reversed to make a plan that will accomplish the final goal.

to the dark grey and the dark green blocks it first encountered. The generalization is accomplished by storing the names of the blocks to be interchanged as variable quantities. The entire action, here called INTERCHANGE, is added to the program's repertory of possible actions as a fixed sequence of the simpler actions GRASP, MOVE and PUT, together with new preconditions and postconditions for the action INTERCHANGE. Because the initial state of the brown and the light green blocks satisfies the preconditions of the action INTERCHANGE the program can immediately achieve the goal state without a search.

A second kind of learning is trial-and-error learning, which is modeled in a program called HACKER written by Gerald J. Sussman of M.I.T. (In the jargon of computer science a hacker is someone who spends much of his time writing computer programs.) HACKER is made up of a planning system similar to the one in SHRDLU, "critics" that monitor the planning and note problems and "debuggers" that formulate new rules for the programs to avoid repeating the errors caught by the critics.

Suppose a dark green block is resting on a dark grey one and a light green block is placed alone on the table. HACKER is asked to build a three-block stack with the dark green block on the top, the light green one in the middle and the dark grey one on the bottom; the program has available only the actions STACK, CLEARTOP and INTERCHANGE. In order to plan its actions HACKER breaks down the goal into subgoals: for the first subgoal it can choose either to place the dark green block on the light green one or to place the light green block on the dark grey one. Assume that the program arbitrarily begins with the wrong subgoal, namely placing the dark green block on the light green one. It saves the information that it can achieve the chosen subgoal by applying the action STACK. Its next subgoal must be to place the light green block on the dark grey one. It cannot pick up the light green block, however, as long as the light green block supports the dark green block because the operation of STACK requires that the top of the light green block be clear. To stack the light green block on the dark grey one the program must remove the dark green block from the top of the light green one, thus "clobbering," or undoing, the subgoal it has just achieved.

The critics in HACKER are programmed to call in the debuggers whenever they detect that a subgoal has been clobbered. The debuggers look for planning options, and in this case they find that if the light green block is first put on the dark grey one, the plan works without clobbering any subgoals. Hence the debuggers can conclude that the clobbering of subgoals can be avoided, at least sometimes, by rearranging them. HACKER saves the conclusion as a new, general debugging method. Sussman's program eventually learned to order the subgoals for a stack made up of any number of blocks.

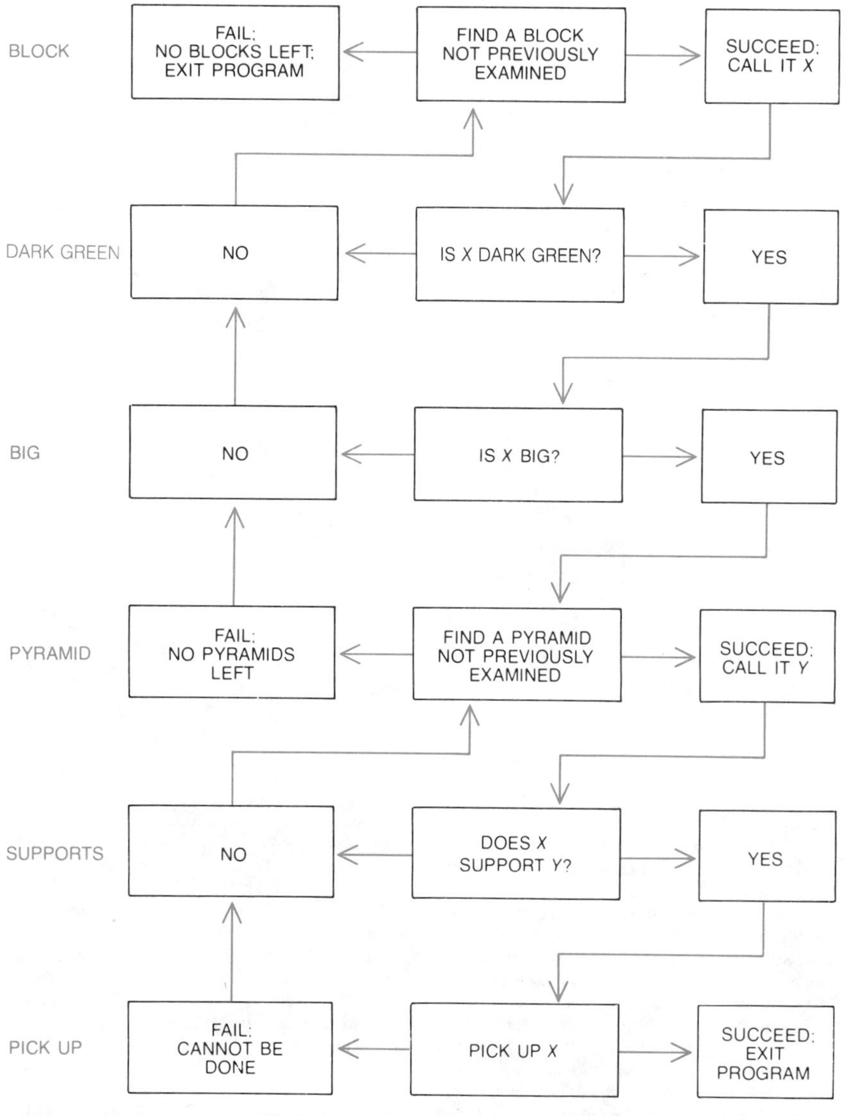

UNDERSTANDING OF COMMANDS is accomplished by the program SHRDLU by following procedures like the one shown in this flow chart. Key words in the command "Pick up a big dark green block that supports a pyramid" initiate a logical series of steps that determine which block the command refers to. SHRDLU will then develop a plan to carry out the command.

Concept Learning

A number of programs enable a computer to carry out an action more competently or to form a more adequate representation of a concept. One of the earliest programs to improve its own performance was a checkers-playing program written by Arthur L. Samuel of the International Business Machines Corporation in about 1960. Learning in the program was designed to simulate the mechanisms of evolution and natural selection. One version of the program played against another version in which the scoring system for evaluating the strength of a position had been altered slightly. In this way a given scoring system and a "mutation" of the system were tested in direct competition, and the winning version was retained as the basis for constructing new variations.

In the late 1960's Patrick H. Winston of M.I.T. wrote a program that successively improves its mastery of certain concepts. A teacher presents the program with a carefully graded sequence of scenes arranged so that the first scene is a good example of the concept the program is to learn. The program analyzes the first scene and builds a "hypothesis" about what components of the scene and what relations among them are essential aspects of the concept. For each subsequent scene the teacher tells the program whether or not the scene is an example of the concept. The program tests and revises its initial hypothesis as each new scene is presented.

Suppose the program is presented with a simple line drawing and told the drawing is an example of an arch [*see illustration on page 84*]. The program notes that the object represented in the drawing is made up of three blocks; two of them stand upright on a table and support the third. Although the program might have guessed many other properties of the example that are true of arches in general, its concept of an arch is kept deliberately impoverished so that the concept can be enriched by analysis of the later scenes.

The second scene is not an arch. The program again constructs a description of the scene and compares the description with the hypothesis it has built up from the first example. If the second scene does not differ from the first one in too many ways, the program can begin to determine which relations are essential to the concept of an arch. If the second scene is identical with the first one except that the block that was on top is now lying on the table, the program infers that in an arch the two standing blocks must support the third block. The program has learned that the relation of support between the lower blocks and the upper block was not an incidental aspect of the first scene, and the hypothesis about the concept of an arch is updated to reflect the finding. As additional scenes are introduced the representation of the concept by the program becomes more adequate for recognizing novel instances of an arch.

Recently a program called AM (for automated mathematics) was developed by Douglas B. Lenat of Stanford that can formulate new concepts and theorems in mathematics from about 100 elementary concepts in set theory. Heuristic principles specify the creation of the new concepts under certain well-defined conditions, and the program then proceeds to investigate the concepts. During one run on a computer AM considered the concept of the divisors of a number. It found several numbers that have four or more divisors (for example, the divisors of 6 are 1, 2, 3 and 6), but the heuristic rules confined the investigation to numbers with only a few divisors.

In considering the numbers with exactly three divisors the program found that all the examples are also perfect squares. Moreover, the program found that the square root of a number with three divisors is always a number with exactly two divisors. Because of the coincidence of the concept square-roots-of-numbers-with-three-divisors and the concept numbers-with-two-divisors, the program raised the priority of both concepts on its agenda and determined to investigate numbers with exactly two divisors in considerably more detail. In this way AM began to explore the rich pattern of mathematical relations that develops from the concept of numbers with exactly two divisors, otherwise known as prime numbers. In about an hour of running time on the computer Lenat's program went on to reproduce several well-known conjectures about prime numbers and guessed that every natural number is the product of a unique set of primes.

Constraint Propagation

The kind of search I have described for chess programs and planning programs is a serial process, and so the size of the tree that can be searched is limited by the time needed to evaluate every node in the tree sequentially. In some cases a process that seems to require a serial tree search can be recast as a parallel process, in which independent aspects of the search are done simultaneously. Much of the signal processing carried out by the brain is done in parallel, and many investigators think programs that incorporate parallel processing will be much better able to simulate human sensory abilities than programs that rely on serial processing. A number of programs in artificial intelligence have experimented with a parallel process called constraint propagation, an early example of which I presented in my Ph.D. dissertation at M.I.T. in 1972. My program was written in LISP, a programming language now employed for most work in artificial intelligence.

One of the things people learn to do almost at a glance is to interpret a two-dimensional line drawing as a three-dimensional scene. In my dissertation I wanted to develop a program that could mimic this skill. Earlier independent

Will you please stack up both of the dark green blocks and either a light green cube or pyramid?
OK.
Which cube is sitting on the table?
The large light green one which supports the dark green pyramid.
Put a small cube onto the light green cube which supports a pyramid.
OK.
Put the littlest pyramid on top of it.
OK.
How many things are on top of light green cubes?
I'm not sure what you mean by "on top of" in the phrase "on top of light green cubes."
Do you mean:
1—Directly on the surface
2—Anywhere on top of?
2
Three of them.
Had you touched any pyramid before you put the light green one on the little cube?
Yes, the light green one.
When did you pick it up?
While I was stacking up the dark green cube, a large dark green block and a large light green cube.
Why?
To get rid of it.
Why did you do that?
To clear off the dark green cube.
Why did you clear off that cube?
To put it on a large light green cube.
Why did you do that?
To stack up the dark green cube, a large dark green block and a large light green cube.
Why did you do that?
Because you asked me to.

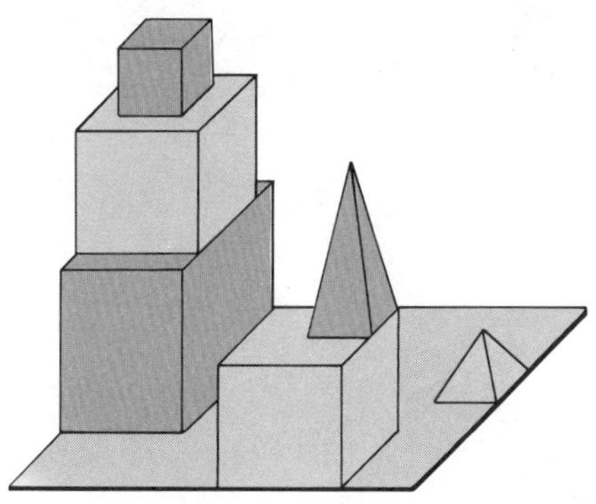

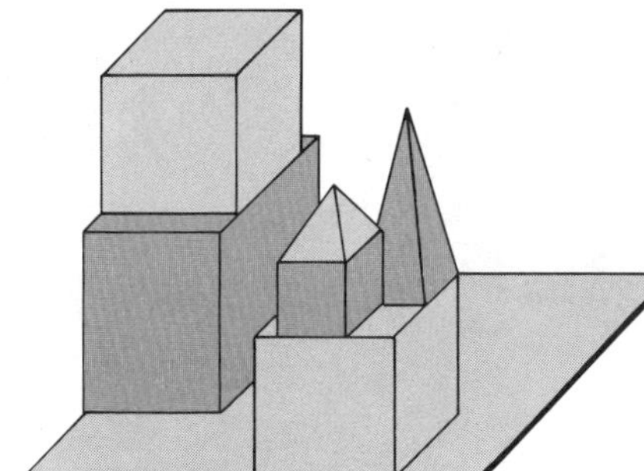

EXTREME SIMPLICITY of the blocks world makes it possible for the program SHRDLU to give a wide and flexible range of responses to questions by the programmer. The program is able to plan and execute the manipulation of the objects in its world on command from the programmer. As the programmer issues the commands listed at the left (*black type*) the initial state of the blocks world (*top right*) is transformed to reflect the results of the actions that carry out the commands (*middle and bottom right*). As the dialogue proceeds the program queries the programmer about an ambiguous question and answers questions about the state of the blocks world, its previous actions and the reasons for its actions (*colored type*). SHRDLU was one of the first programs to combine both language understanding and the simulation of action.

work by David A. Huffman of M.I.T. and the late Max B. Clowes of the University of Sussex had shown, under certain simplifying assumptions, that a line drawing can be interpreted as a three-dimensional scene only if all its vertexes can be labeled consistently from a set of 16 allowable kinds of vertex. The scheme developed by Huffman and Clowes applies only to drawings of objects whose surfaces are all planes and in which no vertex represents the intersection of more than three planes. Each line emanating from a vertex must be labeled as either an occluding edge, a convex edge (pointing toward the viewer) or a concave edge (pointing away from the viewer).

A scene can be labeled consistently if every vertex is labeled and every line is assigned only one label. If two vertexes connected by a single line cannot be labeled in such a way that the line is unambiguously identified, the drawing cannot represent a real three-dimensional object. An example of a drawing that cannot be labeled consistently is the so-

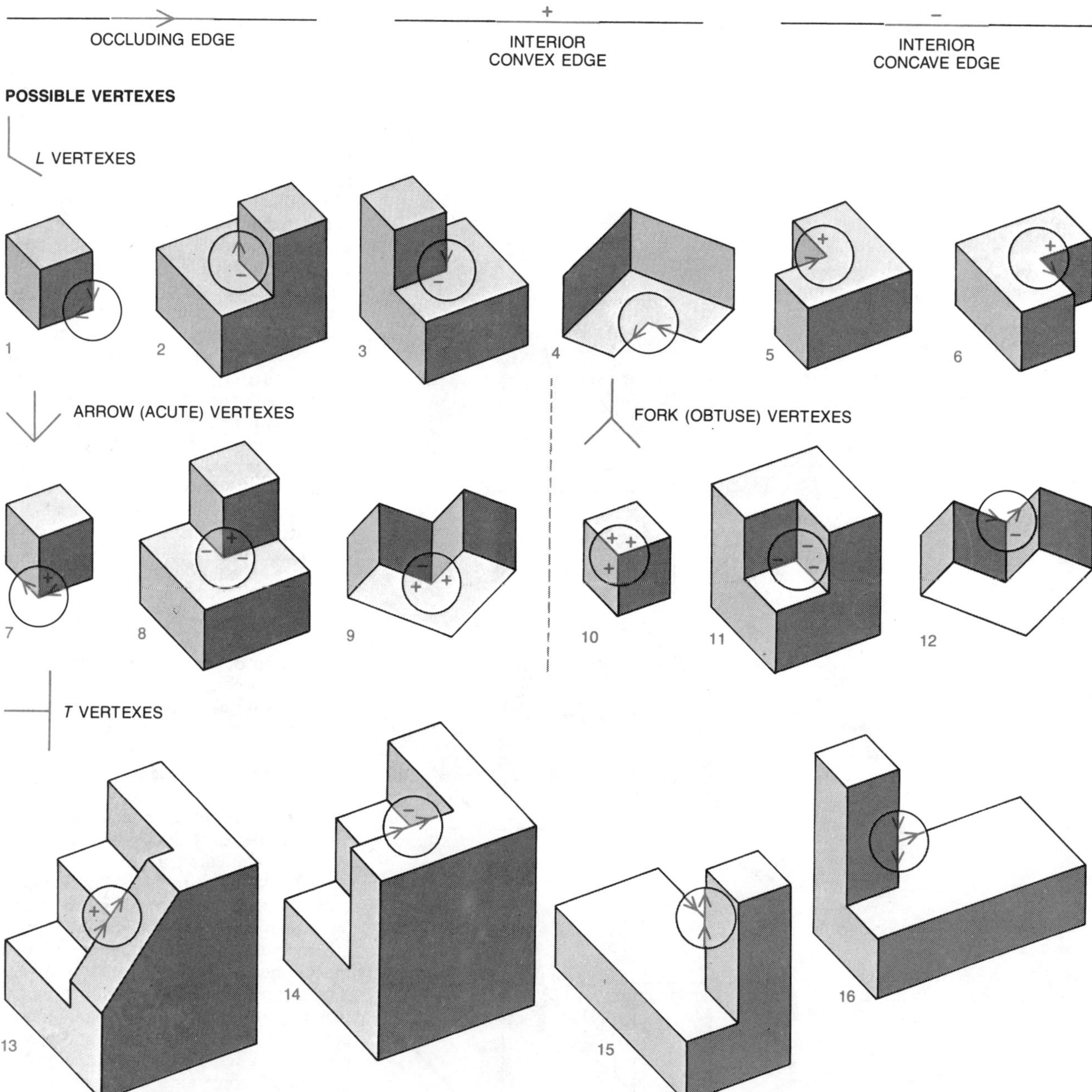

RECOGNITION of a line drawing in two dimensions as a perspective view of a three-dimensional object can be achieved by a computer program that applies a labeling scheme to the vertexes of the drawing. It is assumed that every line segment in the drawing is either an occluding edge of an object in perspective, an edge of the object pointing toward the viewer (a convex edge) or an edge of the object pointing away from the viewer (a concave edge); furthermore, no more than three planes are allowed to meet at any point. An occluding edge is the boundary of an occluding plane, a plane at the exterior of the object or a plane that lies in front of another plane of the object from the viewer's position. By convention an occluding edge is indicated by an arrow, and the occluding plane lies to the right of the edge when it is viewed along the direction of the arrow. There are four categories of vertexes and 16 kinds of vertexes in all; every vertex in the plane figure must be classified as one of the 16 kinds of vertexes before the interpretation of the object as three-dimensional can proceed. The labeling scheme was first proposed by David A. Huffman of M.I.T. and the late Max B. Clowes of the University of Sussex; the scheme was later generalized by the author in order to make possible the recognition of shadows, cracks and other kinds of edges.

called devil's pitchfork, which initially resembles an object but which on closer inspection generates a disconcerting visual paradox. The labeling scheme enables a computer program to rule out the possibility that the drawing represents an object and also helps to dispel the paradox [*see illustration below*].

The first programs for labeling the vertexes of a line drawing ran a serial tree search for consistent labels. Beginning at some arbitrary vertex the programs would assign all possible labels to the vertex. For each label the programs would then proceed to an adjacent vertex and assign all the labels to the second vertex that were consistent with the label chosen for the first vertex. For each consistent label at the second vertex the programs would determine the possible labels for a third vertex adjacent to the second one. The procedure would continue in sequence through all the vertexes until every branch of the tree had been explored. Each branch of the search would end either when no further vertex labeling was possible or when all the vertexes had been labeled consistently. (For some drawings it may happen that consistent labels can be applied to the vertexes in more than one way; such drawings can appear ambiguous to human observers as well.)

Tree-search methods are adequate when the number of vertex labelings is small, but I wanted my program to distinguish cracks, shadows and other kinds of edge that earlier programs could not correctly interpret. When the additional kinds of edge are distinguishable, however, the number of possible labels for each vertex becomes quite

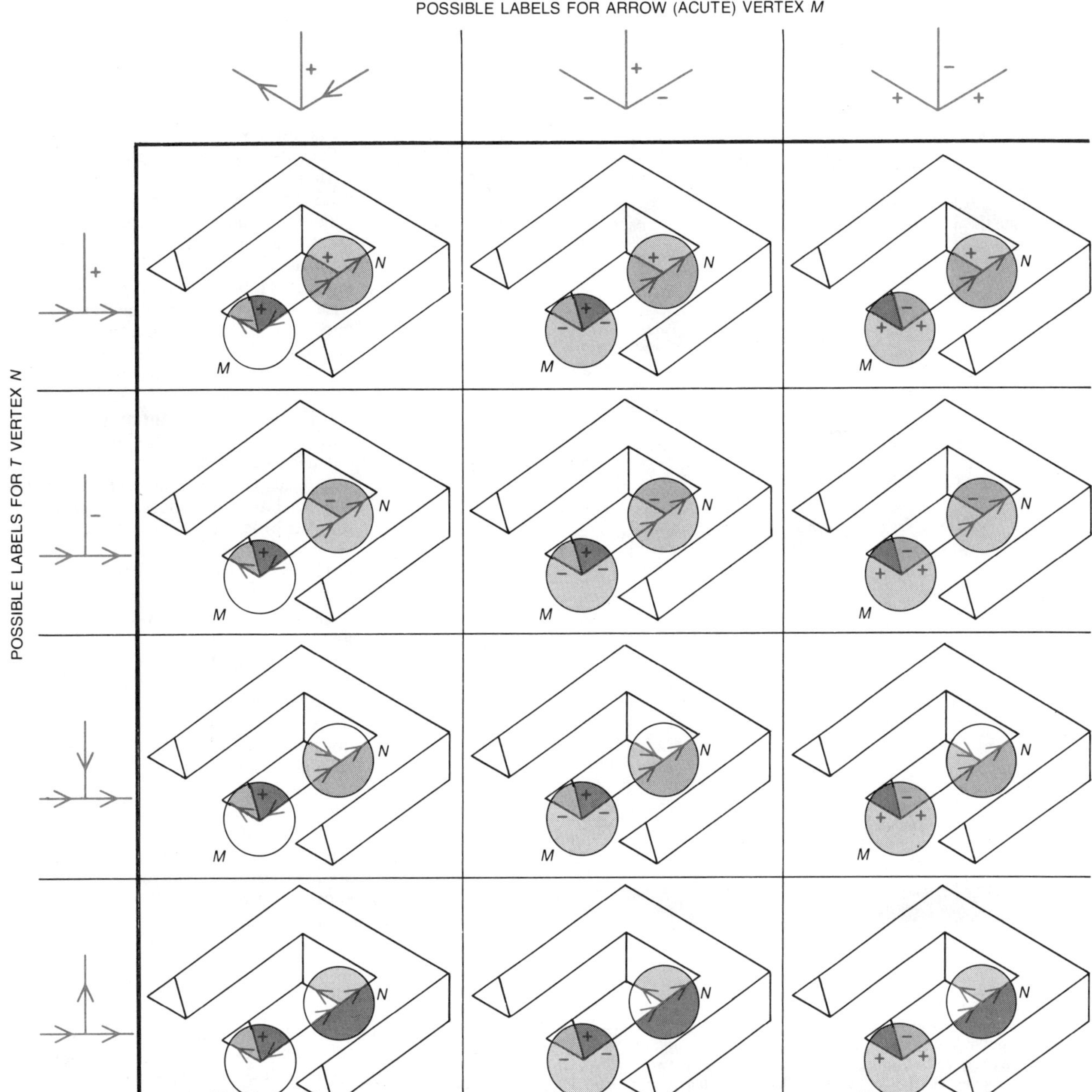

INCONSISTENT LABELING of a line segment, no matter what combination of possible vertex labels is tried, shows that a two-dimensional line drawing cannot be a perspective view of a three-dimensional object. In the drawing of the impossible object called the devil's pitchfork all possible combinations of vertex labels are tried for the ends of the line segment *MN*, but no combination gives the same label to *MN* along its entire length. There are drawings, however, that can be labeled consistently but cannot represent a real object.

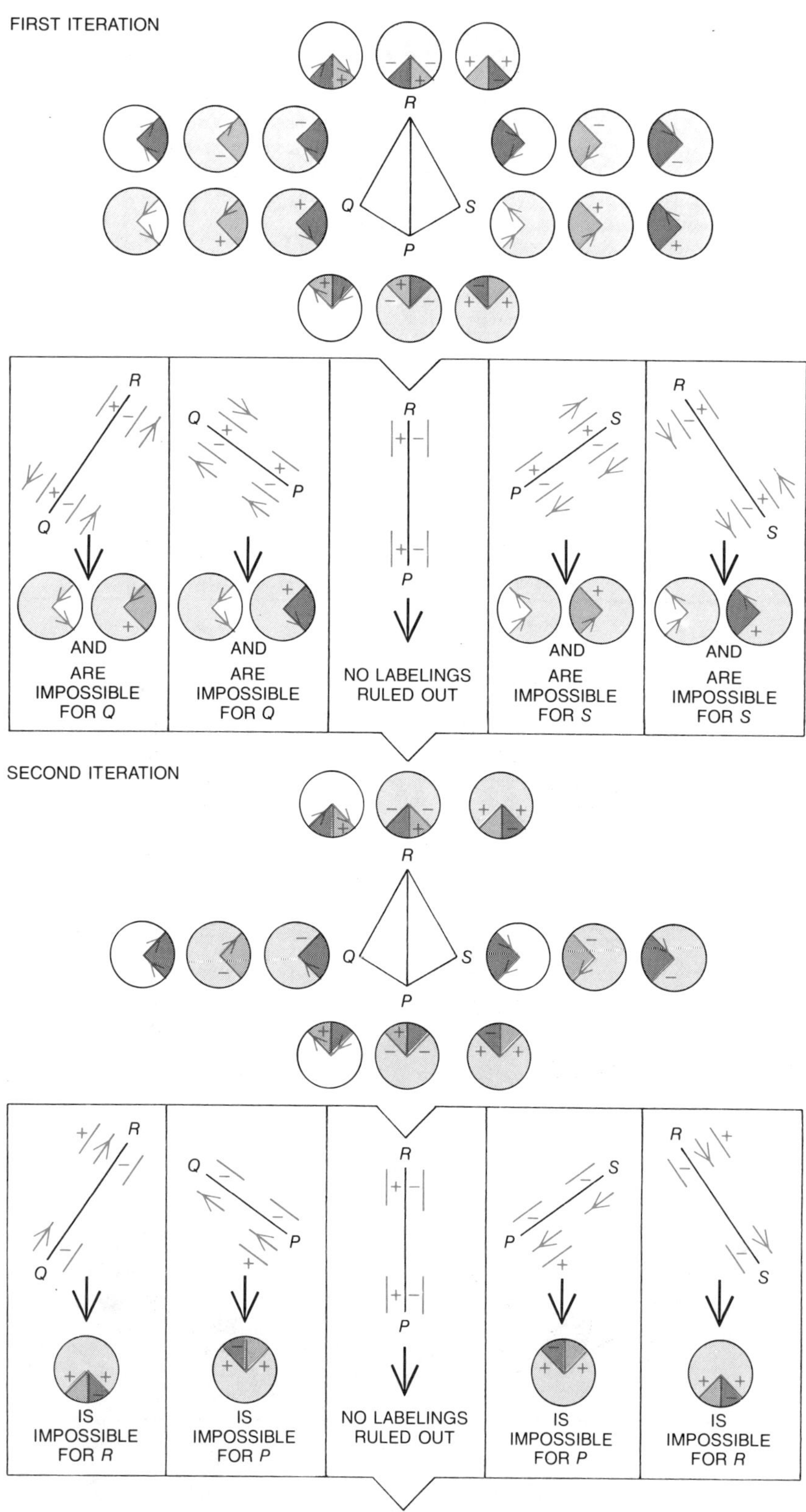

PROPAGATION OF CONSTRAINTS on the labeling of vertexes can be analyzed in parallel, in much the same way as some signals are thought to be processed by the brain. Each vertex is assigned all possible labels, and each possible label is compared with all the possible labels of a vertex at the other end of a line segment connecting the two vertexes. If the line segment cannot be labeled consistently (so that it has the same label at both ends), all the vertex labels leading to the inconsistent labeling are eliminated. The constraints on the labeling of the line segments are given only by the colored symbols; the shading has been added for clarity. Because the process can be done independently for each line segment the segments can all be analyzed simultaneously. Once all the constraints have been determined at each vertex they are combined. The labels that remain are then applied to the vertexes and the procedure is repeated.

large: about 100 for certain kinds of vertex and more than 1,000 for others. For a scene having only four vertexes the number of ways to label the scene can be greater than $1{,}000^4$, or a trillion. Even though a search of the complete tree for such a scene would not have to consider every one of the labeling schemes (if only because many of them would be found to be inconsistent before the last vertex in the scene was examined), the search would still be unmanageable.

I decided, therefore, that my program should eliminate all the impossible labels for each vertex before undertaking a search. The program assigns all the labels that are possible at each vertex. It then examines every pair of vertexes connected by a line. Because of the requirement that the line have a single label some of the labels for the two adjacent vertexes may be eliminated: it may turn out that a label at one vertex is not compatible with any of the labels at the adjacent vertex. Every pairwise examination of labels is independent of every other one, and so the processing in this stage of the program is done in parallel. Once the first round of label eliminations has been completed all the surviving vertex labels are reassigned and pairwise examinations are done in parallel once again. Thus the constraints identified in the first round are propagated to the second and subsequent rounds [*see illustration at left*].

I had originally meant to use the pairwise elimination of labelings simply to cut the tree search down to a manageable size. On the first scene I tried I found that the process reduced the number of labels for each vertex to one. Hence a tree search was unnecessary.

The discovery was a surprise, and indeed I thought there were errors in the program when it first gave unique labelings to scenes. Moreover, if I had not written the program to be run on a computer but instead had attempted the labeling procedure by hand, the dispensability of the tree search would probably not have been discovered. The simplest manual labeling would have called for examining some 10,000 vertex labels; in such a tedious undertaking error is almost inevitable. The possibility of such unexpected findings is seldom appreciated outside the field of computer science, but it is not at all unusual.

Subsequent attempts to apply my program to more realistic scenes have also shown that experiment is an essential aspect of research in artificial intelligence. Although the program turned out to be an elegant and efficient one for the scenes to which it was originally applied, the work has not generalized well to scenes that include curved objects, textures, shiny surfaces and other features of real objects.

The most impressive recent results in computer vision were achieved by the late David C. Marr of M.I.T. Marr modeled the operations of the visual cortex of the brain that may be needed for dealing with scenes in their full complexity. Techniques related to my work, however, have been useful for analyzing electronic circuits, for carrying out stereoscopic correlations of two views of the same scene, for comparing detailed features of a scene with other features nearby and for reducing the ambiguity of certain linguistic phrases.

Language Understanding

The medium for human interaction with computers is often called a language, but programming computers to understand ordinary natural language is one of the most difficult challenges now facing the discipline of artificial intelligence. Even the simplest programs for understanding language are large and complex, and the most powerful programs are still confined to narrow semantic domains in which they attend primarily to the most superficial meanings. Nevertheless, the area is of great importance, not least because a successful program would simulate processes that seem to be close to the essence of human thought.

The earliest work on the understanding of language by computer programs began in the 1950's and was aimed at mechanizing translation. The general approach was to provide a dictionary equivalent for each word in the material to be translated; simple rules were given to reorder the words in the translation and improve its syntax. The effort was a failure. When the sentence "The spirit is willing but the flesh is weak" was translated into Russian and back into English, it is said to have come out as "The vodka is strong but the meat is rotten." Good translation without understanding proved impossible, and by the middle of the 1960's the work had largely been abandoned.

Another early approach to language understanding is a program called ELIZA, written by Joseph Weizenbaum of M.I.T. in 1966. ELIZA bypasses any real linguistic processing and instead relies on a clever system of rather fixed patterns of response that give an imitation of language understanding many people find convincing. The responses of the program mimic those of a psychiatrist; each response is called up from a set of stored sentences or sentence patterns that are associated with words or patterns of words in statements made by a "patient." Whenever the word "mother" is mentioned, for example, the program replies with one of several stock sentences, such as "Tell me more about your mother." If the patient types "I'm feeling a bit tired," ELIZA can embed part of the patient's sentence in its reply: "Why are you feeling a bit tired?"

Although many of the input words are ignored by the program, it still requires a large library of meaning patterns to deal with a large number of potential input statements. Weizenbaum later argued that the program demonstrated the shortcomings of making the simulation of human behavior a criterion for ascribing intelligence to computer programs. ELIZA, he pointed out, operated on an extremely simple and superficial level of language understanding, yet many people were lured by its lifelike responses into reciting their personal problems to the machine just as if it were a psychiatrist.

In about 1970 Roger C. Schank of Yale University introduced programs for processing natural-language sentences about human actions. The programs are based on what Schank calls primitives of conceptual dependency. The primitives include MTRANS, the set of all actions in which there is a transfer of mental information, such as telling, hearing, writing and reading; ATRANS, the set of actions in which there is a transfer of possession, such as buying, selling, giving and taking, and ATTEND, for actions that involve sensing, such as watching, listening, smelling and tasting.

It is possible to represent the meaning of a sentence in a diagram based on conceptual dependencies. It turns out that sentences that are superficially similar but have different meanings have quite different diagrams. Moreover, the diagrams representing the semantic structure of a sentence and a paraphrase of the sentence are similar even though the two sentences may be superficially different. In addition the conceptual dependencies organize the "expectations" a program has after analyzing part of a sentence. For example, after the sentence fragment "John gave" the program expects the sentence to name a recipient of the action as well as an object that was given. The program sets up slots, or blank spaces, in its provisional understanding of the sentence to hold the expected items.

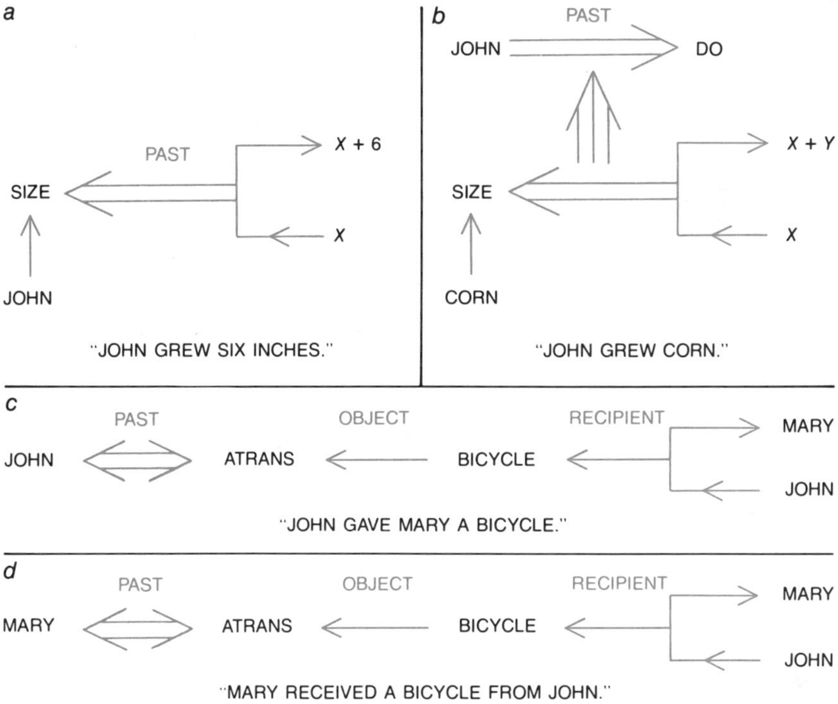

Frames and Scripts

Schank's work was part of a long-term trend toward the view that language understanding is a "top down" process, in which words serve as cues for retrieving expectations from memory and as evi-

DIAGRAMS OF CONCEPTUAL DEPENDENCY represent the semantic structure of a sentence in such a way that sentences that are superficially similar but have different meanings are represented differently (*a, b*). Sentences similar in meaning but superficially different in structure are represented in similar ways (*c, d*). The diagrams show that the sentence "John grew six inches" corresponds roughly to "John's size went from some value X inches to some value $X + 6$ inches" (*a*), whereas the sentence "John grew corn" corresponds roughly to "John did something unspecified that caused the size of the corn to increase from some size X to some size greater than X by the amount Y" (*b*). The sentence "John gave Mary a bicycle" corresponds roughly to "John transferred possession of the bicycle from himself to Mary" (*c*). (ATRANS is a class of verbs that have to do with the transfer of possession.) The sentence "Mary received a bicycle from John" is given a similar representation (*d*), except that Mary is listed as the agent who caused the transfer. The system was developed by Roger C. Schank of Yale University.

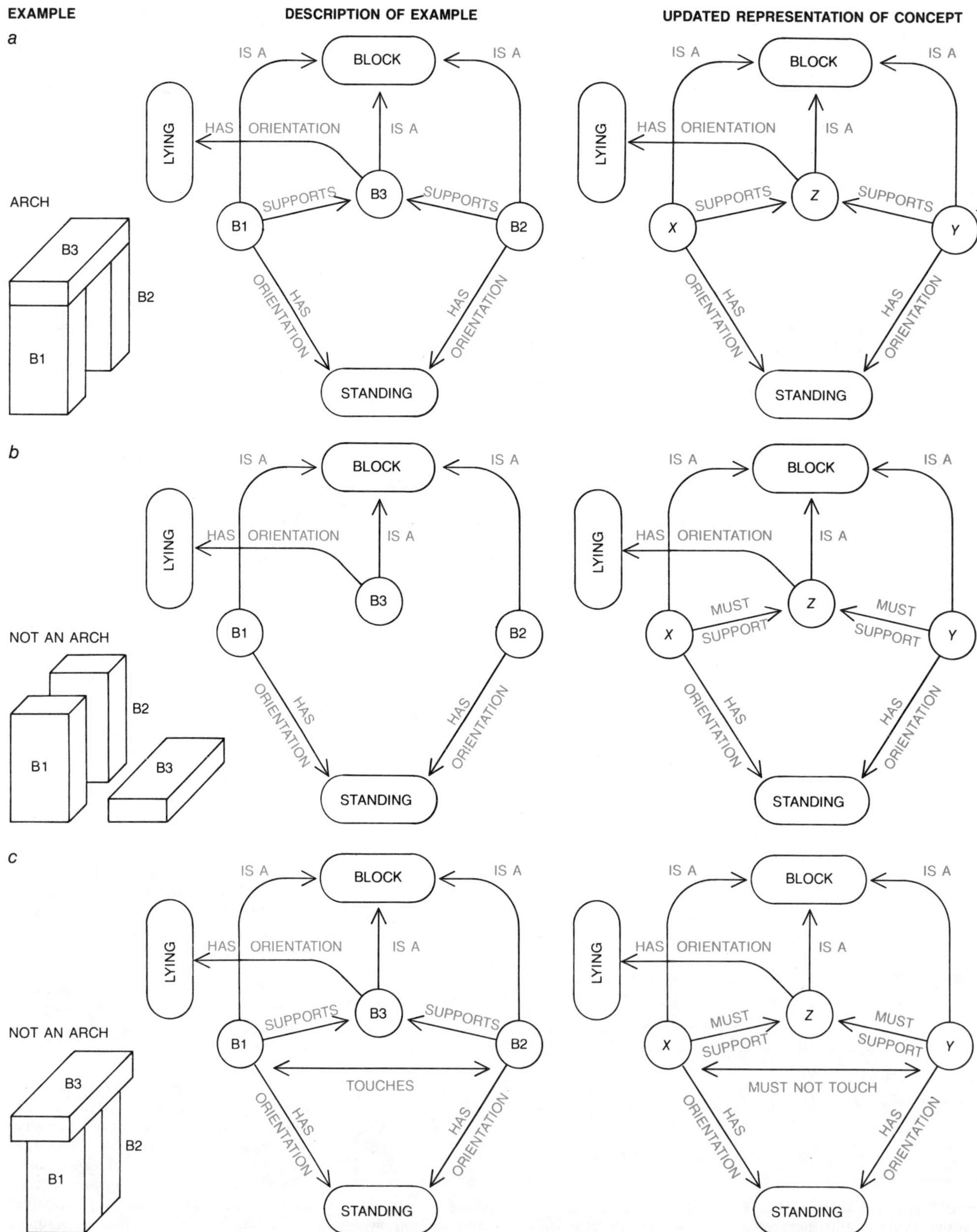

LEARNING A CONCEPT can be understood as the formulation of a hypothesis about the aspects of the concept that are embodied by a particular example and the revision of the hypothesis to accommodate information gained from further examples. To teach a computer program the concept of an arch the teacher presents the program with a picture of what he wants to call an arch (*a*). The program describes the picture by means of a semantic net, or a network of relations among the concepts that are already incorporated into the program. The first hypothesis is a generalized semantic net in which variables are substituted for the particular components of the picture. The teacher then presents the program with additional pictures that are not arches (*b, c*). The program combines a description of each image with the information that it does not represent an arch and thereby revises its original hypothesis. The sequence of examples must be chosen carefully; an example that differs in too many ways from the preceding one will "confuse" the program. It will not be able to discern which aspects of the examples are important and which are incidental. The program was developed by Patrick H. Winston of M.I.T.

dence for or against established expectations. The view is in contrast to an earlier one in which meaning was to be constructed "from the bottom up," that is, from the definitions of words to their meaning in phrases and finally to their likely function in a sentence.

In 1974 Marvin L. Minsky of M.I.T. suggested that not just language but all thinking might depend heavily on processes driven by expected structures of knowledge he called frames. A frame, like a primitive of conceptual dependency, is made up of a core and a set of slots. Each slot corresponds to some aspect of or participant in a concept implicitly defined by the frame. Minsky argued that an important function of a frame is to represent a stereotype. The stereotype is an intuitively plausible model of the process by which people fill in information about a situation that is not explicitly mentioned.

A number of language-understanding programs now exploit this general strategy. For example, a program written by Wendy G. Lehnert of Yale can answer questions about stories such as the following:

John took the bus from New Haven to New York. On the way his pocket was picked. He went to a restaurant and ordered spaghetti. John could not pay the bill and so he washed dishes.

Although the passage states that John merely ordered spaghetti, most people would assume from the story that John also ate the spaghetti. Lehnert's program makes such plausible inferences from a special kind of frame called a script, in which the background expectations most people have about going to restaurants are made explicitly available to the computer.

A program called FRUMP, developed by Gerald F. DeJong II of Yale, can summarize news stories as they appear on the wire service of United Press International. The program includes scripts for many events such as earthquakes, automobile accidents and diplomatic visits. DeJong, who is now at the University of Illinois at Urbana-Champaign, is making additions to the program that will enable it to write its own scripts. The program might be given the text fragment "Mary wanted a new radio; she went to the bank." The program would consult its script for obtaining new objects and its script for going to banks, looking for information that would relate the two parts of the sentence. The program would note that new radios cost money and that people go to banks to withdraw money, and so it would "reason" that Mary probably went to the bank to get the money to buy the radio. Similarly, if the program knew nothing about kidnapping, it could develop a plan to figure out why someone would steal a person. Once the analysis was finished and generalized the plan could be added as a kidnapping script.

Many other issues in language understanding have recently come to the fore. Programs have been developed that attempt to model the understanding of metaphor, the understanding of unstated goals and beliefs of the speaker and the appreciation of the emotions and the underlying motivations of characters in stories. Other programs are intended to deal with inconsistent information and to judge the plausibility of sentences.

The judgment of plausibility is often central to the understanding of ordinary language. Before a program can understand metaphors, humor, lies or exaggerations it has to recognize that the literal meaning of the sentence is implausible for the given situation. Sentences can fail to be plausible for a variety of reasons. For example, the object of the verb may be inappropriate for its action, as in "John ate up the compliments," or a sentence may posit physically implausible events, as in "Mary jumped 10 feet when she heard the news." I regard work on plausibility judgment as an early step toward modeling common sense.

Common Sense

Probably the most telling criticism of current work in artificial intelligence is that it has not yet been successful in modeling what is called common sense. One difficulty in simulating common sense is that a program must link perception, reasoning and action simultaneously, because ultimately the intelligent use of a concept depends on all three domains. The best current programs for language understanding literally do not know what they are talking about; their only contact with the world is through language.

The greatest successes in artificial intelligence have come about where it has been possible to identify narrow, self-contained domains such as the blocks world of SHRDLU. In my opinion, however, experience has shown that such programs cannot simply be enlarged and generalized in a straightforward way. Much conflicting and incompatible knowledge, real scenes and unrestricted processing of language will probably not yield to the engineering techniques that have been applied so far.

This observation does not mean that engineering methods will not be extremely useful in uncovering general principles of intelligence. Nevertheless, substantially better models of human cognition must be developed before systems can be designed that will carry out even simplified versions of commonsense tasks. I expect the development of such models to keep me and many others fascinated for a long time.

9

Multilingual Word Processing

by Joseph D. Becker
July 1984

The advantages of computerized typing and editing are now being extended to all the living languages of the world. Even a complex script such as Japanese or Arabic can be processed

The personal computer has become a familiar fixture in the office and even in the home. It is useful in many ways, and yet for all its novel applications it is probably most useful to the greatest number of people when it serves the function of a typewriter. In that role it enables the user to see text displayed on a screen, so that words can be reviewed and revised before they are ever committed to paper. The kind of computer program underlying such an ability is known as word-processing software.

So far computers have largely been limited to the processing of words in the English language. That is not surprising: most computers have been developed in English-speaking countries, and English is the principal language of international commerce. Yet there is no technical reason for word processing to be confined to English. Indeed, it is possible for word-processing software to handle not only French, German, Italian, Russian, Spanish and other European languages but also more complex scripts such as Arabic, Chinese, Hebrew, Japanese and Korean. My colleagues and I at the Xerox Corporation have been developing multilingual word-processing software for a personal computer work station called Star, which is manufactured by Xerox. Our basic idea is that the computer should deal with a universal notion of "text" broad enough to include any of the world's living languages in any combination.

In effect, therefore, the fascinating diversity of mankind's written symbols must be made to coexist in the computer. At first it hardly seems possible. Arabic script, for example, flows from right to left in curlicues. Thai and other scripts, originally from ancient India, have letters that sometimes step around their neighbors and thus get out of phonetic order. Occasionally a letter even surrounds its neighbors. Korean groups its letters in syllabic clusters. (The Korean alphabet was designed from scratch by a group of scholars in 1443.) Chinese, the most ancient of living writing systems, consists of tens of thousands of ideographic characters. Each character is a miniature calligraphic composition inside its own square frame. It seems the developers of the computer and of word-processing software were coddled by the English language, which happens to have the simplest writing system of all: unadorned alphabetic letters laid out one after the other.

How can computer software originally designed to handle only English text be broadened to encompass the full diversity of the world's writing systems? The many challenges of the task can be divided into three basic realms. There must be a way for text to be represented in the memory of a computer; there must be a way for text to be typed at the keyboard of the computer; there must be a way for the computer to present text to the typist. I shall refer to these realms as encoding, typing and rendering. By rendering I mean both the display of text on the screen of a computer and the printing of text on paper.

Encoding is governed by a single, basic fact: the computer can store only numbers. Indeed, it can store only binary numbers, consisting of strings of 0's and 1's. Hence text is represented in a computer by storing a binary code number for each letter. In the case of the English language the American Standard Code for Information Interchange, abbreviated ASCII, assigns the binary code number 01000001 to the letter *A*, 01000010 to *B*, 01000011 to *C* and so on. Thus when you type an *A* on a computer keyboard, the computer is really being instructed to store the code number 01000001. When the computer comes to display or print a letter encoded as 01000001, its instructions cause it to draw a symbol you recognize as an *A*. As long as the input and output instructions are consistent, you have the illusion that the letter *A* itself was stored.

Computers generally store information in units of bytes, where each byte is a group of eight bits. It therefore seems a sensible strategy to store text as one byte per character. The trouble is, there are only 2^8, or 256, ways in which eight 0's and 1's can be combined in a byte. The living scripts of the world have far more letters than that. A two-byte coding scheme, in which each letter would be identified by two successive bytes, would yield 2^{16}, or 65,536, possible codes; a three-byte scheme would yield 2^{24}, or well over 16 million, codes. But employing two or three bytes per letter where only one byte is needed would waste space in the computer's memory. The answer is to arrange for the encoding to expand to two or three bytes per letter only when necessary. This can be done by setting aside a few bytes as signals to the computer and putting those signals into encoded text.

The first step in establishing a scheme for multilingual text encoding is to assign a binary code number to each of the alphabets of the world. The Roman alphabet is assigned 00000000, Greek 00100110, Russian 00100111, Arabic 11100000 and so on. (The particular choices, like the choices for individual letters, are based on international standards.) Next the code 11111111 is designated the shift-alphabet signal. The

MULTILINGUAL TEXT occupies much of this "screen dump," which shows the content of the display screen of a computer. At the upper right is a "virtual keyboard." It establishes that the Arabic alphabet has been assigned to the standard keyboard attached to the computer. Pressing the *g* key, for example, stores the Arabic letter *lam*. Below the virtual keyboard is a document in Arabic and English. The former reads from right to left, the latter from left to right; the computer enables the typist to embed one language in the other while preserving the directionality of each script. Below the bilingual text is a set of "icons" that represent facilities such as printers. The left is occupied by a document that shows symbols available to the typist.

computer is to start by assuming the text is in alphabet 00000000—that is, in Roman script—but whenever it encounters 11111111, it is to interpret the next byte as the code specifying a new alphabet and the succeeding bytes as codes for letters in that alphabet [*see top illustration on page 90*].

That solves the text-encoding problem for the world's phonetic alphabets. The Chinese ideographs remain: they push the total number of letters above the 65,536 the scheme can encompass. To accommodate all the ideographs one must create another level in the encoding hierarchy. One can consider a group of 65,536 letters to be a "superalphabet" and specify two bytes of 11111111 in succession to be a shift-superalphabet signal. The signal causes the computer to interpret the following byte as the code number of a new superalphabet and succeeding pairs of bytes as codes specifying symbols in that superalphabet. The main superalphabet, designated 00000000, is all one needs except for very rare Chinese characters.

This strategy of "flexible encoding," which was devised by Gael Curry of Xerox's Office Systems Division, opens the computer to a range of more than 16 million characters, including all Chinese ideographs. At the same time it optimizes the storage of text by encoding ordinary (that is, phonetic) alphabets with a single byte per letter. It allows text in any mixture of living languages to be represented economically in the computer as a sequence of bytes.

The sequence of bytes is stored in the linear order in which the text would be spoken, and as such it is isolated from graphical complexities such as the variant forms of letters and the mixing of the directions in which multilingual text might have to be written. This accounts for a fact that may seem surprising: the internal computer processing of multilingual text is not affected by the presence of exotic scripts. Word-processing operations such as the editing of text, the search of text for particular characters or words and the electronic transmission of text depend not on the graphical form of the text but on the internal sequence of bytes that represents its information content. The only real complexities in multilingual word-processing software involve the typing and rendering of text.

I turn next to typing. For most languages the process can be quite simple, since almost any living alphabet will fit comfortably on a standard typewriter keyboard. Indeed, in computerized typing it is easy for the software to change the computer's "interpretation" of the keys so that the typing is in another alphabet. For example, pressing the *A* key can cause the computer to store the Russian letter Ф or the Arabic letter ش, depending on the keyboard interpretation. The computer can even display on its screen a small diagram called a virtual keyboard, which reminds the typ-

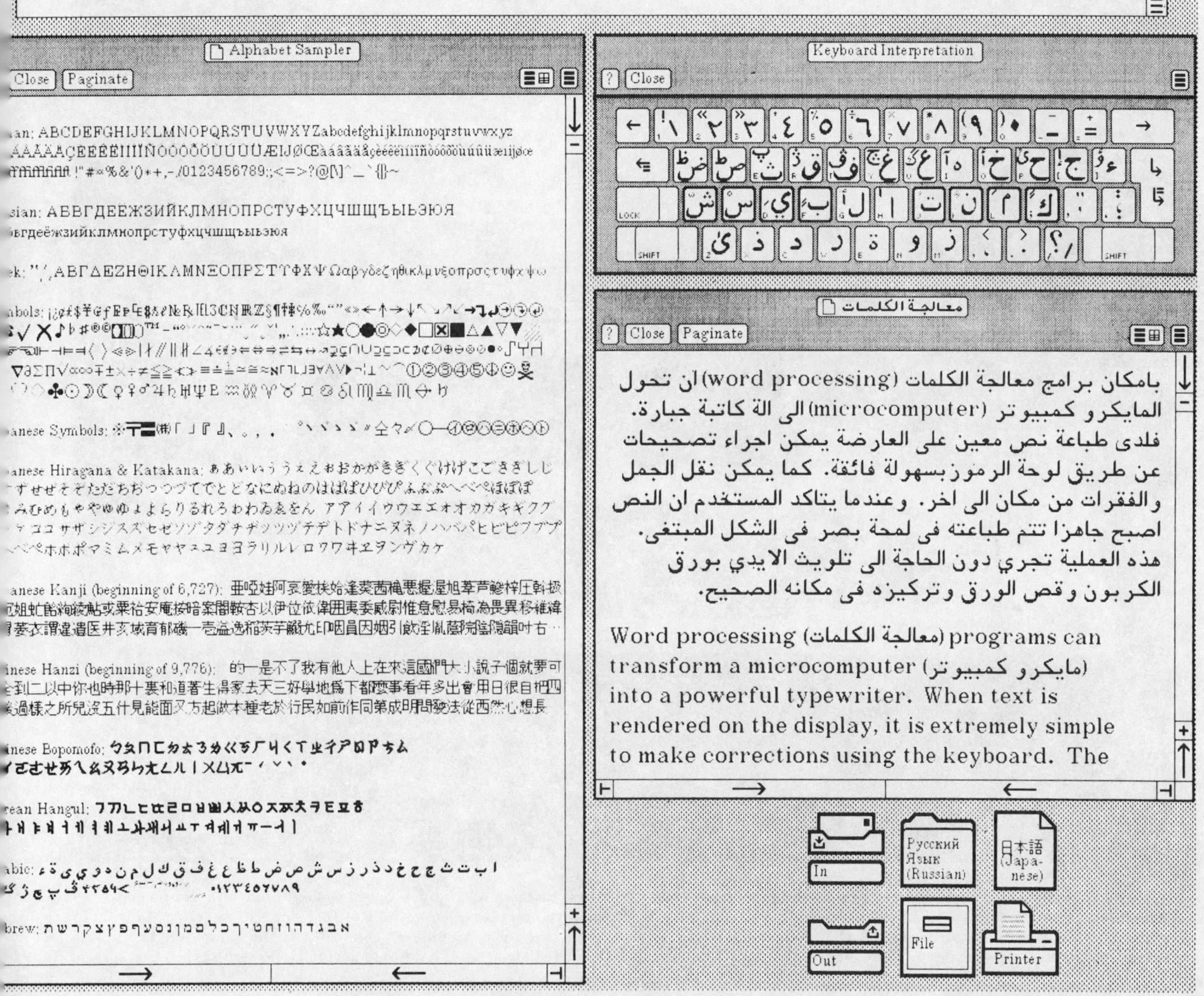

ist what alphabet is currently assigned to the keyboard and which keys correspond to which letters.

For some languages the computer can simplify typing itself. Arabic script, for example, includes a special combination character that replaces the letters *lam* and *alif* whenever the two appear in sequence. On an Arabic typewriter the special character occupies its own key. The computer can automatically render all *lam-alif* combinations as the special character, making the extra key superfluous. The computer can also handle letters that change their appearance depending on their context. With word-processing software for such a script the typist need only enter a natural (that is, phonetic) sequence of characters; the computer will take over the burden of handling the complexities of the script.

There is one living script whose complexity challenges even a computer's capabilities. It is the ideographic system employed in writing Chinese, Japanese and occasionally Korean. The Chinese ideographic characters, which can conveniently be called by the Japanese term *kanji*, originated as pictographs more than 4,000 years ago and assumed their

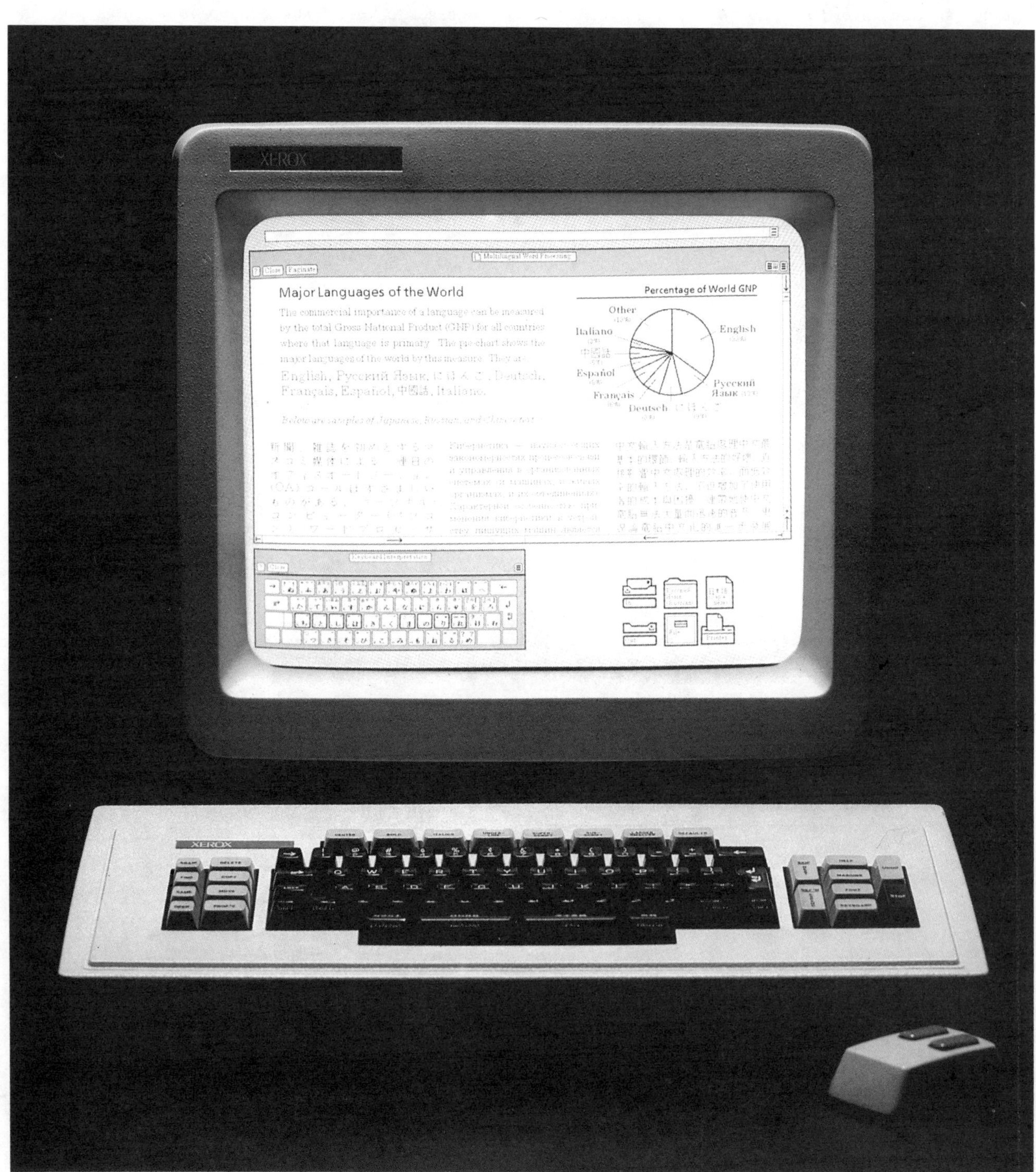

COMPUTER WORK STATION includes the screen whose content was shown in the illustration on the preceding page. The computer itself is part of a computer system called Star manufactured by the Xerox Corporation. The space bar on its keyboard is actually four space bars. In Japanese word processing they specify three Japanese "alphabets" (*katakana*, *hiragana* and *kanji*) or English letters. In front of the keyboard is a "mouse" connected to the computer. The mouse is moved about on a desktop to position a pointer on the video screen.

present form some 2,000 years later. About 500 years after that the Japanese and the Koreans adopted the Chinese language for official and scholarly discourse. For writing the native language they devised phonetic letters: the *kana* (*hiragana* and *katakana*) characters in Japan and the *hangul* in Korea. The Chinese characters were unsuitable from the beginning for writing the native language; now they were also unnecessary. Nevertheless, the prestige of Chinese culture led to hybrid scripts. Today the phonetic alphabets in Japan and Korea are used mainly to write the inflectional endings of words (endings somewhat similar to English inflections such as *-ed* and *-ing*). *Kanji* are used to write word roots, that is, the basic dictionary form of words. In Japan the number of *kanji* commonly seen in published text is declining: it has been cut to about 3,500, about half the number commonly seen in China.

As a result of its curious history the Japanese language has the most complex script in the world: it remains a mixture of *kanji* ideographs and *kana* phonetic letters. Because of this complexity, the Japanese have had no reasonable way to type their own language; more than 90 percent of all documents in Japan are handwritten, or rather handcrafted. A slip of the writer's hand, and a page must be torn up. Moreover, most documents are hard to read unless the writer happens to be an accomplished calligrapher. To be sure, there does exist a *kanji* typewriter, rather like a small typesetting machine, but the device is slow and tiring to use. Professional typists are comparatively rare, and their productivity is typically about 20 characters per minute, or only 10 pages per day.

Hisao Yamada of the University of Tokyo, a scholar of the social history of typing, notes that it is not easy for a society to envision a usable typing system where none has existed. In the U.S. the possibility of high-speed typing never occurred to the inventor of the typewriter; touch-typing (with all 10 fingers potentially in contact with the keyboard) was not devised until 14 years after the typewriter was patented. In Asia the situation is much the same. The initial methods for entering *kanji* into a computer were not well conceived. Some methods employ a keyboard with several hundred keys, where each key has several characters on it. The right hand presses such a key while the left hand manipulates a bank of shift keys to specify a particular character. Other methods require the typist to analyze each *kanji* character and then enter some sequence of code symbols. This turns out to be even more tiresome than searching among hundreds of keys.

In recent years a new *kanji* typing

WORLD'S LIVING LANGUAGES raise problems for multilingual word processing. Mongolian (*a*) is in vertical columns. The specimen reads: *Erte togha tomshi ugei, nogchigsen galab-un urida anu,* or "Once upon a time, countless past ages ago. . . ." Arabic (*b*) is written from right to left in descending curlicues. The specimen reads: *najmu-l-fajri,* or "star of dawn." Hebrew (*c*) is written from right to left in letters that carry markings. The word is *ba'asher,* or "where." Greek (*d*) includes a letter, *sigma* (*colored arrows*), that has a special form at the end of a word. Here the word is *aschimos,* or "ugly." Arabic scripts (*e*) require the combining of certain letters. The word is *al-islam,* or "Islam." Hindi (*f*) has letters written out of phonetic order. The word is *hindî;* the spelling, in effect, is *ihndî.* Thai (*g*) has vowels surrounding consonants. The word is *deuan,* or "month"; the letter *eua* is in three parts. Korean (*h*) is characterized by syllabic clusters. The specimen reads: *han-gug-ŏ,* or "Korean language." Chinese (*i*) is written with thousands of ideographs. The specimens both read: *zhong-guo-hua,* or "Chinese language."

a				
CODE NUMBERS	01000001	01000010	01000011	01000100
MEANING TO COMPUTER	A	B	C	D

b						
CODE NUMBERS	11111111	00100111	00100001	00100010	00100011	00100100
MEANING TO COMPUTER	SHIFT ALPHABET	RUSSIAN ALPHABET	А	Б	В	Г

c						
CODE NUMBERS	11111111	11111111	00000000	01000110 01111100	01001011 01011100	00111000 01101100
MEANING TO COMPUTER	SHIFT ALPHABET	SHIFT SUPER-ALPHABET	MAIN SUPER-ALPHABET	日	本	語

FLEXIBLE ENCODING accommodates all the world's writing systems while minimizing the length of the string of bits, or binary digits (0's and 1's), that represents a multilingual text in the memory of a computer. For English (*a*) a standard scheme, the American Standard Code for Information Interchange, is available. It assigns one byte, or eight bits of code, to each character. For other languages, such as Russian (*b*), the byte 11111111 is designated a "shift alphabet" signal: it instructs the computer to interpret the following byte as the code specifying a new alphabet, and the bytes after that as codes specifying characters in that alphabet. For Chinese and Japanese (*c*) a still more complex scheme is required. Two successive bytes of 11111111 are a "shift superalphabet" signal, the following byte specifies a particular superalphabet and the subsequent bytes, taken in pairs, specify characters in the superalphabet (here ideographs).

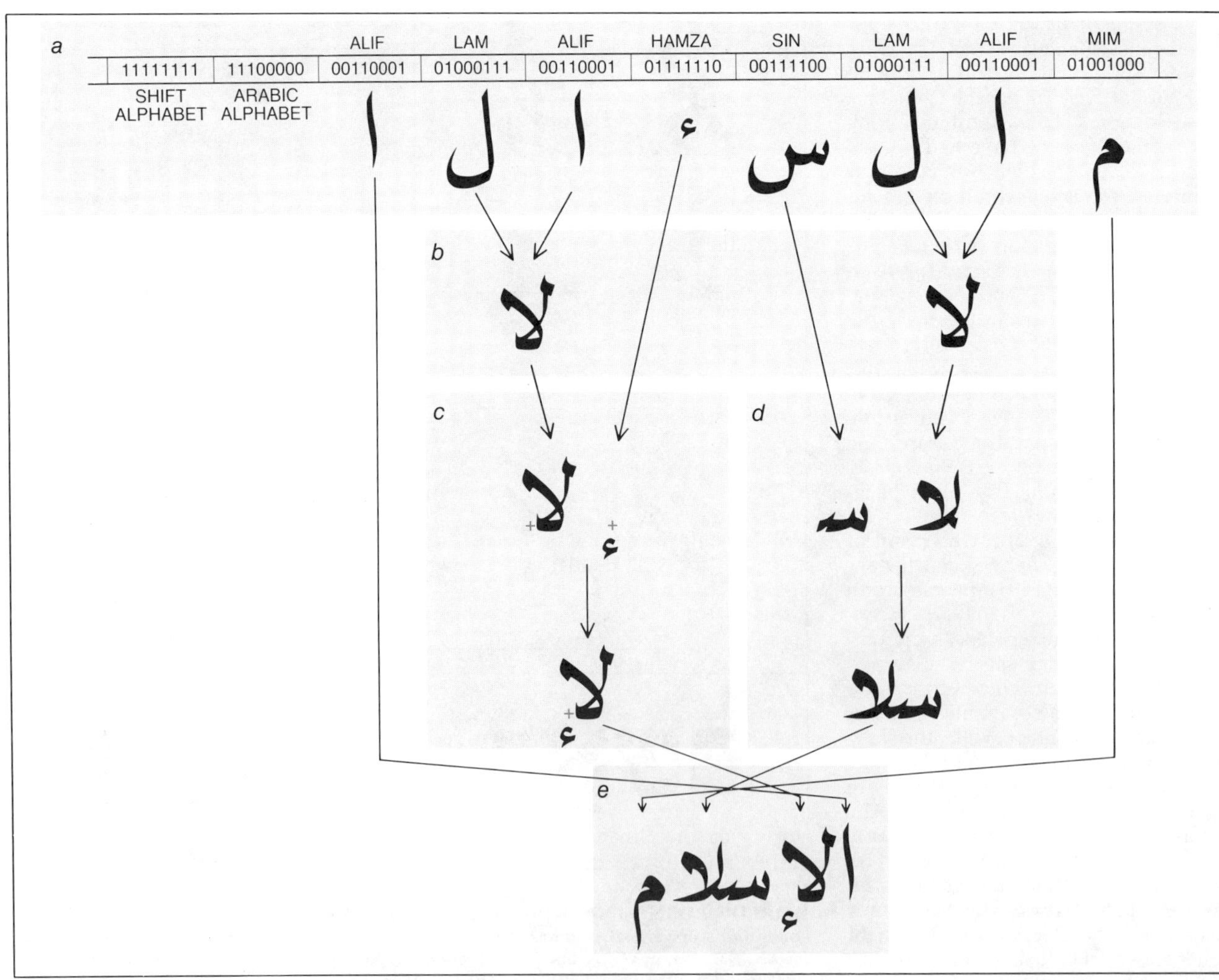

RENDERING OF TEXT means the process of displaying text on a screen or printing it on a page. The rendering of the Arabic word *al-islam* suggests some of the complexities. In storage in the computer's memory the word is simply a sequence of eight letters (*a*). Their proper rendering requires some special computations. First the computer finds two instances in which *lam* and *alif* are neighbors; Arabic script requires that this combination be replaced by a single ligature that looks much like the Greek letter *gamma* (*b*). The computer "notes" this in temporary memory; the stored code for the original text is unchanged. Next the computer searches for small markings such as *hamza,* which have to be positioned above or below other letters. The small crosses in the illustration are registration marks (*c*). Third the computer searches for letters that must be joined to their neighbors. The *sin* and its neighboring *lam-alif* ligature will join, and so they are given special joining forms (*d*). Finally, the computer displays the word or prints it on paper, in proper right-to-left order (*e*).

method has emerged; it suits the average typist so well that it is fast becoming the standard for Japanese manufacturers. Indeed, it makes possible touch-typing at a rate of about 50 characters per minute for the average typist and 150 characters per minute for the best speed typists. Called phonetic conversion, it has three steps that enable the Japanese to type their language phonetically. The typist types a word in phonetic *hiragana* symbols. (This phonetic spelling is learned in childhood by the Japanese.) To change the spelling to *kanji* the typist presses a special "look-up key" and the computer finds the *kanji* spelling in a dictionary it holds on a magnetic storage disk. If several words share the same phonetic spelling or if the word has several *kanji* spellings (this happens about 40 percent of the time), the computer assigns each alternative to a key on a virtual keyboard, and the typist chooses the one wanted.

Phonetic-conversion typing employs a standard typewriter keyboard. The *hiragana* characters fit neatly on such a keyboard; in fact, there is a standard arrangement for them. Yet many Japanese are familiar with the English typewriter keyboard and do not want to have to learn another arrangement. In consideration of their preferences many phonetic-conversion systems offer a *hiragana* typing method called *romaji* conversion. *Romaji* signifies the use of Roman letters to spell Japanese words. *Fuji, sayonara, samurai* and a host of other words are *romaji* spellings well known to Westerners. Most Japanese know them too. To type the word *sushi*, therefore, the typist can simply type *s u s h i*. The computer converts this first into *hiragana* すし and then into *kanji* 寿司. Offered a choice between typing *hiragana* on a standard Japanese keyboard and typing *romaji* on an English keyboard, nine out of 10 Japanese users prefer the latter.

The second step in phonetic-conversion typing—the computer's search in a dictionary—is greatly complicated by the inflectional endings of the Japanese language, which are somewhat similar to those of a European language. (For example, *aruku* means "walk," *aruita* means "walked" and *aruite* means "walking.") The dictionary may contain well over 100,000 word roots. The inflected forms of those words would number in the millions. Plainly the computer cannot store them all. The problem is solved by software that draws on a grammar of Japanese inflections to analyze the phonetic spellings supplied by the typist [*see illustrations on pages 92–94*]. In essence the typewriter is made to know the complete grammar of the language typed on it.

The chief advantage of phonetic-conversion typing is that the typing is analyzed by the computer word by word rather than one *kanji* at a time. Consider the nature of *kanji*. Although each *kanji* character signifies a separate concept, most words in Chinese, Japanese and Korean are compounded from two such concepts (and therefore from two *kanji*), much like English words such as *blackboard* and *railroad*. The compounding allows the creation of far more words than there are *kanji*. In addition it reduces the phonetic ambiguity of the language. For example, a Japanese dictionary lists 64 common *kanji* pronounced *tou* and 53 common *kanji* pronounced *kyou* but only one compound word pronounced *toukyou*, namely 東京, or "Eastern capital," the name of the city Tokyo. In the face of the alternatives each *kanji* in the compound word uniquely determines the other.

Consider, then, the typing of *toukyou*. When 東京 is typed a *kanji* at a time, the typist must somehow pick the desired *tou* from among 64 alternatives and the desired *kyou* from among 53 alternatives. In contrast, phonetic conversion requires merely that the typist enter *t o u k y o u*. The computer will respond with the unique, correct *kanji* pair. The creation of the computer's dictionary bestows on the computer a store of information about *kanji*. This greatly reduces the amount of information the typist must transmit to the computer.

I have treated phonetic-conversion typing in reference to Japanese, the language in which it was first applied, but it is equally effective in Korean and Chinese. For Korean a *hangul* keyboard is likely to be popular; for Chinese the romanized spelling called *pinyin* can serve in the same role as *romaji*. For example, the name of the city Beijing can be typed by simply entering *b e i j i n g*. To be sure, each syllable in Chinese has a particular tonal pattern, and this input does not specify it. Still, that leaves only two dictionary alternatives: 背景, or "background," and 北京, or "Northern capital." It turns out to be far more efficient for a typist to choose among alternatives of this kind than it would be to enter an explicit encoding of the tone for each syllable. Chinese is further complicated by dialects that differ widely in pronunciation, but the standard Mandarin pronunciation is taught worldwide and already is native to 750 million potential typists.

I have described how multilingual text can be typed into a computer and stored in its memory. I turn now to the third aspect of multilingual word processing: the rendering of text that is stored in the computer. For word processing in the English language there is a simple one-to-one correspondence between code numbers in computer storage and rendered characters on a display screen or a printed page. In fully multilingual software, however, that correspondence must be abandoned and replaced by a much richer scheme. When the computer processes a sequence of text codes for rendering, it must be empowered to examine any number of consecutive codes at a time, and it must be allowed to make any computation in order to choose the graphical forms and positions for the characters. In particular, the computer must be provided with variant character forms that it can use to represent the changeable letter shapes characteristic of many writing systems.

An example of the application of these ideas is provided by the handling of the Greek letter *sigma* (σ), which takes on a special shape (ς) when it appears at the end of a word. In the computer every *sigma* is stored as the code for an ordinary *sigma*, even if it comes at the end of a word. Whenever the computer is called on to render a *sigma*, however, it examines the character that follows the *sigma*. If the *sigma* is found to be at the end of a word, the computer renders the variant form instead of the ordinary form of the letter.

Arabic offers a more complex example: most Arabic letters have four forms, depending on whether the letter stands alone or is at the beginning, in the middle or at the end of a word. In addition the rules for joining Arabic letters to their neighbors must accommodate the presence of small markings placed above or below the letters. Nevertheless, the solution is much the same: the computer can be instructed to consider each letter's context before choosing its rendered shape. All the contingencies can be taken into account, given that the computer can make any computation in determining the final appearance of the text.

An important element in rendering is the ligature, in which two or more letters fuse to form a single rendered character. In most English typefaces (including the one in which this article has been typeset) there are ligatures for a few common letter combinations, chiefly *ff, ffi, fi, fl* and *ffl*. Software that takes each letter's context into account can instruct the computer to render the word *office* in four characters—*o, ffi, c* and *e*—while retaining in its memory the six-letter sequence *o f f i c e* required to process the word correctly.

A similar approach can be adopted for accents, or diacritical marks, such as the German umlaut (*ü*) or the French accent grave (*è*). The International Organization for Standards requires such marks to be represented in the computer as separate codes preceding the code for the letter to which the mark is applied. Hence a letter such as *ü* is represented by two bytes. The computer can render the two bytes ¨ and *u* as the single character *ü* by the same process that renders the two bytes *f* and *i* as the ligature *fi*. Some scripts require the application of multiple marks above or below a base character; the computer can handle this problem by a somewhat more complex rendering procedure.

Even the unique syllabic clumps that characterize the Korean *hangul* script can be rendered if the computer is given appropriate software and rendering variants of the Korean letters, which it can build into square groupings. Similarly, the slanting descent to a baseline characteristic of many Arabic fonts can be rendered, freeing Arabic typography from the stricture of a flat horizontal baseline. In the Hindi language the word *hindî* itself has the first vowel (*i*) written out of

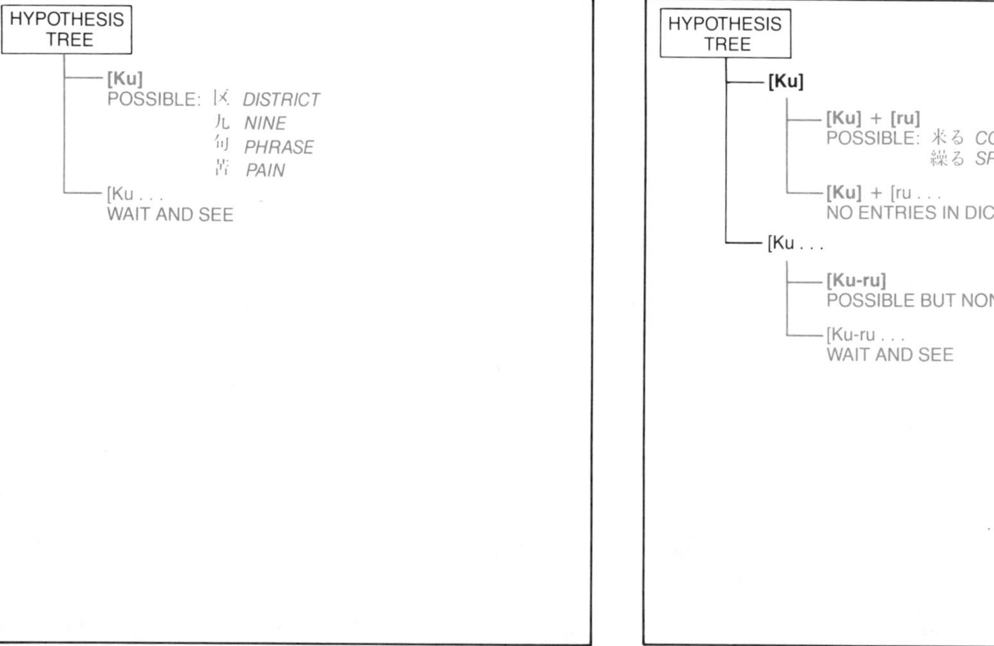

JAPANESE WORD PROCESSING challenges a computer because the Japanese language is a complex mixture of thousands of *kanji* (ideographic symbols borrowed from the Chinese) and dozens of *kana* (indigenous phonetic symbols). Here a typist types *kurumade,* which means "by car." The typing is in *romaji,* that is, it employs a standard English keyboard. Thus the typist begins (*a*) by typing an English *k* and *u*. The computer translates that immediately into a single *kana* character. Meanwhile the computer consults an internal dictionary to find entries consisting entirely of *ku* (*boldface type in square brackets*) and entries beginning with *ku* (*light type with a left bracket*). From the entries it constructs a "hypothesis tree." The processing continues (*b*) as the typist enters the English letters *r* and *u,* completing the second syllable of *kurumade.* Again the computer translates the *romaji* into *kana.* The result is a string of two *kana* characters. Then the computer consults the internal dictionary. The possibilities are more varied. *Kuru* could be a complete word. *Kuru* could be the start of a word. *Ku* could be the root of a word and *ru* could be an inflection, or modification of the root, somewhat like the English *-ed, -ing* and so on. Finally, *ku* could be a root and *ru* could be the start of an inflection. Some of the possibilities are ruled out because the dictionary has no such entries; others remain conceivable. Accordingly the hypothesis tree grows further branches (*color*). The third step in the processing (*c*) occurs when the typist enters the English letters *m* and *a*. The computer now has a string of three *kana,* from which it constructs the corresponding additions to its hypothesis tree. Some of the additions are conceivable but are not preferred. In particular, the root *ku* plus the inflection *ru* could in principle act as an adjective meaning "coming" or "spinning" (in the sense of making thread);

phonetic order: it is placed before the initial consonant (*h*). When the rule for placing the vowel *i* is incorporated into the computer's instructions, however, the typist can enter the word in its normal phonetic order and the computer will automatically place the *i* before the *h* when it renders the word. The same approach can even rationalize the handling of scripts such as Thai, in which vowels can actually split into fragments that surround a neighboring letter.

Equipped with enough flexibility in the rendering process, the computer can handle any instance in which the letters of a script have a contextual effect on one another. The only remaining rendering problem is a broader one:

c

kuruma ⟶ くるま

WORD ROOT DICTIONARY

[Ku-ru-ma]

KANJI	PART OF SPEECH	RELATIVE FREQUENCY	*ENGLISH MEANING*
車	NOUN	8	*CAR*
包ま	VERB STEM	2	*BE WRAPPED*

[Ku-ru-ma . . . MANY ENTRIES IN DICTIONARY

INFLECTION DICTIONARY

[ma]

HIRAGANA	PART OF SPEECH	RELATIVE FREQUENCY
ま	VERB ENDING	9
ま	POLITE VERB ENDING	9

[ma . . . MANY ENTRIES IN DICTIONARY

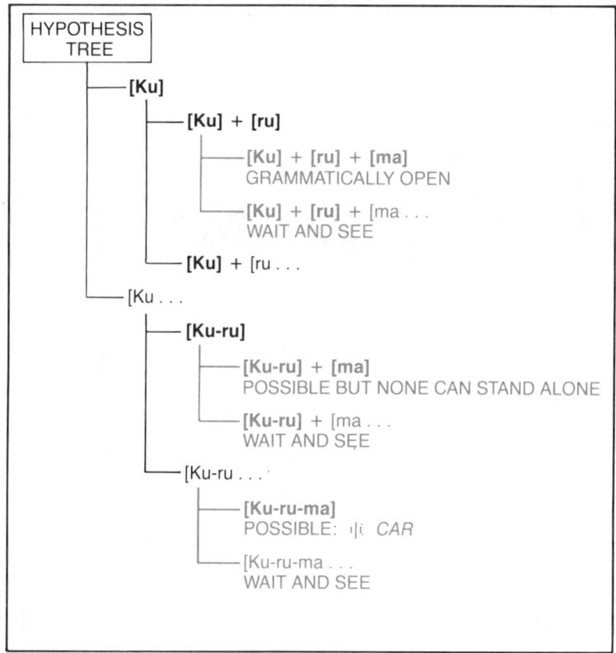

hence it could modify any noun. The computer will revert to this interpretation only if nothing more concrete emerges from further input. The tree is now at its most complex; the typing of further syllables will introduce additional hypotheses, but most of them will be eliminated by linguistic constraints, such as grammatical impossibility. The fourth step in the processing (*d*) occurs when the typist enters the English letters *d* and *e*, which complete the string *kurumade* and supply the computer with a sequence of four *kana*. The computer consults the internal dictionary one last time. The information retrieved from the dictionary constrains the possibilities. The root *ku* followed by the inflections *ru* and *made* is conceivable: it could mean "until coming" or "until spinning." Moreover, the root *kuruma* followed by the inflection *de* is conceivable: it means "by car." The last step in the processing of *kurumade* is shown in the illustration on the next page.

d

kurumade ⟶ くるまで

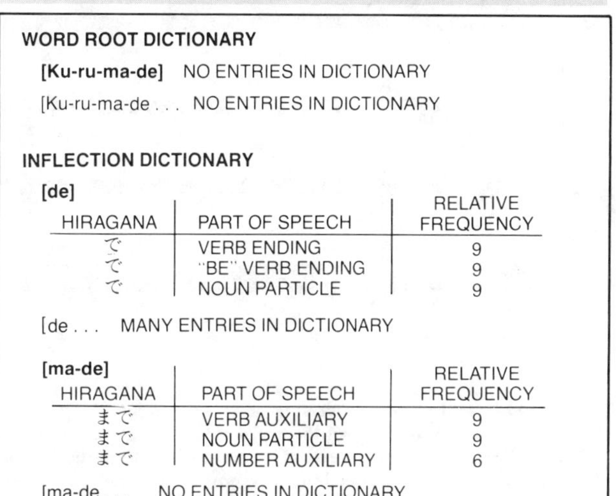

WORD ROOT DICTIONARY

[Ku-ru-ma-de] NO ENTRIES IN DICTIONARY

[Ku-ru-ma-de . . . NO ENTRIES IN DICTIONARY

INFLECTION DICTIONARY

[de]

HIRAGANA	PART OF SPEECH	RELATIVE FREQUENCY
で	VERB ENDING	9
で	"BE" VERB ENDING	9
で	NOUN PARTICLE	9

[de . . . MANY ENTRIES IN DICTIONARY

[ma-de]

HIRAGANA	PART OF SPEECH	RELATIVE FREQUENCY
まで	VERB AUXILIARY	9
まで	NOUN PARTICLE	9
まで	NUMBER AUXILIARY	6

[ma-de . . . NO ENTRIES IN DICTIONARY

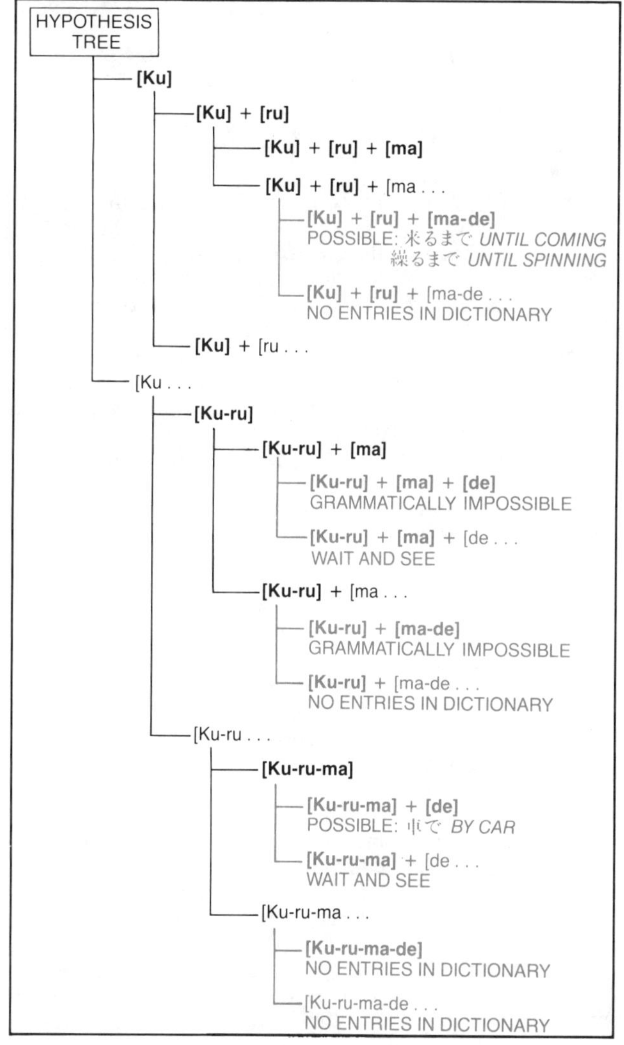

a

くるまで + "LOOKUP"

b

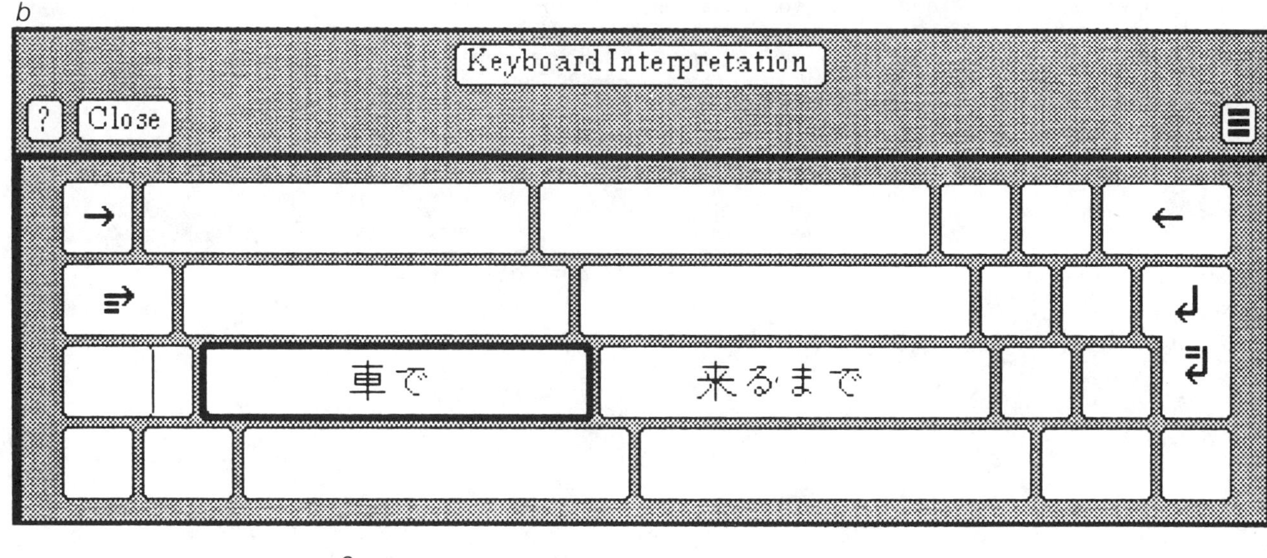

c

車で

FINAL STEP in the word processing of *kurumade* comes after the *romaji* typing of the word, when the typist presses a special "lookup key" (*a*). Inside the computer the dead branches of the hypothesis tree are ruled out. The wait-and-see branches, now superseded, are ruled out. The grammatically unpreferred branches, also superseded, are ruled out. The surviving hypotheses are ordered by the frequency of their appearance in Japanese; then the more likely ones (here the ones that mean "by car" and "until coming") are displayed on a virtual keyboard (*b*). Roots are displayed in *kanji;* inflections remain in *kana*. Extremely unlikely possibilities (here the one that means "until spinning") are not displayed unless the lookup key is pressed again. When the typist chooses an alternative, it replaces the string of four *kana* (*c*).

How is the computer to mix scripts that run in different directions?

A computer cannot do the impossible: there is simply no sensible way to mix vertical text and horizontal text in a single paragraph. Chinese, Japanese and Korean are vertical by tradition. Asian printers, however, have developed the practice of printing these languages horizontally from left to right. Mongolian too is vertical by tradition. Mongolian printers rotate text by 90 degrees when it is necessary to combine it with horizontal text.

In sum, typographical usage calls for all languages to be typeset horizontally at need. The one circumstance that remains for the computer to handle is the mixing of a horizontal left-to-right script such as English with a horizontal right-to-left script such as Arabic. The typist wants to type Arabic in its proper phonetic order and have it appear in its proper right-to-left sequence, even if it is typed into the midst of English text. Conversely, the typist wants an English passage to appear in left-to-right sequence even in the midst of Arabic text.

The problem may seem perplexing, but it looks simpler from the standpoint of the computer. The computer works much faster than the typist; thus the computer spends most of its time waiting for the typist to enter the next character. Between keystrokes the text is simply displayed without change on the screen; the computer has done no more than produce a static text layout. The static arranging of mixed-direction text is handled routinely by printers of books and magazines in which Arabic or Hebrew script appears.

Mixed-direction text can go through remarkable transformations as it is entered into a computer. In most word processors the place on the screen where the next typed letter will appear is indicated by a blinking marker. The marker moves along as the text continues to grow. When a line fills up with type and the marker reaches a margin, the marker automatically drops to the beginning of the next line. For the typing of all-English text the marker moves from left to right. For the typing of all-Arabic text it moves from right to left. For mixed-direction text its activity is novel. Throughout the typing of English text embedded in Arabic the marker must stay put and the newly entered text must slide away from it. The stationary marker cannot, of course, reach a margin. All the same, the filling of a line means that the marker and subsequent words must drop to the next line. The typist has the strange impression that text is falling from the middle of a line. Yet the drop creates the correct layout of the mixed-direction text.

The editing of a mixed-direction text can cause changes that are even more remarkable. Consider the English-Arabic sentence "The words *al-islam* and *al-'arab* mean Islam and the Arabs," where *al-islam* and *al-'arab* are written in Arabic [*see illustration on page* 95]. Suppose in the course of editing the sentence the English word *and* is replaced by the Arabic equivalent; the Arabic words must then switch places, because they are now part of a phrase expressed in Arabic that should read from right to left. Yet the Arabic words themselves were not involved in the editing operation. Indeed, the text in computer storage changes only to accommodate the replacement of the word *and*. The visible permutation of the Arabic words is entirely a consequence of the rendering process.

The encoding, typing and rendering of text are the basic elements of multilingual word processing, but they do not exhaust the challenges that must be faced in designing a multilingual word-processing system. Suppose an oil company's Texas offices are made part of a worldwide network of word-processing

Character	Code
T	01010100
h	01101000
e	01100101
	00100000
w	01110111
o	01101111
r	01110010
d	01100100
s	01110011
	00100000
	11111111
	11100000
ا	00110001
ل	01000111
ا	00110001
ء	01111110
س	00111100
ل	01000111
ا	00110001
م	01001000
	11111111
	00000000
	00100000
a	01100001
n	01101110
d	01100100
	00100000
	11111111
	11100000
ا	00110001
ل	01000111
ع	01000010
ر	00111010
ب	00110010
	11111111
	00000000
	00100000
m	01101101
e	01100101
a	01100001
n	01101110
	00100000
I	01001001
s	01110011
l	01101100
a	01100001
m	01101101

Character	Code
T	01010100
h	01101000
e	01100101
	00100000
w	01110111
o	01101111
r	01110010
d	01100100
s	01110011
	00100000
	11111111
	11100000
ا	00110001
ل	01000111
ا	00110001
ء	01111110
س	00111100
ل	01000111
ا	00110001
م	01001000
	00110000
و	01001011
	00110000
ا	00110001
ل	01000111
ع	01000010
ر	00111010
ب	00110010
	11111111
	00000000
	00100000
m	01101101
e	01100101
a	01100001
n	01101110
	00100000
I	01001001
s	01110011
l	01101100
a	01100001
m	01101101

BILINGUAL TEXT in storage presents no special problems for multilingual word processing. Here the text includes the sentence "The words *al-islam* and *al-'arab* mean Islam and the Arabs," where Arabic words are expressed in Arabic. The sentence is stored in phonetic order (*left*), even though Arabic characters are rendered from right to left whereas English ones are rendered from left to right. Some bytes (*color*) are special codes that shift alphabet and specify a new alphabet. When the sentence is edited (*right*), so that the English word *and* is replaced by its equivalent in Arabic, the only change to the stored text is the removal of the bytes specifying *a, n* and *d,* along with some special shift codes, and the insertion of the code for the Arabic letter *wa.*

computer work stations. An Arabic document arrives electronically from the Middle East, but the computers in Texas do not have the software needed to render Arabic text. The Texas computers must nonetheless handle the text as best they can without "crashing" and without mistaking the Arabic codes for English ones. They must at least render the English portions of a multilingual document. Furthermore, the computers in Texas should be capable of accepting an Arabic-software module, which would add Arabic rendering instructions to the repertory they already have.

The oil company's situation suggests the broad-scale design goals for a multilingual word-processing system. They are compatibility (all the computers in the system must be able to exchange documents in any combination of scripts); open-endedness (each computer must be able to deal sensibly with scripts unknown to it), and modularity (it must be possible to add the capacity for new languages one by one). These goals are difficult, but they can be achieved. The solutions derive in large part from the treatment of text in ways that are broad enough to include any mixture of the world's living languages.

The initial applications of multilingual word processing surely lie in the creation of multilingual documents. After all, as worldwide commerce and politics grow, all kinds of multilingual documents become essential. In addition software that can manipulate multilingual text is certain to bring benefits to language teachers and translators. The automatic translation of documents from one language into another is a far more distant goal. Indeed, at the moment there is little cause to imagine that high-quality machine translation can be achieved. The faithful translation of a passage requires that the translator understand the passage both in its explicit content and in its implications. In a quarter century of intensive research there has been no significant progress in supplying a computer with such an ability. Low-quality translation of texts with circumscribed meaning (such as instruction manuals) is already a reality. Even there, however, the success of machine translation depends heavily on editing by a human proofreader.

The questionable prospects for high-quality machine translation are balanced, I think, by the brilliant outlook for electronic mail: the near-instantaneous transmission of messages or documents by way of private electronic networks or public communication lines. International electronic-mail systems are already in everyday use. They are similar to telephone and postal systems in that their usefulness increases with the extent of the network. It seems inevitable, therefore, that electronic mail services will eventually expand and join to form a single worldwide electronic-mail utility. If this is to come about, one prerequisite is inescapable. The telephone does not require its users to speak only English, nor does a postal system require its users to write only English. Electronic mail will not succeed as a global communication medium unless the text it carries is fully multilingual. To my mind that is the ultimate application for multilingual word processing.

T h e w o r d s ا ل ا ء س ل ا م a n d ا ل ع ر ب m e a n I s l a m a n d t h e ...

T h e w o r d s ا ل ا ء س ل ا م و ا ل ع ر ب m e a n I s l a m a n d t h e ...

The words الإسلام and العرب mean Islam and the Arabs.

The words العرب و الإسلام mean Islam and the Arabs.

RENDERING OF THE STORED TEXT shown in the illustration above yields a remarkable consequence. The change made in the text involves only the English word *and,* as shown at the top of this illustration. Yet in the rendering of the text the words *al-islam* and *al-'arab* must exchange places, because the entire phrase is now rendered in Arabic script, which must be read from right to left.

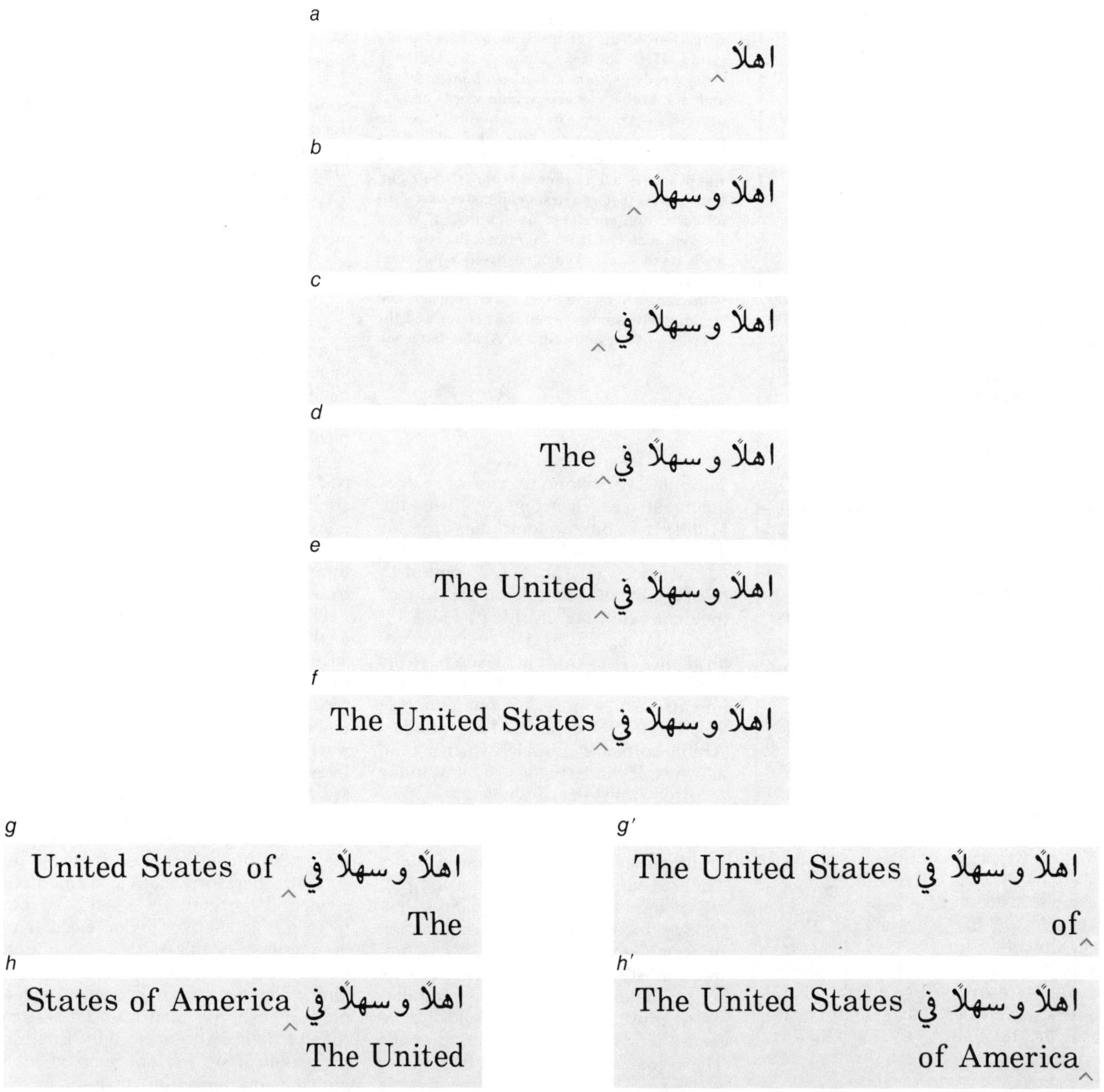

a

اهلاً

b

اهلاً وسهلاً

c

اهلاً وسهلاً في

d

The اهلاً وسهلاً في

e

The United اهلاً وسهلاً في

f

The United States اهلاً وسهلاً في

g

United States of اهلاً وسهلاً في
The

h

States of America اهلاً وسهلاً في
The United

g′

The United States اهلاً وسهلاً في
of

h′

The United States اهلاً وسهلاً في
of America

"WORD WRAP" is the ability of a computer to move a word to the next line of the display screen if the word will not fit on the line being typed. If the text combines a language that reads from left to right with one that reads from right to left, a special problem arises. Here *aḥlan wa saḥlan fi* is typed in Arabic (*a*). It means "Welcome to. . . ." The Arabic characters appear on the screen in right-to-left order; a marker (a caret) has moved to the left to show where the next new character will be entered (*b, c*). The typist then switches to English to type "The United States" (*d, e, f*). Now the caret is stationary; the newly typed characters slide to the left to make room for input. That input ("of America") will require a wrap, but if the computer continues to push text to the left, the words "The United" will be forced down a line (*g, h*), reversing the halves of the English. A more appropriate wrap (*g′, h′*) drops "of America" and the caret onto the next line.

Speech Recognition by Computer

10

by Stephen E. Levinson and Mark Y. Liberman
April 1981

Designing a machine that listens is much more difficult than making one that speaks. Significant improvements in automatic recognition may come only with a better understanding of human speech patterns

Modern computers have prodigious powers, but they would be still more useful if more natural ways of communicating with them were possible. The evolution of spoken language has made it well adapted to the needs of human communication. It is fast and nearly effortless. It requires neither visual nor physical contact and it places few restrictions on the mobility of the body or on the use of the hands. A machine capable of recognizing human speech could combine these advantages with the quite different powers of the computer. Such a machine could provide universal access to large data bases through the telephone network. It could provide for the control of complex machines by vocal command and make possible sophisticated prosthetic devices for the handicapped.

After more than 40 years of research, however, the automatic recognition of natural or conversational speech remains a utopian goal. Current speech-recognition devices have small vocabularies and little ability to deal with fluent sequences of words; usually they must be trained to recognize only one speaker's voice. Even so, the advantages of automatic speech recognition are so great that devices capable of recognizing isolated words or short phrases from a vocabulary of between 10 and 30 words are commercially available and are economically practical in some applications. In research laboratories there are speech recognizers with vocabularies of up to 1,000 words, systems that recognize limited-vocabulary sentences with brief pauses between the words and systems that recognize connected speech with fair accuracy if the vocabulary is small, the syntax is limited and the speaker is careful.

The interaction of technology and economics will undoubtedly lead to speech-recognition systems of greater capability. We cannot accurately predict the pace of such development. We are certain, however, that mere elaboration and extrapolation of current technology will not lead to the development of machines that match the human capacity for recognizing speech. Major progress depends on new discoveries.

Why is the problem of recognition so hard? The core of the difficulty is the complex and variable way linguistic messages are encoded in speech. Spoken language enables people to express their thoughts in sound and to recover messages from the sounds produced by others. This curious two-way mapping between concepts in the mind and vibrations in the air presupposes the participants have some common conceptual framework, so that the message received is at least approximately equivalent to the one that was sent. It is not enough, however, to share knowledge of the things one might want to say. Monolingual speakers of English and of Finnish may have many potential messages in common without being able to understand each other's utterances at all. In order to speak and to understand, people must share a system for encoding messages in sound and for decoding speech sounds to yield meanings. In other words, they have to know the same language.

Speech communication with a computer can be understood in an analogous way. The computer "knows" (in some extended sense of the word) about a domain its users also know about. It is useful for information in this domain to be exchanged, and speech happens to be the chosen medium of communication.

Consider a conversation between a computer and its users concerning the inventory of a warehouse. The computer "knows" how many of each item are on hand and where each article is stored. Its data base also lists costs and suppliers. People probably think about the warehouse and its contents in many ways, but the structure of the computer data base is sufficiently similar to one mode of human thought for certain kinds of communication to be possible. The users have questions that the computer can answer, at least in principle, such as, "Do we have any blue pencils in stock?" The users also have things to say that the computer can profitably "understand," such as, "There is no more room in bay 13." If such communication is to be accomplished through the medium of speech, the computer and its users must agree on how to encode such messages in sound and how to reverse the process. They have to "know" the same language.

We are mainly interested in languages such as English, which are called natural because they are defined implicitly by the everyday usage of ordinary people. Computers now function with formal languages such as FORTRAN, which are defined by an explicit set of rules consciously established by specialists. At least for now, computers do only what they are specifically programmed to do. They do not live in the world of people and learn from everyday experience. Hence for a computer to "know" a natural language, it must be provided with an explicit and precise characterization of the language, or at least with a characterization of what the programmer takes the language to be. In all existing and currently conceived speech-recognition systems the formal description of a natural language covers only a fragment of the language, and the formalism reconstructs the fragment in ways that are probably quite different from the implicit knowledge of a native speaker. Even imperfect linguistic abilities on the part of a computer, however, are enough to make possible useful communication with people.

It will help in understanding various approaches to natural-language recognition if we begin by considering some aspects of language and speech in their own terms. We shall then discuss methods of recognizing isolated words and review some procedures for analyzing connected speech. Finally we shall describe a speech-recognition system developed at Bell Laboratories that attempts to combine the major elements of human speech communication into a single operating unit.

At the center of human language is the word. Sequences of words are generally arranged into phrases according to principles of combination known as syntax; moreover, such sequences are usually intended to mean something. The fact that words are ordinarily part of coherent discourse can help in the recognition of the words themselves by providing a context in which some words are likelier than others. Arranging for a computer to act as if it could "understand" word sequences is formidably difficult. The problem involves not only relations among words but also knowledge and reasoning about the nature of the world.

Although a capacity for understanding language may be the ultimate goal, the enterprise of speech recognition is really founded on the identification of words. The aspect of words that concerns us here is their sound. In this sense a word is an equivalence class of noises: the set of all sounds, however distinct in other ways, that represent (in the context of their utterance) the same lexical unit. The problem in word recognition is to find a mathematically defined space in which such a set of sounds can be effectively delimited. Because the amount of variation within the set of sounds corresponding to a given word is quite large, because the acoustic distinction between words can be quite small and because an adult speaker may know 100,000 words or more, the problem is a difficult one.

In order to understand the sources of variation in the sound of a word and the nature of the distinction between one word and another, it is necessary to grasp two things. First one must understand the basic medium of spoken communication: the ways in which acoustic disturbances of the air can be produced by the human vocal apparatus and perceived by the human auditory system. Second, one has to recognize that speech sounds are elements of a phonological system peculiar to a given language. The

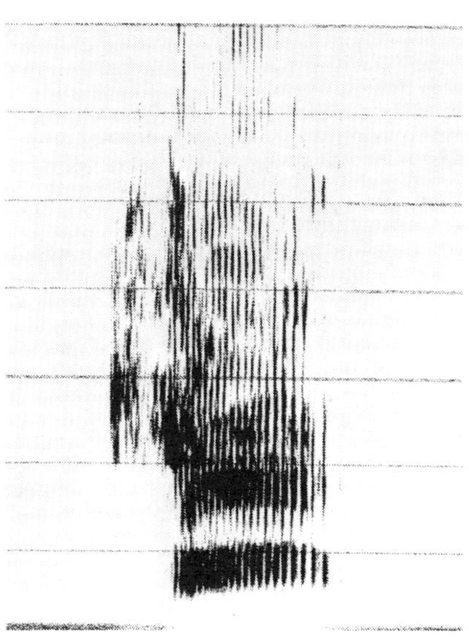

"CAT" SPEAKER 1 MICROPHONE

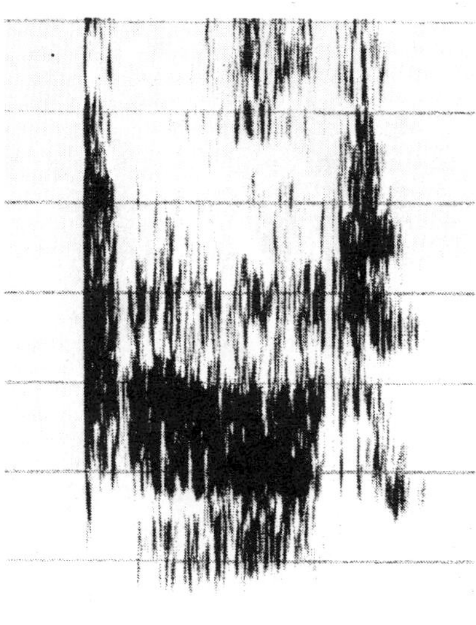

"CAT" SPEAKER 1 WHISPERED

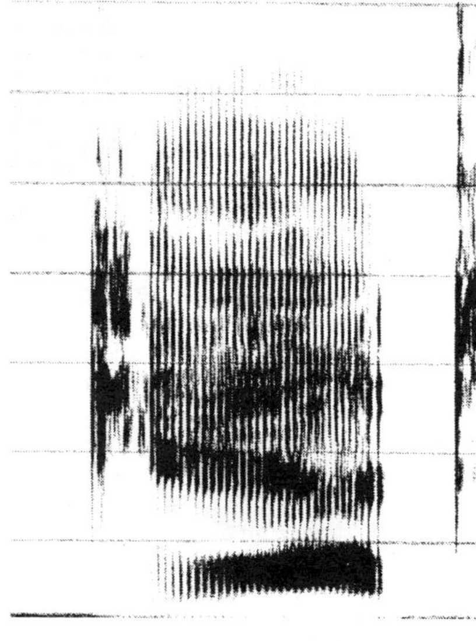

"CAT" SPEAKER 2 MICROPHONE

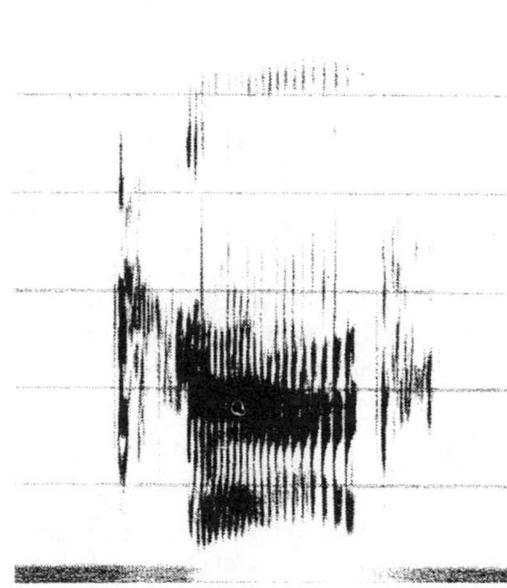

"CAT" SPEAKER 1 TELEPHONE

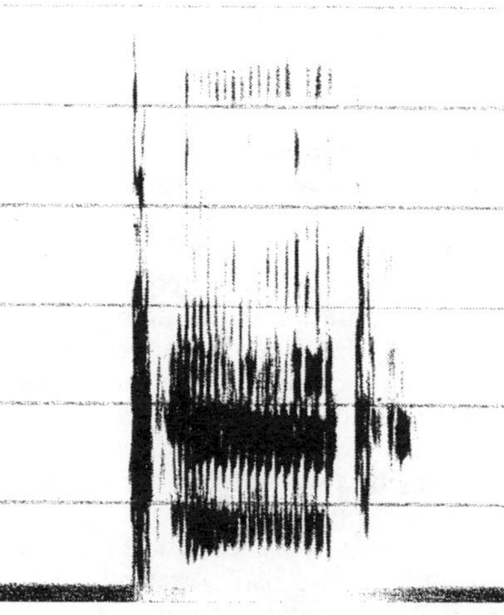

"PAT" SPEAKER 1 TELEPHONE

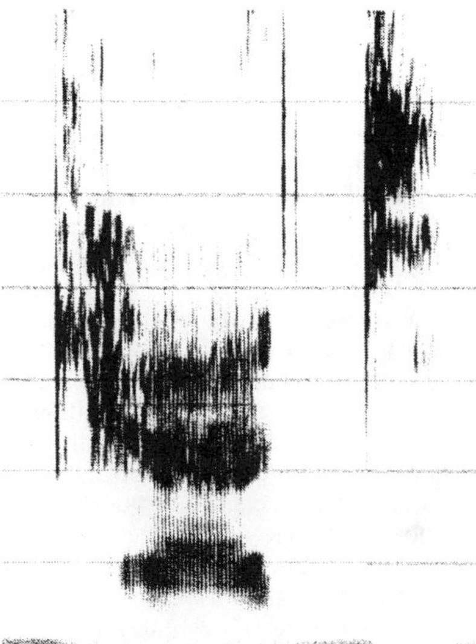

"CAT" SPEAKER 3 MICROPHONE

VARIABILITY OF HUMAN SPEECH, illustrated here by means of sound spectrograms, is one of the principal difficulties encountered in building an automated system for speech recognition. Spectrograms of distinct but acoustically similar words may be more alike than spectrograms of the same word pronounced under various conditions by different speakers. Automatic speech recognition must be able to attend only to relevant spectral differences (when they exist) and must disregard apparent differences that are linguistically irrelevant. The sound spectrogram represents a series of amplitude spectra over time. Time varies along the horizontal axis and frequency varies along the vertical axis. The darker the mark on the graph, the greater the amplitude of the waveform at that frequency and time.

phonological system limits the ways in which the various words of the language can differ and controls in part the ways in which the pronunciation of any specific word in the language can vary.

During speech a flow of air from the lungs passes through the larynx, or voice box, into the throat and out through the mouth. If the velum (the flap of soft tissue at the rear of the palate) is lowered, the airflow also proceeds out through the nose; if the velum is raised, the nasal passages are blocked. The airflow can also be obstructed by closing the lips, by pressing the tongue against the palate or by closing the glottis, which consists of two parallel folds of soft tissue (the vocal cords) within the larynx.

The flow of air through the vocal tract can give rise to sound in three main ways. First, the vocal cords can be made to vibrate in somewhat the same manner as the double reed of an oboe or a bassoon. When the vocal cords are brought together, they stop the passage of air from the lungs, and so pressure builds up below them. The pressure forces the vocal cords apart, but the velocity of the rushing air then reduces the pressure in the space between them. The reduction in pressure and the elasticity of the tissues bring the vocal cords together again, in position for another buildup of pressure. The rate at which this cycle is repeated is the fundamental frequency of the voice, which is heard as pitch.

The second way of generating sound in the vocal tract is to form a constriction in the airway narrow enough to cause turbulence. For example, forcing air past a close contact between the upper teeth and the lower lip causes a turbulent flow that is perceived as the sound "f." Unlike the periodic sounds created by vibration of the vocal cords, the sounds generated by turbulent flow are aperiodic, or noiselike. It is possible for the vocal tract to create both periodic and aperiodic sounds at the same time. Combining vocal-cord vibration with the noise source of an "f" gives rise to the sound perceived as a "v."

A third kind of sound generation takes place when pressure built up behind a closure is abruptly released. Such bursts of acoustic energy occur in the pronunciation of consonants such as "p," "t" and "k."

These three sources of speech sound are shaped acoustically by the changing physical shape of the vocal tract. If the vibrations of the vocal cords were somehow vented directly to the outside air without first passing through the throat, mouth and nose, they would sound rather like a door buzzer and not like speech at all. On passing through the throat, mouth and nose cavities, however, the quality of the buzz is changed profoundly. It is the shape of the vocal tract, including the positions of the larynx, the

```
NFRAM=  396
NO. OF WORDS=  5
CANDIDATES FOR WORD NO.  1  20 FRAMES
WHAT          1   .180
CANDIDATES FOR WORD NO.  2  29 FRAMES
IS            1   .270
CANDIDATES FOR WORD NO.  3  24 FRAMES
NINE          1   .343
ONE           1   .278
SIX           1   .370
SEVEN         1   .242
THE(ALT)      1   .314
CANDIDATES FOR WORD NO.  4  24 FRAMES
SOME          1   .296
FLIGHT        1   .341
ONE           1   .414
THREE         1   .390
CANDIDATES FOR WORD NO.  5  28 FRAMES
NINE          1   .378
OH            1   .390
TIME          1   .291
ONE           1   .411
SEVEN         1   .396
TIMES         1   .315
WHAT IS SEVEN SOME TIME
METRIC=  .1279442E 01
WHAT IS THE FLIGHT TIME
METRIC=  .1396801E 01
THE FLIGHT TIME IS FIVE HOURS AND TWENTY-FIVE MINUTES
```

Machine:	This is the Bell Laboratories flight information system. May I help you?
User:	I want one first-class seat on flight number three one to Denver on Sunday.
Machine:	I am sorry the flight is not available on Sunday.
User:	I would like to leave on Saturday.
Machine:	Flight number three one leaves New York at nine forty-five A.M.; arrives in Denver at one ten P.M.
User:	What is the flight time?
Machine:	The flight time is five hours and twenty-five minutes.
User:	How many stops are there on the flight?
Machine:	This flight makes one stop.
User:	I want a nonstop flight.
Machine:	I am sorry there are no nine A.M. nonstop flights.
User:	I want to go at four P.M.
Machine:	Flight number one six leaves New York at four fifty P.M.; arrives in Denver at seven P.M.
User:	What stops are there on the flight?
Machine:	This flight makes no stops.
User:	Is a meal served on the flight?
Machine:	Dinner is served.
User:	How much is the fare?
Machine:	The round-trip first-class fare is three hundred sixty dollars.
User:	What plane is on the flight?
Machine:	The aircraft is a Douglas DC ten.
User:	I prefer the Boeing seven four seven.
Machine:	The aircraft is a Douglas DC ten.
User:	Please repeat the departure time.
Machine:	The departure time is four fifty P.M.
User:	I will take flight number six five.
Machine:	I am sorry there is no flight six five to Denver.
User:	Please repeat the flight number.
Machine:	The flight number is one six.
User:	I want flight one six.
Machine:	Your reservation on flight number one six to Denver on Saturday is confirmed. Thank you.

TELEPHONE CONVERSATION between man and machine proceeds according to steps that can be displayed on the screen of a computer terminal. The computer counts the number of words in each sentence to be recognized and also divides the entire utterance into "frames" by taking a spectral sample every 15 milliseconds. "NFRAM" is the number of frames in the sentence. It exceeds the number of frames occupied by individual words because the speaker must pause briefly between the words. The candidate words listed for each position in the sentence have been found by comparison with word templates stored in the computer. Only those candidates appear that are grammatically possible in a given position and similar in spectral structure to the spoken word. Not all the candidates to be considered are listed. The numbers following each candidate word are measures of the distance between the word's template and the utterance. The shorter the distance is, the more similar the template is to the utterance. "METRIC" is the unrounded sum of the distance measures for a particular string of words. If the smallest possible METRIC (which necessarily consists of the most likely word in each position) is not allowed by the internal grammar, the grammatically correct string with the smallest METRIC is substituted. A synthetic-voice response to the question by the user is given over the telephone. The complete conversation is transcribed in the computer printout.

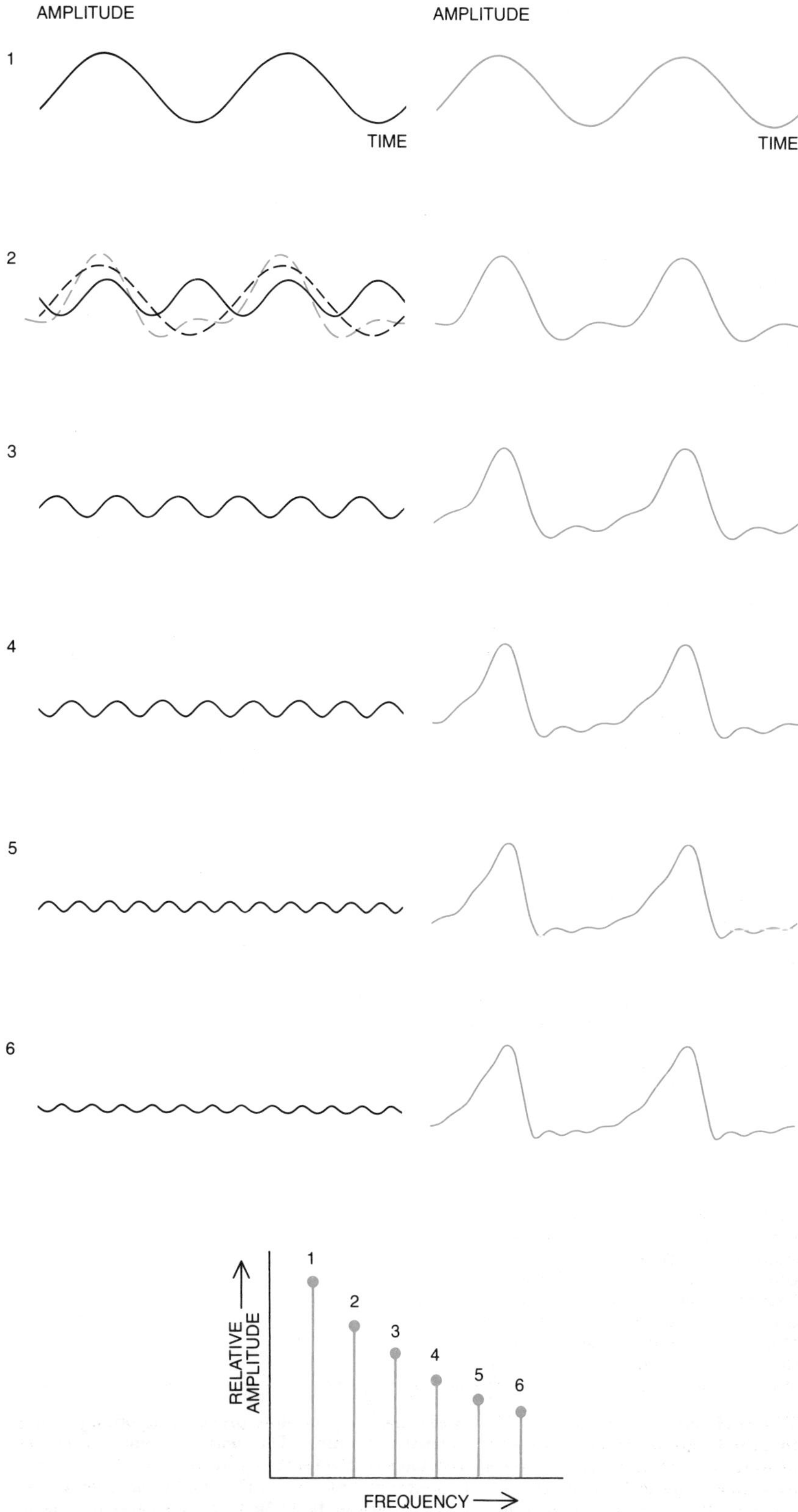

PRINCIPLE OF SUPERPOSITION allows temporal variation in the sound pressure of the signal to be represented as a spectrum of sound amplitude, or energy, at different frequencies. The amplitude spectrum is generally a more useful way of displaying acoustic information. The waveform (here a glottal wave) can be treated mathematically as a pattern that repeats indefinitely in the past and the future at a fundamental frequency. As the French mathematician Jean Baptiste Joseph Fourier showed, any such waveform can be decomposed into a series of sine waves at integral multiples of the fundamental frequency, with various amplitudes and phases. When the sine waves are combined by adding the amplitudes at each point, the result is the original waveform. When the amplitude of each sine wave that makes up the decomposition is graphed as a function of its frequency, the result is an amplitude spectrum.

tongue, the lips and the velum, that distinguishes (for example) the "ee" sound in "me" from the "oo" sound in "you."

One way of understanding this acoustic transformation is the mathematical technique called Fourier analysis. In 1822 the French mathematician Jean Baptiste Joseph Fourier showed that any periodic waveform can be represented as the sum of an infinite series of sine waves. A periodic waveform is one that is repeated at uniform intervals. If the interval of repetition is t seconds, the fundamental frequency of the waveform is $1/t$ hertz. In the Fourier series for a periodic waveform, the frequencies of the component sine waves are harmonics, or integral multiples, of the fundamental frequency of the waveform being analyzed, and they must be assigned appropriate amplitudes and phases. The Fourier transform is a generalization of the Fourier series; it allows analysis of aperiodic waveforms. Thus the noisy hiss of an "f" sound can be represented as a sum of sinusoidal components all along the frequency continuum.

The most obvious way to represent sound waves is to graph the variation of air pressure with time. Fourier's result implies that the same information can also be displayed by a graph that shows amplitude and phase as a function of the frequency of the sinusoidal components. Because phase differences are of little perceptual significance, a speech sound can be represented in practice by its amplitude spectrum, a graph that shows the amplitude of the sine-wave component at each frequency.

What is the acoustic effect of the shape of the vocal tract on the sound emitted? When the sounds are represented by their amplitude spectra, the effects are clear [*see illustration at right*]. The vocal tract acts as a filter on the spectrum of the sound source, enhancing some frequencies and diminishing others. The selective filtering can be described by a mathematical expression called a transfer function; a separate transfer function is associated with each position assumed by the organs of the vocal tract. The transfer function usually has several well-defined frequency peaks, called formants, in which most of the energy from the sound source is concentrated.

It is now possible to state with some precision why it is hard for a computer to make the translation from sounds to words, from an acoustic characterization of an utterance to a linguistic characterization of the intended message. One source of difficulty is that the organs of speech do not take up a series of fixed configurations corresponding to units of the message. Instead parts of the vocal tract are in constant motion along smooth trajectories. Some investigators

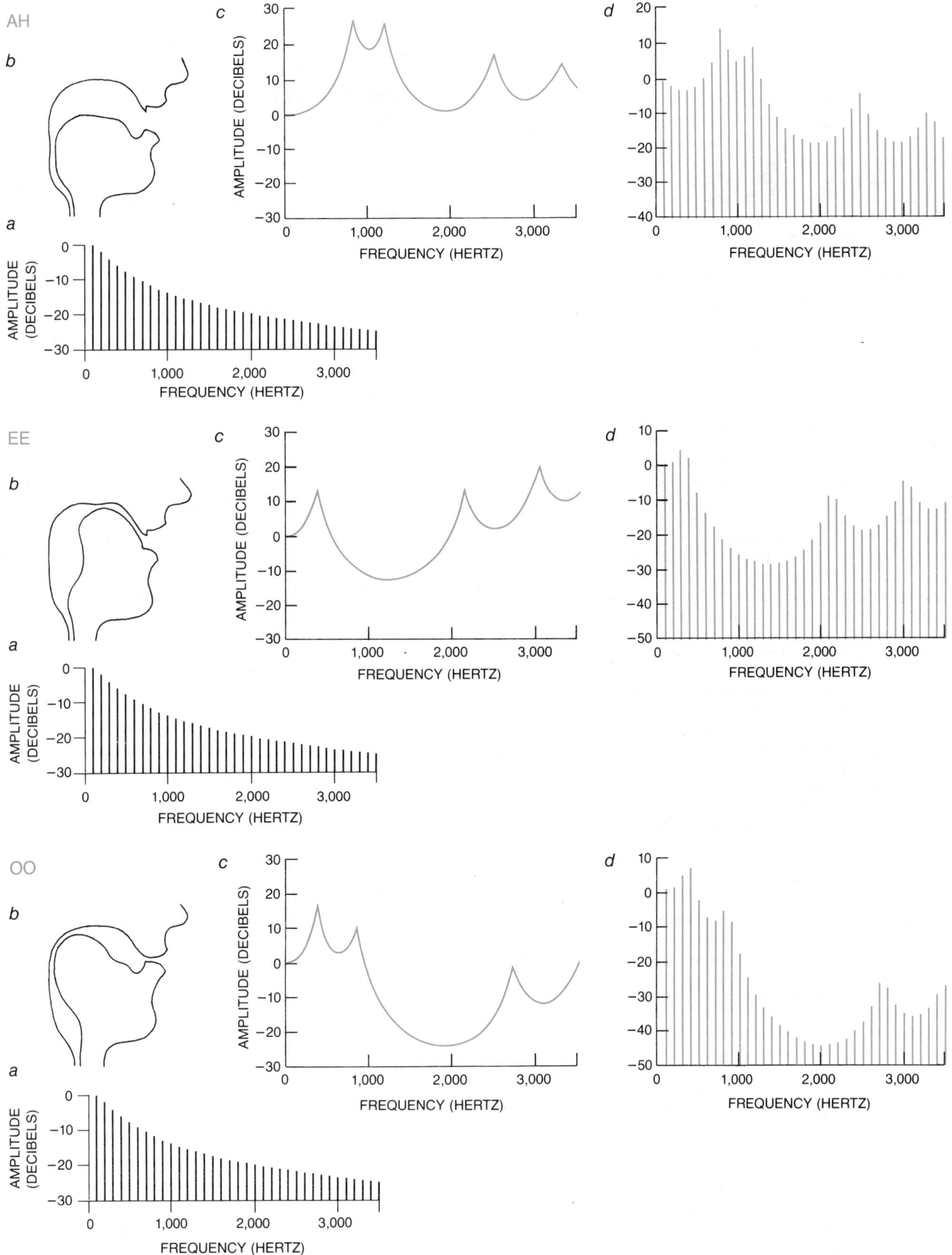

VOWEL SOUNDS result from various configurations of the mouth, lips, tongue and velum (soft palate). The resulting shape of the vocal tract can be modeled by a series of resonating cavities that enhance energy at some frequencies and diminish it at others in predictable ways. Such filter-response characteristics can be represented by a transfer function (*c*) for each position of the model of the vocal tract (*b*). When the input sound energy is periodic (which is almost the case for vocal-cord vibration), both the input spectrum (*a*) and the output spectrum (*d*) are line spectra. In a line spectrum the sound energy is concentrated at harmonics, or integral multiples, of the vocal-cord frequency. An aperiodic sound source such as a whispered vowel has no discrete lines in its spectrum, but the shape of the output spectrum still matches that of the transfer function. Model vocal-tract configurations for vowels "ee," "ah" and "oo" are shown.

believe these motions "flow" through a sequence of target positions defined by linguistic units such as consonants and vowels. Others think even the simplest linguistic units are inherently dynamic. In any case the result is a complex and continual motion, which is inherited by the emitted sound in the form of a constantly changing amplitude spectrum. Such patterns of changing sound quality can conveniently be represented by a sound spectrogram, a graph in which time proceeds from left to right, frequency increases from bottom to top and amplitude increases from white through shades of gray to black.

Motions of the vocal tract that correspond to linguistic units usually overlap and combine with their neighbors. For instance, in saying "coo" the lip-rounding of the vowel "oo" usually precedes the tongue motion of the initial consonant. Hence the acoustic effects of the two motions are combined from the beginning of the word. In fluent speech such amalgamation also applies between one word and the next. The effects are sometimes quite plain to the ear. When the "t" of "cat" combines with the "y" of "your," it makes the phrase "You gave the cat your dinner" sound like "You gave the catcher dinner."

Other variations in the sound of a word result from its position in a phrase, from its degree of emphasis and from the rate at which it is pronounced. The size and shape of the vocal tract vary from individual to individual, and habits of speech differ widely according to age, sex, geographic region and social background. Furthermore, the signal that reaches a speech-recognition device is influenced by various circumstances in addition to the sounds made by the speaker, such as room acoustics, background noise and the characteristics of the transmission channel.

For these reasons it is hard to divide a speech signal into chunks corresponding to the elements of the message the signal conveys, and it is difficult to translate pieces of acoustic information into information about the identity of pieces of the message. People find speech easy to understand, and so the needed information must be present in the signal. The trick is to find it.

A natural starting place is the recognition of words. Words are generally distinct from one another as elements of a linguistic system, and they constitute natural and relatively stable patterns for an automated speech-recognition system. Although speech is more than a sequence of words, it is at least such a sequence, so that a crucial function of a speech recognizer is identifying words. If a speech-recognition system can recognize words accurately, it will succeed; if it cannot, it will fail.

Most speech recognizers now in use are not capable of recognizing words in

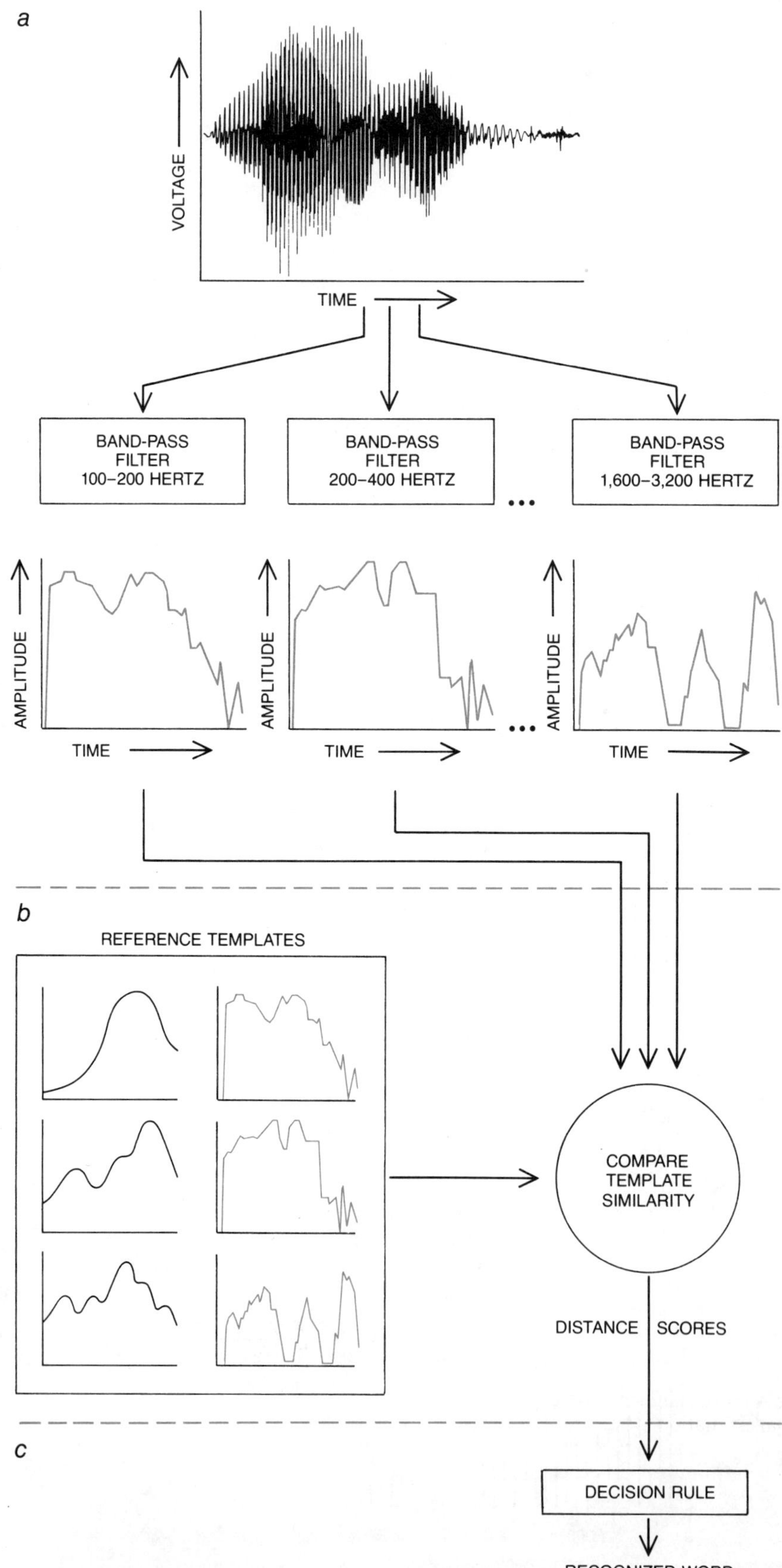

STANDARD METHOD OF WORD RECOGNITION employs the basic principles of pattern recognition to discriminate among acoustic patterns. The speech waveform is measured and analyzed (*a*), in this case by filters that divide the signal into frequency bands, each band being an octave wide. The output of each filter is the energy in its band. The outputs are compared with stored reference templates, and distance scores are assigned to each template (*b*). A decision procedure then classifies the input utterance on the basis of the distance scores (*c*).

connected speech. Instead recognition is carried out on isolated words by a process of acoustic pattern recognition. Generally the user must "train" the machine by speaking into a microphone all the words the system is to recognize. In some cases the training is limited to one utterance of each word by a few of the speakers who will use the system. In other applications every potential user must say each word several times. The result of this training process is a set of stored "templates," which represent typical acoustic patterns for the words in the vocabulary.

When a word is presented for recognition, the machine analyzes the acoustic signal, compares the results of the analysis with the stored templates and decides which one of the templates most closely resembles the spoken word. The machine may also list other possible matches in decreasing order of similarity. Once a classification has been made the machine can respond to the user's utterance or issue an appropriate signal to some other device. Each stage of the template-matching procedure (analysis of the speech signal, comparison with the template and classification of the signal) can be carried out by a variety of techniques.

The aim of all methods of analyzing the speech signal is to characterize the temporal variation of the signal's amplitude spectrum. Perhaps the simplest method of estimating the spectrum is the zero-crossing count. This method consists in counting the number of times the voltage analogue of the speech signal changes its algebraic sign (from plus to minus or from minus to plus) in a fixed interval. The number of such axis crossings is related to the frequency.

One refinement of the zero-crossing method filters the speech signal into three frequency bands. The zero crossings are measured separately in each band to give rough estimates of the first three formant frequencies. Such measurements are useful in classifying vowel sounds, and for small vocabularies of easily distinguished words these measurements alone are sufficient for discrimination. The zero-crossing method is economically attractive because it can be accomplished by simple electronic devices.

A more elaborate procedure for spectral estimation is the filter-bank method. The speech signal is divided by filtering into between 20 and 30 frequency bands, covering the frequency range of human speech. The output of each filter is a measure of the energy in that frequency band. The energy levels are suitable for direct comparison with those of a template. The Fast Fourier Transform provides a general, computationally efficient method for estimating the amplitude spectrum of a signal from its time-domain waveform. This algorithm provides one of several ways to obtain filter-bank information in purely digital form.

Recently a new method for estimating the amplitude spectrum of speech, called linear predictive analysis, has been introduced. Actually statisticians have employed the method for some time under the name autoregressive analysis. The method predicts the amplitude of a speech wave at a given instant from a weighted sum (or linear combination) of its amplitudes at a small number of earlier instants. The coefficients, or weights, that give the best estimate of the true speech wave can then be mathematically converted into an estimate of the amplitude spectrum. For the analysis of speech linear predictive analysis is particularly appropriate because it is mathematically equivalent to treating the vocal tract as a pipe of varying circular cross section, or in other words as a sequence of resonant cavities. The model is quite faithful for nonnasalized, voiced speech. Because it is a model of the vocal-tract resonances and not of vocal-cord vibration, the linear-prediction spectrum is smooth. None of the pitch harmonics are in evidence. Consequently the formant structure of the speech wave, which is important for speech recognition, is brought clearly to the fore.

During the comparison, or template-matching, stage the phonological structure of a word can be exploited in an indirect way. A spoken word consists of a sequence of vocal gestures, which gives rise to a time-varying pattern of sound. The parts of the sound pattern rarely have the same durations in different utterances of the same word, but their sequence is more nearly constant. For example, the word "fable" begins with an "f" noise, which is followed by a pattern of moving formants that show the lips opening out from the "f" and closing again for the "b" while the tongue is moving through the first vowel; next there is a "b" lip closure, and finally there is another pattern of spectral motion as the lips open and the tongue moves into the final "l." On different occasions the timing of these patterns may vary considerably, but they must all be present in the described order if the utterance is to count as a reasonable rendition of the word "fable."

Because of differences in timing, the various parts of a word may be badly out of alignment with the corresponding parts of the template it is to be matched against. Since the order of events is fairly constant, the misalignment can be corrected by stretching the template in some places and compressing it in others so that a mathematically optimum match is found. Nonuniform temporal alignment is accomplished by means of a procedure called dynamic programming. Dynamic programming was developed by Richard E. Bellman of the University of Southern California School of Medicine for solving problems in the design of servomechanisms. It is a technique for mathematical optimization that is often carried out with the aid of a computer, but it should not be confused with computer programming itself.

Comparison implies some estimate of the degree of similarity between the sound of the input and the sound represented by the stored template. The final aspect of processing common to all word recognizers is a decision strategy, which is usually based on a statistical measure of closeness of fit. Each template is assigned a point in an abstract space; the position of the point is defined by the spectral characteristics of the template. The utterance to be classified is represented as a point in the same space. The recognizer calculates the distance in the space between the utterance and each of the templates. It then picks either the template closest to the utterance or the equivalence class of templates that is closest to the utterance in a statistical sense.

The performance of automatic recognition systems in identifying isolated words is poor compared with that of people. Even for the most powerful word recognizers the number of errors rises rapidly as the vocabulary increases to more than a few hundred words. The error rates get worse still when unknown speakers and acoustic conditions are introduced. In a recent experiment isolated words from a 26,000-word vocabulary were spoken by a variety of speakers unknown to the listener; the words were identified with an error rate of less than 3 percent. Human word-recognition abilities are also remarkably tolerant of background noise: conversation can be understood even at a noisy party. No existing recognition system can approach this level of performance.

In attempts to recognize continuous speech the disparities between human and computer performance are even more evident. People generally find it easier to recognize words in context, but for an automated system the recognition of fluent speech is far more difficult than the recognition of words in isolation. One of the crucial problems is coarticulation, which causes the blending at the boundaries between words and makes the spectral patterns to be recognized highly complex and unstable. In fluent speech there are no clear acoustic signs of word boundaries and direct template-matching becomes extremely difficult. In essence every template must be aligned with every possible interval of the utterance by means of a variant of the dynamic-programming method.

The computational burden is somewhat reduced by the requirement that

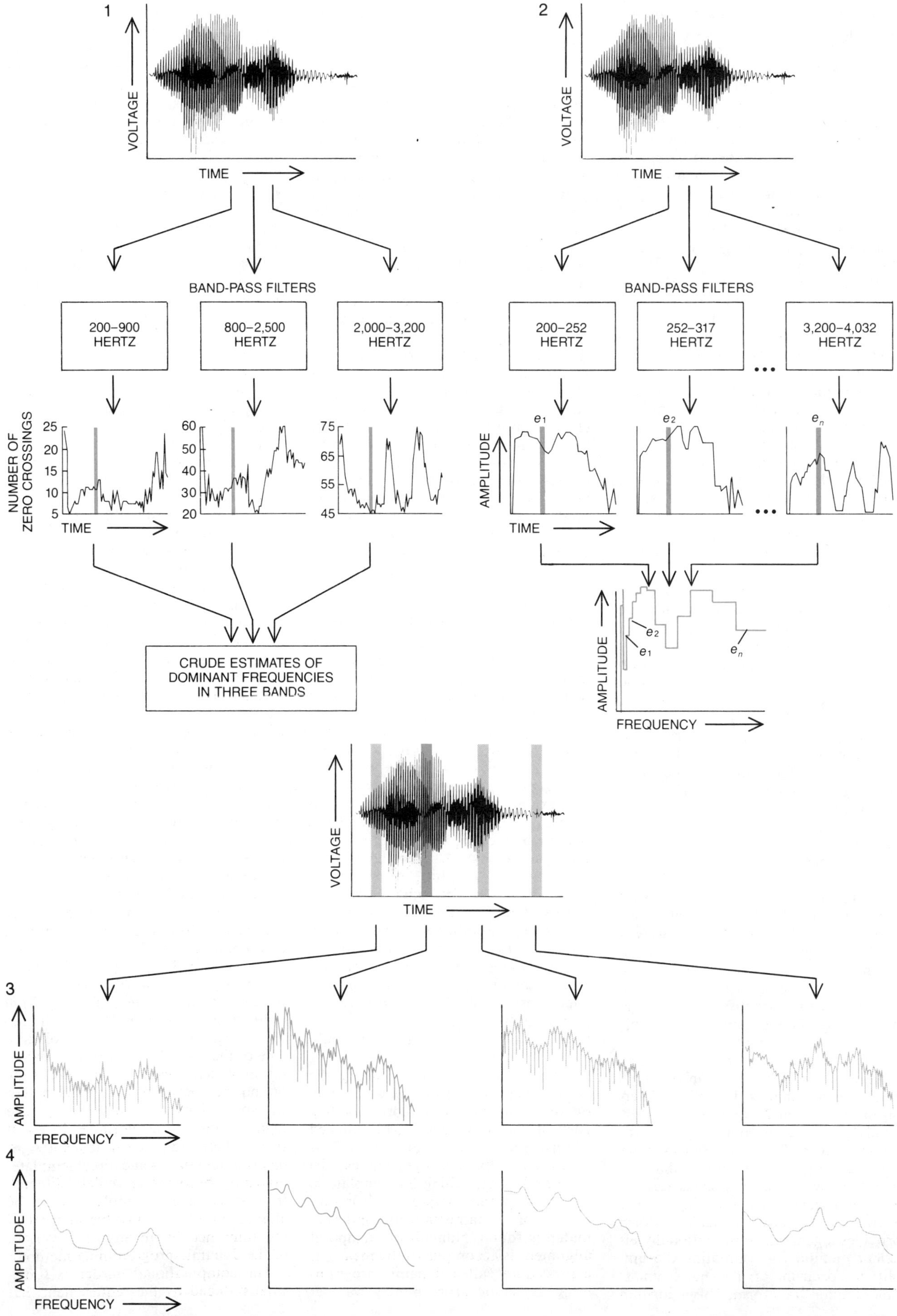
1
VOLTAGE
TIME
BAND-PASS FILTERS
200–900 HERTZ
800–2,500 HERTZ
2,000–3,200 HERTZ
NUMBER OF ZERO CROSSINGS
TIME
CRUDE ESTIMATES OF DOMINANT FREQUENCIES IN THREE BANDS
2
VOLTAGE
TIME
BAND-PASS FILTERS
200–252 HERTZ
252–317 HERTZ
3,200–4,032 HERTZ
AMPLITUDE
TIME
e_1
e_2
e_n
AMPLITUDE
FREQUENCY
VOLTAGE
TIME
3
AMPLITUDE
FREQUENCY
4
AMPLITUDE
FREQUENCY

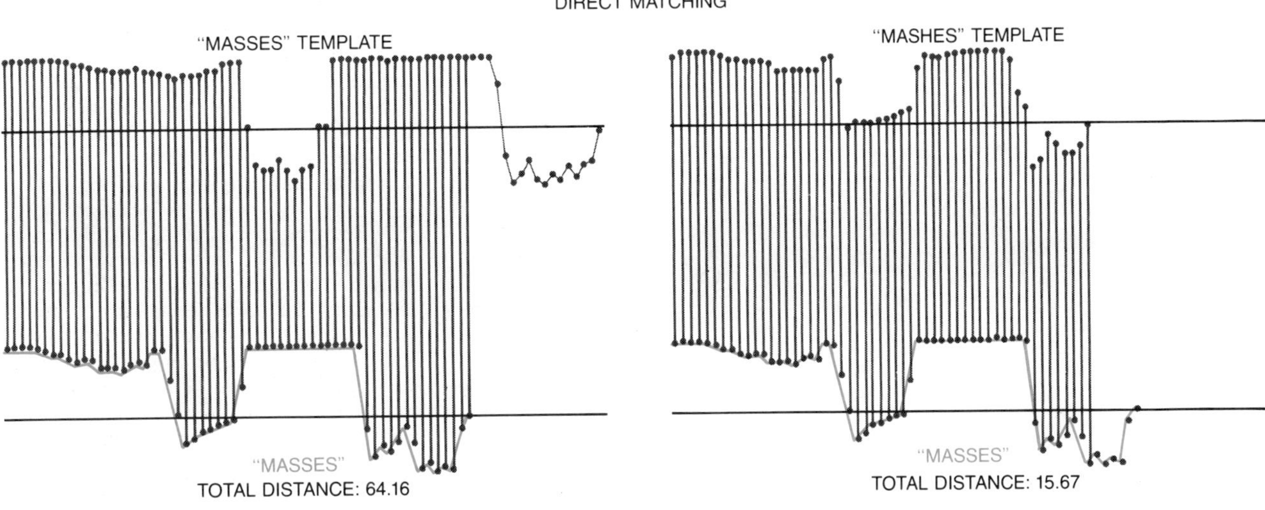

MATCHING BY DYNAMIC PROGRAMMING

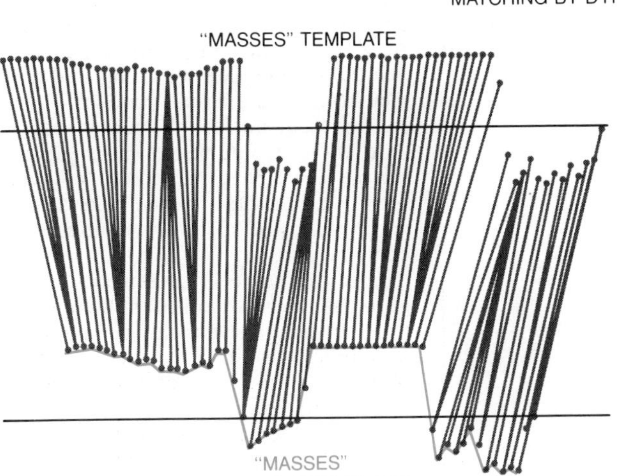

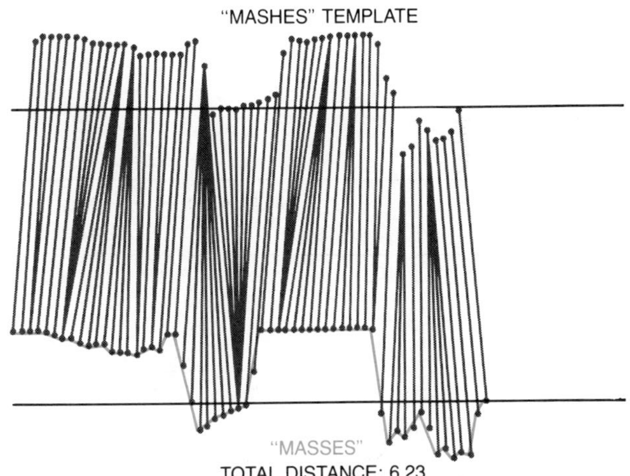

COMPARISON STAGE of word recognition is carried out by compressing and stretching stored templates according to an optimization process called dynamic programming. For each stored template, dynamic programming seeks to associate every frame of the input word with some frame of the template in such a way that a distance measure of overall fit between the input and the template is minimized. The nonuniform time alignment of the stored template with the spoken word allows for variations in the rate of speech and in the relative lengths of the vowels and consonants in a word. Here matching the templates (*black*) to the input (*color*) without dynamic programming yields a misidentification, indicated by the distance scores, that is corrected when the compression and expansion procedure is applied. Dynamic programming is often done with the aid of a computer but should not be confused with computer programming.

the intervals be contiguous, so that the end of one word meets the beginning of the next. Still, the combinatorial complexity of the process increases too fast for it to be considered a practical solution to the general problem of recognizing continuous speech. Direct template-matching can be useful only where the range of possible utterances is small. With present technology the technique can work in real time (that is, as fast as the utterance is spoken) for sequences as many as five words long, drawn from a vocabulary of about 20 words.

Instead of looking for every possible pattern everywhere in the signal, a continuous-speech-recognition system can search for linguistic units in a more constrained way, such as in sequence from the beginning of the utterance to the end. The speech signal is divided into intervals that correspond to specific acoustic patterns, and the intervals are classified in a way that matches the categories of a potential linguistic message as closely as possible. We shall call such techniques segmentation and labeling. The processes of segmentation and labeling can be carried out in many ways, and the intervals to be found can correspond to words or to smaller linguistic units such as syllables, phoneme pairs or phonemes.

The easiest way to achieve automatic segmentation and labeling is to require the user to pause briefly between words. The pauses that appear as intervals of

METHODS OF ESTIMATING the amplitude spectra of short intervals of a word (here the word "language") all seek to highlight linguistically relevant information in a computationally efficient way. Zero-crossing counts exploit the fact that as the frequency increases, the number of times the voltage analogue of the acoustic signal changes its sign increases as well. In the band-pass-filter method the signal is divided into several frequency bands and the amount of energy in each band is measured. These measurements yield an amplitude spectrum for the interval. The Fast Fourier Transform is a general, computationally efficient algorithm for estimating the amplitude spectrum of the signal from its time-domain waveform. It is one of several ways of computing filter-bank information in digital form. The rough appearance of the spectrum is caused by pitch harmonics or other fine structure in the spectrum. The fourth method of spectral estimation, called linear predictive analysis, employs a model of the vocal tract to generate successive frequency spectra. Its advantage is that a smooth, continuous spectrum is generated for each sample. The spectra in dark color are all constructed from the same interval of the time-varying signal. Several other methods of spectral estimation are also in use.

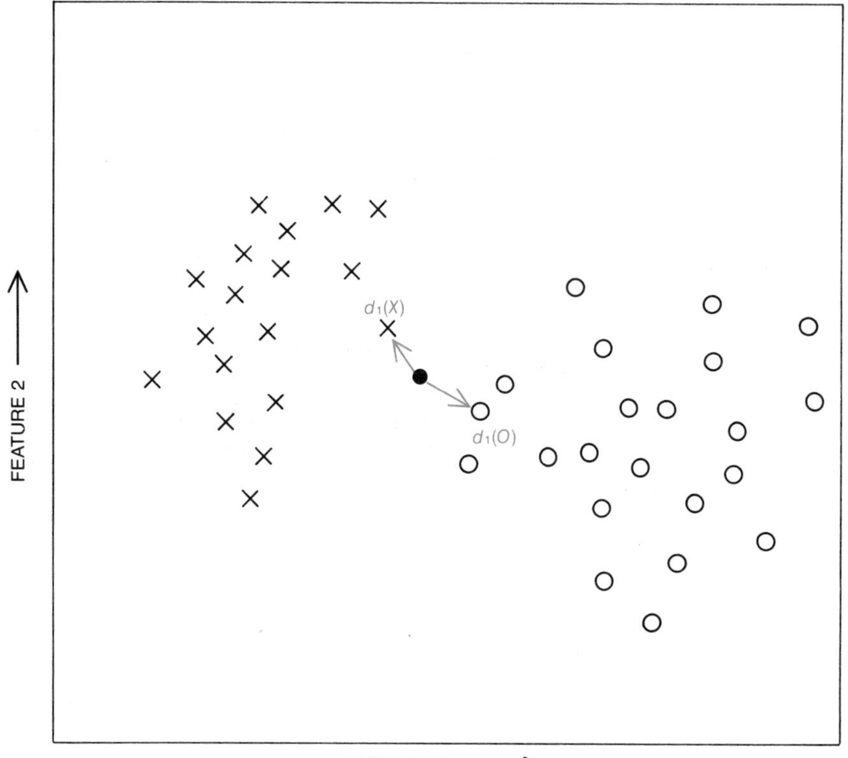

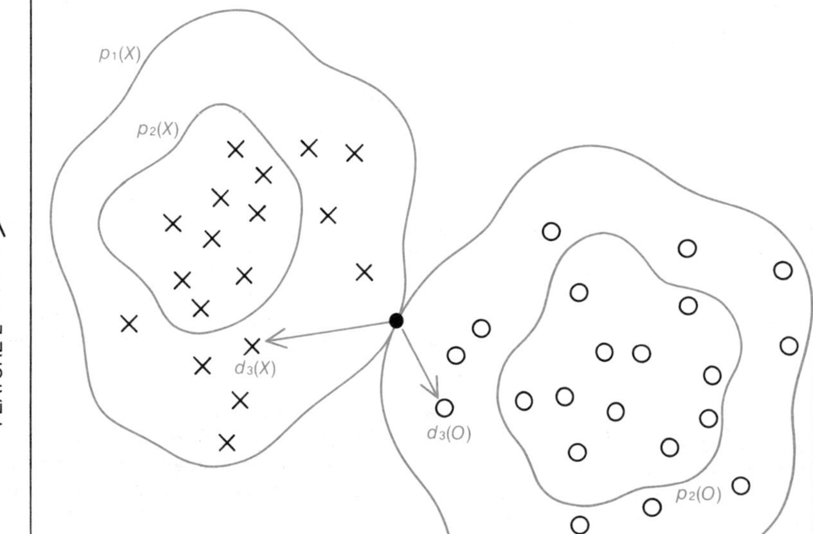

CLASSIFICATION OF AN INPUT SOUND consists in finding the shortest distance in a space of acoustic features from the input (represented by a dot) to a stored template or class of templates (represented by *X*'s and *O*'s). The simplest decision strategy picks the closest template (*upper graph*), and so the input is classified as the sound "ah" (an *X*). When several templates represent linguistically equivalent sounds (as when the computer must recognize the voices of several speakers), the decision strategy may take account of entire classes of templates. One method calculates the distance from the input to the third-nearest neighbor in each class (*lower graph*); here the input is classified as the sound "aw" (an *O*). Under certain conditions it is possible to draw equal-density contours along which the number of template samples per unit area is constant. The highest-density contour that passes through the input can then be found; because $p_1(X)$ is greater than $p_1(O)$ the input is classified as the sound "ah" (an *X*).

low sound energy are a reliable indication of word boundaries. Once the words have been segmented they can be analyzed independently. Although this method works well, it does not really address the question of fluent speech recognition. Other methods of segmentation and labeling are available.

Discontinuities in the spectrum, peaks and valleys in the energy of certain frequency bands and other acoustic signs provide clues to articulatory events: the closing or opening of the vocal tract or the beginning or ending of laryngeal vibration. This suggests that segmentation and labeling might be carried out on the basic phonological units of which words are constructed.

Blending and the diffusion of acoustic information across boundaries affect the acoustic shape of the smaller speech units even more than they affect words. As a result such units are difficult to identify by template-matching, and segmentation errors would probably be at least as frequent for the smaller speech units as they would be for words. Nevertheless, there may be reason to favor segmentation into smaller units as the vocabularies of speech recognizers become larger.

There are some 300,000 words in English, far too many for all of them to be tested by template-matching. Moreover, it is difficult to allow for the effects of blending at the boundaries of words when word templates are employed. English syllables number some 20,000, which is still too many for them to be identified easily and reliably. In addition the effects of blending at boundaries are even more disruptive to template-matching with syllables than they are with words. In contrast, there are only about 40 English phonemes (basic linguistic elements such as consonants or vowels), and the phonemes can be further decomposed into about a dozen phonological features that specify distinctive characteristics of vocal-tract shape and larynx control. Such features can also be combined directly into syllable-like units. As the set of linguistic units is reduced in number, however, the relation of the units to patterns of sound becomes more abstract, more complex and less well understood. Segmenting and labeling such small speech units by currently available techniques leads to high error rates. Still, if constraints imposed by the linguistic code can compensate for the errors, or if more reliable methods of analysis can be found, the small number of the basic phonological units will give them a decided advantage as the fundamental elements of a recognition system.

There is one difficulty that is common to all segmentation and labeling procedures: the probability of error is much higher in making a number of independent classifications than it is in making a single classification. In a three-word phrase, even if the probability of recognizing the correct word in any given position is .8, the probability of recognizing the entire phrase correctly is only about one-half (.8 × .8 × .8).

One way of offsetting this effect is to introduce constraints imposed by the linguistic code, such as allowable sequences of words in a sentence or allowable sequences of syllables in a word. An area of mathematics called formal-language theory provides several methods for specifying and using such constraints. By applying some of the elementary principles of formal-language theory it is possible to write precise and efficient descriptions, or formal grammars, of linguistically possible sequences of sounds and words. One can also write computer programs that utilize these grammars to recognize formally correct linguistic sequences.

One simple way of exploiting grammatical structure makes use of a mathematical construction called a state diagram. A state diagram defines every possible sentence the machine can recognize. Each path from the starting point of the diagram to the end points represents an acceptable sentence. From acoustic measurements the recognizer assigns a probability to each transition in the diagram. A probability can then be calculated for each path by forming the product of the probabilities of all the transitions that make up the path. The sentence chosen is the one represented by the path with the highest probability. This technique can significantly reduce the error rate in sentence recognition: it can choose a word with a relatively low probability in a given position in order to enhance the likelihood that the overall transcription is correct.

Such a reduction in the error rate was demonstrated in a phoneme-based system for the recognition of fluent Japanese, which was tested at Bell Laboratories and at the Nippon Telegraph and Telephone Electrical Communication Laboratories. The segmentation and labeling of phonemes was correct only 60 percent of the time. Syntactic processing, however, led to a 70 percent success rate for the recognition of sentences with an average length of 25 phonemes. Although 70 percent recognition is not adequate for reliable communication, the result is remarkable in view of the small probability of finding a correct sentence without syntactic processing: it comes to about one chance in three million.

A state diagram can also improve the efficiency of continuous-speech recognition by nonlinear time alignment. Instead of matching every template to every interval in the input sentence, the recognition system tests only those templates that fit admissible sequences described by the state diagram. This procedure eliminates much wasted computation, since only a small subset of the words in the vocabulary can appear at a given position in a sentence. A device employing syntax-directed time alignment can recognize connected sentences of more than 20 words composed from a vocabulary of more than 100 words.

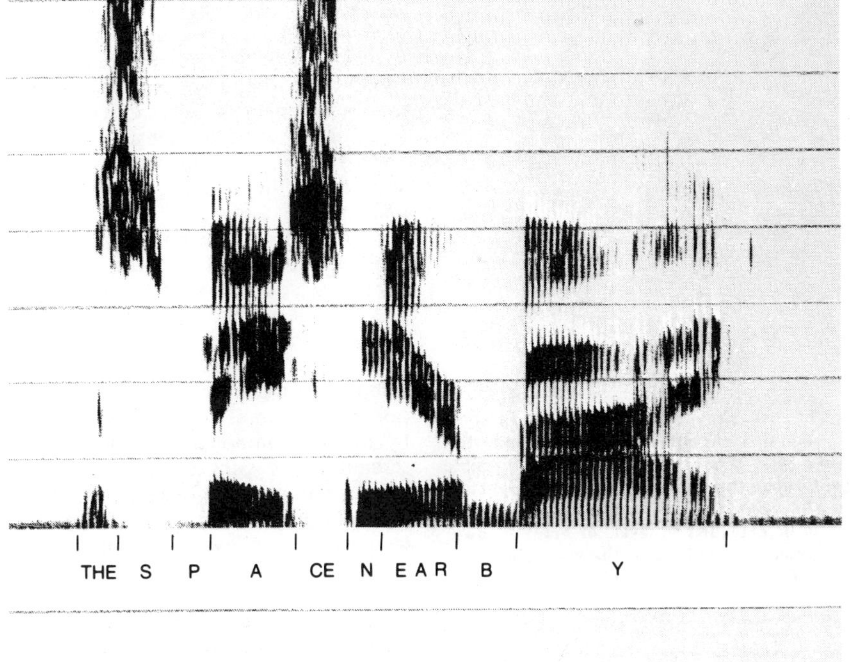

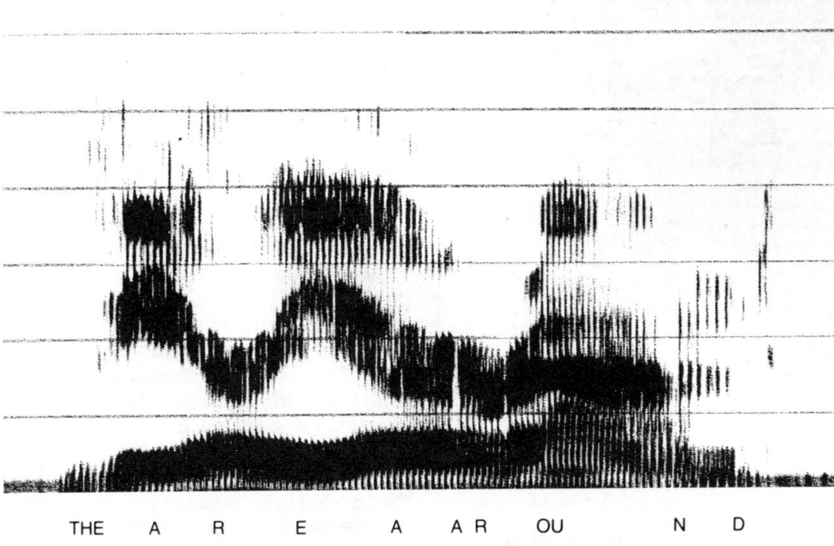

SEGMENTATION OF ACOUSTIC PATTERNS into words or other linguistic units is difficult because of the temporal smearing of speech sounds. Certain sounds, however, exhibit more spectral discontinuity than others. The alternation of the consonants and vowels in the phrase "The space nearby" shows up in relatively clear discontinuities. The smooth sequence of blended vowels in the phrase "The area around" makes segmentation more difficult.

So far we have described the phonological symbols that correspond to the acoustic reality of speech and the grammatical organization of the symbols into words and phrases. These form the linguistic code of speech. The purpose of the linguistic code is to convey meaningful messages: semantic information. Hence semantic information imposes additional constraints on the way the symbols of a language can be combined to form messages.

A machine that processes the semantic information encoded in speech attempts a much more complex and subtle task than a machine that merely recognizes words. In order to deal with meaning a machine not only must recognize acoustic patterns but also must manipulate abstract representations of reality. In other words, it must simulate at least some important aspects of human intelligence.

At Bell Laboratories we have incorporated a rudimentary semantic proc-

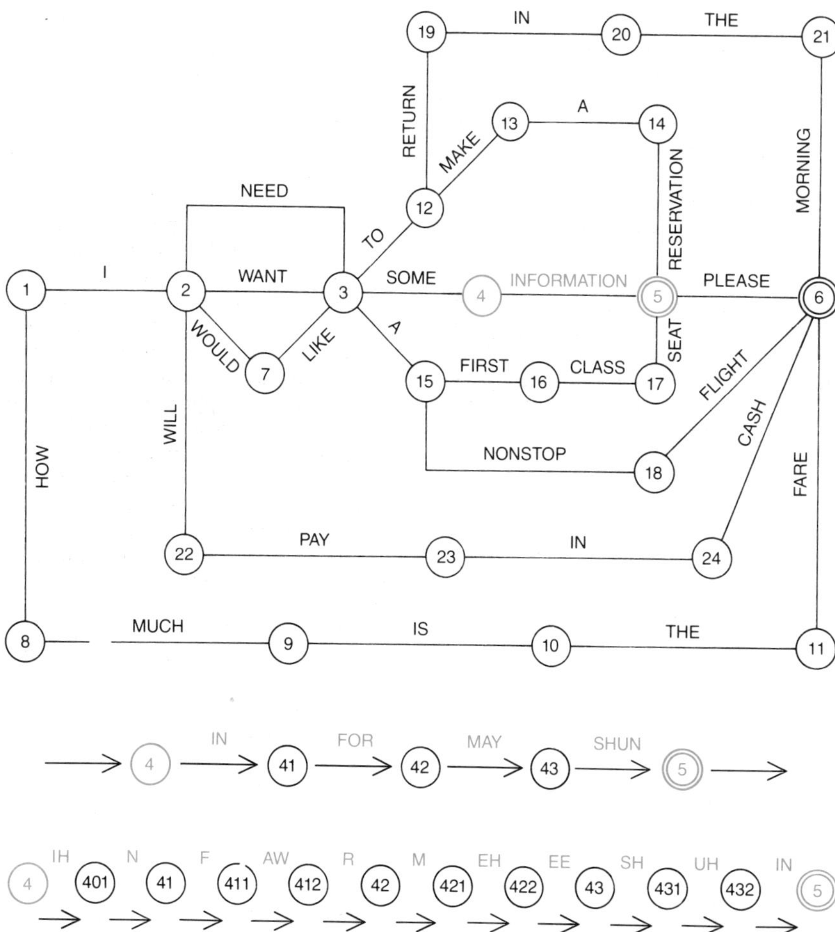

FINITE-STATE GRAMMAR is computationally the most straightforward means of imposing syntactic (or word-order) constraints on the recognition of sentences. The grammar diagrammed here would force the computer to classify every sequence of acoustically possible words as one of the 26 sentences that can be traced through the state diagram, starting at state 1 and ending at state 5 or 6. For instance, one possible sentence is "I would like a first-class seat, please." The principles of the diagram can also be extended to levels of analysis lower than the level of the word, such as the syllabic and phonemic analyses of the word "information." The grammars of experimental recognition systems allow for billions of sentences.

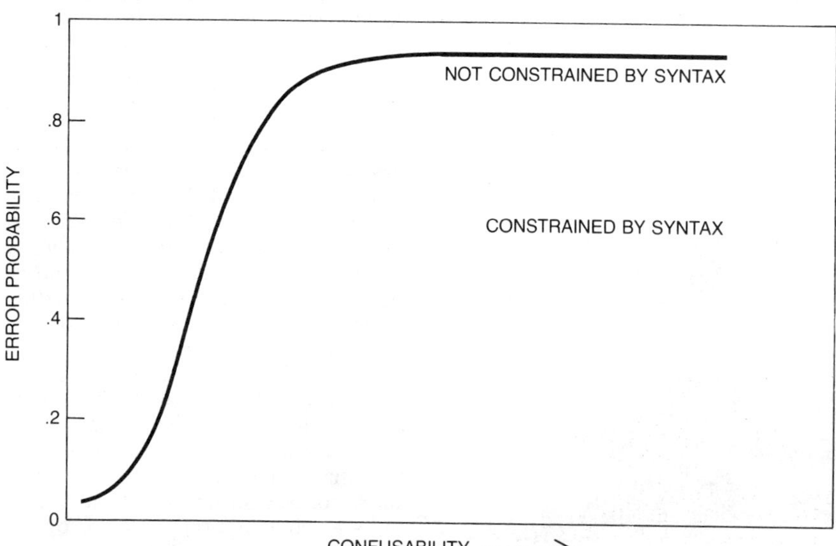

CONFUSABILITY OF A SPEECH SIGNAL is a complex function of the size of the input vocabulary, the acoustic similarity of the elements to be discriminated, the number of speakers to whom the system must respond and the amount of noise in the communication channel. Errors tend to become more frequent as confusability increases. Syntactic contraints can significantly reduce the effect. This error pattern is as true for human listeners as it is for machines.

essor in a system designed to emulate the entire process of human speech communication. The user communicates with the system by telephone. The computer, which is intended to function as an airline ticket agent, responds in a synthetic voice. The integration of the necessary functions into a single device has enabled us to study the interaction of the subsystems and their control.

As a complete simulation of human communication the Bell Laboratories machine is the most advanced system known to us. The individual components, however, are less advanced than those of experimental systems in other laboratories. There are speech-recognition systems that work with vocabularies much larger than the 127 words our machine recognizes, and there are systems with a more flexible syntax. There are more sophisticated semantic processors that accept typed input instead of speech. There are processors that respond faster than ours does. A question that is asked in 10 seconds receives a reply on our system after about 50 seconds. We hope to improve the performance of all the building blocks of our system.

In the airline-information system the acoustic processor and the syntactic parser are coupled, so that the acoustic processor tests each hypothetical word-identification made by the parser for agreement with spectral information. The rest of the system, with the exception of two memory units that are shared by all the components, is devoted to semantic processing.

The semantic processor incorporates a world model, whose state can be changed as a conversation progresses, and a memory module, which cannot be altered. The world model is based on a set of concepts, each of which can take on a number of values. Among the concepts are "destination," "departure day" and "departure time." During a particular conversation these categories might be assigned the values "Boston," "Tuesday" and "5:00 P.M.," whereas another state of the world model might correspond to the values "Chicago," "unknown" and "unknown." The semantic processor determines a new state from its present state, from the words in the input sentence and from the transitions in the state diagram that were employed in generating the sentence. The need for the latter two sources of information reflects the fact that semantic content is a function both of the words and of their relations in a sentence.

The memory units store two kinds of information: facts and procedures. Facts are of two types. Airline schedules are stored as a portion of the *Official Airline Guide,* but relations among the concepts in the *Airline Guide* must also be stored. If the system is asked the elapsed time of a flight, it can calculate the time from the listed departure and arrival times; for it to do so, however, the time zone of each city must be available. (In the *Official Airline Guide* all times are local.)

Procedures are special-purpose programs that use stored facts to derive new information from an input and from the current state of the world model. For example, one program is a perpetual calendar, which can find the day of the week for any given date. The conversion is needed because a question may specify only a departure date, whereas the *Official Airline Guide* is organized by day of the week.

When an internal instruction calls for a reply to the user, the system activates a linguistic encoder. The semantic analyzer tells the encoder what concepts are to be communicated from the world model. Then the encoder retrieves grammar and vocabulary from memory and transforms the concepts into a sequence of symbols. The speech synthesizer transforms the sequence into speech [see "The Synthesis of Speech," by James L. Flanagan, *Scientific American*, February 1972].

In what ways can the art of speech understanding be advanced? We see two basic aims. For the near term it is important to seek a better grasp of the fine structure of speech communication. This should include detailed information about the kind of signal analysis done by the human ear and a better understanding of the relation between sound symbols (such as phonemes and syllables) and actual sounds. More efficient ways of exploiting this information must be developed and incorporated into recognition systems.

For the long term several areas of investigation may bring significant advances. We have stressed that the speech code includes a number of coexisting kinds of structure, such as phonology, syntax and semantics. A general theory of such complex codes is needed, particularly so that the interactions of the levels can be coordinated and controlled. It is also desirable to gain a better understanding of the processes by which people acquire a language. Although present speech recognizers are "trained," the training is rudimentary and cannot be altered through "experience." We believe this lack of adaptive abilities is a serious disadvantage. The best design strategy is not to program a computer directly with the wealth of descriptive detail that constitutes a natural language but rather to give it the basic set of expectations and abilities that are needed to learn a language.

It is hard to predict how well these investigative strategies can ultimately succeed in approximating natural speech communication. Whatever the rate of progress, this goal will continue to be pursued. Some success is guaranteed, and wisdom will be required in its application.

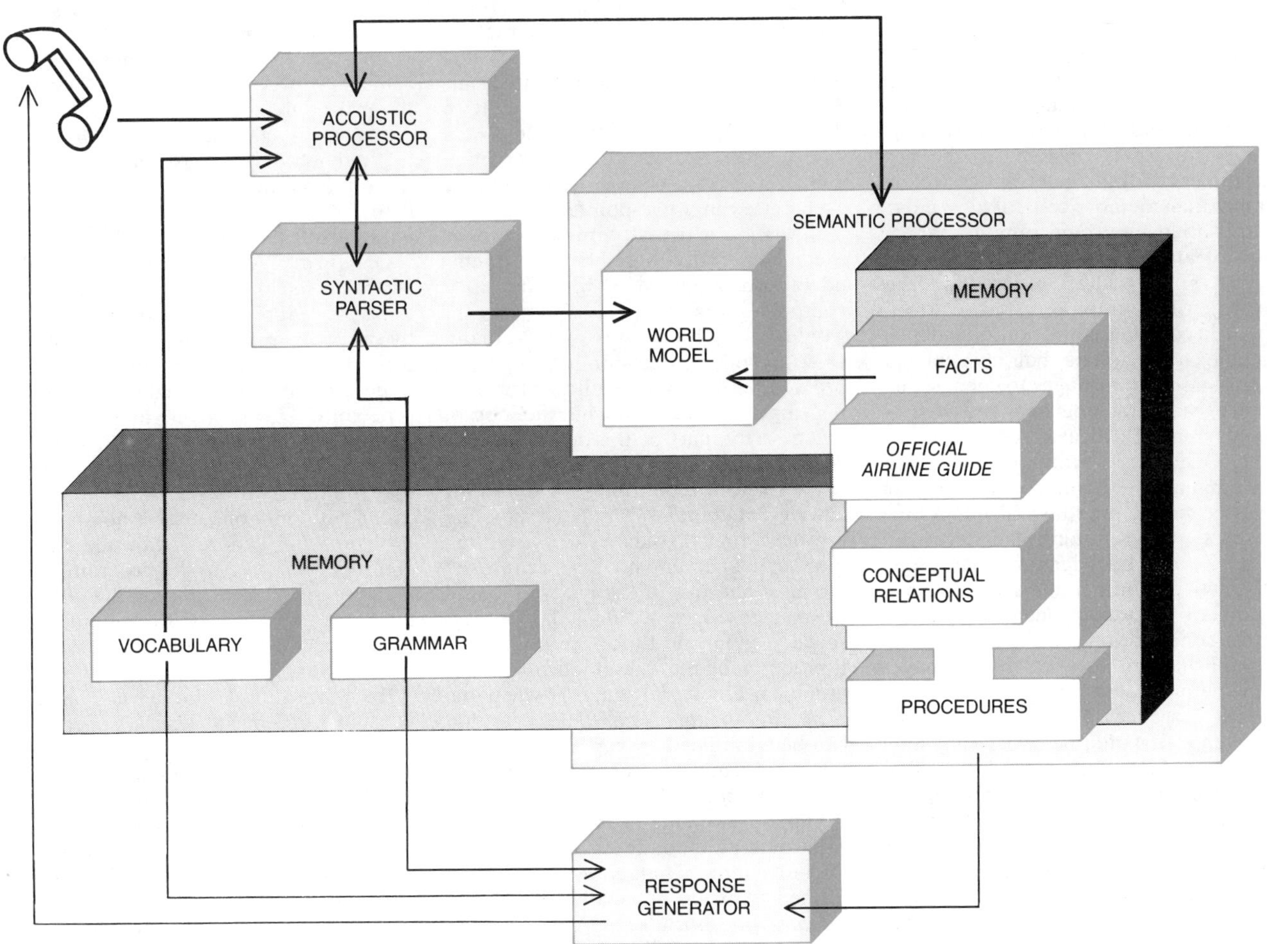

COMPLETE SIMULATION of human speech communication is attempted by an automated system constructed by the authors and their colleagues at Bell Laboratories. Functional relations among major parts of the system are shown here in a block diagram. The user asks for information about airline timetables over the telephone, and the computer replies in a synthesized voice. Heavy arrows trace the flow of information related to speech recognition. The generation of a response is traced by lighter arrows. Memory modules concerned with semantic processing include facts and procedures related to flights and reservations. Nonsemantic memory stores vocabulary templates and grammatical rules used both in speech recognition and in speech synthesis. The semantic processor also includes a world model, which is constantly updated with data based on the user's questions and on the information in the semantic memory.

11 Programming Languages

by Lawrence G. Tesler
September 1984

They offer a great diversity of ways to specify a computation. A language transforms the computer into a "virtual machine" whose features and capabilities are determined by the software

A programming language is more than a notation for giving instructions to a computer. A language and the software that "understands" it can totally remake the computer, transforming it into a machine with an entirely different character. The hardware components of a typical computer are registers, memory cells, adders and so on, and when a programmer writes in the computer's native language those are the facilities he must keep in mind. A new language brings with it a new model of the machine. Although the hardware is unchanged, the programmer can think in terms of variables rather than memory cells, of files of data rather than input and output channels and of algebraic formulas rather than registers and adders. A few languages even give the computer a split personality: it becomes a collection of independent agencies that do their own calculations and send messages to one another.

Programming languages and their dialects number at least several hundred, and possibly a few thousand. The natural languages of human communication may be more numerous still, but in some respects programming languages are more diverse. Each language has its own distinctive grammar and syntax, its own manner of expressing ideas. In principle most computational tasks could be accomplished with any of the languages, but the programs would look very different; moreover, writing a program for a given task would be easier with some languages than with others. Here I shall describe some of the programming languages in common use and attempt to give an impression both of the elements they have in common and of the features that distinguish them.

The illustration on page 112 shows several stages in the development of a short program in Logo, a language devised in the late 1960's by Seymour Papert and his colleagues at the Massachusetts Institute of Technology. One interesting feature of Logo is the ability to control a "turtle," a small robotic device that can move forward and backward, turn in place and raise or lower a pen that leaves a trace of the turtle's path. In many cases the turtle is not a real device but instead is simulated on a video display.

The initial version of the program consists entirely of commands to the turtle. First the pen is lowered, then the two commands *forward 50* and *right 144* are repeated five times and then the pen is raised. When the turtle follows the instructions, it draws a five-pointed star. The command *forward 50* causes it to draw a straight line 50 units long; *right 144* specifies a clockwise turn through 144 degrees, the change of heading at each vertex in a five-pointed star.

If writing a list of commands to be executed serially were the only method of conveying one's intentions to a computer, creating a complex program would be all but impossible. Actually Logo and other programming languages provide a number of facilities for simplifying and generalizing instructions. In this case the part of the program most conspicuously in need of improvement is the fivefold repetition of the *forward* and *right* statements. Whenever possible a programmer avoids writing anything more than once, and not just because the typing is onerous. If the program could be condensed, it would take up less space in memory. Furthermore, repetition increases the likelihood of a typographical error, particularly when the program is being revised. The repetition can be eliminated by replacing the five turtle-movement commands with the statement *repeat 5 [forward 50 right 144]*.

Suppose now the programmer wants to draw a nine-pointed star with edges 80 units long. That could be accomplished by means of a statement such as *repeat 9 [forward 80 right 160]* but it is apparent the same basic program structure is being duplicated, with differences only in detail. A better solution is to define a more general procedure in which the number of points and the length of a side are given as variable quantities. In Logo the word *to* introduces a procedure definition. Thus the phrase *to star* indicates the instructions that follow should be stored as the method for drawing a star. Thereafter *star* becomes a new command in the language, one that can be entered into a program just as the built-in commands *forward* and *right* would be.

The variables in the *star* procedure are of the kind called parameters, which are "passed" to the procedure at the time it is invoked. In Logo the name of a parameter is preceded by a colon. Hence the procedure would be defined with a phrase such as *to star :size :points;* typing *star 80 9* would assign a value of 80 to the parameter *size* and a value of 9 to *points,* thereby generating a nine-pointed star 80 units on a side.

One further refinement might be added to the *star* procedure. In Logo a defined procedure can be called not only by the programmer but also by another procedure. This is an important source of power, but it increases the hazard of a procedure's being given inappropriate parameters. For example, in the intricacy of a program one might not realize that the turtle would be asked to draw a star with only one or two points. The problem can be addressed by adding the clause *if points* > *2* to the program. The *if* clause serves as a "guard" that allows the turtle to draw only if the number of points specified is greater than two.

From the example above it can be seen that Logo has at least a superficial resemblance to a natural language such as English. It has a vocabulary of words, numbers and other symbols (collectively called tokens) that can be strung together to form larger constructs analogous to sentences. Some of the tokens are "key words" with a fixed meaning; others are defined by the programmer. Some of the tokens act as verbs; others function as nouns, modifiers or marks of punctuation. The rules governing how tokens can be combined constitute a grammar.

The sentences of a programming language are generally classified as declarations and statements. A declaration defines what something is, what it means or how it is structured. In the Logo program, *to star :size :points* is a declaration that defines *star* as the name of a procedure and defines *size* and *points* as variables that serve as parameters to *star*. A statement, on the other hand, generally describes part of an algorithm; it specifies some action to be taken. In most cases a statement has the form of an imperative: it begins with a verb, which is followed by an object or a modifiei. In the *repeat* statement *repeat* itself is a verb, the number following it serves as an adverb and the material in brackets is the object of the verb.

The vocabulary and the syntax of the *star* procedure are peculiar to Logo, but the mechanisms that control the flow of execution through the procedure can be found in the great majority of programming languages. In the absence of any explicit control statement, execution is sequential. If one imagines the computer as reading the program, it reads the lines from top to bottom, so that unless the flow is altered each statement is executed exactly once.

One program element that alters the flow of execution is the *repeat* statement, which is an example of a looping, or iterative, construct. When the computer encounters *repeat n* followed by a group of statements in brackets, it reads and executes the material in brackets *n* times. Another way of controlling the computer's progress through a program is conditional execution, which in Logo (as in many other languages) is embodied in the *if* statement. The statements governed by an *if* are executed only if some specified condition is met.

There are many variations on the basic ideas of iterative and conditional execution. The *repeat* statement is useful only if it is known before the loop is entered how many times it is to be executed. Other constructs allow the termination of the loop to be controlled by events within the loop itself; in essence a conditional expression is incorporated into the loop. In a number of languages a statement beginning with the key word *while* is repeated as long as a stated condition remains true. Another way of diverting program flow is an "unconditional jump," or *goto* statement, which simply shifts execution to a new point in the program. In recent years the *goto* statement has been in some disrepute among computer scientists on the grounds that programs with many such jumps are difficult to follow (for the human reader, not for the computer).

The notion of procedure definition itself is a vital element of programming. It is the chief mechanism of abstraction, the process of converting specific instances (a five-pointed star 50 units on a

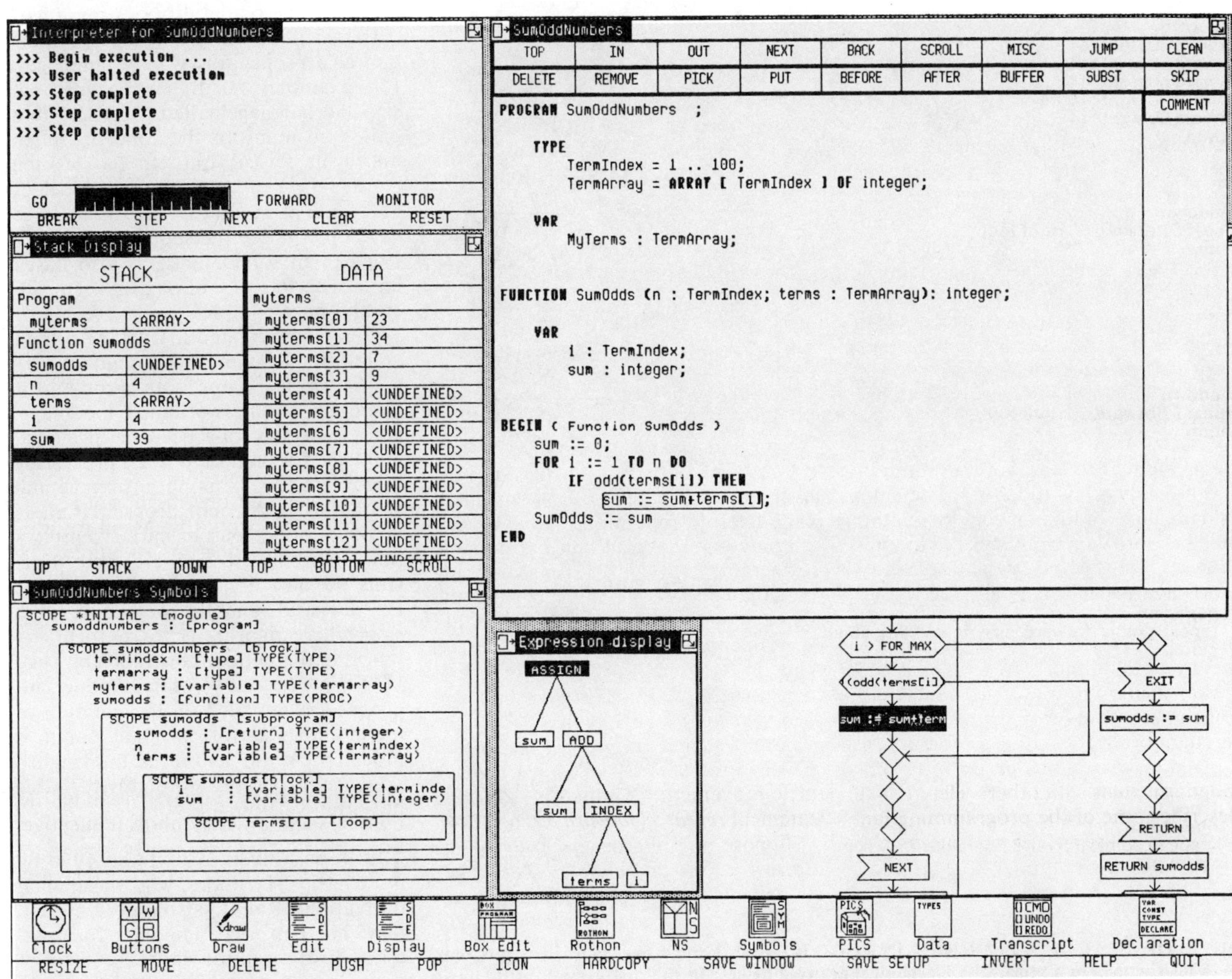

SNAPSHOT OF A PROGRAM in execution is given by a program-development system called PECAN. Most of the source text, or original program, is displayed in the large window at the upper right; it is a program in the Pascal language for summing the odd terms in an array of integers. Commands controlling the execution of the program are given in the window at the upper left. Execution has been stopped at the statement where the actual calculation of the sum is done; the statement is enclosed in a box in the source-text-display window. Below the source text, part of a flow chart for the program is visible, and to the left of that is a binary tree showing the logical structure of the assignment statement. The nested boxes at the lower left indicate the scope of symbols in the program. The stack-display window gives a view of the program's data structures. PECAN was developed by Steven P. Reiss of Brown University, who also created this illustration.

side) into general concepts (a star with any number of points and any size). A procedure is defined only once and is stored in memory only once, but it can be invoked from many places in a program, thereby allowing a product of mental labor to be used many times. Each time a procedure is called, execution transfers to the area in memory where it is stored; when the procedure has been completed, execution resumes with the instruction immediately following the call. A specialized kind of procedure, a function, returns a value of some kind to the calling program. The tangent function, for example, is given an angle as a parameter when it is called, and it returns a value equal to the tangent of the angle.

Among the hundreds or thousands of programming languages only a dozen or so are in widespread use. The illustrations on pages 28 through 30 show the same problem programmed in six languages: BASIC, Pascal, COBOL, Forth, APL and Lisp. These six were chosen in part because they are well-established languages with a sizable population of programmers fluent in their use. They also illustrate well the great diversity of ways a single idea can be expressed. In each case an attempt has been made to write in a style that would be natural or comfortable to a programmer accustomed to the language.

The problem is not one of great intrinsic interest. It was chosen because a solution can readily be programmed in all the languages and because it demonstrates the essential mechanisms for defining variables and procedures and for controlling iterative and conditional execution. The problem is to sum the odd numbers in a set of integers.

The BASIC programming language was developed in 1965 by John G. Kemeny and Thomas E. Kurtz of Dartmouth College, primarily as a language for introductory courses in computer science. It has since fallen from favor somewhat in the academic world, but it has become popular in other contexts, notably the programming of microcomputers. In BASIC every line is identified by a number, and the control of flow through the program is based largely on references to the line numbers. The heart of the sample program is a loop in which all the statements between a *FOR* statement and a *NEXT* statement are executed repeatedly. The actual calculation is done in an assignment statement, which begins with the key word *LET* and gives a new value to a variable.

Pascal was designed in about 1970 by Niklaus Wirth of the Swiss Federal Institute of Technology in Zurich. It is another language meant for teaching that has been adapted to many other purposes. Pascal, unlike BASIC, requires the programmer to declare each variable and to specify its type; in this case the variables are integers and arrays of integers. Procedures and functions are referred to by name rather than by line number, which improves the readability of programs.

Pascal has been particularly important as a progenitor of later languages. For example, Wirth has recently designed a language called Modula-2 that builds on many of the concepts introduced in Pascal but emphasizes the construction of a program as a set of independent modules. Ada, a language developed under the sponsorship of the Department of Defense, is also based largely on Pascal, although it is considerably more complex.

COBOL was created in 1960 by a joint committee of computer manufacturers and users. The name is an acronym for Common Business-oriented Language, and COBOL has long been the principal language for large-scale data processing in government, banking, insurance and similar areas. A COBOL program is made up of four divisions, or parts: identification, environment, data and procedure. Only the data division, where variables are declared, and the procedure division, where algorithms are set forth, are shown in the bottom illustration on page 114. Whereas many programming languages are modeled on the notation of mathematics or formal logic, COBOL is modeled on the syntax of the English sentence; programs are highly readable but often verbose.

Forth was invented in about 1970 by Charles H. Moore, who was then at the National Radio Astronomy Observatory. The aim was a language for process control, in particular the control of telescopes, but again the language has been extended to other domains. It has been adopted for many minicomputer and microcomputer applications, in part because Forth programs tend to take up little space in memory. In contrast to COBOL, Forth programs are difficult

```
pendown
forward 50 right 144
forward 50 right 144
forward 50 right 144
forward 50 right 144
forward 50 right 144
penup
```

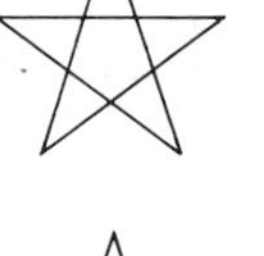

```
pendown
repeat 5 [forward 50 right 144]
penup
```

```
pendown
repeat 9 [forward 80 right 160]
penup
```

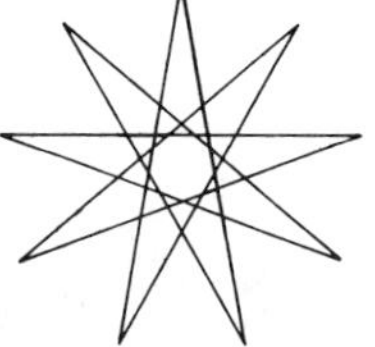

```
to star :size :points
  pendown
  repeat :points [forward :size right 720/:points]
  penup
```

```
to star :size :points
  if :points > 2
    [pendown
     repeat :points [forward :size right 720/:points]
     penup]
```

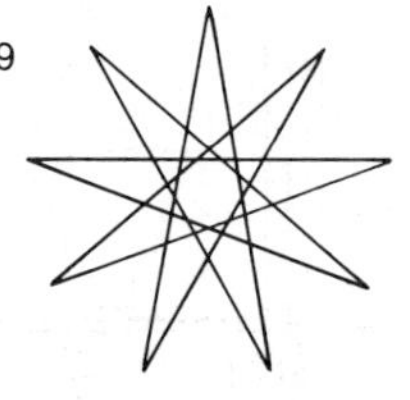

DEVELOPMENT OF A PROGRAM IN LOGO is traced through five stages. The program gives instructions to a "turtle," a mechanical drawing device. In the first version of the program all the instructions for drawing a five-pointed star are given explicitly. The *repeat* statement in the second version condenses the program and reduces the likelihood of error. The third version has the same basic program structure but draws a larger star with nine points. In the fourth version a procedure is defined in which the length of a side and the number of points are variable quantities. In the final version of the program an *if* clause allows the procedure to execute only if the number of points specified is greater than two. The *repeat* and *if* statements are examples of control structures important in virtually all programming languages.

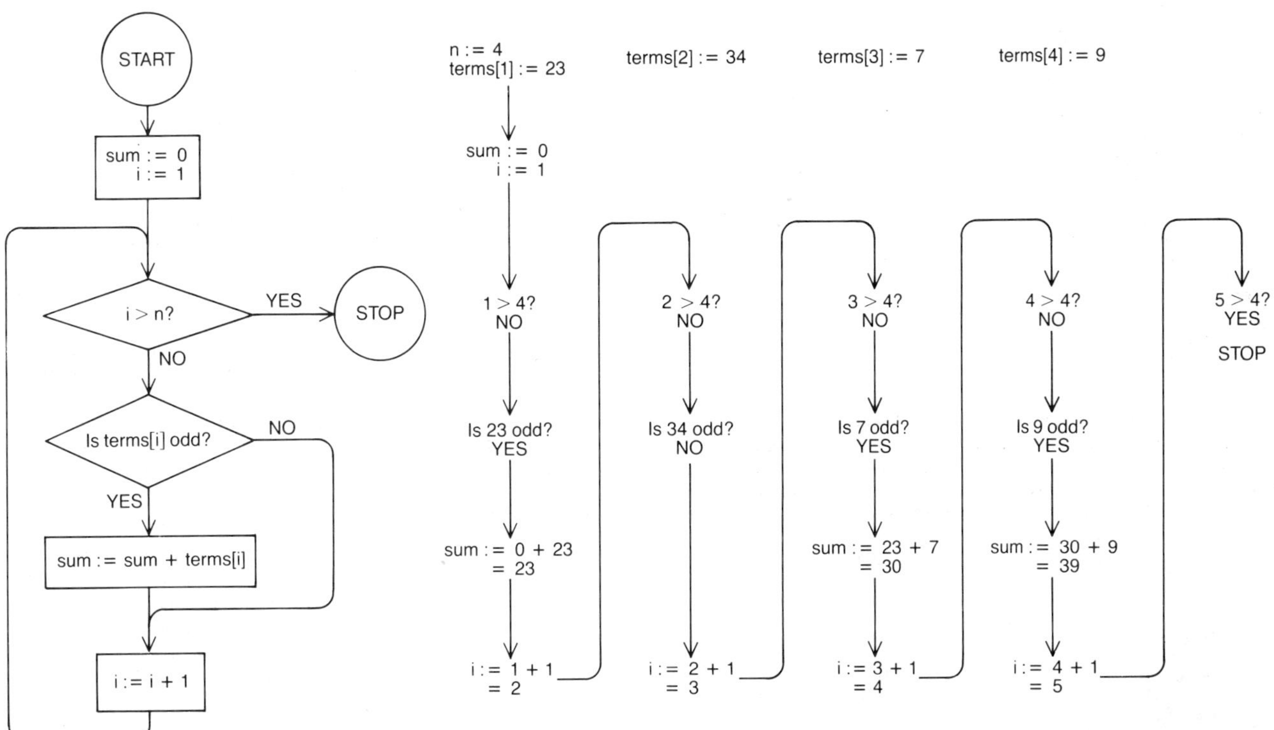

SAMPLE CALCULATION employed to illustrate the characteristics of several programming languages finds the sum of the odd elements in an array of *n* integers. The algorithm outlined in the flow chart at the left is embodied directly in the Pascal, BASIC and COBOL programs shown on the next page. The heart of the algorithm is a loop executed *n* times. On each passage through the loop a term of the array is examined; if it is an odd number, it is added to the running total. At the right the successive values assumed by the variables in the procedure are traced as the calculation is done for an array of four numbers. The symbol ":=" gives to the variable on the left the value computed on the right. A number in brackets, as in *terms*[*1*], is equivalent to a subscript: it identifies an element of the array *terms*.

to read and extremely terse; several key words are mere marks of punctuation.

In Forth the central facility of the computer is the "stack," an area of memory organized like a stack of cafeteria trays, so that the first item put on the stack is the last one removed. In the Forth version of the sample program it is assumed that the array of numbers and its size are at the top of the stack when the function is called; all calculations are done on the stack, and the value of the function is returned at the top of the stack. No variables are defined.

APL has a syntax even more concise than that of Forth. The initials stand for A Programming Language, but in 1961, when a book on APL was first published (by Kenneth E. Iverson of the International Business Machines Corporation), the language was merely a notation for expressing problems in applied mathematics; implementation on a computer came later. A distinguishing feature of APL is that it can deal as easily with an entire array of numbers as with a single value; a command that adds two numbers can be applied without change to arrays with thousands of elements. The sample APL program sums the odd elements of an array in a single statement. Taking the remainder of each number modulo 2 identifies the odd elements, which are then extracted from the array and added.

Lisp is in some respects the simplest of the languages considered here. It has only one kind of statement, namely a function call; its great source of power is that the value returned by a function can be another function. Lisp was developed in the late 1950's by John McCarthy, then at M.I.T., and since then it has been the preeminent language of those pursuing the goal of artificial intelligence. The name is derived from "list processing"; both programs and data are structured as lists.

The sample program could be written in Lisp as an iterative loop, but a Lisp programmer would be more likely to choose a recursive technique, in which a procedure calls on itself; the called procedure then issues another call to itself, and so on. Some means of escape must be provided or the recursion will become an infinite regress. The usual means is a conditional statement within the procedure: when the condition is satisfied, execution returns to the next-higher level.

In the sample program the set of numbers takes the form of a linked list. If the list is empty, the function returns a result of zero. Otherwise if the first element of the list is odd, it is added to the sum, and the function calls on itself with an argument consisting of the list that remains after the first element is removed. Eventually all the elements are stripped off in this way, at which point the entire chain of pending calculations is completed.

In general computers are not built to "understand" Logo or BASIC or other languages that operate at a similar level of abstraction. The circuitry of the computer recognizes only the electronic embodiment of binary numbers. A program stored in a form that can be executed—the form called machine code—is a sequence of such numbers. Some of them represent instructions to the central processor, some of them are data and some are addresses in memory.

It is possible to write a program directly in machine code, but it is tedious, and the probability of completing even a small project without error is slight. (The computer has no trouble distinguishing 01101001 from 01011001 and remembering what each code means, but the human eye and mind are not used to best advantage in such tasks.) In the late 1940's and early 1950's, in an attempt to reduce the toil of writing machine code, programmers invented a notation called assembly code. Instead of writing down the binary digits for each machine instruction, the programmer wrote a short word or abbreviation, such as ADD, SUB or MOVE. Similarly, the address in memory where a variable is stored was replaced by a

```
program SumOddNumbers;
type TermIndex = 1..100;
     TermArray = array [TermIndex] of integer;
var  myTerms: TermArray;
function SumOdds(n: TermIndex; terms: TermArray): integer;
  var i: TermIndex;
      sum: integer;
  begin
    sum := 0;
    for i := 1 to n do
      if Odd(terms[i]) then
          sum := sum + terms[i];
    SumOdds := sum;
  end;
begin
  myTerms[1] := 23; myTerms[2] := 34; myTerms[3] := 7; myTerms[4] := 9;
  WriteLn(SumOdds(4, myTerms))
end.
```

PASCAL PROGRAM for summing the odd numbers in an array employs a function named *SumOdds* with two parameters: an integer *n* and an array *terms*. The function consists of the statements in the panel of color; the remainder of the program sets up a particular array on which *SumOdds* operates. In Pascal every variable must be introduced in a declaration that gives the variable's type. Some types, such as *integer*, are built into the programming language; others, such as *TermIndex*, are defined by the programmer. The loop is designated by the *for... to... do...* statement and the conditional is designated by the *if... then...* statement.

```
 100 DIM T(100)
 200 READ N
 300 FOR I = 1 TO N
 400    READ T(I)
 500 NEXT I
 600 GOSUB 1100
 700 PRINT S
 800 GOTO 2000
 900 DATA 4
1000 DATA 23, 34, 7, 9
1100 REM MAKE S THE SUM OF THE ODD ELEMENTS IN ARRAY T(1..N)
1200 LET S = 0
1300 FOR I = 1 TO N
1400    IF NOT ODD(T(I)) THEN GOTO 1600
1500    LET S = S + T(I)
1600 NEXT I
1700 RETURN
2000 END
```

BASIC PROGRAM employs a subroutine to add up the odd terms in an array. The subroutine, indicated by the panel of color, has no name but must be referred to by line number; it is called by the *GOSUB 1100* statement. A BASIC subroutine also has no parameters; values are assigned to "global" variables, which the subroutine can then access. A variable does not have to be declared in BASIC unless it has subscripts, as in an array; in this example the *DIM* (for "dimension") declaration states that the array *T* can have as many as 100 elements. The *FOR... NEXT...* statement defines a loop and the *IF... THEN...* statement defines a conditional.

```
DATA DIVISION.
WORKING-STORAGE SECTION.
01 NUMERIC-VARIABLES USAGE IS COMPUTATIONAL.
    02 TERMS PICTURE 9999 OCCURS 100 TIMES INDEXED BY I.
    02 N PICTURE 999.
    02 SUM PICTURE 999999.
    02 HALF-TERM PICTURE 9999.
    02 RMDR PICTURE 9.
PROCEDURE DIVISION.
EXAMPLE.
    MOVE 23 TO TERMS(1).
    MOVE 34 TO TERMS(2).
    MOVE  7 TO TERMS(3).
    MOVE  9 TO TERMS(4).
    MOVE  4 TO N.
    PERFORM SUM-ODDS.
SUM-ODDS.
    MOVE 0 TO SUM.
    PERFORM CONSIDER-ONE-TERM VARYING I FROM 1 BY 1 UNTIL I > N.
CONSIDER-ONE-TERM.
    DIVIDE 2 INTO TERMS(I) GIVING HALF-TERM REMAINDER RMDR.
    IF RMDR IS EQUAL TO 1; ADD TERMS(I) TO SUM.
```

COBOL PROGRAM for the sum-of-the-odd-numbers calculation uses a procedure named *SUM-ODDS* that calls another procedure named *CONSIDER-ONE-TERM*. A COBOL procedure cannot have parameters, and so before *SUM-ODDS* is called by a *PERFORM* statement, values are assigned to *N* and to the first *N* elements of *TERMS*. The key words *PERFORM... VARYING...* define the loop and *IF...* introduces the conditional clause. In the data division the numbers 01 and 02 designate two levels in a hierarchy of data structures. *PICTURE* specifies how values are to be displayed. Only an excerpt from the complete program is shown.

name assigned to the variable. Numerical values were expressed in decimal notation. The words representing instructions were chosen to be more easily remembered than binary values, and so they came to be known as mnemonics.

At first the translation from assembly code to machine code was done by hand. It is a straightforward process: a table records the unchanging correspondence between instruction mnemonics and their binary codes, and a similar table can be constructed for the variable names appearing in a program. The process is clearly suitable for mechanization, and programs called assemblers were soon written to do the translation.

Some programming is still done in assembly code, because it offers direct access to all the facilities of the computer. Carefully written assembly code is fast and efficient, and if a compromise must be made between speed of execution and program size, the programmer is in direct control of such decisions. Modern assemblers are sophisticated translation programs. Nevertheless, there is still a rough one-to-one correspondence between lines of assembly code and machine instructions, so that programs tend to be quite long, and the possibilities for error are legion. The control structures available in most assembly codes are primitive. What is most important, assembly code remains closer to the computer's language than to the programmer's. Algorithms must be expressed in terms of what the machine is to do rather than in whatever terms might be natural to the problem at hand. (An assembly-code version of the odd-element-sum calculation is shown in the top illustration on page 117.)

In planning the solution to a problem one is unlikely to think in terms of registers and memory addresses; rather, the problem itself suggests the appropriate notation. If the problem is one in physics, the design of a program might begin with an equation such as $F = ma$; in business the formula chosen might be *profit* = *revenue* − *expenses*. The operations specified by the formula are then translated into explicit instructions to the machine. Early programmers recognized that this translation too might be mechanized. In that idea is the genesis of languages such as FORTRAN, BASIC and Pascal. For some years languages of this kind were called high-level languages; it now seems appropriate to refer to them simply as programming languages, because machine code and assembly code do not really qualify as languages.

Since 1960 most software has been written with the aid of programming languages. They have many advantages over lower-level representations. Because one statement can give rise to many machine instructions, programs tend to be shorter, which both reduces the labor invested in writing them and improves their clarity. Working with concepts pertinent to the problem rather than with those defined by the machine also reduces the chance of error. Furthermore, it introduces the possibility of "machine independence," of writing a single program that can be run on many computers.

It is important to distinguish between a programming language and an implementation of the language. The language itself is the notation, the set of rules that define the syntax of a valid program. An implementation of a language is a program that converts the high-level notation into sequences of machine instructions.

There are two main kinds of language implementation: compilers and interpreters. A compiler translates the entire text of a high-level program in one continuous process, creating a complete machine-code program that can then be executed independently of the compiler. Working in a compiled language generally has three stages: the program text is created with a text editor or word-processing program, then the text is compiled and finally the compiled program is executed. The term compiler was coined in 1951 by Grace Murray Hopper, then at Remington-Rand Univac, to describe her first translator program. As part of the translation process the program retrieved standard sequences of machine instructions from tables stored on magnetic tape and compiled them into a complete program.

An interpreter executes a program one statement at a time, transforming each high-level construct into machine instructions on the fly. The difference between a compiler and an interpreter is analogous to the difference between a translator of literary works and a conversational interpreter. The translator takes a completed manuscript and delivers a new text in another language. The conversational interpreter renders each phrase or sentence as it is spoken. Actually most interpreter programs do some initial processing of the text before execution begins; key words are converted into shorter tokens and variable names are replaced by addresses. Still, the two kinds of implementation remain distinct: for an interpreted program to be executed, the interpreter must be present in main memory, whereas once a program has been compiled the compiler is no longer needed.

In principle any programming language could be either interpreted or compiled, but in most cases custom has made one or the other kind of implementation more common. FORTRAN, COBOL and Pascal are generally compiled; Logo, Forth and APL are almost always interpreted; BASIC and Lisp are widely available in both forms. The chief advantage of compilation is speed; because an interpreter must determine a suitable sequence of instructions each time a statement is executed, an interpreted language is almost inevitably slower. On the other hand, an interpreted language is often more convenient for the programmer; it is well suited to an interactive style of program development. Sections of a program can be written, tested and executed without leaving the interpreter, and when an error is found, it can be fixed immediately, without the need to return to a text-editing program and then compile the program again.

The inner mechanism of a compiler or

```
: SUMODDS
 0 SWAP 0
  DO
    SWAP DUP 2 MOD
      IF +
      ELSE DROP
      THEN
   LOOP
;
23 34 7 9 4 SUMODDS .
```

WORD	STACK							COMMENT
23	23							
34	23	34						
7	23	34	7					
9	23	34	7	9				
4	23	34	7	9	4			
SUMODDS	23	34	7	9	4			Call SUMODDS.
0	23	34	7	9	4	0		
SWAP	23	34	7	9	0	4		
0	23	34	7	9	0	4	0	
DO	23	34	7	9	0			Remove loop-control values.
SWAP	23	34	7	0	9			
DUP	23	34	7	0	9	9		
2	23	34	7	0	9	9	2	
MOD	23	34	7	0	9	1		
IF	23	34	7	0	9			TOS = 1; do IF to ELSE.
+	23	34	7	9				
ELSE	23	34	7	9				Skip past THEN.
DROP	23	34	7	9				Skipped.
THEN	23	34	7	9				Skipped.
LOOP	23	34	7	9				Return to DO.
DO	23	34	7	9				
SWAP	23	34	9	7				
DUP	23	34	9	7	7			
2	23	34	9	7	7	2		
MOD	23	34	9	7	1			
IF	23	34	9	7				TOS = 1; do IF to ELSE.
+	23	34	16					
ELSE	23	34	16					Skip past THEN.
DROP	23	34	16					Skipped.
THEN	23	34	16					Skipped.
LOOP	23	34	16					Return to DO.
DO	23	34	16					
SWAP	23	16	34					
DUP	23	16	34	34				
2	23	16	34	34	2			
MOD	23	16	34	0				
IF	23	16	34					TOS = 0; do ELSE to THEN.
+	23	16	34					Skipped.
ELSE	23	16	34					
DROP	23	16						
THEN	23	16						
LOOP	23	16						Return to DO.
DO	23	16						
SWAP	16	23						
DUP	16	23	23					
2	16	23	23	2				
MOD	16	23	1					
IF	16	23						TOS = 1; do IF to ELSE.
+	39							
ELSE	39							Skip past THEN.
DROP	39							Skipped.
THEN	39							Skipped.
LOOP	39							No more iterations.
;	39							Return from SUMODDS.
	<empty stack>							Print the result.

FORTH PROGRAM for summing the odd numbers in an array declares no variables or other data structures but works exclusively with values on a "pushdown stack." When *SUMODDS* is called, the elements of the array are expected to be on the stack, with the number of elements at the top. The line below the procedure definition would be typed to execute the program with an array of four elements. A complete trace of the program's execution is then given, showing the content of the stack after each word is executed. A numeric "word" such as 0 or 2 pushes the number onto the stack; *SWAP* exchanges the top two elements; *DUP* pushes a copy of the top element onto the stack; *DROP* discards the top element. Operators such as "+" and *MOD* replace the top two elements on the stack with the result of the operation. The loop construct *DO* removes two elements (say i and j) from the stack and executes the words up to *LOOP* a total of $i-j$ times. The conditional *IF* executes the words between *IF* and *ELSE* when the top of the stack (TOS) is nonzero and otherwise executes the words between *ELSE* and *THEN*.

an interpreter is a subject too large to be covered here, but the structure of a typical compiler can be described in outline. There are at least three phases in the compilation process. The first phase is a lexical analysis, in which the compiler identifies the various symbols in the text of the program and classifies them as key words, numerical values, variable names and so on. The next phase is parsing, in which the compiler determines the syntactic relations of the key words and builds a skeleton representation of the program's structure. Each *if*, for example, is associated with a subsequent *then*. In the third phase machine code corresponding to the parsed structure is generated. Some compilers add a fourth phase of optimization, in which the code is revised to improve its efficiency.

Over the past 30 years much careful thought has been given to the design of compilers, and there is now a well-developed methodology for their construction. The first step is to define the language itself in a completely explicit form. It is now common practice to specify the grammar in terms of "production rules" that can be applied recursively to generate all the possible statements of the language. The creation of the compiler is then a comparatively straightforward job of programming; there are even compiler compilers that can automate part of the task.

The idea of a programming language has been around almost as long as there have been large-scale digital computers. In 1945 the German mathematician Konrad Zuse invented a notation he called Plankalkül. Statements in the language had a two-dimensional format: variables and their subscripts were aligned vertically and operations on them were laid out along the horizontal axis. Zuse wrote Plankalkül programs on paper—including one that made simulated chess moves—but he did not implement the language. Many of the ideas he developed, however, have been introduced into modern languages.

Surely the most influential of all programming languages was FORTRAN, developed by John Backus and his colleagues at IBM between 1954 and 1957. The name stands for "formula translation," and the language was intended for scientific and numerical calculations, for which it is still in use. At the time the project was greeted with considerable skepticism. Computing machinery was then a scarce and valuable resource, with the result that much emphasis was put on program efficiency. It was assumed that a higher-level language would inevitably compromise efficiency, but Backus and his group performed an extraordinary feat: they created a compiler whose output was equal in quality to a hand-coded program.

At about the same time, Hopper and her co-workers at Remington-Rand Univac developed a programming language called Flow-Matic for business data processing. It was less sophisticated than FORTRAN, but experience gained with it over a period of several years was the main inspiration for COBOL. Another major language introduced in the late 1950's was Algol (which stands for "algorithmic language"). Algol-58, the first version, was designed by an international committee that drew on both the pragmatic syntax of FORTRAN and the more elegant notation of Plankalkül. The result was a language that is both readable and practical and that has had an important place in the genealogy of later languages, including Pascal.

Quite a number of other languages trace their roots to the same era. COMIT was created for text analysis and APT for the control of machine tools. JOVIAL, a derivative of Algol, was the first widely used multipurpose language; it was suitable for both scientific and business applications. In the early 1960's Lisp appeared and so did the notation (but not an implementation) of APL.

The rapid proliferation of languages troubled many observers. After all, most mathematics is done with a single, universally accepted notation. Implementing a new language is a major undertaking, and becoming comfortable as a programmer in it also takes time. Soon several projects were launched to design a new language so complete and versatile that it could serve as the universal argot of programming. All such endeavors have failed. The partial success of PL/I, developed under the sponsorship of IBM in 1965, made it clear that a language for all purposes is likely to be both hard to learn and hard to implement. Moreover, as the techniques of computing became more diverse, people realized that new languages would continue to be needed to address special application areas.

In a sense, all programming-language research since 1957 has been motivated by attempts to correct flaws in FORTRAN. Indeed, FORTRAN itself has been re-

```
    ∇SUM ← SUMODDS TERMS
[1]  SUM ← +/(2|TERMS)/TERMS
    ∇
SUMODDS 23 34 7 9

              TERMS ← 23  34  7   9    Initial value assignment.
           (2|TERMS) ←  1   0  1   1    Array of remainders.
     (2|TERMS)/TERMS ← 23      7   9    Compression of two arrays.
   +/(2|TERMS)/TERMS ← 23   +  7 + 9    Reduction by addition.
                 SUM ← 39               Assignment of result.
```

APL PROGRAM calculates the sum of the odd elements in an array with a function whose operation is specified in a single line. The function has one parameter, *TERMS*, an array that "knows" how many elements it has, so that *N* need not appear in the program. An APL statement is executed from right to left except where parentheses alter the order of evaluation. In this example the expression (*2*|*TERMS*) is evaluated first; it calculates the remainder left after dividing each element of *TERMS* by 2 and creates an array of the same size as *TERMS* to hold the remainders. The symbol "/" can indicate two different operations, both of which appear in the example. In the expression (*2*|*TERMS*)/*TERMS*, "/" is a "compression" operator that creates a new array in which each element of *TERMS* appears only if the corresponding element of (*2*|*TERMS*) is nonzero. In the symbol "+/," "/" is a "reduction" operator that reduces the array to a single number by inserting a "+" between each pair of elements.

```
(DEFUN SUMODDS
  (LAMBDA (TERMS)
    (COND
      ((NULL TERMS) 0)
      ((ODD (CAR TERMS)) (PLUS (CAR TERMS) (SUMODDS (CDR TERMS))))
      (T (SUMODDS (CDR TERMS))))))

(SUMODDS '(23 34 7 9))

(SUMODDS '(23 34 7 9))
  = (PLUS 23 (SUMODDS '(34 7 9)))
    = (PLUS 23 (SUMODDS '(7 9)))
      = (PLUS 23 (PLUS 7 (SUMODDS '(9))))
        = (PLUS 23 (PLUS 7 (PLUS 9 (SUMODDS '( )))))
      = (PLUS 23 (PLUS 7 (PLUS 9 0)))
    = (PLUS 23 (PLUS 7 9))
  = (PLUS 23 16)
= 39
```

LISP PROGRAM calculates the odd-element sum by means of a function that calls on itself recursively. A Lisp function is a list, where the first element (called the *CAR*) is the name of the function and the remainder of the list (the *CDR*) gives the parameters. *DEFUN* is a function-defining function and *LAMBDA* precedes the names of the parameters; here the only parameter is the list of numbers *TERMS*. *COND* is a conditional function that evaluates the *CAR* of the lists that form its parameters. If the result is *T*, or true, the *CDR* of the list is evaluated; otherwise *COND* goes on to the next list. Here there are three possibilities. If *TERMS* is an empty list, *NULL* is true and *SUMODDS* returns a value of zero. If the *CAR* of *TERMS* is odd, the *CAR* is added to the running total and *SUMODDS* is called to evaluate the *CDR* of *TERMS*. If neither of these conditions is true, the *T* clause (which must be true) is reached; it simply calls *SUMODDS* with (*CDR* (*TERMS*)) as its parameter. Calculations are left pending during each call.

MACHINE CODE	LABELS	ASSEMBLY CODE INSTRUCTIONS		COMMENTS
00100100 01011111	SUMODDS	**MOVE.L**	(A7)+,A2	Pop return address from the stack into A2.
00100010 01011111		**MOVE.L**	(A7)+,A1	Pop address of first term into A1.
00110010 00011111		**MOVE.W**	(A7)+,D2	Pop n into D1.
01000010 01000010		**CLR.W**	D2	Assign a value of 0 to the sum in D2.
01001110 11111010 00000000 00001110		**JMP**	COUNT	Jump to the end of the loop to test if n = 0.
00001000 00101001 00000000 00000000 00000000 00000001	LOOP	**BTST**	0,1(A1)	If the term addressed by A1 is even...
01100111 00000010		**BEQ.S**	NEXT	...then go to NEXT
11010100 01010001		**ADD.W**	(A1),D2	...otherwise add the term to the sum in D2.
01010100 01001001	NEXT	**ADDQ.W**	#2,A1	Set A1 to the address of the next term.
01010001 11001001 11111111 11110010	COUNT	**DBF**	D1,LOOP	Decrement D1; unless it is −1, go to LOOP.
00111110 10000010		**MOVE.W**	D2, −(A7)	Push the sum from D2 onto the stack.
01001110 11010010		**JMP**	(A2)	Go to the return address.

MACHINE CODE AND ASSEMBLY CODE specify the steps of the odd-element calculation in terms of the hardware resources of the computer. The code is necessarily specific to a particular machine, in this case the Motorola 68000 microprocessor. The algorithm employed is much like that of the Pascal procedure *SumOdds*, although it is more compact than the code that would be generated by a Pascal compiler. Parameters are passed to the procedure on a stack and the result is returned on the stack; the address at which execution is to resume when the procedure is finished is also on the stack. The assembly-code version of the program, in which instructions take the form of "mnemonic" abbreviations, can be translated directly into the binary machine code executed by the microprocessor.

vised several times. The original version put certain arbitrary constraints on the programmer—for example, a variable name could be no longer than six characters—and offered only limited capabilities for defining data structures. Perhaps the most serious deficiencies were in the facilities for controlling program flow. All branch points had to be defined by line numbers, and unless care was taken the function of a program could be made quite obscure by a tangle of *GOTO* statements. Later versions introduced control structures that encourage a more readable programming style.

All the languages I have discussed so far can be classified as procedural, or prescriptive. A program written in such a language tells how to get a result; it says first do this, then do that, and so on. There are also nonprocedural, or descriptive, languages, and they are becoming increasingly important. A descriptive program states what result is

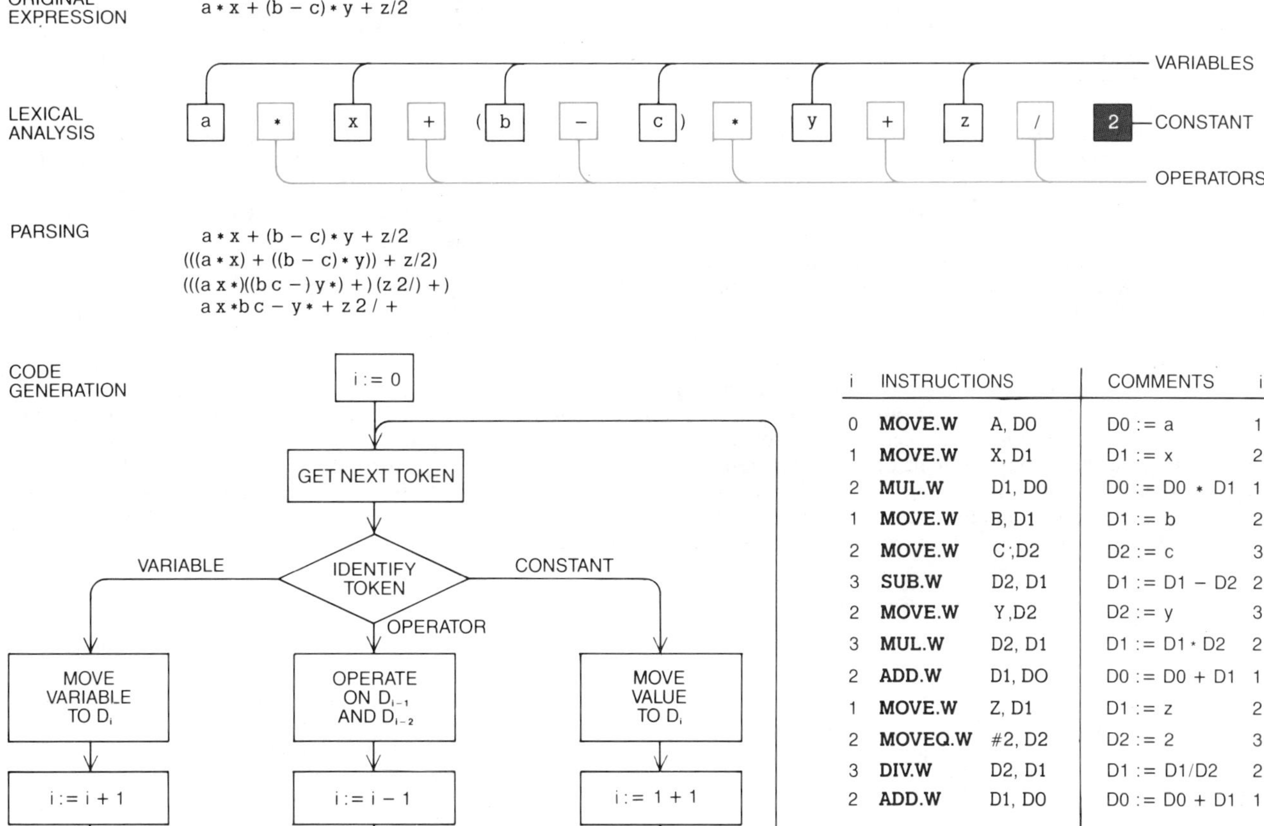

OPERATION OF A COMPILER, or translator, for a programming language has at least three stages. They are shown here for the particularly simple case of an arithmetic expression in Pascal. In lexical analysis the tokens, or symbols, that make up the program are identified and categorized. Parsing defines the semantic relations among the tokens. In an arithmetic expression the major task of the parser is to determine which operands are associated with each operator. It is done here by comparing the precedence of adjacent operators (assuming that multiplication precedes division, which precedes addition, and so on); parentheses are added around the operation of higher precedence. The expression is converted into "postfix" notation by exchanging the operator and the second operand in each subexpression. The parentheses are then removed, yielding an expression that can be evaluated from left to right. Code generation transforms the parsed expression into machine instructions, employing a simple algorithm for assigning each variable to a hardware register.

wanted without specifying how to get it. The program sets forth relations rather than the flow of control, and so the programmer is relieved of responsibility for working out the steps of an algorithm and specifying their order.

The most conspicuous nonprocedural languages are the spreadsheet programs, such as VisiCalc and MultiPlan, that have become popular with the rise of personal computers. In MultiPlan a calculation is specified by writing formulas, much as in BASIC or FORTRAN. The order in which the formulas are to be evaluated, however, is determined by the implementation rather than by the programmer. To some extent temporal relations are replaced by spatial ones. In a conventional language the output of one procedure might serve as input to the next procedure; the analogous concept in a spreadsheet makes the value of one cell depend on the value of another.

There is even less sense of defining procedures in the language Prolog, a derivative of Lisp that has lately attracted the attention of many workers in artificial intelligence. In Prolog no formulas are written; instead relations between objects and quantities are defined. The language consists of declarations only and has no statements. Thus the relation (*product height width area*) describes the equality *area* = *height* × *width*, but it does not specify that the height and the width are the given quantities or that the area is to be computed. The same relation can serve to find the height when the width and the area are known.

Another trend in the evolution of programming languages is the growth of interest in notational systems called object-oriented languages. As mentioned above, the statements of most programming languages are imperatives: the entity being addressed is not named, simply because there is only one possibility, an abstract embodiment of the computer as a whole. In an object-oriented language the computer is conceptually divided into objects that can be addressed individually. Furthermore, the objects can communicate with one another by sending messages.

The notion of software objects was introduced by Ole-Johan Dahl and Kristen Nygaard of the Norwegian Computing Center in Oslo in Simula 67, a language derived from Algol 60. The idea did not attract widespread attention, however, until the development of the language Smalltalk in the 1970's by Alan Kay and a group of colleagues (of whom I was one) at the Xerox Palo Alto Research Center. Smalltalk consists exclusively of object-oriented constructs, which makes the language specification small and very general; on the other hand, because everything in the language is an object, some important data-structuring mechanisms cannot be implemented efficiently.

A software object consists of both data structures and algorithms. Each object "knows" how to carry out operations on its own data, but to the rest of the program the object can be treated as a black box whose internal workings are immaterial. Indeed, various objects may employ quite different algorithms to accomplish tasks the programmer identifies by the same key word. Just as penguins, horses and centipedes clearly have different methods for the activity identified generically as walking, so objects whose data consist of integers, arrays and complex numbers would employ different methods for the operation of addition.

My colleagues and I at Apple Computer, Inc., have developed a language called Clascal that adds the concept of classes of objects to the underlying structure of Pascal. Clascal, Smalltalk, Simula and some other object-oriented languages allow the objects in a class to inherit properties from a superclass to which they belong, so that each class does not have to be built up from scratch. Only those traits that distinguish the individual class need to be specified. Thus penguins, horses and centipedes share the concept of legs; they differ in the number of legs and the details of the method of locomotion. Inheritance is another abstraction mechanism, allowing the properties of a class to be reused by many subclasses.

Inheritance turns out to be particularly useful in the design of interactive graphics software, another realm where there is much current activity. Entire programming languages can be built out of graphic images. Indeed, even certain computer games that rely heavily on graphics have some of the characteristics of a programming language. A notable example is a game called Robot Odyssey I, recently introduced by the Learning Company; "robots" programmed by connecting electronic logic gates and other components on a video screen can incorporate the concepts of conditional execution and procedure definition. A complete visual programming language tentatively named Mandala is now under development by Jaron Z. Lanier and his colleagues at VPL Research in Palo Alto. An example of what a Mandala program might look like is shown on the cover of this issue.

Another direction in which programming languages are expanding is the exploitation of parallel computation in computer systems made up of multiple processors. It would seem that 100 processing units ought to be able to solve a problem 100 times faster than a single processor of the same intrinsic speed, but the gain can be realized only if the software is able to break the problem into many pieces that can be worked on simultaneously.

Some languages provide an explicit mechanism for designating tasks that can be done in parallel; an example is the language called Occam, developed by the British semiconductor manufacturer Inmos. Other languages leave it to the compiler to analyze the program and discover opportunities for parallel execution. One such language is COMPEL (for "compute parallel"), on which I collaborated with Horace J. Enea in 1969. A COMPEL program consists entirely of assignment statements, which are not necessarily executed in the sequence in which they are written; the compiler is expected to deduce which calculations must be completed first. No compiler for COMPEL programs was ever written, but languages with a similar mechanism (called data-flow languages) have since been implemented.

The great diversity of programming languages makes it impossible to rank them on any single scale. There is no best programming language any more than there is a best natural language. "I speak Spanish to God, Italian to women, French to men and German to my horse," said Charles V (presumably in French). A programming language too must be chosen according to the purpose intended.

```
add (Adam is-parent-of Cain)
add (Adam is-parent-of Abel)
add (Eve is-parent-of Cain)
add (Eve is-parent-of Abel)
add (Cain is-parent-of Enoch)

which (x : x is-parent-of Abel)
Adam
Eve
No (more) answers

which (x : Eve is-parent-of x)
Cain
Abel
No (more) answers

add (x is-ancestor-of y if x is-parent-of y)
add (x is-ancestor-of y if z is-parent-of y and x is-ancestor-of z)

which (x : x is-ancestor-of Enoch)
Cain
Adam
Eve
No (more) answers

which (x : Adam is-ancestor-of x)
Cain
Abel
Enoch
No (more) answers
```

NONPROCEDURAL LANGUAGE called Prolog has no statements but consists entirely of declarations. In other words, a Prolog program gives no explicit instructions to carry out an operation; it merely states relations and makes inferences based on them. The illustration shows a program in a dialect called Micro-Prolog. The first five declarations set forth certain parent-child relations. The system can then answer questions about the established facts, for example identifying the parents of Abel and the children of Eve. Two rules of logical inference are then introduced to define the relation "ancestor of" in terms of the relation "parent of." The system can apply the rules to find all the ancestors or all the descendants of an individual.

THE AUTHORS

JOSEPH D. BECKER ("Multilingual Word Processing") writes: "I am currently manager of international advanced development at the Xerox Office Systems Division in Palo Alto, Calif. I got a B.S. from the Massachusetts Institute of Technology in 1966 and a Ph.D. in computer science from Stanford University in 1970. I worked at Bolt, Beranek & Newman, Inc., on semantic networks and intelligent robots until 1975 and then went traveling around the world, stopping in Taiwan to study Chinese for several months. In 1976 I joined the Xerox Palo Alto Research Center to help create the Fuji Xerox '8012-J Star' Japanese-language professional work station. I spent two years living in Tokyo testing the cultural acceptability of J Star there. After returning to the United States I helped to bring Arabic, Chinese, Korean, Russian, and other languages to the Star system. After having devoted nearly 10 frustrating years to the pursuit of machine translation and artificial intelligence I was pleasantly surprised to find challenging practical problems in multilingual word processing."

DEREK BICKERTON ("Creole Languages") writes: "I acquired my B.A. from the University of Cambridge in 1949 but did not start my academic career until 1964, when I taught English literature at the University College of Cape Coast in Ghana. In 1966 and 1967 I studied linguistics at the University of Leeds before becoming senior lecturer in the English language at the University of Guyana, where I remained for four years. I taught briefly at the University of Lancaster in England and joined the University of Hawaii at Manoa in the fall of 1972. In the British system it isn't necessary to have a doctorate but in the American it is, and so I took advantage of a regulation that enables graduates of Cambridge to submit published work instead of a regular dissertation. The work I submitted was *Dynamics of a Creole System* (Cambridge University Press, 1975). I obtained my doctorate in 1976, I have held the rank of full professor at Hawaii since the same year. I have also written several novels, the most recent of which was *King of the Sea* (Random House, 1980)."

PETER D. EIMAS ("The Perception of Speech in Early Infancy") is professor of psychology at Brown University, where he has taught since 1968. He took his B.A. at Yale University in 1956 and received his M.A. in 1959 and his Ph.D. in 1962 from the University of Connecticut. His work on infant speech perception has been funded since 1970 by the National Institute of Child Health and Human Development. Eimas would like to thank Joanne L. Miller for her comments on an early version of his article and for a collaboration of 10 years. He would also like to thank Alvin M. Liberman for encouragement and helpful comments as well as for making available the facilities of the Haskins Laboratories.

WALTER A. FAIRSERVIS, JR. ("The Script of the Indus Valley Civilization"), is professor of anthropology at Vassar College. He received an associate of arts degree from the University of Chicago in 1953. He went on to obtain his bachelor's degree at Columbia University and his doctorate in anthropology from Harvard University. His professional career has been divided between teaching and leading anthropological expeditions to the Middle East and Far East. He has led expeditions to Afghanistan, Pakistan, Iran, and India, some of them under the auspices of the American Museum of Natural History, of which he is a research associate. He held academic appointments at New York University and the University of Washington before moving to Vassar in 1968. Fairservis writes: "I have an implicit belief that in the origins of civilization we are dealing with something we do not completely understand. My whole career has been aimed at increasing our understanding of that."

NORMAN GESCHWIND ("Specializations of the Human Brain") is James Jackson Putnam Professor of Neurology at the Harvard Medical School and director of the Neurological Unit at Beth Israel Hospital in Boston. He is also professor in the department of psychology and in the School of Health Sciences and Technology at the Massachusetts Institute of Technology. He obtained his bachelor's degree from Harvard

College and his M.D. at the Harvard Medical School and then received postgraduate training in Boston and London. Geschwind's research has focused on the relation between the anatomy of the brain and behavior, including the cerebral organization of language, aphasias, emotional changes resulting from brain lesions, the evolution of language, and the functional asymmetry of the brain.

STEPHEN E. LEVINSON and MARK Y. LIBERMAN ("Speech Recognition by Computer") are on the technical staff of Bell Laboratories. Levinson has a B.A. in engineering sciences from Harvard College and an M.S. and a Ph.D. in electrical engineering from the University of Rhode Island. Before going to work for Bell Laboratories in 1976 he taught computer science for several years at Yale University. Liberman's Ph.D., in linguistics, is from the Massachusetts Institute of Technology. He has been at Bell Laboratories since 1975, except for a semester of teaching at M.I.T. in 1978.

DENISE SCHMANDT-BESSERAT ("The Earliest Precursor of Writing") is assistant professor of art at the University of Texas at Austin and assistant director of the university's Center for Middle Eastern Studies. Born in France, she studied at the Ecole du Louvre in Paris and came to the United States in 1964 to do research on the Near Eastern archaeological collections at Harvard University's Peabody Museum. In 1969, while a fellow at the Radcliffe Institute, she began an investigation of the earliest uses of clay in the Middle East. Since then she has studied unpublished early clay collections in museums of the United States, Europe, and the Middle East and done fieldwork in France, Iran, and Israel.

LAWRENCE G. TESLER ("Programming Languages") manages a software-development group in the Macintosh Division of Apple Computer, Inc. While studying at Stanford University for his bachelor's degree, which he got in 1965, he founded a small software company. He remained in business for five years, then joined the Stanford Artificial Intelligence Laboratory, where he did research in cognitive simulation and document formatting. In 1973 he moved to the Xerox Corporation's Palo Alto Research Center, where his work focused on software for personal computers. He began his career at Apple in 1980 as manager of applications-software development for the Lisa computer. Tesler writes: "Although I have worked in many areas of software engineering and computer science during the past 24 years, a recurring theme has been the user interface: making it easier for people to get computers to do their bidding."

DAVID L. WALTZ ("Artificial Intelligence") is professor of electrical engineering at the University of Illinois at Urbana-Champaign and research professor at the Coordinated Science Laboratory there. He earned three degrees in electrical engineering from the Massachusetts Institute of Technology: a B.S. in 1965, an M.S. in 1968, and a Ph.D. in 1972. After a year of postdoctoral work at M.I.T. he moved to Illinois. He has been interested in the possibility of mimicking the action of the human nervous system since his days at M.I.T. He writes that his "early interests at the M.I.T. Artificial Intelligence Laboratory included the design of a touch-sensing system for robot hands." When he went to Illinois, he became interested in the utilization of existing human languages as a means of instructing computers. He writes that his "group designed and constructed an experimental English-language question-answering system called PLANES that served as a front end for a large base of Navy aircraft flight and maintenance data." Waltz adds that outside the laboratory his interests include "playing baritone saxophone (moderately well) in a concert band."

WILLIAM S-Y. WANG ("The Chinese Language") is professor of linguistics at the University of California at Berkeley and director of its phonology laboratory. He is also director of the Project on Linguistic Analysis, which he founded in 1961 with support from the National Science Foundation. Wang received his early education in China, was graduated from Columbia College and obtained his Ph.D. from the University of Michigan. He and several colleagues have developed a computerized dictionary of Chinese dialects. In phonology his special interest is in the nature of tones; the work has taken him to many areas where tone systems are found, including Japan, Mexico, Yugoslavia, Southeast Asia, and Scandinavia. He is editor of the newly established *Journal of Chinese Linguistics*. "On the lighter side," Wang writes, "I try to play the flute occasionally, limiting myself mostly to its middle register. During his more tolerant moments my son will do flute duets with me, which I enjoy especially much."

TERRY WINOGRAD ("Computer Software for Working with Language") is associate professor of computer science and linguistics at Stanford University. He is a graduate of Colorado College and the Massachusetts Institute of Technology, where he received his doctorate in applied mathematics in 1970. He taught at M.I.T. until 1973 and then joined the Stanford faculty. Since 1973 he has served concurrently as a consultant at the Xerox Corporation's Palo Alto Research Center. Winograd pursues his research interests—artificial intelligence, computational linguistics, and cognitive modeling—at Stanford's Center for the Study of Language and Information, and in addition he is a member of the National Executive Committee of Computer Professionals for Social Responsibility.

BIBLIOGRAPHIES

1. Specializations of the Human Brain

EMOTIONAL BEHAVIOR AND HEMISPHERIC SIDE OF THE LESION. G. Gainotti in *Cortex,* Vol. 8, No. 1, pages 41–55; March, 1972.

SELECTED PAPERS ON LANGUAGE AND THE BRAIN. Norman Geschwind. D. Reidel Publishing Co., 1974.

THE INTEGRATED MIND. Michael S. Gazzaniga and Joseph E. Ledoux. Plenum Press, 1978.

RIGHT-LEFT ASYMMETRIES IN THE BRAIN. Albert M. Galaburda, Marjorie LeMay, Thomas L. Kemper, and Norman Geschwind in *Science,* Vol. 199, No. 4311, pages 852–856; February 24, 1978.

2. The Perception of Speech in Early Infancy

INFANT SPEECH PERCEPTION: A CRITICAL APPRAISAL. P.W. Jusczyk in *Perspectives of the Study of Speech,* edited by Peter D. Eimas and Joanne L. Miller. Lawrence Erlbaum Associates, Inc., 1981.

ON FINDING THAT SPEECH IS SPECIAL. Alvin M. Liberman in *American Psychologist,* Vol. 37, No. 2, pages 148–167; February, 1982.

3. Creole Languages

BIOLOGICAL FOUNDATIONS OF LANGUAGE. Eric H. Lenneberg. John Wiley & Sons, Inc., 1967.

RULES AND REPRESENTATIONS. Noam Chomsky. Columbia University Press, 1980.

ROOTS OF LANGUAGE. Derek Bickerton. Karoma Publishers, Inc., Ann Arbor, 1981.

ISLE DE FRANCE CREOLE. Philip Baker and Chris Corne. Karoma Publishers, Inc., Ann Arbor, 1982.

4. The Earliest Precursor of Writing

AN OPERATIONAL DEVICE IN MESOPOTAMIAN BUREAUCRACY. A. Leo Oppenheim in *Journal of Near Eastern Studies,* Vol. 17, pages 121–128; 1958.

GLYPTIQUE SUSIENNE. Pierre Amiet in *Mémoires de la Délégation archéologique en Iran,* Vol. 43; 1972.

AN ARCHAIC RECORDING SYSTEM AND THE ORIGIN OF WRITING. Denise Schmandt-Besserat in *Syro-Mesopotamian Studies,* Vol. 1, No. 2; July, 1977.

5. The Script of the Indus Valley Civilization

THE SCRIPT OF HARAPPA AND MOHENJODARO AND ITS CONNECTION WITH OTHER SCRIPTS. G. R. Hunter. Kegan Paul, Trench, Trubner & Co., Ltd., 1934.

A DRAVIDIAN ETYMOLOGICAL DICTIONARY. T. Burrow and M. B. Emeneau. Oxford University Press, 1961.

THE INDUS CIVILIZATION. Sir Mortimer Wheeler. Cambridge University Press, 1968.

THE ROOTS OF ANCIENT INDIA. Walter A. Fairservis, Jr. The University of Chicago Press, 1975.

THE INDUS SCRIPTS—TEXTS, CONCORDANCE AND TABLES. I. Mahadevan. Memoirs of the Archaeological Survey of India No. 77, Manager of Publications, Government of India, 1977.

A SKETCH OF COMPARATIVE DRAVIDIAN MORPHOLOGY. Kamil V. Zvelebil. Mouton Publishers, The Hague, 1978.

6. The Chinese Language

A GRAMMAR OF SPOKEN CHINESE. Yuen Ren Chao. University of California Press, 1968.

CLIBOC: CHINESE LINGUISTICS BIBLIOGRAPHY ON COMPUTER. William S-Y. Wang and Anatole Lyovin. Cambridge University Press, 1970.

THE COMPUTER IN CHINESE LINGUISTIC RESEARCH. William S-Y. Wang, Stephen W. Chan, and Benjamin K. Tsou in *Proceedings of the USA-Japan Computer Conference,* 1972.

DOC, 1971: A CHINESE DIALECT DICTIONARY ON COMPUTER. Mary L. Streeter in *Computers and the Humanities,* Vol. 6, No. 5, pages 259–270; May, 1972.

A SYNCHRONIC PHONOLOGY OF MANDARIN CHINESE. Chin-Chuan Cheng. Mouton Publishers, 1973.

7. Computer Software for Working with Language

UNDERSTANDING NATURAL LANGUAGE. Terry Winograd. Academic Press, 1972.

METAPHORS WE LIVE BY. George Lakoff and Mark Johnson. University of Chicago Press, 1981.

NATURAL LANGUAGE PROCESSING. Harry Tennant. Petrocelli Books, Inc., 1981.

THE MENTAL REPRESENTATION OF GRAMMATICAL RELATIONS. Edited by Joan Bresnan. The MIT Press, 1982.

LANGUAGE AS A COGNITIVE PROCESS. Terry Winograd. Addison-Wesley Publishing Company, Inc., 1983.

TEX BOOK. Donald E. Knuth. Addison-Wesley Publishing Company, Inc., 1983.

8. Artificial Intelligence

ARTIFICIAL INTELLIGENCE AND NATURAL MAN. Margaret Boden. Basic Books, 1977.

ARTIFICIAL INTELLIGENCE: AN MIT PERSPECTIVE. Patrick Henry Winston and Richard Henry Brown. The MIT Press, 1979.

MACHINES WHO THINK. Pamela McCorduck. W. H. Freeman and Company, 1979.

THE MIND'S I. Douglas R. Hofstadter and Daniel C. Dennett. Basic Books, 1981.

PERSPECTIVES IN COGNITIVE SCIENCE. Edited by Donald A. Norman. Ablex Publishing, 1981.

9. Multilingual Word Processing

WRITING SYSTEMS OF THE WORLD. Akira Nakanishi. Charles E. Tuttle, 1980.

A HISTORICAL STUDY OF TYPEWRITERS AND TYPING METHODS: FROM THE POSITION OF PLANNING JAPANESE PARALLELS. Hisao Yamada in *Journal of Information Processing,* Vol. 2, No. 4, pages 175–202; February, 1980.

10. Speech Recognition by Computer

ON HUMAN COMMUNICATION: A REVIEW, A SURVEY AND A CRITICISM. Colin Cherry. The MIT Press, 1966.

TRENDS IN SPEECH RECOGNITION. Edited by W. A. Lea. Prentice-Hall, Inc., 1980.

11. Programming Languages

FORTH: AN INTRODUCTION TO THE FORTH LANGUAGE AND OPERATING SYSTEM FOR BEGINNERS AND PROFESSIONALS. Prentice-Hall, Inc., 1981.

HISTORY OF PROGRAMMING LANGUAGES. Edited by Richard L. Wexelblat. Academic Press, 1981.

THE IMPACT OF ABSTRACTION CONCERNS ON MODERN PROGRAMMING LANGUAGES. Mary Shaw in *Studies in Ada Style* by Peter Shaw, Andy Hisgen, Jonathan Rosenberg, Mary Shaw, and Mark Sherman. Springer-Verlag, 1981.

PROGRAMMING LANGUAGES: DESIGN & IMPLEMENTATION. Terrence W. Pratt. Prentice-Hall, Inc., 1984.

INDEX